Butterworth Architecture Legal Series

Towards Sustainable Architecture

Towards Sustainable Architecture
EUROPEAN DIRECTIVES AND BUILDING DESIGN

Brian Edwards

Butterworth Architecture

Butterworth Architecture
An imprint of Butterworth-Heinemann Ltd
Linacre House, Jordan Hill, Oxford OX2 8DP

A member of the Reed Elsevier plc group

OXFORD   LONDON   BOSTON
NEW DELHI   SINGAPORE   SYDNEY
TOKYO   TORONTO   WELLINGTON

First published 1996

© Butterworth Architecture 1996

All rights reserved. No part of this publication
may be reproduced in any material form (including
photocopying or storing in any medium by electronic
means and whether or not transiently or incidentally
to some other use of this publication) without the
written permission of the copyright holder except
in accordance with the provisions of the Copyright,
Designs and Patents Act 1988 or under the terms of a
licence issued by the Copyright Licensing Agency Ltd,
90 Tottenham Court Road, London, England W1P 9HE.
Applications for the copyright holder's written permission
to reproduce any part of this publication should be
addressed to the publishers

British Library Cataloguing in Publication Data
Towards Sustainable Architecture: European
  Directives and Building Design –
  (Butterworth Architecture Legal Series)
  I. Edwards, Brian II. Series
  720.47094

ISBN 0 7506 2492 2

Library of Congress Cataloguing in Publication Data
Edwards, Brian, MSc
  Towards sustainable architecture: European directives and
  building design/Brian Edwards.
  p.   cm.
  Includes bibliographical references and index.
  ISBN 0 7506 2492 2
  1. Architecture – Environmental aspects – Europe.
  2. Environmental impact analysis – Europe. I. Title.
  NA2542.35.E35
  720'.47'094 – dc20   95–37487
                                                     CIP

Typeset by Scribe Design, Gillingham, Kent
Printed in Great Britain

Contents

Foreword by Ken Collins   vii

Acknowledgements   ix

List of contributors   xi

Introduction   xiii

Part 1 Perspectives on the Environment

    1   The environmental context   3
    2   The implications of the Maastricht Treaty on design   8
    3   Maastricht and the architect   11
    4   A layman's guide to EC law   16

Part 2 Construction Products and Professional Services

    5   The Construction Products Directive   21
    6   The Architects' Directive: mutual recognition of qualifications   26

Part 3 Energy and Pollution

    7   The construction industry and global warming   31
    8   CFCs, HCFCs and other ozone depleting gases   39
    9   Reducing air pollution by better design and urban development   41
    10   An overview of energy and building design   47
    11   Technical factors in the design of sustainable commercial buildings   61
          Lori McElroy
    12   Renewable energy   78
    13   The potential of wind power   88
          Lawrie O'Connor

Part 4 Environmental Impact

    14   Environmental impact assessment   97
    15   Predicting visual impacts by computer aided visual impact analysis   104
          Professor Thomas W. Maver and Dr Jelena Petric
    16   Environmental audits   111
    17   Protecting Europe's cultural heritage   118
    18   A–Z of environmental impacts of commonly used building products,   121
          processes and services and related design issues

Contents

Part 5   Environmental Health and Safety

   19   Environmental health and pollution problems with buildings   129
   20   Environmental health and building occupation   132
   21   Environmental health and safety on building sites   135
   22   An overview of environmental safety and the architect   138
       Dr Paul Yaneske

Part 6   Recycling

   23   Waste management and recycling   147
   24   Contaminated land use   154

Part 7   Ecology

   25   The EC eco-labelling scheme   163
   26   Biodiversity   168
   27   Ecology energy and building: the importance of landscape   174

Part 8   Sustainable Development

   28   Sustainable development: EC and UK policy and international agreements   181
   29   Case studies of sustainable urban development   189

Part 9   The Future of Design

   30   New laws, new responsibilities   201

Glossary   213

Bibliography   215

Index   217

Foreword

Greening the Future

Ken Collins

European society is largely urban. It is estimated that approximately 80 per cent of the population live in cities and towns. The problems of urban areas vary enormously as some face problems of rapid growth while others face those of economic decline while still others face both types of problems. However, most cities and towns share major difficulties such as the decay of the urban environment through congestion, water and air pollution, deterioration of housing and derelict land, and the disappearance of useful open space.

In 1990, at the initiation of the European Parliament, the Commission published a Green Paper on the Urban Environment proposing actions that might be taken at the European level to address this decay. One major conclusion of the Green Paper is that policies must take a holistic approach. This means integrating and internalizing environmental consideration into policies covering urban planning, transport, historical preservation, building design, energy management, waste management and social initiatives.

The interdependence of these areas requires a fusing of policies to stimulate economic activity with those policies encouraging conservation and environmental protection. In practice this means that directives on urban waste water or car emissions, for example, will be more successful in the long term if they take adequate account of environmental and public health factors. Policies ranging from urban mobility and building design to household and industrial waste policy should all have an environmental dimension. The Green Paper alone cannot begin to solve these problems. It marked the beginning of urban environmental policy-making at the European level. Now more must be done.

'Horizontal' measures such as environment policy that can be integrated into 'vertical' legislation covering transport and building design have already been established. The European Union (EU) has set quality objectives and standards through various directives for air, water, waste and noise pollution, for example. Legislation requires environmental impact assessments for many major development projects, and guarantees better access to environmental information (having an important influence on the success of environmental improvement projects). Now with the establishment of the European Environment Agency, the EU can begin to provide better monitoring for the execution of legislation. These measures will increasingly impact upon the life of design professionals in the building industry.

The further development of environmental policy for urban areas requires the consideration of two additional factors: the cost of non-environment and the benefits of a proactive environment policy. If we are to move progressively to address the new challenges of cities and towns, we will need to adopt a new model of development, one that is more environmentally friendly, which creates and sustains more jobs and which take more account of the quality of life. Architectural design will increasingly be judged by its ability to deliver these objectives.

Looking around us we see that the current pattern of production and consumption across Europe today not only diminishes the quality of life in some areas for this and future generations, it also can pose threats to the life-supporting systems of the planet in the form of global warming, ozone depletion and the loss of biodiversity.

The absence of an efficient environmental policy across the European Union will cost us dearly in the future. Money saved today by a lack of environmental protection will be later spent many times over on the treatment of human ill health and the cleaning up of a degraded environment: costs that are simply too important to ignore. Investing today in sound environmental policies is not only sensible, but financially practical and prudent.

While noting the high cost of ignoring the environment, we need also to focus on the benefits of a proactive environmental policy. There is a clear connection between

Foreword

resource use, economic growth and environmental policy and it is a connection that we ignore at our peril. Environmental measures often directly create new jobs and indirectly promote sustainable growth because in the long run, only environmentally-friendly products will remain successful in the marketplace of the future.

As urban areas are the places where the problems of the environment touch most people's quality of life, European policies should affect us in our towns and cities as well as our homes. Public transport systems should be made more efficient and cheaper *vis-à-vis* private auto use by reflecting the true costs. Public participation in promoting green spaces and car-free shopping and living areas should be promoted. Cities and towns should be encouraged to provide these increased services without, however, expanding the physical boundaries of the city. Sustainable development within our urban areas should be fostered in a way that makes better use of our current land and resources.

These are some of the challenges that Europe must face if we are to escape from the dilemmas of our present model of development and turn toward a new model which shows greater respect for the balance of nature, creates more jobs and strengthens our common bonds.

Land use, local planning and building design decisions should of course remain the responsibility of Member States' regional and local governments. Nevertheless, policies and strategies developed and decided at European level do have a strong impact on land use, physical planning and architecture within the Member States. A positive approach to encourage the development of urban environmental strategies would be the agreement of policy and guidelines which, if followed by local authorities in Member States, would command financial support from the European Union. Additional support should derive from demonstration projects and pilot projects serving as models for wider application. A European Union approach along these lines would be welcome. It is certainly long overdue.

Ken Collins MEP,
Chairman of the European Parliaments Committee on the Environment, Public Health and Consumer Protection

Acknowledgements

As principal author of this book I am indebted to many people, organizations and journal editors. Besides those who have contributed chapters with little complaint (Dr Yelena Petric, Lori McElroy, Professor Thomas Maver, Dr Paul Yaneske and Lawrie O'Connor) I have to acknowledge the assistance in particular of the writings in *The Architects' Journal* of Barrie Evans. The various technical papers, case studies of 'green' buildings and articles on unfolding European Law written by Barrie Evans in his capacity as Technical Editor of the *AJ* have proved an invaluable and reliable archive of material upon which to draw.

Other journals, principally *Architecture Today*, *RIBA Journal*, *Building*, *The Surveyor*, and *Planning Week* have provided insights and ideas which I have freely used. Such is the span of this book and the speed of unfolding European regulation that it is to journals rather than books that the authors' have turned for information or case law.

Many other organizations have proved helpful in timeously posting or faxing information. Three in particular are worthy of special thanks – the West Yorkshire European Business Information Centre (WYEBIC) based in Bradford, the CBI's Environment Business Forum, and the Department of the Environment for its monthly *Construction Monitor*.

The principal author wishes to thank the University of Huddersfield for a Small Project Grant to help pay for the costs of writing and researching the book. Also to Geoffrey Calderbank, Dean of Study at the University, for providing time from an increasingly heavy faculty teaching load for writing the book. A special word of thanks is due also to Mrs Judith Shaw who patiently and with no hint of complaint typed, retyped and recorrected the manuscript.

Finally, I would like to thank Linda Stanley for her support, encouragement and patience.

Contributors

Lori McElroy is Technical Director of EDAS, Energy Design Advisory Service, run for the Department of Energy by the University of Strathclyde with European funding.

Dr Jelena Petric is an architect and lecturer at the University of Strathclyde specializing in Environmental Impact Assessment and computer-aided design.

Professor Thomas Maver is Professor of Building Science at the University of Strathclyde with a special interest in the use of computers in Environmental Impact Assessment.

Dr Paul Yaneske is a senior lecturer at the University of Strathclyde specializing in Environmental Health and Building.

Lawrie O'Connor is a building services engineer with a special interest in wind energy, and teaches at the University of Huddersfield.

Ken Collins is the MEP for Lanarkshire North and is chairman of the European Parliament Committee on the Environment, Public Health and Consumer Protection.

Introduction

Environmental protection and sustainable development are important areas of interest for the European Community (EC). Various directives and research funding programmes seek to improve the quality of life by ensuring that environmental matters are taken into account. Other fields of EC policy making and development in general are now required to consider the impact they have upon the physical, biological and, increasingly, aesthetic environment of Europe. To ensure that environmental policies are based upon solid scientific and technical knowledge, the EC funds a number of research programmes, many of interest to the building industry.

The scale of impact of development upon the physical and social environment has necessitated growing legislative intervention by the European Parliament. Much of the activity has been scorned by the British Parliament in Westminster which in 1994 argued that European 'red tape' prevents industrial recovery and the creation of jobs, and that the British system of planning and building control is without equal amongst Member States.

Energy in particular remains a vital problem for Europe. The EC is keen to ensure that the Community has energy security in the widest sense, and the environmental damage caused by fossil fuel consumption is reduced to acceptable levels. In 1992 the Community adopted a target of stabilizing CO_2 emissions at 1990 levels by the year 2000. Questions of sustainable development impact significantly upon the energy field and hence environmental policy and energy policy are increasingly related to each other in terms of new legislation and research funding. Buildings have a key role to play as they are one of the major sources of energy consumption, and development is one of the biggest factors changing the environment of Europe. Construction is also Europe's second biggest industry in terms of people employed, and hence environment policy will have an impact upon hundreds of thousands of building workers – both professional and manual. In the EC about half of total energy use is building related and buildings are responsible for land loss to agriculture, for other areas of resource depletion, and for much of Europe's pollution and carbon dioxide production. Buildings also impact significantly upon the health and safety of people at work and in the home. Here too European legislators have been busy enacting regulations and directives to provide a measure of protection for the users of buildings.

Two important principles enshrined in EC law change the relationship between clients and their professional advisers on the question of pollution. Under EC law the principle that the 'polluter pays' exposes clients and architects to risk of litigation from third parties. If the best environmental knowledge and skills are not employed, those who specify products or who design and procure buildings may be at risk from injured third parties. Such liability extends to those who merely use buildings (as

Table 1
International milestones of environmental agreement or awareness

Year	Event
1972	'The Limits to Growth' Report
1972	Stockholm Conference on the Human Environment (UN)
1979	Berne Convention on Habitat Protection (Council of Europe)
1979	Geneva Convention on Air Pollution (UN)
1980	World Conservation Strategy (IUCN)
1980	Global 2000 Report (USA)
1983	Helsinki Protocol on Air Quality (UN)
1983	World Commission on Environment and Development (UN)
1987	Montreal Protocol on Substances that deplete the Ozone Layer (UN)
1987	Our Common Future (Brundtland Commission on behalf of the UN)
1990	Green Paper on the Urban Environment (EC)
1992	Rio Summit Agreements (UN)
1992	Our Common Inheritance (UK)

Introduction

Table 2
Summary of principles of EC environment policy

- Prevent pollution at source
- The polluter pays for environmental damage
- Environmental policy to be integrated with economic and social policy
- Environmental effects of development to be taken into account at technical planning and decision-making stage
- Environmental knowledge should be improved
- One Member State should not cause degradation of the environment of another
- Effects of EC policy on global environment should be taken into account
- The EC should take an international lead in environment policy
- Environmental protection is a responsibility of all the Community
- Specific levels of action should be introduced to remedy specific types of pollution
- Environmental policy must be consistent between Member States
- EC environmental policy should be harmonized with national policy

Source: Paraphrased from *The European Community and the Environment* (3rd Edition) European Documentation 3. 1987, Office of Official Publications of the European Community.

against own them) or who suffer from a building's pollution at some distance away. The second important principle is that pollution should be dealt with at source, rather than by remedial action later. Clients need to be aware of these duties when commissioning buildings (and to be advised of them by their architects). They also need to be aware of their liability with regard to environmental clean-up costs.

The Single European Act of 1986 and the European Union (EU) signed at Maastricht in 1992 tie Britain irretrievably into the European culture of environmental protection. Though Britain may be in the slow lane in terms of enthusiasm for the flood of directives emanating from Brussels, UK architects, engineers, contractors and building product manufacturers cannot avoid their implications. The new laws apply across Europe, requiring new skills, new design approaches and a fresh philosophy. It is now necessary to design with benign impacts in mind, to reduce the footprint a building leaves upon the environment and the health of those who occupy it. If Britain's construction industry does not adjust to the new environmental imperative, then those from France, Germany and Holland will undertake a disproportionate share of Europe's new construction projects. Environmental care is not only a matter of changing emphasis and the adoption of new ethical codes, it also makes good sense in terms of market penetration.

Architects and environmental responsibility

Architects have a larger share of responsibility for the world's consumption of fossil fuel and global warming gas production (CO_2) than any other professional group. In the UK and also the world at large half of all energy used is in relation to heating, lighting, cooling and the ventilation of buildings. The structures architects and engineers design, the way buildings are serviced, and how they are adapted over time, all directly influence the volume of fossil fuels consumed and lead indirectly to the tonnes of CO_2 released into the atmosphere, raising planetary temperatures. Decisions about buildings, towns and their spatial distribution are the key to creating a future built upon the concept of 'sustainable development'. If buildings are responsible for half of total energy use, the transport needed to get to them and to move supplies from rural to urban areas accounts for another half of the remaining half of energy consumption. Hence, the urban scene with its complex matrix of buildings, activities, services and transportation consumes 75 per cent of the world's energy resources and produces the vast bulk of its pollution and climate changing gases. Decisions made by architects are crucial to the achievement of a sustainable future.

Politicians in the 1990s have begun to realize the magnitude of the problem facing the human race. An increase in world temperatures of only 1.5°C threatens to flood large areas of productive land (in Holland and Bangladesh for example) through the thawing of polar ice and the thermal expansion of global waters. World cities such as London, New York and Sydney are also threatened by sea level rises. In parallel, the thinning of the ozone layer due to chlorofluorocarbon (CFC) use is leading to a big increase in skin cancers (60 000 a year in the UK alone) and a loss of productivity in oceanic plankton. This will affect fish and bird populations, and since plankton is also a carbon dioxide absorber (as are other photosynthesizing plants) the loss of plankton will tend to increase CO_2 in the atmosphere.

Both global warming and ozone depletion are directly the result of decisions made by architects. Faced by the problems posed, world leaders agreed at the Earth Summit at Rio de Janeiro in 1992 to take measures to reduce carbon dioxide (CO_2) emissions, to develop a strategy of sustainable development, to protect surviving rainforests, and to maintain the biodiversity of world eco-systems. The UK government and the European Community were

Table 3
Key provisions of EC treaties and law for construction industry

Title	Date	Key provisions
Founding treaties	1951, 1952	• free movement of goods • free movement of labour • free movement of capital • common policies on agriculture • harmonization of laws • establishment of social fund • setting up of Investment Bank
Single European Act	1986	• completion of Internal Market • removal of trade barriers • adoption of environment policies • improvement of working conditions • strengthening economic and social ties
Maastricht Treaty (Environment provisions only)	1992	• extension of environment policies • encouragement for renewable energy • integration of environment and social policy • adoption of 'sustainable development' • adoption of 'polluter pays' principle • adoption of 'pollution control at source' principle

signatories to the Earth Summit. Political response to environmental concerns in Europe has been led by the EU rather than separate Member States except perhaps in Germany where green issues remain a motor for progressively stricter legislation. Various EC directives have sought to restrict energy use, to make designers more conscious of the environmental impact of their decisions, to maintain biodiversity, and to limit the use of CFCs, a half of which are employed in the European construction industry. In parallel, a broadening of environmental policy has begun to embrace questions of health and environmental safety.

Sustainable development, formalized into EC policy via the Maastricht Treaty, can only be achieved by architects, engineers, designers, town planners and manufacturers of building products working co-operatively. The energy and ecological impact of development is great, more significant than any other sector of the economy including the motor industry. Energy is embodied in the materials employed in construction and used in the running of buildings. As fossil fuels are irreplaceable and their burning contributes directly to global warming, designers need to think deeply about the materials they specify and the heating and lighting systems they employ. Other countries such as Germany, Denmark and Holland have stricter energy and environment building codes than the UK. Professionals familiar with working in these areas have an advantage over those in the UK as Europe as a whole moves towards greater emphasis upon sustainable development. As the European Community adopts ever stricter controls on energy use and environmental protection, those designers with expertise in these areas will gain a greater share of construction work. Britain's comparatively backward building industry, which has been encouraged to consume energy wastefully by relaxed building regulations and a planning system which has not equated energy with land-use policy, may well find the balance of trade in both professional services and building products tipped unfavourably to the advantage of continental competitors.

The adoption by the Government in 1992 of global responsibilities at the Earth Summit and the publication in 1994 of the UK Strategy for Sustainable Development augurs a new era for design and construction. As the case studies in this book show it is possible to design in a sustainable fashion. Sustainability will not, however, be achieved overnight and in certain fields such as transportation perhaps never, but to meet the flood of European directives and the green consciousness of the client body at large, construction professions need to adapt rapidly to changing conditions. This book is an attempt to describe those conditions by examining the main areas of European environment law which impact upon building,

Introduction

Introduction 1
Mixed use development in Dublin's Temple Bar designed by Murray O'Laorire Architects and built with the assistance of an EC Thermie grant. Not only does the building contain a variety of activities (housing, offices and shops) it also seeks to generate its own energy. Buildings such as this point to the future of architecture in Europe. (Murray O'Laorire©.)

Introduction

Introduction 2
This energy demonstration village known as Ecolonia in Holland is built upon ecological principles which range from the landscape design to the selection of building materials. It was grant aided under the EC Thermie Scheme. (Novem©.)

discussing their implications for design, and suggesting through case studies how certain exemplar projects can be a guide to the future.

Since environment, health and safety are major preoccupations of European legislators, an ethical shift is required by those involved in building. New duties are rapidly unfolding and old practices are quickly becoming obsolete. This book is aimed at those who practise, teach, procure or are merely interested in the design of buildings and the management of urban areas. A visually rich, environmentally responsive, and socially just architecture will emerge under the dictates of the new laws. The comprehensive new measures introduced by the European Commission strengthen certain national laws already in place (such as nature conservation) and have led to the setting up in the UK of an Environment Agency. Rather than bemoan the increasing trend towards European control and standardization, new 'green' legislation offers fresh employment opportunities for those with the skills required in the new environment age.

Part 1
Perspectives on the Environment

1

The environmental context

The European Commission's Green Paper on the Urban Environment (1990) was a turning point in environmental awakening. It was primarily concerned with establishing the broad framework for effective community action on a diverse range of environmental problems from energy to noise, and global warming to water pollution. The Green Paper prompted municipal authorities and national governments to face up to the declining quality of urban life in Europe. For many, such as the UK Government, it led to a reorientation of policy towards environmental quality. The prime value of the Green Paper was its general approach, crossing sectorial boundaries and asking EC governments to address the growing problem of deteriorating urban life with attendant risks from pollution to health, safety and global climate change.

More than 80 per cent of Europe's population (i.e. about 250 million people) live in urban areas whose quality of life is worsening under 'heavy environmental burdens'.[1] Since cities are where the population, buildings and activities are concentrated, it is here that pollution is concentrated, and where European policy is increasingly focused. Improvement to environmental conditions in cities, particularly with regard to the by-products of energy use, will have major benefits for the world eco-system. The release of greenhouse gases, acid rain and ozone depleting chemicals are all the results of modern city life which affect global conditions generally.

The Green Paper provided a framework for action rather than specific remedies. Its function was to be a catalyst encouraging national governments and town councils to begin to address the environmental problem. As described in the Paper 'environment' was a broad issue. It embraced a complex web of activities and interests from transport to water management, waste to historical character. One benefit of the approach was to show the interdependency of policy areas, suggesting for instance that tackling the rise in car ownership (at present Europe has about 400 cars for every 1000 inhabitants) through greater road building had implications for the preservation of historic buildings and landscapes, on the one hand, and health on the other. The Paper not only confronted government with difficult policy choices, it also raised the importance of European cities to European culture. Under the single market of 1992 cities will, it was predicted, be forced to offer a better and more competitive environmental quality and standard of living. Not all Member States have accepted the idea of environmental quality determining the success of their cities yet places such as Glasgow and Barcelona are testimony to the value of design and heritage-led economic regeneration. The Green Paper raised for the first time at such a level the imperative of restricting private car access to historic centres. It sought a reappraisal of public transport both as a means of addressing the social, health and environmental ills of European cities and as a way of creating user-friendly areas attractive to inward investment.

The Green Paper predicted a change of emphasis in the cities of Europe from being manufacturing bases to becoming post industrial centres. Such a change would allow the cities to revert to their vital role as places where people can meet and enjoy the rich social and cultural exchanges of the past. The declining industrial base will in time give way, according to the Green Paper, to a new urban order based upon sound environmental principles. The transition period of today is one where action can be taken to reorganize and reshape the urban landscape through green measures such as the establishment of city forests.

The Green Paper lists seven important areas of action or policy change to facilitate the transition necessary in European cities.

- *Urban planning* – The abandonment of land-use zoning principles and the adoption of policies by Member States which encourage mixed use and denser development. In such areas the car will be an option not, as in the suburbs, a necessity. Emphasis is also placed upon the reuse of contaminated urban

---

[1] Carlo Ripa Di Meana, Keynote Address, *Green City: Conference Report* Glasgow, March 1991, p 3.

The environmental context

Figure 1.1
Europe has arguably the richest man-made environments in the world. The European Union Green Paper on the Urban Environment reminds Member States of their duties towards conserving the cultural heritage of towns and villages. (Brian Edwards ©.)

land and the environmental assessment not only of major projects, but policies, plans and programmes.
- *Urban transport* – A switch from investment in road to support for public transport is sought. The EC itself will favour grants under the structural fund which incorporate balanced judgement between roads, development and public transport. Linked to its support of public transport, the Green Paper introduced the idea of pilot projects which integrate environmental management with transportation.
- *Historical character* – The identity of Europe is bound up in her towns and cities. Such places are, the Green Paper states, an important symbol of the Community's rich cultural diversity and its shared historical heritage. Questions of historic character impinge upon Europe as a whole and extend beyond the boundaries of that city's own citizens or the interests of individual Member States. Consistency in protection and restoration measures, supported by EC funds, is mooted for the first time.
- *Natural environment* – The protection and improvement of open spaces in towns is recommended to enhance the visual pleasure of urban areas, to improve the microclimate of cities, and to reduce air pollution. The adoption of 'green' plans by municipal authorities is mentioned as a pilot project for EC funding.
- *Urban water management* – In 1984 a survey of Member States found that over half of organic pollutants were entering Europe's waters untreated. The Green Paper encourages municipal authorities and national governments to give the treatment of waste water from urban areas a priority for the maintenance of ecological diversity, human health and amenity.
- *Energy consumption* – The need to reduce air pollution and use energy more efficiently is central to environment strategy in the Green Paper. The benefits in terms of human and global health are emphasized. Two main fields are addressed in the Green Paper – building design of both new and existing buildings and urban energy planning. The former is of concern to architects and surveyors, the latter to town planners and transport engineers. Amongst suggestions made are the standardizing of energy and insulation measures throughout Europe, the dissemination of good practice guides, and more detailed energy planning in our cities.
- *Urban waste* – The emphasis here is on the avoidance of waste at source, and greater reuse and recycling. Resource constraints are beginning to limit consumption. The Green Paper identifies the importance of urban and architectural design that favours the sorting of waste at source and finding new uses for urban waste, particularly that resulting from construction.

The Green Paper makes the case that the European Community's urban policy needs to be concerned over a wide front with reducing the impact of human activities, including those from buildings, on the environment. It represents an important awakening of interest in energy conservation and environmental matters – concerns which have grown in the 1990s as problems of health, global warming and ozone thinning have deepened. The Green Paper also marks a shift at EC level from concerns with agriculture and rural communities to a recognition that the urban population matters. In many ways the European

The environmental context

Figure 1.2
Large modern cities are the focus of environmental and ecological problems whose effects are often global. (Scottish Development Agency©.)

policy reports which have followed, such as that on sustainable development in 1992 and subsequent directives, stem from environmental initiatives mooted in the Green Paper.

The next significant development was the publication in 1992 by the European Commission of a Task Force report on the environment.[2] It recognized that the quality of urban life matters; that important links exist between health, environment and amenity. It also raised the issue of consistency of environmental regulation to prevent regions with lax law attracting inward investment to the detriment of other European areas. As infrastructure

---
[2] Published by the EC and inspired by Commissioner Carlo Ripa Di Meana of the Environment Directorate and DGX1.

projects are often EC funded, the Task Force report asked that the environmental consequences – on biodiversity, health and energy consumption, be evaluated alongside economic and social justifications. Again subsequent policy of the EC has moved in this direction.

The Task Force report gave great weight to the link between community health and environmental quality. Lung cancer rates are higher in urban areas than rural ones, ambient lead concentrations in the air are higher in towns than the countryside, with a consequence that death rates are also 10 per cent higher. The report advised the European Parliament to address this relationship in its allocation of Community funds and in future directives. Since environment was emerging as one of the issues of the age, the report argued for greater cohesion in European policy across fields such as energy, transport,

The environmental context

Figure 1.3
As concerns over the environment grow and new laws are enacted buildings begin to take on new form. This energy-efficient office was designed by Building Design Partnership. (BDP©.)

health, agriculture and development. The Maastricht Treaty with its introduction of the concept of sustainable growth respecting the environment was one important consequence.

Both the Green Paper and the Task Force report mark milestones in European political perceptions. Their effect has been twofold: first, to pave the way for the inclusion of environmental policy into the Maastricht Treaty (see Chapters 2 and 3). Second, they signal to national governments and municipal authorities the importance of the environment as both a resource to be protected and a problem to be addressed in terms of active intervention to renew and repair the damage of earlier generations. As Ken Collins noted at a Green Conference in Glasgow in 1991 a 'healthy city is an environmentally-friendly city and an environmentally-friendly city is likely to be a prosperous city'.[3] The triangular relationship between environment, health and development has emerged as one of the most important global issues of the nineties.

Under the influence of such documents architects and engineers have begun to accept planetary responsibility for the decisions. There is emerging a new morality based upon benign environmental impacts. The need for life cycle assessment, of thinking holistically about design, of establishing a methodology of environmental measurement, have caught the imagination of many in the construction professions. The creation of green cities with

---

[3] *Green City: Conference Report* Glasgow, March 1991, p 13.

The environmental context

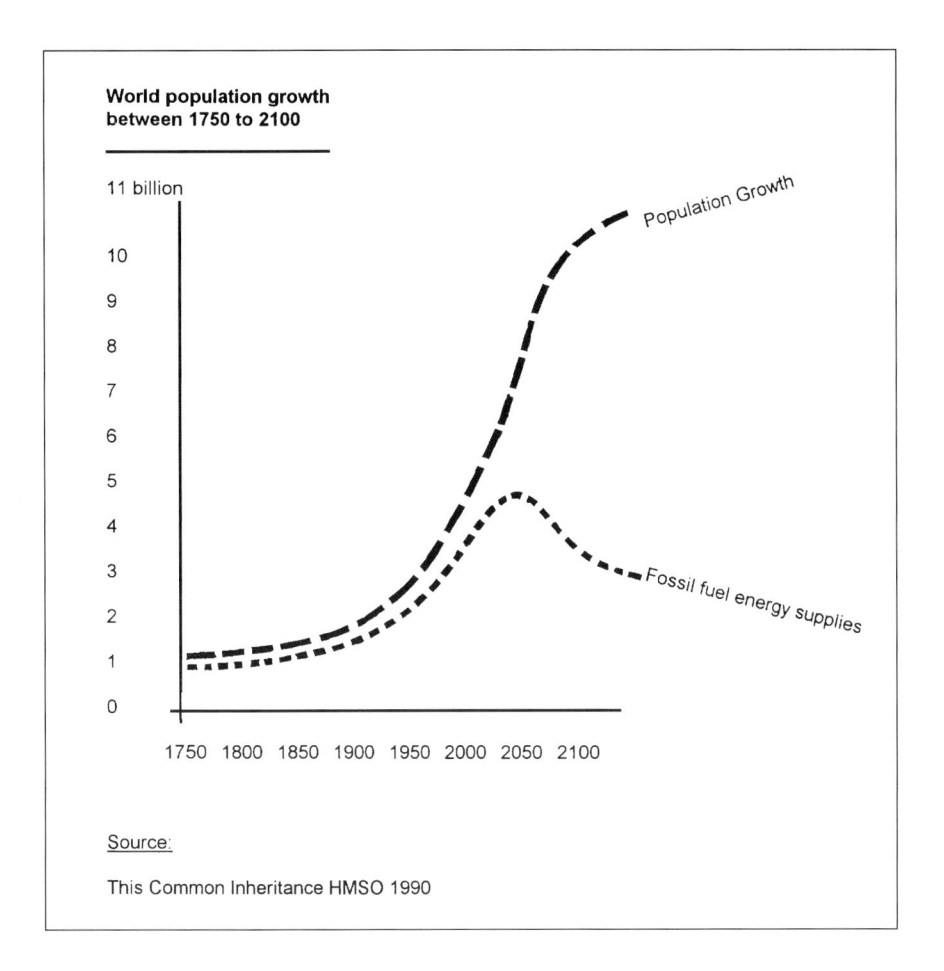

Figure 1.4
World population growth and fossil-fuel energy supplies.
Source: *This Common Inheritance*, HMSO, 1990.

green buildings for green people requires 'circular' not 'linear' thinking: design which embraces cycles of sustainable development and change. It will happen if designers adopt the simple principle that development should not compromise the ability of future generations to meet their needs. Such a premise is itself dependent upon equity and participation – equity in the sense that there should be equality of access to resources within and between classes, regions, countries and generations, and participation which embraces the 'notion of democracy and community involvement in decisions over resource use.'[4] Cyclical thinking is how nature operates with its pattern of growth, decay and renewal, and its dependency upon seasonal change. Green development to which many in Europe aspire accepts the principles of nature, seeks limits to corporate growth and personal consumption, and uses the minimum of resources to achieve the maximum in environmental quality.

---

[4] David Gee, 'Are green cities possible' in *Green City: Conference Report* Glasgow, March 1991, p 33.

2

The implications of the Maastricht Treaty on design

The Maastricht Treaty has been seen in some quarters as primarily an act dealing with economic co-operation and monetary union. It is, however, much more than this with extensive provisions covering a portfolio of new laws, articles and agreement on matters as diverse as citizenship, education and training, the 'flowering' of culture, public health, consumer protection and the environment. Many of the provisions adopted as part of the Maastricht Treaty signed on 7 February 1992 (and formally adopted by Britain after bitter Parliamentary debate on 3 August 1993) have implications for the practice of architecture in both the medium and short term.

Article 130v allows for the strengthening of laws on the environment through the introduction of policies for preserving, protecting and improving the quality of the environment; protecting human health; encouraging the prudent use of natural resources; and facing up to the international dimension to environmental problems.[1] The words 'environment' and 'sustainable development' occur widely in the Treaty, marking a significant shift in EC philosophy and one which has profound implications for the future of Europe's construction industry.

In the medium term this will lead to greater controls at national level through changes to the planning, building and public health acts. In the short term also the strengthening of environmental controls embodied in the Maastricht Treaty will give greater strength to those who have sought to use Environmental Assessment (EA) procedures to measure the potential adverse effects, direct and indirect, of major development. Maastricht now places a duty upon EC governments to 'aim at a high level of protection' based upon the 'precautionary principle ... that preventive action should be taken, that environmental damage should be rectified at source'.[2] As buildings are the source of much environmental pollution, there is a role here for architects and engineers, both in the design of new structures and in the modification of existing ones.

Although the Maastricht Treaty ratifies the provisions of the Single European Act (1986), it also extends and clarifies certain provisions. In the environmental field new responsibilities are placed upon Member States and upon the EC itself. Maastricht requires for the first time that environmental protection must be integrated into other community policies. Such powerful fields as agricultural and economic policy are now to be redrafted to ensure a measure of environmental control. Maastricht, in spite of comment that the Treaty has little worth in terms of monetary union, promises a shift in culture, at least at an environmental level.

The Maastricht Treaty also introduced the concept that the EC had international or worldwide environmental responsibilities. The new recognition of global problems allows the EC to legislate on fossil fuel emissions (and hence the effect on global warming), on ozone depletion, rainforest destruction, and the loss of biodiversity. In the long term architects will be affected by directives allowed under these new provisions.

Another measure which may concern architects is the recognition that town and country planning, land-use planning, and the management of water resources are matters in keeping with European environmental law. Article 130s effectively legitimizes these activities and provides the framework for their extension across Europe. It also encourages Member States to introduce energy plans as part of the rational use of natural resources, and (under Article 130u) to foster 'sustainable' economic and social development in developing countries.

The word 'sustainable' occurs in several contexts of the Maastricht Treaty probably as a direct response to the commitment to 'sustainability' signed by various European governments at the Earth Summit at Rio in 1992. In Article B of the Common Provisions the task of the EC is to 'promote economic and social progress which is balanced and sustainable'.[3] Neither 'balanced' nor 'sustainable' are defined, thereby providing perhaps the

---

[1] The Maastricht Treaty, Article 130r.1.
[2] *Ibid.*, Article 130r.2.

The implications of the Maastricht Treaty on design

Figure 2.1
Engineering and architecture have an enormous environmental impact. Here in northern France road and rail intersections are well integrated with nature conservation. (Paul Andreu©.)

necessary flexibility for the policy to be implemented by the 15 Member States. Subsequent to the signing of the Maastricht Treaty the UK Government published a consultation paper on 'Sustainable Development'[4] which attempts to draw together the various strands of argument. In terms of environmental impact assessment the word 'significant' is also employed without supporting definition. Notwithstanding those criticisms, the Treaty and the Single European Act upon which it is based, signal a new direction for architects. The environmental consequences of development, and to some extent the social ones, are now to be evaluated in general terms, and could be used as a basis to challenge UK development decisions in the European courts.

Looking outside the new provisions covering the environment, other important measures have been introduced which may impact upon the life of the architect or building engineer. As readers will be aware, under Article 57 of the Maastricht Treaty 'mutual recognition of diplomas, certificates and other evidence of formal qualifications' opens UK professional services to new competitive forces. To safeguard the interests of architects and the general public an earlier EC Directive (85/384) prescribed the content of architectural education, thereby ensuring that such diplomas had a common competency basis. Those concerned with education will have noticed that the Directive takes a wider and arguably more liberal view of architectural training than that exercised formerly by ARCUK and the RIBA.

Under Article 128 the Community wishes to contribute towards 'the flowering of the cultures of the Member States'. It hopes to do this by encouraging the dissemination of knowledge of the 'culture and history of the European

---

[3] The Maastricht Treaty, Common Provisions Article B.
[4] *UK Strategy for Sustainable Development: Consultation Paper* Department of the Environment, London, July 1993.

Peoples' and by supporting the 'conservation and safeguarding of cultural heritage of European significance'. Such a policy, if supported by adequate funds, offers further work for those specializing in the repair, restoration and presentation of historic buildings. The Article also encourages non-commercial cultural exchanges, and the creation of artistic and literary output. The effect of these provisions could be to foster greater trans-European architectural co-operation at an art historical level, and to promote the concept of architecture as artistic creation. Consumer protection increases in importance under Article 129a of the Maastricht Treaty. Although a number of directives had been issued earlier, such as those on dangerous substances, the Treaty on European Union signed at Maastricht now adopts the policy that Member States are to 'protect the health, safety and economic interests of consumers'. In time the consumer interest in the built environment, particularly health aspects and energy consumption of buildings, could lead to specific directives on matters such as energy labelling and a carbon tax. Maastricht provides the legal basis for such action.

Under Article 130g greater provision is made for technological development and demonstration programmes between research centres and universities. Matters such as energy projects and new environmental management systems are likely to be encouraged. Linked to a university, an enterprising architectural practice could receive funds to help construct a building testing the latest smart window technology or biological waste treatment plant.

Although the environmental provisions are likely to affect the life of British architects most, other articles of the Maastricht Treaty will have indirect impact. The signing at Maastricht of the Treaty on European Union and its subsequent ratification by the UK Parliament offers, in the medium and long term, a refocus for professional activity. The concerns over environmental quality and protection, the importance attached to consumer rights, the idea of a flowering of European culture, and the importance of research and technology, all bode well for an architecture of greater responsiveness

3

Maastricht and the architect

The Treaty on European Union signed at Maastricht on 7 February 1992 has wide ranging implications for the future practice of architecture. The Treaty contains the statement that one of the basic tasks of the European Commission is the promotion of 'sustainable and non-inflationary growth respecting the environment'.[1] Although the principle of 'subsidiarity' allows Member States to interpret or compile their own environmental policies within this general framework, the Maastricht agreement places considerable responsibility on the shoulders of government to ensure that development is compatible with the ability of the environment to sustain it.

In spite of John Major's opt-out clauses on the social chapter, the Maastricht Treaty was subject to considerable close scrutiny by the UK Parliament. That the environmental responsibilities were finally adopted suggests that the UK Government feels confident that its own regulations do already (or could be adapted to) meet its new European duties. Although Maastricht was an important turning point for the introduction of more rigorous environmental standards, the agreement also ratified and extended earlier commitments. The most important of these was the Single European Act of 1987 which introduced in general terms the concept that environment protection was to be part of EC policy. Under this Act the EC published a number of 'integrative documents' relating to areas of importance to architects such as energy, the urban environment, tropical rainforests, transport and carbon dioxide emissions.

Another important milestone before Maastricht was the Declaration on the Environment signed by EC heads of state in 1988 which stated that 'sustainable development must be one of the overriding objectives of all Community policies'. This declaration was one of the first to employ the, as yet ill-defined, term 'sustainability'. The Maastricht Treaty defines 'sustainability' in terms of four broad objectives:[2]

- preserving, protecting and improving the quality of the environment;
- protecting human health;
- prudent and rational utilization of natural resources;
- promoting measures at international level to deal with worldwide and environmental problems.

Perhaps the willingness of the UK Government to sign such an agreement reflects the elasticity of the concepts and definitions employed. The frequency of the use of the word 'sustainable' in EC law and elsewhere suggests some urgency in defining the term, especially in the different contexts in which it is frequently employed.

The Maastricht Treaty alters the central philosophy underpinning European development. The 1957 Treaty of Rome talked of 'continuous and balanced expansion' yet by 1992 heads of state signed an agreement which stated that 'sustainable development' was to be one of the new planks of Community policy. Also whilst earlier legislation had called for the introduction of environmental policies across Europe, the Maastricht Treaty declared that Community action on the environment 'shall aim at a high level of protection'.[3] It was no longer permissible to talk of general environmental concerns; after Maastricht Member States were required to introduce specific policies and objectives into their local laws. A further important innovation at Maastricht was the so called 'precautionary principle' which introduced into EC law the precept that preventive action was to be taken whereby environmental damage was to be rectified at source. This could be construed as implying that the architects' responsibility is one of dealing with pollution at the building, rather than dissipating its pollutants into the wider environment. Another principle ratified at Maastricht was that the polluter should pay for rectifying environmental damage, thereby shifting the emphasis away from government to the environmental contaminator. Again in terms of building this could place a duty upon the architect to design and specify in a benign

---

[1] David Wilkinson, Maastricht and the environment *Journal of Environment Law*, Vol 4, No 2, 1992, p 223.
[2] Treaty on European Union (the Maastricht Agreement), Article 130r.

[3] *Ibid.*, article 130r (2).

environmental fashion, thereby reducing the risk of long-term environmental costs to be borne by the building owner, operator or wider community.

In terms of UK legislation three fields will need to be modified to reflect the Maastricht agreement:

- Town and Country Planning Acts
- Building Regulations
- Health and Safety Acts

How far the Government intends to go remains to be seen. The matter has potential sensitivity, and over-ambitious environmental policies could, some claim, undermine Britain's competitive edge. The latter argument was the main basis for Britain's opt-out of the social chapter and could readily be employed to justify moving to the slow lane on environmental policy making.

If the Maastricht Treaty gave new teeth to environmental policy-makers, the introduction of the principle of 'subsidiarity' means that a clearer boundary is drawn between EC policy-making and the duties of Member States, and local and regional authorities. Subsidiarity restricts Community action to those situations where it is more effective than national or local action. However, whilst subsidiarity was seen as a welcome introduction by countries such as Britain wary of too much centralized environmental legislation, the reality is that many environmental impacts necessarily require Community-wide action. The international scale of problems such as global warming, the raising of sea levels, ozone depletion, the loss of wildlife sites for migrating birds, the destruction by Europe's building industry of the tropical rainforests, etc., means that the harmonizing of European environmental standards is imperative. Such national concerns, as they exist and are legitimized by Maastricht, will more than compensate for the constraints imposed by the subsidiarity clause.

It is becoming increasingly clear that environmental protection is one area where action needs to be international or at least trans-European to be effective. The harmonization of building product standards and their environmental impacts on the one hand, and of conserving Europe's cultural heritage on the other, requires legislation which is consistent in spirit no matter how it is worded at a local level. Policies aimed at eliminating chlorofluorocarbons (CFCs) in building must apply across Europe otherwise one Member State could gain a competitive advantage by short cutting environmental controls. A similar case could be made for the recycling of waste and the provision of measures to eliminate acid rain at power plants. Arguments which relate to reducing environmental damage apply equally well to protecting heritage resources. The cross-European interest in conserving Norman architecture, for instance, means that protection policies in France and England need to share common

Figure 3.1
Greater ecological awareness, whether measured in terms of building impacts or landscape sustainability, will figure more largely in the building design of the future. This computer centre for the Halifax Building Society by Abbey Hanson Rowe works with nature using trees to provide solar protection and water to modify external environmental conditions. (Abbey Hanson Rowe©.)

principles if the total stock of buildings is to be adequately preserved.

The Maastricht Treaty recognizes that environmental action must be across national boundaries. In spite of the UK opt-out clauses engineered under the general umbrella of subsidiarity, a 'variable speed Europe' cannot ignore the environmental consequences of urban development. Moreover, because majority voting is the basis for environmental policy making by the Council of Ministers, neither the European Parliament nor the European Court will uphold national objections to legislative changes. Hence, the UK Government will be forced to introduce changes to planning, building, and health and safety laws.

Design, construction and urban development face a new, fundamental change in direction. The capacity of the environment, both globally and locally, to absorb

Table 3.1
EC Building and Civil Engineering regulations and directives of interest to architects and engineers

Subject	Reference	Date adopted
Building sites		
Limitation of noise emitted by excavation,	86/662	1986
loaders, etc.	89/514	1990
Falling-object protective structures for		
certain construction plant	86//296	1990
Lifting and mechanical handling appliances	84/528	1986
	87/354	1987
	88/665	1988
Electrically operated lifts	84/529	1986
	90/486	1990
Temporary and mobile sites	89/391	1989
Hotels		
Protection of existing hotels against fire	86/666(RR)	1986
Construction materials		
Construction products	89/106	1991
	93/5068	1993
Eco-label award scheme	880/92(R)	1992
Health and safety at work		
Protection from ionizing radiation	76/579	1976
	79/343	1979
Provisions of safety signs at work	77/576	1977
	79/640	1979
Exposure to chemical, physical and	80/1107	1982
biological agents	88/642	1988
Exposure to asbestos	83/477	1987/90
	91/382	1991
Exposure to noise	86/188	1986
Information on safety, hygiene and health at work	88/383	1988
Improvements in the safety and health of		
workers in the workplace	89/391	1992
Minimum standards for use of machines,		
equipment and installations	89/655	1989
Minimum standards for work with visual		
display units (VDUs)	90/270	1992
Procurement		
Public procurement	89/440	1989
	90/380	1990
	90/531	1990
Utilities Directive	93/38	1994
Works Directive	93/37	1993
Professional services		
Professional services	92/5050	1992
Architects' Directives	85/384	1987
	85/614	1987
	86/17	1988
	90/685	1990

R = Regulation
RR = Recommendation

Table 3.2
EC environment regulations and directives of interest to architects and engineers

Subject	Reference	Date adopted	Secondary UK Legislation
Air pollution			
Health protection standards for SO$_2$	80/779	1980	
	89/427	1989	S1 317/89
	91/692	1991	
Chlorofluorocarbons in the environment	80/372	1980	
	594/91	1991	
Combating air pollution from industrial plants	84/360	1984	S1 319/89
	91/692	1991	
Air quality standards for nitrogen dioxide	85/203	1985	S1 319/89. See
	85/580	1985	also Environ-
	91/692	1991	ment Act 1995
Protection of forests against atmospheric pollution	3528/86(R)	1986	Section 80
Environmental pollution by asbestos	87/217	1987	
	91/692	1991	
Chlorofluorocarbons and halons which deplete ozone layer	3322/88(R)	1988	
	594/91(R)	1991	
Water pollution			
Pollution caused by certain dangerous substances discharged into the aquatic environment	76/464	1976	Water Industry Act 1991
			Water Resources Act 1991
	91/692	1991	
Quality of water for human consumption	80/778	1980	Water Industry Act
91/692	1991	1991	
Waste			
Toxic and dangerous wastes	78/319	1978	Environment Act
	91/692	1991	1995 Section 57
Recovery and reuse of waste paper and board	81/972(RR)	1981	
Dangerous substances			
Control of certain industrial activities	82/501	1982	
against major accident	87/217	1987	
	88/610	1988	
Pollution by asbestos	87/217	1987	
Protection and management of the environment			
Protection of the architectural and natural heritage	75/65(RR)	1975	
Environmental assessment of public and private projects	85/337	1985	
Conservation of natural habitats and wild flora and fauna	92/43	1992	
Recycling			
Encouragement of recycling measures	75/442	1975	Environment Act
	91/156	1991	1995 Section 92
	91/692	1991	
Noise			
Airborne noise from household appliances	86/594	1986	
Noise produced by construction plant and equipment	79/113	1979	
	81/1051	1981	
	85/405	1985	
Permissible sound levels of tower cranes	87/405	1989	
Sound levels for hand-held concrete breakers, etc.	85/409	1985	

R = Regulation
RR = Recommendation
SI = Statutory instrument

development will become over time the major basis for development consent. Buildings which are benign in terms of environmental impact, non-damaging to the health of users, frugal in the use of finite resources, will gradually become not the rarity they are now but commonplace. Maastricht promises to shape the future of building design as much as the introduction of public health law in the nineteenth century or planning controls in the twentieth. The concept of sustainable development across EC boundaries, of a building industry in Europe committed through legislation and moral imperative to green principles, is the direction in which today's designers and engineers need to be moving.

Practical effects of the Maastricht Treaty

Although the practical effects of the Maastricht agreement are likely to emerge gradually, the new commitment to the environment will have both external and internal ramifications. Externally, environmental protection is now required to be integrated into other EC policies. Hence, industry, agriculture, tourism, education and economic policy-making will all need to examine the environmental consequences of their actions. Internally, British building and development legislation will need to address more squarely the concepts of sustainability listed earlier.[4] The three main vehicles for introducing sustainable policies into British building legislation are under the planning acts, building law, and health and safety provisions.

Under the Town and Country Planning Acts, circulars have to provide a methodology for incorporating the concept of sustainability into the development plan and control procedures of British planning law; this is to continue with increasing emphasis under the Maastricht Treaty. Specifically, the Environmental Assessment (EA) procedures incorporated into legislation (England and Wales) under Circular 15/88 require a measure of prediction of the anticipated effects of development upon the local, and where appropriate, wider environment. As concerns over matters such as global warming grow, an expansion of EA project categories to embrace more types and scales of development looks inevitable. Also with greater emphasis placed upon conserving Europe's cultural heritage under Article 128 of the Treaty on European Union, more weight will be placed on examining the physical and sometimes visual impact of development. Such matters, though an obvious constraint upon how we build, should provide new opportunities for professionals in tune with Europe's environmental commitments.

The UK building regulations will also need to respond to the new EC directives. As the construction and use of buildings has a large environmental impact (in terms of finite resources such as energy and land) development will come under greater scrutiny and control. It is already evident that some areas of building law will be relaxed whilst others will be strengthened. To satisfy the EC's environmental concerns there is already a tightening of legislation dealing with thermal performance, the encouragement of greener methods of ventilation in office buildings, use of more natural materials, and greater fiscal flexibility to encourage the adoption of solar heating in housing. In time it is possible that legislation will be introduced to encourage the recycling of building components, the use of biological methods of human waste disposal, and guidance on self-sheltering layouts to improve local microclimates.

Health and safety legislation has already moved some way in protecting the welfare of workers in buildings, and in promoting an environment which is benign to human health. Certain building types such as hospitals and factories continue to pose environmental problems and fresh legislation will be required to meet the agreements signed at Maastricht. Measures here will, no doubt, focus upon more critical hazards such as toxic waste handling and disposal, radioactive exposure, and atmospheric toxicity in the workplace.

These various fields open up new areas of work for the building professional. The impact of buildings upon the global environment and its use of resources, the effect of buildings locally upon pollution and community health, mean that legislation affecting buildings will be crucial in meeting the Maastricht agreements. The practice of architecture, the education of Europe's future building professionals, and the wider building industry, will need to adjust rapidly to meet Brussels' if not Westminster's perception of environmental problems. If they do not, then under the Single European Market, professionals from outside Britain will win the lion's share of environment work in the UK. Increasingly, too, the pendulum will swing from environmental protection to environmental repair, thereby opening up further areas of work for the architect. The importance of this shift in the ethical basis of architecture promises to have implications not just for practice and education, but in creating a climate of greater inter-professional co-operation in the building industry.

---

[4]An important step is *UK Strategy for Sustainable Development: Consultation Paper* published by the Department of the Environment, July 1993 and the subsequent *UK Strategy for Sustainable Development* published with amendments in January 1994.

4
A layman's guide to EC law

Community Law (i.e. EC law) cannot be readily defined within accepted legal classifications. It represents a new legal order and is made up of:

- that part of international law governing treaties, etc.;
- EC Treaties and their Annexes;
- secondary legislation such as Directives made by Community institutions;
- that part of national law (i.e. UK law) implementing Community provisions.

The main primary sources of EC law are the Foundation Treaties, Conventions, Merger Treaties and Acts. Secondary sources of EC law consist of Obligatory Acts (i.e. Regulations, Directives and Decisions introduced to implement primary sources of law) and Non-obligatory Acts (i.e. Opinions, Recommendations, etc.). Specifically, 'Regulations' are general in scope and binding in their entirety without the need for further national implementation. 'Directives' are binding on each Member State, though national governments may choose how to implement them. Implementation, however, must be completed within a specified time period. Failure to implement a Directive into national law will normally lead to enforcement proceedings by the EC. 'Decisions' are binding in their entirety and may be addressed to Member States, individuals or corporations.

Hence, EC law consists of primary and secondary sources which apply equally to all 15 Member States (in 1995), 27 Member States possibly by the year 2000. Each element of legislation is given a specific number by the Community so that it can be readily identified. This normally consists of an official number and a year. For example, the harmonization provision governing the formation and exercise of the architectural profession is known as Directive 85/384/EEC.

The Maastricht Treaty which entered into force on 1 November 1993 established a European Union (EU). The EU consists of:

- The European Community (EC) – this is the formal title given since Maastricht to what was the European Economic Community (EEC);
- The European Coal and Steel Community (EECSC);
- The European Atomic Energy Community (EUROATOM);
- Inter-governmental Co-operation on Community Foreign and Security Policy (CFSP);
- Inter-governmental Co-operation in the Field of Justice and Home Affairs.

The EU does not replace the EC: it simply embraces the EC within a larger Union. However, since the EC is the main source of European legislation and the body responsible for its effective implementation, the title 'community' rather than 'union' is the most appropriate for outlining environmental concerns, initiatives and policy.

New European law is fraught with difficulties. The timescale between the initiation of directives or

Table 4.1
Chronology of key events in the European Community

Year	Event
1948	Organisation for European Economic Co-operation (OEEC)
1957	Treaty of Rome and Establishment of EEC
1959	European Free Trade Association (EFTA)
1973	Denmark, Ireland and UK join EC
1976	Discussion on European Political Union and Economic Integration
1978	European Monetary System (EMS) established
1986	Single European Act (SEA)
1991	Agreement on Economic Co-operation between EEC and EFTA
1992	Maastricht Treaty Extending Powers of EC

Source: Based on chronology in Rebecca Wallace and William Stewart (eds) *Butterworths Guide to the European Communities*, Butterworth, London, 1992.

Table 4.2
Chronology of membership of the EC

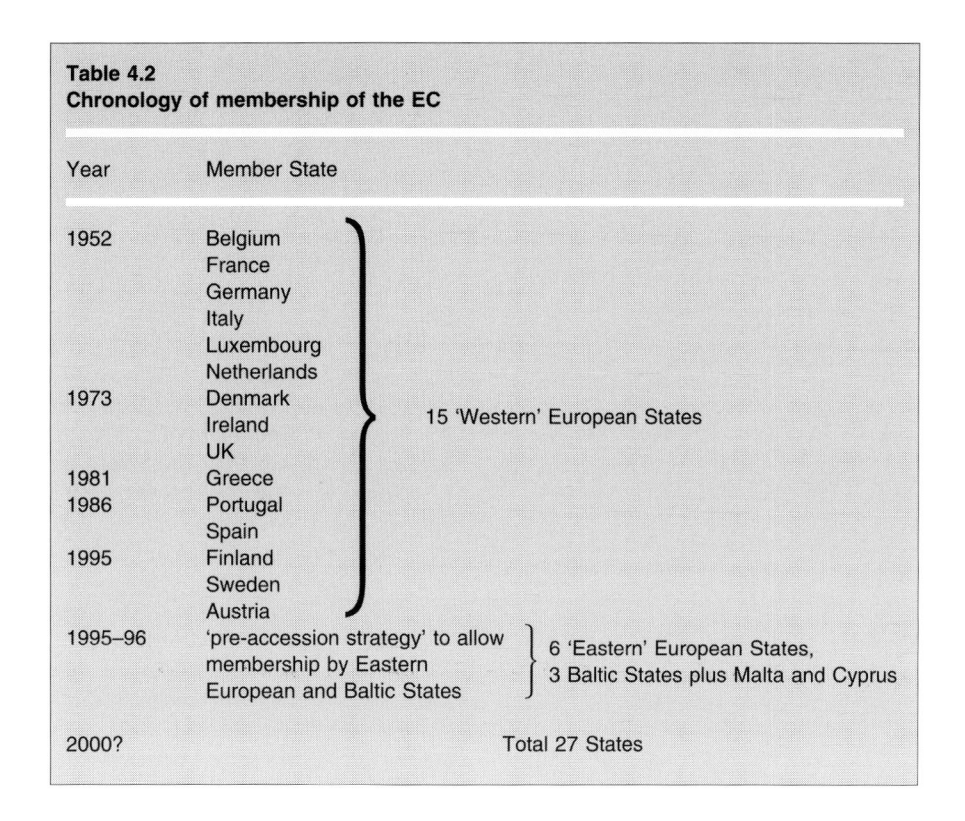

Year	Member State	
1952	Belgium, France, Germany, Italy, Luxembourg, Netherlands	
1973	Denmark, Ireland, UK	15 'Western' European States
1981	Greece	
1986	Portugal, Spain	
1995	Finland, Sweden, Austria	
1995–96	'pre-accession strategy' to allow membership by Eastern European and Baltic States	6 'Eastern' European States, 3 Baltic States plus Malta and Cyprus
2000?		Total 27 States

regulations and their adoption in national legislation can be as much as two or three years. However, as the timescale of many construction projects is long, many proposed directives can be law by the time projects become the reality of a busy construction site. Judging what is relevant may not be easy – the thrust of European legislative policy is not always clear and directives themselves have a habit of influencing matters outside their immediate subject. For instance, company directives could be of significance to the architect/contractor relationship, and product safety directives could influence the layout of domestic or office interiors.

To date, most EC environmental legislation has been in the form of *Directives*. While these are binding, they are implemented through national legislation which allows some discretion in how a directive is implemented. This has lead to a number of problems and it is possible that the EC will adopt more environmental measures through *Regulations* which apply in all Member States without need for national legislation.

Useful sources of information

Finding information quickly is by no means simple, especially for draft directives of consultative documents which seek to implement EC law in terms of UK national legislation. The principal government department is the Department of Trade and Industry (DTI) which has a useful information hotline 01179-444888. Sadly, it is not a freephone number and for long distance calls can be expensive for the small practitioner. The Department of Environment (DOE) produces 'Construction Monitor' on a monthly basis. It is particularly useful on changes to building and construction product information and can be contacted on 0171-276-3146. The Health and Safety Commission (HSC) publishes a bi-monthly newsletter which contains a useful introduction to new European codes. The HSC publications department can be contacted on 01787-881165 and the Health and Safety Executive (HSE) has a free leaflet line on 0114-289-2346.

The scope of directives is changing continuously and following the Maastricht Treaty of 1992 one can assume an acceleration in the scale and content of EC regulations. For the architect or engineer, the technical press plus the Construction Directorate of the Department of Environment, the Department of Trade and Industry, and professional bodies are obvious points of contact. The RIBA for instance maintains a European Office where members can obtain up-to-date advice. It also publishes (in 1993) a series *Architectural Practice Europe* with volumes devoted to France, Spain, Germany, Italy and Portugal. These cover building and planning law, contract procedures and procurement policy in each of the

Table 4.3
Hierarchy of main European documents for architecture

Treaties	General principles of the European Community or Union
Resolutions	Policy statement by the European Council
Regulations	Made by European Community to be adopted directly by governments of Member States
Directives	Made by European Community to be adopted by governments of Member States by secondary legislation
UK Acts and Regulations	Made by UK Government when new legislation is needed to implement a directive
Interpretative Documents	EC's explanation of the requirements of certain directives
Mandates	Order from the Commission for Harmonized Standards to be prepared by the European Standards body (CEN)
ENs	European Standards (such as Eurocodes)
ETAs	European Technical Approvals

countries. The Builder Group also publishes an excellent range of booklets and guides readily available at the Building Bookshop in Store Street, London. These, and the directives, regulations and decisions themselves, provide an essential starting point for those wishing to practise in Europe or to understand future directions in practice at home.

Besides directives, building professionals should consult also with the directorates dealing with the development of new proposals of the EC and the enforcement of existing directives. Particularly relevant are Directorate DGIII responsible for the Internal Market and Industrial Affairs, DGV for Employment, Industrial Relations and Social Affairs, DGXI for Environment, Nuclear Safety and Civil Protection, DGXII for Science, Research and Development, and finally DGXVII for Energy. The various directorates of the Directorate Générale are the main policy-making bodies of Europe.

All UK directives and subsequent national legislation are available from the HMSO. For speed of ordering it is important to quote the directive number as well as title. The HMSO also has available the *Official Journal of the European Communities* usually known as *OJ*. It is divided between the 'L' series which contains the full texts of legislation, the 'C' series of proposed legislation, and the 'S' series of notices of public contracts.[1]

---

[1] Barrie Evans, Keeping on top of Europe, *The Architects' Journal* Vol 13, January 1993.

Table 4.4
EC institutions and powers

Title	Members and location	Key powers
The Council	Ministerial representatives of Member States (usually one per country) Brussels	• EC's main legislative body • adopts legislative measures proposed by Commission • agrees levels of taxation
The European Parliament	Members elected from Member States (MEPs) Strasbourg	• controls EC budget • scrutinizes proposed legislation • supervises EC institutions (including the Commission)
The Commission	Representatives of Member States (usually one or two per country) Brussels	• guardian of EC Treaties and Laws • proposes fresh legislative measures • deals with complaints • has power to fine those who break EC Laws (including Member States)
The European Court of Justice	Judges appointed by Member States (Court consists of 13 judges) Strasbourg	• interpretation of Treaties and EC Laws • gives judgement on EC Law to national courts of Member States

Part 2
Construction Products and Professional Services

5

The Construction Products Directive

The Construction Products Directive (89/106/EEC) is one of the most important EC Directives for the architect. The Directive was enacted by the Construction Products Regulations (SI 1991 No 1620) which came into force in December 1991. Usually known as CPD, it requires that any construction products or components offered for sale must allow the building works to satisfy six essential requirements:

- mechanical resistance and stability;
- safety in case of fire;
- hygiene, health and environment;
- safety in use;
- protection against noise;
- energy economy and heat retention.

The main purpose of the Directive is to provide for the unencumbered and equitable circulation of building products throughout the EC which meet minimum standards of performance (and hence bear the CE mark). The intention is to encourage free trade of suitable construction products within the Community, and to ban products which are not fit for use. The Directive applies only to products for permanent incorporation into buildings and other civil engineering works. The wide ranging Directive has implications for the whole construction industry from those who design and specify materials to those who manufacture and supply products.

The Directive is worded in a fashion which allows the layman to readily understand the intentions. Each of the six essential requirements is supplemented by 'Interpretative Documents' which give a set of criteria or standards against which products may be assessed. The technical standards in each allow manufacturers to judge the conformity of their products and to self-certify or present their product for type-testing by an approved body. For the architect, surveyor or engineer, a product bearing the EC Conformity Mark (displaying the symbol CE) can be presumed to satisfy the technical requirements of the Directive. The approval of product quality depends upon the meeting of either:

- harmonized European Standards for construction products (few of which currently exist);
- a European Technical Approval (ETA);
- an agreed national standard.

Only if a product meets one of the above can it bear the CE mark. Manufacturers of non-building products can display the EC Mark under an 'Attestation of Conformity' clause if its quality is guaranteed by independent inspection and if the factory production control system is maintained under a quality assurance scheme such as BS5750. However, these arrangements are not available for construction products. At present the scheme is voluntary, but when the CE mark becomes mandatory (in 1977) then all construction products will need to conform. It is an expensive and time-consuming process and may well disadvantage small manufacturers and those towards the craft end of the market.

The CPD is a major step towards the removal of trade barriers in the construction industry. The vast majority of construction products are covered, including mechanical and electrical services, but the Directive excludes temporary site equipment such as scaffolding and shoring. As the CPD required Member States of the Community to remove regulatory barriers by June 1991, the UK Building Regulations and British Standards have had to adapt to the new Directive. The criteria of performance, however, accepts (under Article 3.2) that throughout Europe different geographics, climate and ways of life alter the reasonable life of products leading to official acceptance of recognized classes of performance of products in use.

Assessment of fitness under the European Technical Approval (ETA) scheme is a second route to the EC Mark and serves much the same function as the former Agrément Certificates issued by the British Board of Agrément (BBA). In time European harmonization will standardize assessment of products except where no common European Standard exists whereby designated bodies of Member States will carry out the assessment.

The long-term effect of the Directive is likely to be twofold:

- to facilitate the free flow of construction products across national boundaries;
- to lead to a standardization of the design and construction of buildings and civil engineering works across Europe.

The latter point may worry those who are keen to ensure a regional identity in construction for aesthetic, cultural and social reasons. The local patterns of building, distinctive craft traditions, and regional colour palettes in parts of Europe may all be subsumed by a directive intent for economic reasons to harmonize construction products.

The six essential requirements mentioned earlier are requirements of buildings, not necessarily requirements of products. Hence a dilemma exists between the need for buildings to offer mechanical resistance and stability or to conserve energy, and the ability of the approved or certified product to deliver such requirements. As buildings or engineering structures are often one-offs it is tempting to apply prototype testing, yet the Directive places the duty of assessment upon the manufacturer of products not the design of buildings. Materials used could be poorly specified, incorporated in conjunction with defective design, stored or installed badly, or attacked by pollution outside the designer's control. Hence, the broad Directive is supported in the UK by specific BS Codes of Practice to ensure correct design and workmanship, and in France DTUs (documents techniques unifées) perform a similar function.[1]

The six essential requirements

The six essential technical requirements of the Directive are explained with the help of Interpretative Documents under Article 3.1. Each is aimed at explaining how the fundamental objective of the removal of trade barriers can be realized whilst also ensuring that buildings and engineering works are healthy, safe, stable, energy conserving and protected against noise. The interpretative documents seek to:

- harmonize the terminology and technical bases of specifications;

- indicate classes of levels of performance;
- establish the technical standards for product assessment.

The main objective of such documents is to allow each Member State to harmonize their own building standards to those of the EC. Certain countries such as Greece with more open-ended building and product control will have to introduce national legislation to meet CPD requirements. Other countries such as Britain and Germany are, on the whole, able to correlate the essential requirements with existing provisions of their own building law.

Mechanical resistance and stability

This essential requirement is concerned to ensure that construction work is designed and built in such a fashion that when under load it will not collapse, deform or lead to damage to works or fittings. It largely duplicates Part B of the 1985 Building Regulations for England and Wales.

Safety in case of fire

Construction works must be designed and built so that in the event of fire the load-bearing capacity can be assumed for a specific period, the spread of fire and smoke is limited internally and to neighbouring structures, occupants can escape safely, and that the safety of rescue teams is taken into consideration. The requirements correspond with Parts B and J of the 1985 Building Regulations.

Hygiene, health and the environment

Construction works must not pose a threat to the hygiene or health of the occupants or neighbours, or damage the environment. The essential requirement lists the giving off of toxic gas, the presence of dangerous particles or gases, the emission of radiation, pollution or poisoning of the water or soil, faulty elimination of waste water, smoke, solid or liquid wastes, the presence of dampness in buildings. The wide ranging set of requirements reflects the growing concern about the effect of the built environment upon the health of occupants. In terms of the 1985 Building Regulations, the requirements correspond approximately with Parts C, D, F, G and H of UK building law and Parts 18 and 22 of German Model Building Ordnances.[2]

Safety in use

Construction works must be designed and built to prevent risk of accidents. These provisions replicate Parts D and K of the 1985 Building Regulations.

---

[1] John Osborne (ed.) *The Construction Products Directive of the European Communities*, London, p 10.

[2] *Ibid*, p 42.

Protection against noise

Construction works must be designed and built to reduce noise to a level which does not threaten the health of occupants or people nearby, and will allow them to sleep, rest and work in satisfactory conditions. These requirements are partly met by Part E of the 1985 Building Regulations, and Parts 17 and 24 of the German Model Building Ordnance.

Energy economy and heat retention

Construction works and their heating, cooling and ventilation installations must be designed and built to conserve energy, having regard to environmental conditions and the economic working life of the building. These essential requirements are met by Part L of the 1985 Building Regulations and subsequent amendments introduced in 1991.

The CPD and design

It is worth noting that the interpretative documents refer consistently to the 'design and building' of construction works. Design is of crucial importance to ensure the performance standards of construction products and buildings generally are met. Although a British architect or engineer would look normally to the UK building regulations and relevant British Standards for guidance on construction provisions, these may not embrace the full range of parameters in the essential requirements.[3] Until full harmonization between the Directive and national construction law is achieved it seems prudent to go to the higher legal authority, i.e. the Construction Products Directive (CPD).

For the UK architect engaged upon a construction project in Europe a grasp of the EC Directive should provide at least a broad appreciation of the likely building law on the ground. For the CPD not only harmonizes standards for the supplier, it also sets an agreed performance level for the designer to take into account. In this regard the Directive helps ensure not only the removal of trade barriers for the building product manufacturer but helps in the free trade of professional services.

Consumer and environmental consequences of the Directive

Whilst harmonization has many benefits for the supplier and designer, it also helps protect the consumer of buildings. The standardization of health, safety, fire protection and energy measures provides potential benefits in areas where, for political or historical reasons, building law has tended towards the *laissez-faire*. British holiday-makers in Spain or Greece will in future be protected by more rigorous hotel fire safety standards, and workers in certain toxic industries will enjoy higher standards of workplace environment. For the construction professional such standardization of performance criteria will open up new areas of work previously closed through lack of consistency in national legislation.

As mentioned earlier the promotion of free trade in construction products threatens to remove further the individuality of places. The traditional townscapes and landscapes of Europe are the result of the use of local building materials, regional craft traditions and methods of construction. Harmonization threatens to erode regional character. The prospect of bricks manufactured in England being used as a facing material in Brittany or Provence, or tiles made in Germany being used in Scotland, could undermine the visual diversity of Europe.

In some ways the standardization of product specifications and standards undermines moves towards a sustainable pattern of building. In the past the construction traditions of different European countries and their regions were shaped by the availability of raw materials to manufacture building products. In Sweden an abundant supply of timber crops led inevitably to houses and schools being constructed of wood, in Northern Italy good brick making clays led to an architecture of brick houses, in central France generous deposits of limestone led with equal inevitability to a stone landscape of houses and barns. In all these cases a domestic tradition grew from the building materials locally available. With little need to import construction products from afar and with manual labour rather than machines being mainly used on site, Europe developed quite naturally a sustainable method of building. Compared to today where the UK imports 95 per cent of its construction timbers and nearly all of its building stones, the pattern of the past has valuable lessons for the future. Whilst the Construction Products Directive has benefits for free trade across Europe, its effects may thwart moves towards sustainable development at the local level.

If the Directive is to promote trans-European trade in building products, it may inadvertently stifle the manufacture of local craft-based materials such as hand-made bricks or floor tiles since these may not meet the required technical standards. Many areas of Europe have a domestic building industry dependent upon cottage-based production of decorative building elements. These are not only important in terms of maintaining an 'identifiable regionalism' but also in helping to conserve old towns and landscapes. Whilst the Directive does not deliberately seek in its technical standard to thwart local production, there are no clauses exempting the Directive from applying to

---

[3] The list of essential requirements can be found in 'The Construction Products Directive', *European Directory of Energy Efficient Building*, J Owen Lewis and John Goulding (eds) London, 1993.

construction products for use in conservation. The Construction Products Directive needs, therefore, to be balanced by an equal effort to protect the often intangible characteristics of the local environment. Hence, EC environment law and construction law will need to enjoy equal priority in terms of the development of national legislation. If the economic arguments which underpin the Construction Products Directive take priority over those seeking environmental protection or the development of local building character, then the visual richness and diversity of Europe will be the loser.

How 'green' is the Construction Product Directive

The Directive is also somewhat in conflict with the Maastricht Treaty commitment to 'balanced and sustainable development'. It is hardly 'green' to manufacture cement in Italy and then transport it for use in say Holland or Denmark. The harmonization of construction products to encourage free trade between Member States carries obvious environmental and energy costs. The energy needed to manufacture a bag of cement could propel a family car for 80 miles, yet under the CPD countries are encouraged to transport that bag several hundreds of miles across Europe. It would be more balanced and sustainable to restrict use to the region in which the cement is manufactured. The concept of manufacturing and using a construction product locally whilst thinking globally does not appear to have influenced the spirit of the Directive.

The Directive is, therefore, paradoxical with regard to energy conservation. The need to conserve energy use in the operation of buildings is the sixth essential requirement yet full life-cycle energy assessment is not suggested. Had it been so then the costs of manufacture and transportation would have joined the equation of product harmonization. The effect may have been to highlight the huge energy and environmental costs in say the production, transportation, use and disposal of an everyday building product such as a concrete block or brick. The problem for politicians is that the complexities of the full equation of costs and benefits may mitigate against the laudable objective of removing barriers to trans-European trade. However, without the introduction of life-cycle assessment of construction products European Commissioners are allowing economic arguments to deflect them from the broader target of 'balanced and sustainable development'.

The CPD and changing professional duties

The Directive will have a growing impact upon the method of work of construction professionals. Many architects will need to shift their specification referencing away from British Standards to the new performance criteria of the Directive. Although as stated earlier BS and CPD are interconnected, the main defence in litigation is by ensuring construction products and usage meet CPD standards, not necessarily British standards.

New European specifications will gradually replace national standards, especially in the larger offices undertaking work in Europe or employing contractors from outside Britain. Although the application of the CPD will vary in each Member State, the principles and broad brush of practice will remain the same. As Europe-wide standards are introduced British building regulations and British Standards will be amended or withdrawn. Hence, there is the need to update and upgrade the knowledge of construction professionals to deal not only with the evolving legislation, but also to keep abreast of new construction products available through Community-wide trade.

A good example is 'Eurocode 2: design of concrete structures' which is one of a growing number of structural Eurocodes which demonstrate compliance of building and engineering works with the essential requirements of the CPD listed earlier. To help UK specifiers the British Cement Association (BCA) introduced the 'Concise Eurocode' in September 1993 to provide information on the design of reinforced and pre-stressed concrete buildings. It helps interpret Eurocode 2 setting out the options for designers and departures from UK Codes of Practice.[4]

The CE Mark and Eurocodes

Under the Construction Products Directive (CPD), the European Community's conformity symbol, the CE Mark, will become a common stamp on building products. By 1997 all products traded will carry the Mark whether destined for the home or European market. The main purpose of the CE Mark is to remove barriers to trade by providing a guarantee of quality and fitness for purpose. As long as the building product in question meets one of the essential requirements of the CPD, it will carry the Mark.

The fact that a product carries the CE Mark does not guarantee it is of a high standard; merely that it is adequate for the task. Designers will need to check that the product meets their own, sometimes higher standard. Under the old Agrément system, the certification of product standard was often voluntary. With CPD certification it is mandatory upon both the manufacturer and specifier of a product. In order to standardize performance criteria across Europe the Comité Européan de Normalisation (CEN) has specified requirements against

---

[4] A summary guide is available in *The Architects' Journal* 22 September 1993, p 8.

> **Table 5.1**
> **Summary of provisions and likely effects of the Construction Products Directive**
>
> The Directive covers all construction products in building and civil engineering works, including mechanical and electrical services, but excluding temporary products or installations.
>
> The Directive will lead to European performance standards replacing national standards, based upon 'six essential requirements.
>
> Periodic changes in the technical aspects of the Directive will require regular updating of the skills of the building professional.
>
> New standards of performance will gradually be used in contract documents and employed as a datum point in litigation.
>
> Designers will have a greatly enlarged range of construction products from which to choose.
>
> The standardization of construction products throughout Europe will lead to the collapse of the vernacular building tradition unless other measures are taken.
>
> The lack of life-cycle assessment in the technical provisions of the Directive will have the effect of discouraging 'green' product specification.
>
> Although the Directive will have an initially big impact upon the producers of construction products, over the 5–10 year time period the emphasis will be upon the engineer and designer using the Directive to improve the service to clients through wider product availability and simplified specification clauses.

which products are tested before they receive the CE Mark. The CEN has the task of liaising with Member States (in the case of the UK with the British Standards Institution and the British Board of Agrément) to help translate European product standards into local tests and measurements.

The documentation available at the completion of standardization will indicate which levels or classes of performance the CE marked product meets. It will allow specifiers in the UK to prescribe a material made say in Italy with confidence. Various levels of attestation of conformity to the CPD exist from third party certification based upon independent testing to a manufacturer's declaration of performance and factory quality control.[5]

The implication of the CPD and its CE Mark system is to influence not only design but maintenance and after-sales service. The main task of the standard is to ensure that products, processes and systems do their job properly.[6] They are in the interest of clients who have the task generally of dealing with suspect materials, and ultimately of designers. Customer confidence, the reassurance of the designer, and the well-being of the contractor are also safeguarded by the CE Mark. Ultimately, standardization will simplify the production of information to produce a building, it will provide guarantees across European boundaries, and it will ensure that health, safety, environmental controls and energy conservation are dealt with consistently.

In parallel to the introduction of the CE Mark, a series of Eurocodes are being developed for the building construction and civil engineering fields. Structural design codes are being developed by the European Committee for Standardization (CEN/TC 250) for introduction in 1995. Drafts of the first parts of Eurocodes 2, 3, 4 and 5 on the design of concrete, composite steel and concrete, and timber structures were made available in 1993. The Eurocodes, when introduced, will cover both EC and EFTA states. Structural design codes depend upon standard measures for materials and products. The CE Mark is not suitable in many cases (since the essential requirements only deal marginally with structural strength) and a parallel set of European Standards (known as ENs) are therefore being developed.

The effect of all of this standardization is to provide reliable quality control of materials and structural systems across European frontiers. The CPD has at its heart the free movement of goods and the removal of barriers to trade through misplaced national standards. Eurocodes, the CE Mark and ENs effectively smooth the way for more consistent criteria on environmental performance, if only through the back door of the essential requirements on health, safety and energy conservation. When the full raft of standards is in place in 1995, it will provide a framework, should the EC think it necessary, to introduce measures to make building products more ecologically benign and environmentally friendly.

---

[5] *The Architects' Journal* 12 May 1993, p 25.
[6] *Ibid.*

6

The Architects' Directive: mutual recognition of qualifications

The Architects' Directive (85/384/EEC)[1] establishes a common basis across Europe for architectural qualifications and training. To achieve the objective of freedom of movement for professional workers and to provide design services in one Member State by those qualified in another, the Directive provides for the mutual recognition of qualifications. The Single European Act, building upon Article 57 of the Treaty, is the legal basis for this and other professionally orientated directives. In the construction industry both architects and engineers have their own directives, though that for the engineering profession is more general in nature.

The Architects' Directive is based upon a minimum standard of education, split between 'the theoretical and practical aspects of architectural training'.[2] Students of architecture (and related architectural subjects such as building design engineering) have in their training to have acquired:

1. An ability to create architectural designs that satisfy both aesthetic and technical requirements.
2. An adequate knowledge of history and theories of architecture and the related arts, technologies and human sciences.
3. A knowledge of the fine arts as an influence on the quality of architectural design.
4. An adequate knowledge of urban design, planning and the skills involved in the planning process.
5. An understanding of the relationship between people and of the need to relate buildings and the spaces between them to human needs and scale.
6. An understanding of the profession of architecture and the role of the architect in society, in particular in preparing briefs that take account of social factors.
7. An understanding of the methods of investigation and preparation of the brief for a design project.
8. An understanding of the structural design, constructional and engineering problems associated with building design.
9. An adequate knowledge of physical problems and technologies and of the function of buildings so as to provide them with internal conditions of comfort and protection against climate.
10. The necessary design skills to meet building users' requirements within the constraints imposed by cost factors and building regulations.
11. An adequate knowledge of the industries, organizations, regulations and procedures involved in designing concepts into buildings and integrating plans into overall planning.

There are two general points of interest. First, the wording makes a distinction between 'hard' and 'soft' areas of architectural education. For example, in the design fields the student is required to demonstrate 'an ability to create' and to display the 'necessary design skills' yet in the softer areas of history or fine arts the student is expected merely to display 'an adequate knowledge' or simply have 'knowledge of'. A distinction should also be drawn between the acquisition of knowledge and demonstrating 'an understanding of' which suggests a higher educational objective. Matters relating to the preparation of briefs, environmental standards, human needs, structural design and the social role of the architect (all requiring an understanding) seem to be given higher priority than history, theory and technology which are covered by knowledge acquisition alone.

One should not suspect a hidden agenda here, the Directive merely reflects the pattern of education common outside Britain. In Britain, the RIBA syllabus makes no distinction between understanding and knowledge, and places technology as highly as social and environmental skills. As worded, the Architects' Directive reinforces the general thrust of policy making in Europe with its emphasis upon social and environmental concerns. It also follows

---

[1] See also Directives 85/614/EEC, 86/17/EEC, 89/48/EEC and 90/685/EEC.
[2] The Architects' Directive (85/384/EEC) Part 11.2.

more closely the French and German pattern of architectural education which less readily makes a distinction between architecture, town planning and structural engineering design. In these countries (and others) the specialization of the architect grows from a more broadly based common curriculum dealing with the built environment. The various professional groupings, of which architecture is one, emerge from the generalist core mainly as specializations in the first degree and are developed further (to RIBA Part 2 level) in postgraduate studies.

The eleven points to be covered in education under the Directive are unlikely to be taught to the same level of competence in all Member States. Our own training in the UK has a distinctive bias, most noticeably in its emphasis upon technological teaching and its avoidance of the discipline of cost and building regulation (item 10 in the Directive). The UK building industry also has specialists not widely recognized in Europe, such as quantity surveyors (cost) and building control officers (regulations). No doubt anomalies exist elsewhere in Europe.

The Architects' Directive is fraught with difficulties at both educational and practice levels. Not all Member States have (in 1993) adopted the measure, and in Britain the deregulation of the architectural profession adds further confusion to a muddled situation. Like the Construction Products Directive, the adoption of measures to promote free trade across Europe finds itself in conflict with traditional practices and governments bent upon protecting the interests of their own manufacturers or professional associations. The difficulty in architecture has been partly resolved by the First General Directive on Mutual Recognition of Professional Qualifications (89/48/EEC) requiring the mutual recognition of all higher education diplomas awarded on completion of professional education and practical training. In effect this Directive, adopted in 1991, ensures that all professionals regulated by the state (including architects, engineers, town planners, surveyors, teachers, lawyers, accountants, etc.) may apply to another Member State to have their qualifications recognized. The term 'regulated by the state' applies to self-regulating bodies such as the RIBA or RICS. The chartered professional bodies exercise delegated powers under the Directive, but as with the Architects' Directive, lack of consistency of title, function and regulatory control mean that qualifications are not always recognized between Member States. UK quantity surveyors, for instance, do not have obvious equivalents in most Member States where building economists are often prohibited from undertaking design work. Also in Germany the architect undertakes work normally done in the UK by structural engineers and frequently fulfils the site management function of a building contractor.[3]

Both the Architects' Directive and the General Directive are important if consultants are wishing to put together multi-disciplinary project teams. EC projects, particularly those open to tender through widened procurement procedures, are likely to involve groups of different professionals, perhaps from different European countries. Mutual recognition is not only important in facilitating such arrangements, but in providing an understanding of the skills provided by construction and design professionals from different cultural backgrounds.

The effects of mutual recognition of qualifications are likely to lead to:

- Greater standardization in the educational and training programmes of construction design professionals.
- Students will adopt the shortest pathways to qualification even if it means shopping around between Member States.
- Technology teaching in UK schools of architecture may have to give ground to social, environmental and economic subjects thereby broadening the base of architectural education.
- With standardization of courses and qualifications, Europe may end up with a greater consistency of design quality but also a further loss of regional differences both in practice and in the built environment.
- The European pattern of broadly-based first degrees with specialisms emerging to serve different professional needs (architecture, structural engineering, town planning, etc.) may become the basis for UK design education.

Public procurement and professional services

The completion of the internal market requires the opening up of public procurement contracts to competition from non-national firms. The Commission believes that such competition would amount to a saving of 0.5 per cent of Community GDP[4] creating some 350 000 additional jobs. As public sector contracts amount to 15 per cent of Europe's GDP (30 per cent of this is devoted to building and civil engineering work) the new Directive carries the potential of additional work for UK contractors.

The Public Works Directives (89/440/EEC and 90/380/EEC) cover civil engineering and building work of over ECU 5 million but exclude mechanical installations such as power lines or railway track laying. All public bodies from state level to local authorities have a responsibility to open contracts to competitive tender from outside their own country. Another Directive

---

[3] N F Spencer Chapman and C Grandjean *The Construction Industry and the European Community* 1993, p 172.

[4] *The Architects' Journal* 18 August 1993, p 71.

(90/531/EEC) as revised by COM 91/347 and COM 92/292 subjects the water, energy and transport sectors to similar competitive pressures, introducing parallel measures in these fields.

Professional services

Design and consultancy services are also embraced within Directives of similar spirit. The internal market spans professional as well as construction services. Opposition from certain government and professional organizations limited the scope of the proposed Directive issued in December 1990.

However, as implemented Directive 92/5050/EEC follows the same pattern of other public procurement directives with the need for advance notices, provisions on technical specifications, award procedures, calls for competition, criteria for selection of tenderers, etc., worded much as before. The Directive proposed the split of professional services between Annex 1A services (where the full provisions of the Directive associated with professional services apply) and Annex 1B services (where limited provisions apply). Annex 1A services embrace not only architectural design, but town planning consultancy, technical and scientific consultancy, engineering services, etc. Annex B lists amongst others legal services, education, health, recreational and cultural services.

The new responsibilities require public authorities to open design services of a certain size (the threshold is ECU 200 000 about £180 000) to trans-European tender. It would, for instance, be illegal for a government department to let, without competitive tender, the design of a major project to say the PSA or directly to a major private design consultancy such as BDP. The effect is to erode well-established linkages between public clients and private design firms, and between public clients and their own public design services. Such a pattern, commonplace in the UK until recently, remains the norm in much of Europe where design and consultancy work is frequently carried out without this fresh air of competitiveness by government agencies of various kinds.

The Directive may have the effect of encouraging the broadening of professional services on offer to the UK architect. The adoption of more comprehensive forms of professional service procurement should reverse the trend towards exclusivist design services witnessed in the growing use of 'signature' architects. The Directive requires a rich mix of services with old fields abandoned by British architects included (such as town planning) as well as new ones such as facilities management. Potentially, as *The Architects' Journal* observed, the architects' position in society may be enhanced by the new measures.[5]

The proposed Directive also legitimizes design competitions operated by certain countries for major buildings by removing geographical barriers on entries. An architect who successfully tenders for such work under the Directive is required to abide by European technical standards (particularly the Construction Products Directorate 89/106/EEC) and European formats for contract documentation.

To take advantage of the new work opportunities in Europe, the UK architect or engineer will need to familiarize himself or herself with advance notices of forthcoming public procurement tenders for professional services. The calls for competition require a keen eye to be kept on public notices in the country of origin. Familiarity with EC technical standards, award procedures and the different criteria for the selection of tenderers is also important. The opening of design and consultancy services is a two-way process. Whilst Sir Norman Foster may win prestigious projects in France such as the new museum at Nimes, Santiago Calatrava may take a lion's share of the more glamorous engineering design work in the UK such as the East London River Crossing. If the liberalization of trade between Member States is achieved by such directives, so too the level of design is likely to be raised. For designers will be set against each other in a fashion which embraces a broader cultural or philosophical mix than was formerly the case. In the field of professional services, tenders are a mixture of financial bids and design proposals. The inclusion of quality of design into the equation can only help the flowering of culture which the EC seeks to achieve under Article 128 of the Maastricht Treaty.

[5]*The Architects' Journal* 11 August 1993, p 29.

Part 3
Energy and Pollution

7

The construction industry and global warming

In the interaction of mankind and the environment, it is often the inter-relationships of activity which matter. In the construction industry the complex web of responsibilities spanning town planning, building design, site operations, refurbishment and demolition mean that good environmental practice to reduce global warming needs to cross the boundaries of professional interests. One could go further and suggest that solutions to our energy and environmental problems should be sought in the connections between activities as well as in the activities themselves. A case in point is that of a detached solar house which, though efficient in terms of energy use for space heating, may well impose additional infrastructure and energy costs through transportation, the delivery of

Figure 7.1
Buildings and transport are together responsible for three quarters of energy use and hence CO_2 production in the UK. (Susan Pritchard, University of Huddersfield©.)

The construction industry and global warming

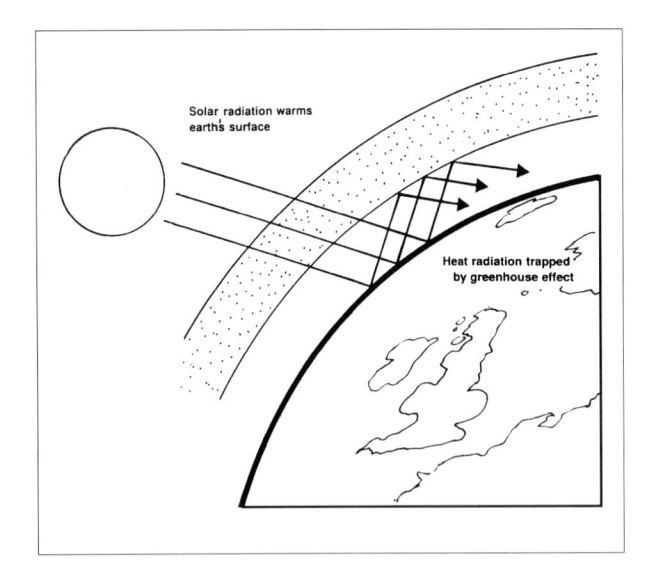

Figure 7.2
How global warming occurs.

**Table 7.1
Main greenhouse gases**

Greenhouse gases	Warming effect (%)
Carbon dioxide	50
Methane	19
CFC 12	10
Tropospheric ozone	8
CFC 11	5
Nitrous oxide	4
Water vapour	3
Other CFCs	2

Source: Environmental Issues in Construction: Volume 2: Technical Review CIRIA Special Publication 94, 1993 p 25

public utilities, and other environmental costs associated with rural or suburban living. Achieving the EC's energy targets outlined directly and indirectly in various regulations and directives (see later) requires a broad appreciation of the effects of development on global warming.

Currently in the UK the heating, lighting and ventilation of buildings consumes about half the total energy consumption of the nation. The pattern of development and the trend towards urban dispersal for which planners, engineers, designers and site operators are partly responsible, also has significant impact through fossil fuel use in transportation. Greenhouse gases are the by-product of this profligate consumption of energy. Taken together, the fossil-fuel derived energy used first to produce building materials, then in the construction process, and subsequently by the users of buildings throughout their 50–60 year lifetime, is a source of large amounts of carbon dioxide (CO_2). Though not the most damaging of the greenhouse gases, carbon dioxide is the one produced in the largest quantities. Other gases associated with construction are more damaging but produced in smaller quantities, but here decisions made by architects, planners and clients, can be significant in terms of environmental impact. The climate changes triggered by these decisions are beginning to require changes in building design construction practice and in post-climate change modifications to existing buildings.

Global warming is arguably the most urgent environmental problem we face. Since the main contributor to the 'greenhouse effect' is carbon dioxide (CO_2), energy and how it is used is the key environmental issue of our day and should be at the forefront of priorities for all those in the construction industry. The damaging cocktail of greenhouse gases has grown in potency since the Second World War. Although carbon dioxide has only increased by 25 per cent in the past hundred years, methane has increased by 100 per cent and other damaging gases such as CFCs and nitrous oxide have been introduced into the atmosphere for the first time. Many of these are widely used in the construction industry.

CO_2 is exchanged naturally between the big deposits of carbon in the oceans, atmosphere and the living world. Various biological processes on land contribute 110 000 million tons of carbon as CO_2 into the atmosphere each year. This considerable volume of carbon is balanced by photosynthesis from the oceans, forests, etc. By burning fossil fuels man artificially adds nearly 6000 million tons of CO_2 a year and a further 2000 million tons by the clearing of forests. It is this excess in atmospheric CO_2 which is primarily responsible for climate change. However CFCs, though usually condemned for their ability to thin the ozone layer (see Chapter 8), contribute 17 per cent towards the warming effect of the world's climate.

Greenhouse gases work by regulating the relative penetration of short- and long-wave radiation from the sun. The atmosphere allows the short-wave radiation to pass through whilst absorbing the long-wave radiation which the Earth emits. Without this barrier to Earth-based radiation the surface temperature would become too cold to support life. The problem with man's activities is that the naturally occurring greenhouse gases in the atmosphere are being added to at about 5 per cent every eight years thereby altering the climatic balance. CFCs are totally new greenhouse gases and their effects in the upper atmosphere are not fully understood (their damage in terms of ozone destruction and ultra-violet light penetration will be

Figure 7.3
Much twentieth-century development has paid little regard to energy conservation or the environment. These flats in Glasgow were designed by architects with the direct encouragement of the government of the day. (Brian Edwards©.)

discussed later). The new greenhouse gases and the greater concentration of old ones means that the temperature of the Earth will rise between 1° and 4°C over the next twenty-five years and perhaps by as much as 6°C in 100 years.[1] A destabilized world climate potentially threatens man's survival, at least in terms of current population levels and expectations of lifestyle.

The consequences of greatly increasing the levels of CO_2 in the atmosphere have only recently been computed with any measure of international agreement. The doubling of CO_2 would increase the temperature by 1°C but set in motion other climate changes which themselves alter global temperatures. A warmer atmosphere holds more water vapour which is itself a greenhouse gas. Extra water vapour increases temperature by 50 per cent. Higher temperatures reduce snow and ice cover so reducing the reflectivity of the earth allowing more sunshine to be absorbed increasing temperatures by a further 50 per cent. These changes then increase cloud cover and cloud distribution adding a further 2°C to world temperatures. Taken together the chain reaction is a 4°C increase, possible in theory within twenty-five years unless urgent action is taken. There will be local variations and one geographical region may benefit at the expense of another. The UK, for instance, will be warmer but wetter with changes in the pattern of rainfall.

Such global temperature rise will have profound impact upon the Earth's climate and the distribution of land to sea. As the temperature rises sea levels will increase by 0.3 m to 0.7 m. As many of the world's cities are at sea level (London, Amsterdam, New York, Sydney, etc.) the consequences are enormous. Not only do such cities face a

---

[1] Department of the Environment *Environment in Trust: Global Atmosphere and Air Quality* HMSO, London, 1992.

The construction industry and global warming

Table 7.2
Good practice principles to reduce the production of greenhouse gases

Urban and landscape design
- Maximize the use of public transport by concentrating development in existing urban areas and along transport corridors
- Minimize land-use separation by integrating building uses and maintaining development densities
- Create green space in towns to improve urban microclimates, enhance air quality and reduce engineering costs of storm water drainage
- Use dense planting in large belts to protect the urban edge from adverse weather conditions
- Avoid new suburban and greenfield development and increase densities around existing suburban transport nodes
- Create attractive and safe cycle and footpath systems
- Exploit waste land in towns for development
- Encourage combined heat and power for electricity generation

Building design
- Maximize use of renewable energy especially solar and wind power
- Minimize fabric heat loss by maximizing wall, roof and floor sharing
- Build in self-sheltering groups open to solar gains
- Design with high thermal mass rather than lightweight construction
- Use planting to improve microclimate at the building edge and fabric edge
- Avoid deep plan buildings and where unavoidable employ atria
- Use atria to promote stack-effect natural ventilation
- Design with long life, loose-fit, low fossil-fuel energy use, and minimum ecological impact in mind
- Insulate and control draughts in existing buildings
- Reuse buildings rather than build new
- Improve insulation levels to well above minimum regulatory standards
- Avoid building over four storeys high
- Use natural light, ventilation and cooling
- Reduce building services to minimum compatible with health and safety

Construction and building services
- Use materials which are locally manufactured
- Use materials such as stone and timber where the environmental costs of production are low
- Consider the 'cradle to grave' energy costs involved
- Avoid tropical hardwoods
- Avoid using materials involving CFCs or halons
- Use low-energy lights
- Use construction techniques which allow for dismantling and re-erection
- Use steel rather than *in situ* concrete frames
- Use lime mortar in masonry construction to facilitate the reuse of bricks, blocks and stonework
- Use natural rather than synthetic materials

greater risk of street-level flooding, but their supporting underground services of subway railways, sewers, water supplies, electric, telecommunication and fibre-optic cabling would be temporarily or permanently impaired. A similar bleak outlook faces farmers. As sea levels rise much fertile land will be lost to flooding. In Britain the agricultural heartlands of East Anglia face inundations, in Holland the intensively farmed landscapes once claimed from the sea will be unsustainable, and in much of the Indian sub-continent the rice fields of estuary deltas will prove unworkable.

Sea level rises will be accompanied by a change in the pattern of rainfall and the severity of storms. Greater climatic disturbance means more damaging storms from the tropics sweeping Western Europe and the eastern seaboard of the USA. From Miami to Glasgow hurricanes will damage buildings, destroy forests and crops, and make the achievement of an acceptable urban-microclimate difficult to achieve. As the frequency and severity of storms increase for some areas, others will see their rainfall diminish. In Africa temperature rises will lead to an expansion of deserts as rainfall evaporates before it can reach the centre of the continent. As the Sahara enlarges whole nations will become dependent upon food aid. Even in parts of Europe, used to regular patterns of rainfall and dryness, the changing climate could lead to long periods of

The construction industry and global warming

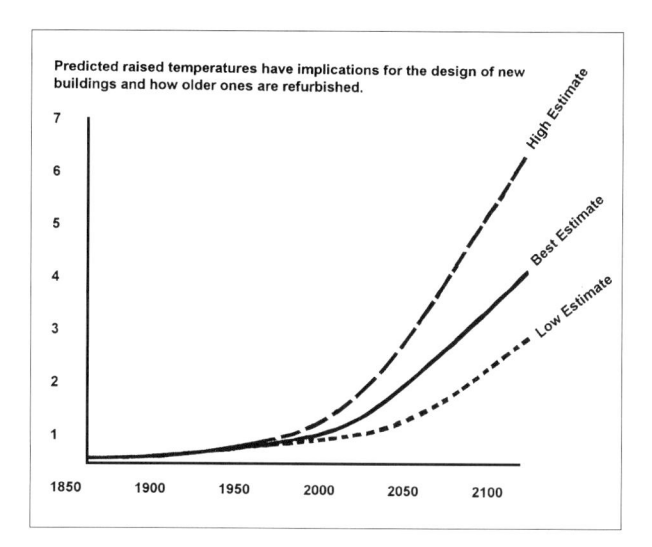

Figure 7.4
Predicted temperature rises (in °C) over the lifetime of today's buildings. *Source*: *Our Common Inheritance*, HMSO, 1990.

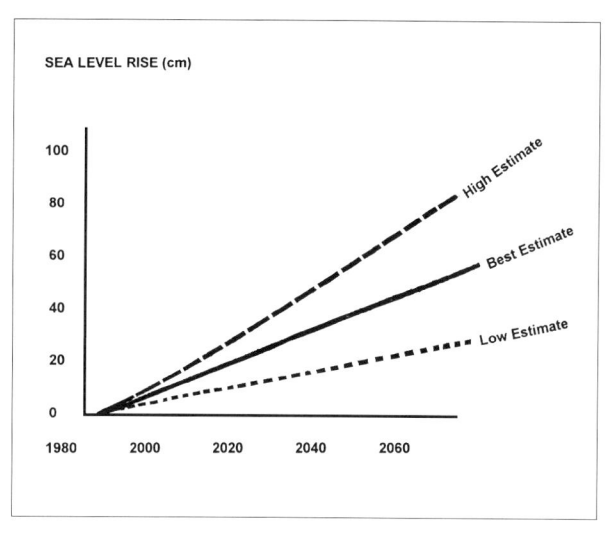

Figure 7.5
Predicted sea level rises over the lifetime of today's buildings. *Source*: *Our Common Inheritance*, HMSO, 1990.

summer drought with important consequences for the management of water.

Decisions on energy use and building design made in the affluent areas of the world have, it is now realized, an effect upon the whole eco-system of the planet. Those who design buildings, those who procure them, and those who manufacture the components and erect them, all need to think about the environmental consequences of their actions. The regulators have an important role as well: they protect the public and the wider environmental interest. Supported by adequate laws, the building and planning regulators have the task of examining the connections and inter-relationships in the complex web which we call the construction industry. Buildings are central to any legislative strategy the UK Government can introduce to reduce the emission of global warming gases. The Government's Energy Efficiency Office in 1992 set a target of 20 per cent energy reduction over the next ten years though observers think a saving of 25 per cent is readily achievable with the introduction of new energy technologies. More recently the UK Government announced its intention of achieving a 15 per cent reduction in energy use over a five year period (1993–98) in its own estate of properties. After the announcement by John Gummer in August 1993, the Environment Secretary said he expected health authorities and local authorities to match that figure.

In Britain levels of carbon dioxide emission have recently begun to fall as government measures (and educational programmes) have started to have impact. In Europe as a whole, however, a small rise is still detectable and the USA, though it continues to achieve efficiency

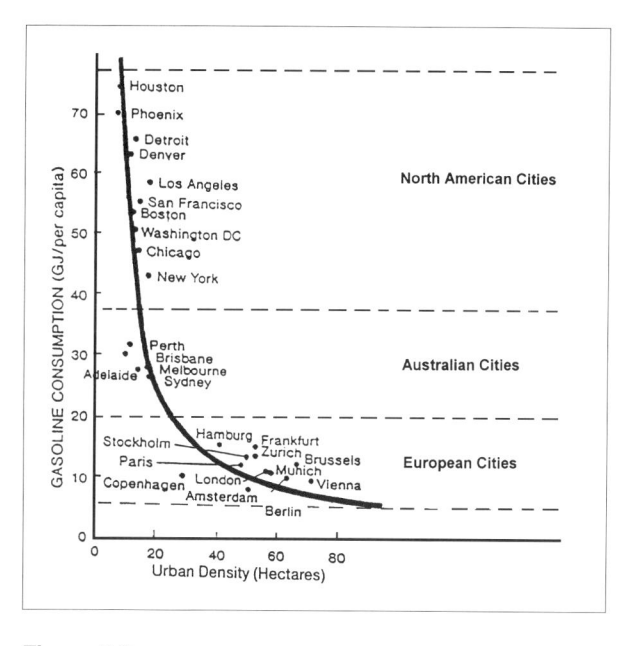

Figure 7.6
Relationship between urban density and gasoline consumption. The graph shows that traditional European cities are less damaging in terms of CO_2 production than newer cities. However, as Britain moves towards American patterns of development the volume of greenhouse gases will increase. *Source*: P Norman and J Kenworthy *Cities and Automobile Dependence* 1989.

35

The construction industry and global warming

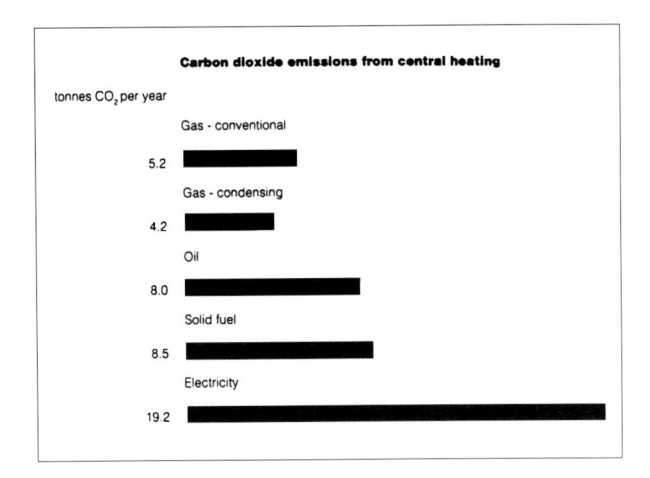

Figure 7.7
Carbon dioxide emissions from central heating in the UK. (British Gas©.)

Figure 7.8
Make up of global warming. The figures represent percentages. (*RIBA Journal*©.)

gains, is still by far the world's biggest producer of global warming gases. As Asia's economy grows, so too does their use of fossil-fuel energy supplies. Although a person in Asia consumes only a tenth of the amount of fossil-fuel energy as an American, the gap is closing rapidly. The worldwide picture is therefore less than encouraging with an annual growth of global warming gas production currently at 6 per cent perhaps increasing to 8 per cent by the year 2000. There are no easy solutions to the problem: agencies such as the UN could give renewed effort to promoting the benefits of a stable world population, and governments could encourage greater telecommunications-led decentralization, allowing more people to work from home. This would reduce the demand for new buildings and greatly curtail the need for travel. The introduction of a carbon tax, mooted within the EC, will also focus attention upon the relationship between the design of buildings and global warming gas production.

Britain's construction industry produces 300 million tonnes of carbon dioxide per year which is about a half of national output. Since energy is only one aspect of environmental impact, the magnitude of the construction industry's effect upon land, water resources, communities, landscapes and cities is enormous. Global warming gas production is an important measure of the scale of impact buildings have upon the wider environment, but it is by no means the only issue to consider.

Design, ethical and legal responsibilities for global warming

In general the building industry impacts upon energy consumption and global warming in four separate ways:

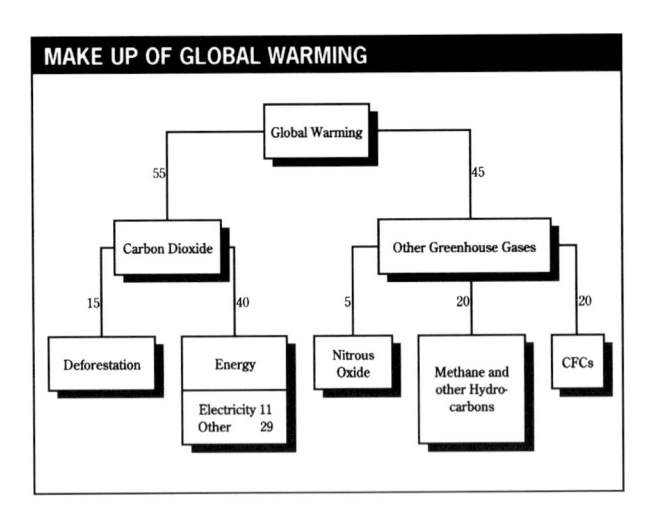

- the production of materials and products used to make a building or structure;
- the fabrication and construction process;
- the heating, lighting, cooling and ventilation of buildings in use;
- the infrastructure and transport costs of servicing buildings.

The first three on this list are direct impacts, whilst the fourth is indirect, though by no means insignificant.

In evaluating global warming impacts it is crucial to consider the full life-cycle energy cost. For instance, though some materials such as aluminium and glass have high energy costs, they can significantly reduce heating demand when used in a building because of their potential for passive solar gain or their ability to produce draught-free openings. Also both materials are capable of being re-cycled, in whole or in part, so once the price of the initial impact has been paid, there should be few additional costs in global warming terms.

There are complex legal parameters in which designers and manufacturers are required to work. Various building laws (particularly part L of the UK Building Regulations), Town and Country Planning Acts, and a plethora of EC directives and regulations, require the physical, environmental and energy impact of development to be taken into account. Whether they are adequate to address the key fields of design impact and professional interaction is open to debate. One could cite the growth of suburban supermarkets in the early 1990s as an example of the failure of regulations to deal adequately with slowing down the rate of carbon dioxide emissions. The typical single storey, windowless supermarket surrounded by an ocean of car parking, poorly served by public transport, and constructed of materials of high energy cost, is now commonplace on the periphery of most English towns. Although aspects of legal control shape such buildings, their impact upon the conservation of total energy used is marginal. The energy consumed to light the deep-plan supermarkets, to ventilate them, to run the refrigeration plants (often utilizing CFCs), to power the lorries which keep the shelves filled and the customer cars which take away the produce, all add up to major global warming gas production. If laws cannot control such gas guzzling retail systems, then those who pay for, or procure, design or manage such buildings must adopt a new ethical stance. Companies with the power and authority of Sainsbury's need to undertake an environmental audit of their whole operation, perhaps in order to see how much of the UK's 600 million tonnes of annual carbon dioxide production is the result of their activities.

Legal imperatives are at present insufficient to draw attention to these environmental injustices. Perhaps the introduction of a carbon tax with full environmental assessment of projects (to include primary and secondary energy use) will be needed before society faces up to the climate damage caused by out-of-town development. At the time of writing the EC is investigating the introduction of a carbon tax applied to Europe's construction industry. The tax would operate simply by measuring the amount of fossil fuel burnt by each building. It would have the effect of encouraging fuel-efficient houses and allow consumers to judge the energy efficacy of different building design.

Environmental audits

Those schemes which are available to help undertake an environmental audit and to issue labels of good practice (such as the BREEAM scheme) are an important first step. The BREEAM scheme is based upon the accumulation of 'credits' which examine the impacts of the design of a building upon the global, local and internal environment. The wide spread of the BREEAM viewpoint is valuable since it embraces fields of activity from across the building industry and allows the inter-relationships to be evaluated. The scheme also looks at other environmental issues (such as worker health and neighbourhood disturbance) and hence begins to become a synthesizing model of use to designers rather than a sectoral blueprint of value to only one professional interest group.

The life-cycle complexities of energy use in a building are not yet fully understood. The construction, use over 50–60 years, demolition and recycling of parts, represents a complicated network of energy impacts. The evaluation of the energy and environmental cost of producing a simple building product, such as brick, is a complex process; imagine how complicated it is to evaluate a whole building. With a brick the costs involve land lost to agriculture (potential loss of food production and increase in energy-expensive imports), energy used in baking the clay into a brick, in transporting the brick to a building site, in erecting the brick in a wall. Once erected the brick helps conserve energy since it allows the wall to perform its function as an insulator. So the initial cost of producing the brick (enough fossil-fuel energy is embodied in the brick to drive a family car seven miles) is gradually offset through energy conserved in the life of the building. Added to this the brick could be salvaged and reused in another wall of another building.

The complexity of an energy audit from 'cradle to grave' should not deter asking questions at present. Information is currently being gathered to allow comprehensive energy audits to be introduced, perhaps as an expansion of the worthwhile groundwork established by the BREEAM scheme. In the meantime designers, builders and clients need to abide by the principles of good practice outlined in Table 7.2.

The timescale of decision making

Since the rate of building replacement is less than 1 per cent per year, existing buildings are of greater importance than new ones in terms of total carbon dioxide (CO_2) production. Any strategy for global warming must therefore pay considerable regard to the energy performance of the existing stock of offices, hospitals, schools, universities, houses, etc. Energy-conscious refurbishment is of fundamental importance and needs to be undertaken on a regular basis – at least once per decade. Even the buildings designed today with carbon dioxide reduction to the fore will need to undergo modification as standards and awareness increase during the lifetime of the building. Energy and environmental audits are, therefore, matters of consequence for both the design of new structures and the upgrading of existing ones. Design decisions made today affect the performance of the building over a long period of time. A building which is badly orientated or located has to carry the burden of poor tactical decision making over a long period. Likewise, a hospital with a deep plan imposes energy costs and hence global warming consequences no matter how well the building is refurbished from other environmental points of view. Just as many of our inherited buildings, such as high rise flats from the 1960s and deep plan sealed envelope office developments of the 1980s, seriously restrict our room to improve their energy performance, so too do our decisions affect the future generation's opportunities for improvement.

What is certain is that buildings designed and constructed today will face an energy crisis within their life span. In such a scenario it is prudent to specify well above the minimum regulatory insulation standard, and to design within the broad parameters of building height and depth which can be readily lit, ventilated and to some extent heated, by natural means. To achieve these changes in architectural culture there will need to be an ethical shift in the design professions and the construction industry at large. Just as the social programmes of the Welfare State led to a distinctive architectural landscape after the Second World War, so too the urgency of current environmental problems will create its own characteristic style and pattern of building. Clues to what this will be can be found in some of the older towns and buildings constructed before energy was cheap and building products were factory made and transported great distances. Historic towns such as Bath, York and Edinburgh contain valuable lessons, as do the arts and craft buildings by C F A Voysey, Edward Prior and William Lethaby.

Evidence is emerging in Europe of a holistic philosophy of design which places the 'green' agenda at the forefront of creative and constructional activity. Global warming is both a problem and an opportunity to improve the poor energy performance of much of the building stock of British cities. It also provides the justification to think afresh about how to address some other problems of the post-industrial cities of the West, such as the decline of the inner cities and the lack of social cohesion. 'Greening' urban areas will not only improve the visual landscape of towns but create fresh employment opportunities, eradicate blighted areas, provide a sense of purpose for those in deprived neighbourhoods and, through well-directed development, gradually reduce global warming. In this regard the imperative of environmental policies can mesh with social ones to achieve the visually rich, socially diversified and energy-efficient cities of the future.

8

CFCs, HCFCs and other ozone depleting gases

Of equal concern to global warming is the problem of the thinning of the ozone layer with a corresponding increase in the penetration of damaging ultraviolet light. European Directive EEC 80/372 and Regulation 3322/88/EEC which sought to control the use of ozone-destroying chlorofluorocarbons (CFCs) and hydrochlorofluorocarbons (HCFCs) have now been repealed by stronger measures in Regulation 594/91/EEC. As about a half of all CFCs are used in buildings, the legislation has the effect of limiting their use in construction where they are frequently employed in the production of insulants and cooling systems. In 1987 the Montreal Protocol,[1] to which the UK was a signatory, established an international agreement to phase out the production of various types of CFCs by 1996. Within the EC a subsequent agreement signed in 1990 prohibits the manufacture and import of CFCs after 1 January 1995. In spite of these measures CFC levels are in 1994 still rising by 4 per cent per year.

CFCs have the effect of destroying the earth's delicate stratospheric ozone layer which protects the planet from potentially dangerous ultraviolet radiation. The thinning of the ozone layer, and particularly the holes discovered over both the Antarctic and Arctic has allowed a big increase in ultraviolet light to reach the earth's surface. This has two main adverse effects: it is leading to a rapid increase in skin cancers in humans (a 1 per cent increase in ultraviolet radiation leads to a 5 per cent increase in cancer), and it is slowing down the earth's productive rate particularly in the oceans where plankton growth is being retarded. There is also evidence that crop growth is being stunted by the increase in ultraviolet radiation, following an 8 per cent reduction in the density of the ozone layer over the past twelve years. Recent research also implicates an increase in ultraviolet radiation in the suppression of immune systems.

Governments worldwide have acted fairly quickly to phase out CFC use and to restrict the use of the related but

[1] *The Montreal Protocol* Foreign Office Command Paper, Treaty Series No 19, HMSO, 1990.

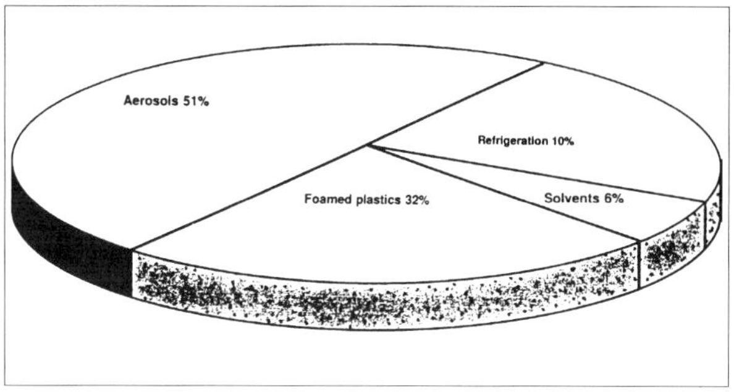

Figure 8.1
How CFCs are used in Europe. The stippled area represents the main building uses in 1994.

less damaging transitional substance HCFCs. The latter, being based upon hydrogen, have a reduced adverse effect upon the ozone layer and the current plans under the 1991 EC Regulation are to restrict their use to 10 per cent of 1996 levels by 2015. Other ozone depleting gases are also damaging the balance of the stratosphere including nitrogen oxide (NO_2) introduced by car exhaust systems, and halons used in fire-fighting agents in buildings.

With CFCs being phased out by the end of 1995 and HCFCs on a slower timescale, the construction industry in the UK has had to rapidly adjust to the introduction of new, less damaging materials. Whilst companies such as ICI have developed alternative materials (some of which although they are not ozone damaging are still greenhouse gases), it is important to eliminate the need for air conditioning refrigerants in the first case by better design. Though substitutes to CFCs have been created by the chemical industry, designers, engineers and clients should ask whether the dependence upon total air conditioning in the workplace is necessary for the environmental damage caused. It is often argued that staff satisfaction and air quality control depends upon mechanical ventilation and total air conditioning in noisy, urban areas, but in fact mixed mode systems of ventilation and cooling utilizing the stack effect can be equally effective. The over-ambitious specification of many commercial projects has led to highly expensive offices being built when most users would have been satisfied with lower running costs and greater flexibility. Better design consists often of avoiding wasteful and unnecessary uses of CFCs.

Most CFC and HCFC use in buildings is in conjunction with air conditioning where the material provides the refrigerants. Elsewhere these substances form the foaming agent in plastics and many insulants (see Table 8.1), and were formerly widely used in aerosol propellants. CFCs continue to be widely employed in domestic refrigerators though ICI has developed a less damaging chlorine-free substitute (HCFC 134a). Since 50 per cent of CFC use is building related,[2] designers and engineers have a large influence upon reducing demand. The main measures which could be taken in the construction industry to phase out CFC and HCFC use are:

- designing buildings to avoid employing air conditioning;
- avoiding specifying insulation materials which utilize CFCs or HCFCs in their production;
- avoiding halon-based fire control agents;
- designing commercial buildings to maximize natural light and ventilation;
- upgrading existing CFC air-conditioning systems, avoiding the repeated use of CFC related materials including HCFCs.

Not all uses of CFCs are evident to those who specify construction materials. Many extruded polystyrene and phenolics employ CFCs as blowing agents and a wide range of rigid urethane foams were formerly based upon CFCs. The lack of an eco-labelling scheme has had the effect of obscuring CFC use to those whose concern for the environment would normally have introduced a measure of caution. Similarly, the wide use of CFCs as refrigerants in vapour-compressed chillers was not as openly advertised as one would have hoped for a material which by the mid-1980s had developed a reputation for global damage. As a consequence many designers and specifiers continued the use of a product in ignorance of the damage it was causing to the delicate stratospheric ozone layer. Britain's property boom of 1985–89 was predicated upon the commercial benefits of the climatically sealed, air-conditioned, CFC-employing office block. Buildings such as Canary Wharf in London Docklands are typical of the type of architecture which emerges when concerns for global warming and ozone destruction fail to be seen as a priority.

Figure 8.2
Modern buildings with sealed envelopes are responsible for half the CFC and HCFC use in the UK. (Brian Edwards©.)

Many buildings constructed in the past decade face refurbishment in order to recover and destroy the CFCs employed. As new, less damaging substances become available, pressure grows to review air-conditioning technology of existing buildings. Such reviews may well entail the introduction of heat pumps, the substitution of CFCs, and other modifications to increase energy efficiency. They may also review the need for air conditioning at all. Various recent reports provide guidance on how to recover CFCs and avoid their loss to the atmosphere.[3] As with other environmental concerns, the damage inflicted by an earlier generation is leading to new areas of work for today's building professionals.

---

[2]S R Curwell, R C Fox and C G March *Use of CFCs in Buildings* Fernsheer Ltd, 1988.

[3]See for instance Building Research Establishment: CFCs and Buildings. Digest 358, 1992 Edition, Building Research Establishment Information Paper PD8/93 *Guidance on the Phase-Out of CFCs for owners of air-conditioned systems*, Department of Trade and Industry, 1993; *CFCs and Halons. Alternatives and the scope for recovery for recycling and destruction* HMSO, 1990.

9

Reducing air pollution by better design and urban development

A number of directives are targeted at reducing the level of air pollution with its consequent potential damage to human health, biological health and the global environment. Air pollution is a general concern of the Sustainable Development clauses of the Maastricht Treaty and a specific concern of the wide raft of EC legislative measures listed in Table 9.1.

For the construction professional there are four main fields of activity which should be addressed to reduce air pollution:

- better building plant design and management;
- the design of more efficient buildings from an energy and resources point of view, exploiting technical innovation to reduce pollution and waste;
- the creation of patterns and types of development which lead to less energy transport use;
- the use of renewable sources of energy.

As pollution in the form of complex interactions such as acid rain is a by-product of combustion, the designer will need to conserve energy by looking at both the demand and supply side of fossil-fuel use. The architect influences demand by their broad design strategy and has the chance to modify supply by providing within the building localized facilities for the generation of power and by taking advantage of renewable sources of energy. The two sides of the equation (supply and demand) can be brought neatly together in small-scaled Combined Heat and Power (CHP) installations. Here the waste heat of locally generated electricity is turned to the advantage of nearby buildings rather than lost to the atmosphere as in conventional power stations. Though generating efficiencies are less (32 per cent as against 40 per cent at a modern power station) two-thirds of the waste heat can be employed for district heating, leading to overall improvements in efficiency and, incidentally, greater control over supply and usually reduced cost to the customer.

There are many well-documented means by which designers can take advantage of renewable supplies of

Table 9.1
Air pollution directives

Exhaust systems	Directives	92/5097/EEC
		82/890/EEC
		88/297/EEC
		86/594/EEC
		91/542/EEC
		79/694/EEC
		87/56/EEC
		89/235/EEC
Gaseous pollutants	Directives	77/102/EEC
		78/665/EEC
		93/5059/EEC
		90/55/EEC
		87/219/EEC
		91/692/EEC
		91/441/EEC
Industrial plants and large combustion plants	Directives	82/459/EEC
		91/692/EEC
		91/692/EEC
		85/580/EEC
		91/692/EEC
		88/609/EEC
		89/369/EEC
		89/429/EEC
	Decision	81/462/EEC
	Regulations	1613/89/EEC
		2157/92/EEC
Lead	Directives	77/312/EEC
		85/210/EEC
		91/692/EEC
		87/16/EEC
		85/581/EEC
		88/609/EEC
Nitrogen dioxide	Directive	91/692/EEC
Ozone depletion	Directives	88/540/EEC
		91/359/EEC
	Regulations	594/91/EEC
		3952/92/EEC
Sulphur dioxide	Directives	91/692/EEC
		89/427/EEC

41

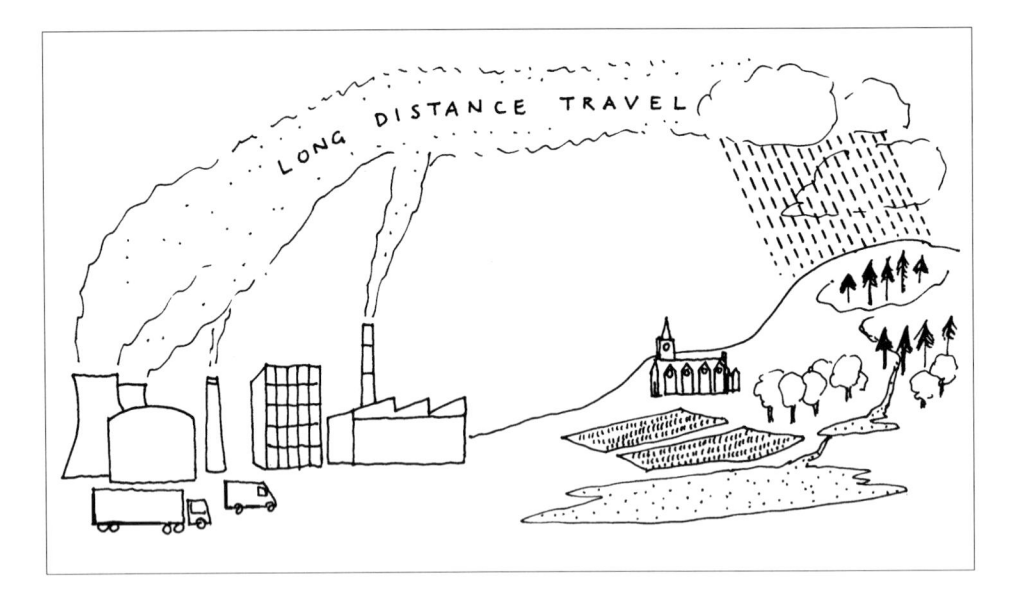

Figure 9.1 Chemical transformation in the atmosphere of acid emissions from fossil-fuel combustion (CO_2, SO_2, NO_x) falls as 'acid rain' some distance away. It adversely affects trees, lakes, farming and buildings.

energy (see Chapter 12). The most obvious and cost efficient is to utilize solar power to either reduce the demand made upon more traditional forms of heating or to promote natural ventilation through the stack effect. Wind, wave and waste power are also important sources of low-cost energy which can be utilized according to building type, circumstances of use, and location. Renewable energy use reduces the demand made upon fossil-fuel burning either at the power station or in the building, and hence has great benefit in bringing down levels of air pollution. By exploiting technical innovation and modern materials, the designer can balance the use of renewable energy with greater efficiency in building plant design.

Patterns and types of development

Directly and indirectly buildings contribute towards energy use through the transport implications of the form, type and location of development. The trend towards widely dispersed, single-use development, has had the effect of separating the demand for goods and services from the supply. To connect the two, people travel increasingly by car and goods are often transported great distances by lorry. The phenomena of out-of-town shopping centres, suburban or green field business parks, large car-based tourist developments, have collectively meant that vehicle-contributed carbon dioxide (CO_2) emissions in the UK have risen from 13 per cent in 1979 to 23 per cent in 1993.[1] As CO_2 is one of the most important global warming gases, the increasing influence of road transport on the global environment has naturally concerned the EC and national governments alike, leading to some of the directives listed in Table 9.1. The growth in transportation has continued in spite of the availability of cheap technology which some predicted would lead to telecommunications-led decentralization. However, the trend toward 'telecottaging' where working people share modern telecommunications such as fax machines and modems, advocated as a green answer to rural living, has yet to reduce the demand for car-based travel.

Britain's agreement at the Rio conference in 1992 to cut CO_2 emissions by one quarter by the year 2000 has profound consequences for the way we design the environment. The matter spans many professional interest groups from town planners to highway engineers and vehicle designers. However, it is clear that architects in their broad design role have a part to play in reversing this upward trend and in meeting the concerns expressed in the UK's Planning Policy Guideline (PPG) 13 on Transport and Planning[2] which sets a framework for energy reduction over the next 10–15 years (see Chapter 28).

During the 1980s and 1990s Britain has seen a shift away from major urban areas towards new employment opportunities created in smaller towns, green field locations, and along certain motorway corridors such as the M4 and M3. Coupled with changes in working locations, Britain has followed the American model of out-of-town shopping centres, major motorway-linked retail parks and tourist attractions. The effect has been to

---

[1] Glynn Jones, Planning and the reduction of transport emissions, *The Planner* July 1993, p 15–18.

[2] Department of the Environment and Transport *Reducing Transport Emissions Through Planning* HMSO, London, 1993.

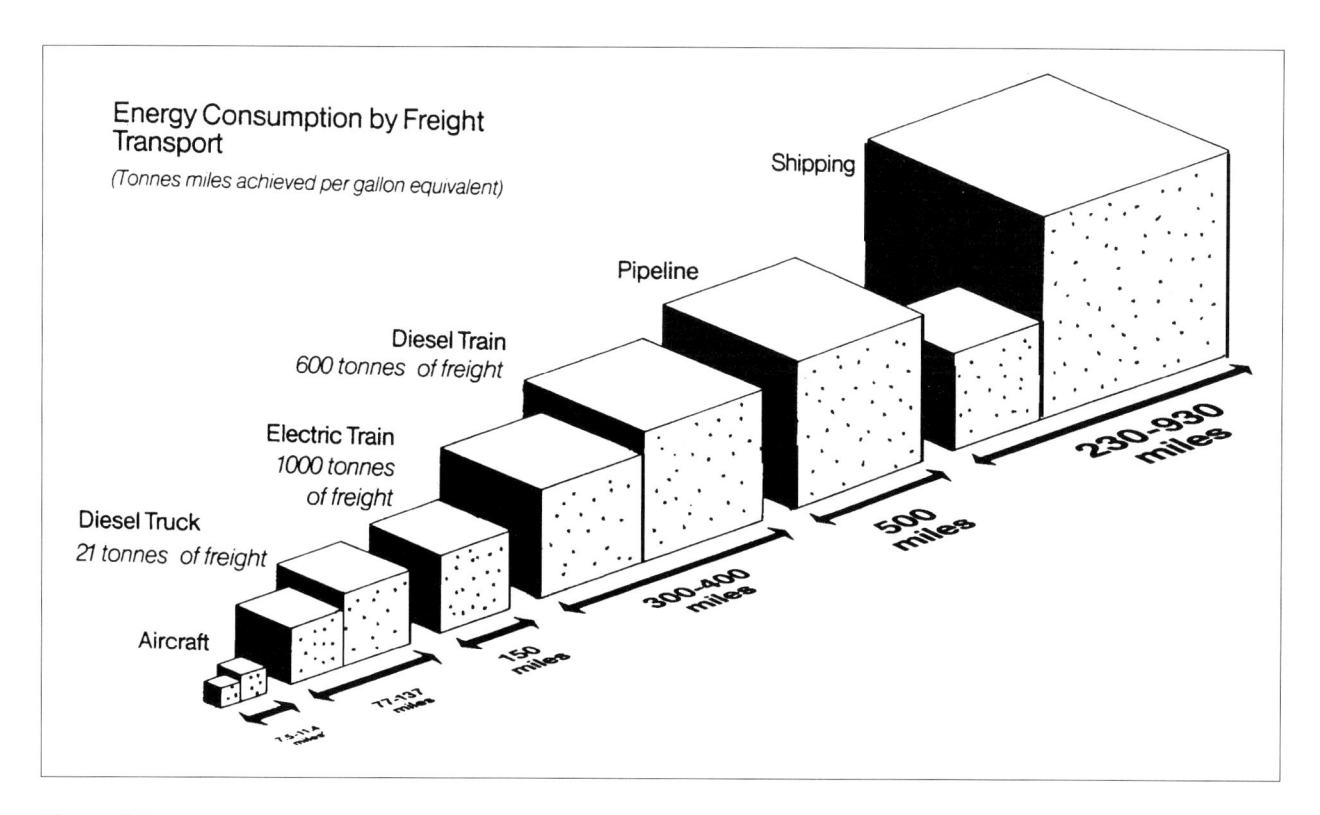

Figure 9.2
Energy consumption in freight transport. (Lothian Energy Group©.)

increase the level of car usage both for commuting to work and travelling to buy goods or to seek entertainment. The decentralization and spatial segregation of services and attractions has meant that the motor car has become the predominant means of joining home with workplace and leisure facilities. Added to this spatial separation, developments have tended to be for single land use with the result that it is difficult to combine a trip to the supermarket with a visit to the town hall or local swimming pool.

Architects, surveyors and engineers have participated in the creation of these essentially 'ungreen' environments. Aided by a new generation of developers and a largely compliant alliance of local and central governments, the retail and physical landscape of Britain (and much of Western Europe) has undergone profound changes. With CO_2 emissions from transportation contributing to nearly 30 per cent of global warming gas production in the UK, the environmental consequences of such large-scale physical segregation can no longer be condoned. There are also increasing worries over the 3 per cent annual increase of ozone pollution – low level air pollution due to a combination of nitrogen oxide and volatile organic compounds mainly attributed to vehicle exhausts. This is endangering asthmatics, retarding crop growth and destroying roadside trees and urban forests.

Elements of a 'green' development strategy

As many architects have long realized, high density, mixed use development leads to the creation of attractive, socially cohesive, low-energy environments. The move towards higher density living with employment, shopping and leisure provided locally (as against regionally) sustains a largely public-transport focused means of movement. Urban size, density of occupation and richness of land-use mix are key ingredients of the sustainable city. A combination of regional centres and more local neighbourhood centres tends to satisfy most trip needs which, with good design and layout, supports access by light rail, bus, bicycle or walking. Clearly, if such a pattern became commonplace again, CO_2 emissions would begin to fall in line with Britain's international commitments. Also compact forms of development mean that the heat lost from one apartment becomes the heat gain for another, as against heat gain for the regional or global environment. Compaction is also a prerequisite for the introduction of combined heat and power schemes with their potential saving of 80 per cent in usable energy over conventional power stations (see Chapter 12).

Wherever possible architects and developers should, therefore, seek to create developments with high levels of

Figure 9.3
Creating safe, direct, well-lit routes for pedestrians encourages people to walk rather than using other forms of transport, thereby saving on energy and maintaining personal health. (Peter Lathey, University of Sheffield©.)

Figure 9.4
Forming attractive urban spaces is essential if the resources of cities are to be fully exploited. Here in London Docklands a close mix of cafes, shops, offices and apartments restricts energy usage in transportation. (Brian Edwards©.)

residential use which support and sustain other activities nearby such as offices, workshops, shops and leisure facilities. They should also seek to retain density of population and employment in existing urban areas. They should specifically avoid the decentralization of population or services to suburban areas or green field locations. Where existing infrastructure of public transport exists, at for instance suburban railway stations, the population and levels of activity should be increased to generate usage and to create concentrated localized diversity. Where suburban development takes place it should be conceived as an 'urban village' with supporting services and employment provided within the development. Such development should also include cycleways and public paths to encourage non-car trips. Where existing retail and business parks exist in the countryside these should be urbanized by creating new high density housing areas around the buildings, and also by extending the public transport network to them.

Architects and engineers can also do much to make existing urban areas more attractive and safe to live and work in. Measures such as traffic calming, cleaning and floodlighting of buildings, transfer of wastelands to parkland, have obvious benefit. Better environmental conditions at a physical level can lead to improved performance in terms of energy conservation, and greater durability of the building stock. Attractive, well-used towns tend to be occupied at night by people who are happy to take a bus, walk or cycle to visit their friends or to shop. Pleasing places are generally both safe, green and durable.

The EC's 1990 Green Paper on the Urban Environment attempted to define universal solutions to Europe's cities based upon the integration of transport and land-use

Reducing air pollution by better design and urban development

Figure 9.5
Compact development with well integrated public transport will be important elements of future cities. (James Stirling, Michael Wilford and Associates©.)

policies on the one hand, and linked questions of health and deprivation on the other. Though much criticized, the Green Paper has helped to identify cities as the focus for environmental action, and has cast a critical light upon current transport policies. Amongst the new policy initiatives encouraged by this paper is the greater weight now attached to the health, well-being and public safety interests of those who live along the transport routes in the inner city. The Green Paper also legitimized the demand in urban areas for safe streets for walking and cycling. Unlike earlier European policy, the Green Paper sought to give expression to the role of cities as cultural and social entities, expressing in their built form and character those things which were typically European. Such a perspective inevitably led to a questioning of transport policy and the assumption that those who travel into towns from the rural hinterland had interests which exceeded those who live there all the time. This has encouraged a new interest in integrated transport policy where various modes are considered and their ability to reduce vehicle emissions and provide improvements to the wider environment are equated.

By diversifying the package of land uses within a development, the need for car-borne trips is greatly reduced. Single-use development such as a modern city-edge supermarket presupposes a high level of car use and hence damaging levels of CO_2 emissions. It is no surprise to find that many out-of-town shopping centres offer land-use variety in the form only of a cheap petrol filling station. Mixed use development in town centre and city edge implies mixed mode travel (cars, buses, cycling, walking) and mixed use architecture. Such variety spans a wide spectrum of environmental concerns and professional interests.

The Belgian 'Greenbus'

Recent directives on exhaust systems, particularly 88/77/EEC and 91/542/EEC, have encouraged the development of less polluting buses to ease Europe's chronic urban air quality problem. In Belgian prototype buses powered by liquid hydrogen have been developed with the aid of a grant of £5.2 million from the European Union.[3] Named Greenbus, the new buses have been jointly developed by the German industrial gas firm Messer Griesheim and the Belgian engine maker VCST - Hydrogen. They seat 88 passengers and have a range initially of 70 km with the prospect of increasing the operational distance to 300 km once the safety problem of hydrogen storage has been solved.

There is nothing unconventional about the appearance or behaviour of the bus. It is based upon a standard bus chassis and MAN diesel engine, both modified for hydrogen power, storage of hydrogen tanks, novel fuel mixture system and associated ignition. Four towns in Belgian including Geel where trials were undertaken have had their buses adapted from diesel to hydrogen power. The justification for the use of liquid hydrogen as a fuel is not one of cost but environmental quality. With oil costing (in 1994) about $20 per barrel, the move to hydrogen is to improve air cleanliness and public health, not to enhance operational costs. Without subsidies from the EU, prototype development would have been hard to justify in a market economy. In the USA it is estimated that 1000 buses utilize the alternative engine specialists Detroit Diesel's natural gas engines which burn a mixture of methane and hydrogen. In the USA, as in Europe, grants

---

[3]Marcus Gibson, Hydrogen bus holds the promise of cleaner air, *The European* 19–25 August 1994, p 20.

from regional and local governments are a prerequisite to the development of green transport. Once buses have proved their worth, it is predicted that fleet cars and government vehicles could be converted to hydrogen (probably two to five years later) with private cars following in a further five to ten years.[4]

Hydrogen powered vehicles do not eliminate dangerous emissions but they do cut pollution problems significantly compared to diesel or petrol. With consumption at around 0.32 litres of hydrogen per kilometre for a bus, the total global warming gas production is reduced to about a quarter and other gases such as nitrous oxide are eliminated altogether. The justification for the Belgian 'green-bus' experiment is one of both global health and public health.

If buses are to become green and to be more widely accepted as a form of transport within towns, the pattern of use will need to reflect the pattern of urban development. An ideal city plan is to have a grid of compact corridors along which bus, tram and light rail trains travel. The conventional dispersed town with randomly distributed sub-centres does not suit public transport. The move back to public transport carries implications for urban form. Corridors linked by a matrix of environmentally friendly public transport separated by a walking distance of about a kilometre will gradually become established. Such an urban pattern will mean nobody is further than 12–15 minutes walk from a bus or tram stop, and every six or so stops on the bus will lead to a sub-centre where shops, parks, medical centres and schools are located. In an ideal world public transport and urban development will be developed in tandem. More generally where towns are already developed, urban renewal provides the means to link questions of urbanism to issues of environment and transport.

New settlement patterns

There will always be a demand for genuine inter-urban development servicing several locations. Distribution warehouses and major visitor attractions may come into this category. To reduce carbon dioxide emissions, such facilities should be served not only by modern roads but also by efficient public transport. Hence, a sports stadium to serve a network of smaller towns should be located, not necessarily by the major roads which connect them, but alongside a rail line where a new station could be formed.

At a detailed level developers and their architects could do more to reduce the dependence on the motor car. If cycling is to be encouraged then cycleways are needed in suburban housing schemes and cycle storage areas within houses. If the local authority wishes to encourage cycle use, then it needs to provide safe and attractive cycle routes through the town; road space may have to be given up or new cycle priority traffic management schemes introduced. Likewise, if walking as a mode of transport is to be encouraged then routes need to be provided, perhaps utilizing redundant railway lines, canal tow paths or derelict industrial sites. Also pavements may need to be widened, not dotted with traffic signs to serve the motorist, and at road crossings pedestrian-friendly routes need to be provided. As pedestrians and cyclists are often at risk from speeding motorists, barriers need to be provided between car and body. Trees make useful barriers, both physically and psychologically, and the use of road space as tree-planted corridors could do much to improve the visual and air quality of towns. Elements of a green transport strategy developed at the building level can extend upwards thereby complementing green policies at a regional level. The type of modal shifts outlined here (essential if Britain's international responsibilities are to be met), requires a fundamental reconsideration of the development assumptions of the past two decades.

A rival argument, popular in some quarters – especially the USA – extols the benefit of rural living with social and intellectual contact undertaken through modern telecommunications. The concept of a rural or suburban idyll made possible by telecommunication-led commuting derives some authority from Frank Lloyd Wright's 'Broadacre City' proposals. In such communities residents will grow their own food, build their houses out of local materials and the indigenous skills of country people, generate their own electricity by biomass and correspond by fax or through telematics. The benefit in terms of reduced fossil-fuel use are obvious, but in a world of rapid population growth such a vision is only accessible to a wealthy, well-educated few. The scarcity of land, the need for social contact, welfare and health care, the loss of industrial or economic productivity, would lead in time to Western nations taking on the characteristics of the Third World. The rural retreat is an attractive, romantic option for a few, not a reality for the majority.

---

[4]*Ibid.*

10

An overview of energy and building design

About a half of all UK energy consumption and a similar proportion of carbon dioxide emissions is associated with buildings. Of this the majority (about 60 per cent) is used by the housing stock, the remaining 40 per cent being made up of offices (7 per cent), warehouses (5 per cent), hospitals (4 per cent), shops (5 per cent), educational buildings (7 per cent), sports facilities (4 per cent), hotels, public houses, clubs and other (8 per cent).[1] Although various directives (see Tables 3.1 and 3.2) impact indirectly upon energy use, there is limited specific reference in EC law to energy consideration and design. The most conspicuous is the need to achieve 'energy economy and heat retention' as one of the 'six essential requirements' of the Construction Products Directive.

The importance of housing

Energy used in dwellings is central to any strategy to conserve fossil-fuel supplies and reduce current global warming problems. Of the 1820 PJ used in housing about 61 per cent goes on space heating, 22 per cent on water heating, 7 per cent on cooking, 10 per cent on lights and appliances.[2] As space heating is by far the largest component it is here that much attention is focused in terms of increasing levels of insulation, reducing unwanted air movement, and improving the performance of heating systems. However, as energy use is largely determined by the density of layout, location, orientation, etc. of the original design, architects and builders have great influence in their initial decisions on the opportunities for improvement later. The decision, for instance, to face a house to the south can reduce heating bills by 15 per cent without any additional insulation, and the adoption of terraced houses as against semi-detached groupings can save the householder a further 25–30 per cent in heating bills. Such relatively simple strategic decisions could have enormous significance in achieving sustainable development if such layouts were to be the norm.

Although space heating is of vital importance, the effect of lighting should not be underestimated in terms of greenhouse gas emissions. Lighting is delivered by electricity for which carbon dioxide levels are high per unit of power. As a result the carbon dioxide contribution of lighting is 25 per cent whilst the total energy used for lighting is only 10 per cent. Hence, a different pattern emerges when global

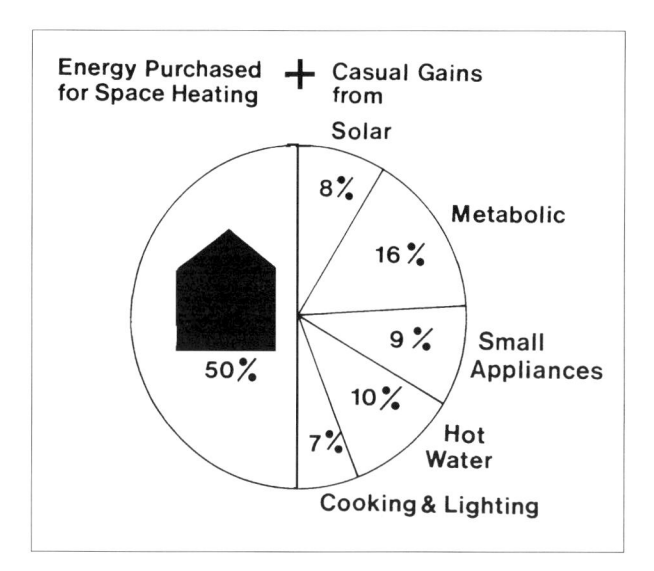

Figure 10.1
In homes 'purchased' energy represents only about a half of all energy needs for space heating. Houses can be made more efficient by cutting down losses and maximizing casual gains. (Lothian Energy Group©.)

---

[1] *Environmental Issues in Construction* CIRIA Special Publications, No. 94, 1993, p 32.
[2] *Ibid.*, p 30.

An overview of energy and building design

warming gases are computed rather than just fossil-fuel use. As gas is mainly employed for space heating, the contribution of this category falls from 61 per cent to 50 per cent when carbon dioxide emissions are taken into account.

What emerges from these figures is the importance of designing with both energy conservation and carbon dioxide reduction in mind. A balance has to be struck between a well-insulated wall and an opening to let in light and to provide natural ventilation. Good guiding principles for residential design are:

- use compact forms with maximum sharing of party walls, floors and roofs;
- use high volume to perimeter surface ratios;
- ensure solar aperture and exploit solar gains;
- build in self-sheltering layouts;
- use roof space for accommodation;
- use planting to achieve shelter and mid-summer solar protection;
- provide high insulation levels to conserve energy and improve comfort levels;
- use low-energy lighting;
- provide occupant with control over personal environment;
- provide the opportunity for raising insulation standards later;
- provide space for working from home;
- provide space for cycle storage;
- differentiate window areas between south and north elevation;
- use hipped rather than gable roofs in exposed locations.

Figure 10.2
Rediscovering the social benefits of urban housing is essential if sustainable patterns of development are to be established. (Brian Edwards©.)

Figure 10.3
Traditional terraced housing is one of the more energy efficient building types. People living in such houses generate only a third of the greenhouses gases produced by detached houses of comparable size.

An overview of energy and building design

Figure 10.4
Low-energy terraced housing built at Milton Keynes in 1986. (Milton Keynes Development Corporation©.)

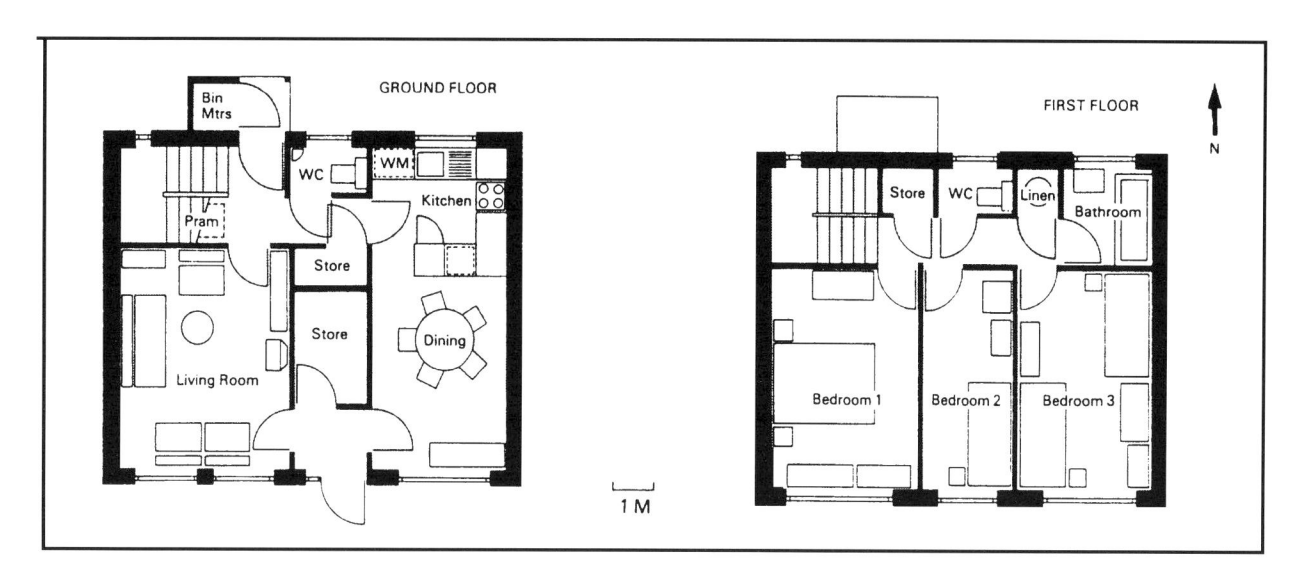

Figure 10.5
Plan of wide-fronted low energy housing at Pennyland, Milton Keynes. Note the differential window sizes between south and north elevations. (Milton Keynes Development Corporation©.)

An overview of energy and building design

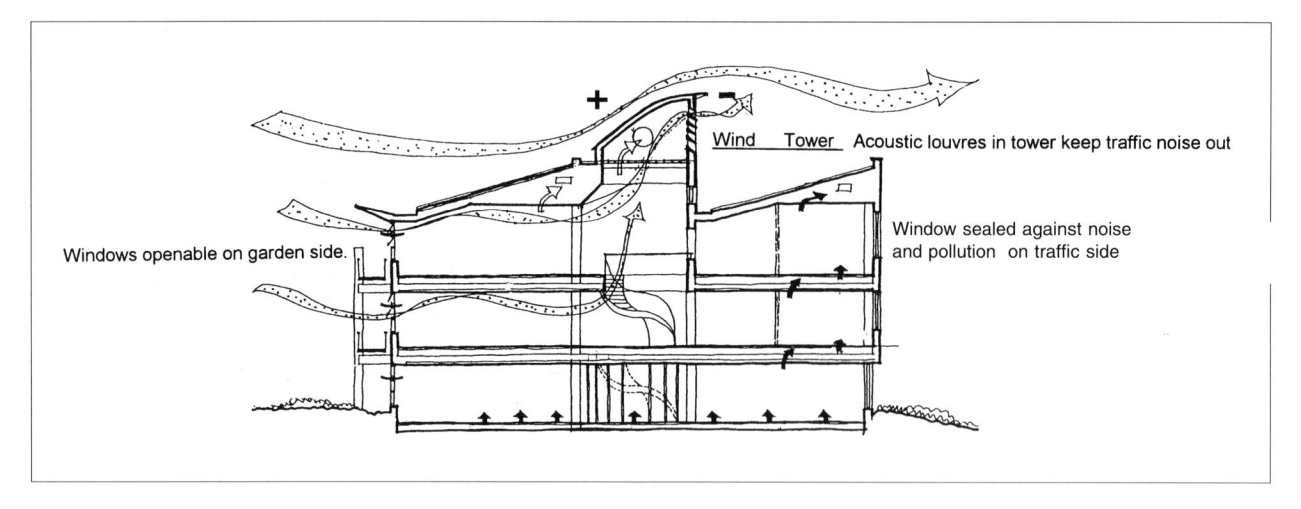

Figure 10.6
The ventilation diagram of the Ionica Building, Cambridge shows the relationship between the wind tower and both naturally ventilated elevation (left) and sealed elevation (right). (R H Partnership©.)

Such a checklist suggests houses quite different in character and form to those built by most volume house builders or designed by many of today's architects. The growth of suburban estates in Britain over the past ten years and the neglect of potential 'brown field' sites in existing urban areas has led to the increase in carbon dioxide emissions in spite of better insulation standards and heating systems. This is because the suburbs contain a higher proportion of detached and semi-detached houses and the dispersed layout encourages journeys by car rather than bus or train. Although there have been improvements in design and construction, the tendency has been to consume more energy as expectations rise.

Energy and other building types

Offices

The structural change in the economy of Britain from one of manufacturing to service industries has profound consequences for how energy is used and what sources of supply are employed. New service industries of banking, insurance, management, design, etc. require the support of energy supply based upon electricity, not coal, oil or gas as in the days of heavy industry. The well-lit office interiors, heavily cabled floors and extensive use of computers are made possible by electrical power. Although the total energy consumed in buildings in the manufacturing sector has remained fairly constant, the shift from oil and gas to electricity in the services sector carries enormous consequences for carbon dioxide emissions. As already noted the same unit of energy supplied by electrical cable produces about two-and-a-half times the volume of greenhouse gases as other fossil fuels. The inefficiencies of conversion and losses in transmission make electrical power both expensive in cost and particularly damaging in terms of global warming. Whilst the change from coal to gas-based electricity production has benefits for acid rain production by reducing sulphur dioxide emissions (SO_2), there are only marginal improvements in carbon dioxide output.

A service economy based upon electricity carries therefore the threat of rapid growth in global warming gas production. Although the use of nuclear sources of electricity has the potential to solve the carbon dioxide problem, nuclear power is by no means free of problems of its own. A UK government committed to cutting CO_2 emissions by 2005 to 1990 levels has an uphill slope to contend with in office buildings. Not only are floor plates generally deeper than can be lit by natural means, but the heat generated as a by-product of electrical use in VDUs means that most office buildings cannot be ventilated naturally, even if air quality could be sustained by such means.

Artificial lighting is a substantial consumer of energy in offices and can account for 50 per cent of electrical consumption. With deep plan offices more energy may be needed to light the building than heat it. As a consequence in the summer months artificial lighting leads to the consumption of additional energy for mechanical cooling. The substitution of daylight for artificial lighting (by the introduction of atria and shallow plan building depths) may save 40 or 50 per cent of the energy consumed. Although lighting is a particularly important element of office design, other building types such as hospitals (25 per

An overview of energy and building design

Figure 10.7
Regional traditions of building usually embody green principles as in this recent development in Edinburgh by architects Campbell and Arnott. Here high thermal mass and small windows contribute towards the energy strategy. (Campbell and Arnott©.)

cent), factories (20 per cent) and schools (15 per cent) consume large amounts of electricity in artificial lighting.

Whilst the information needed to undertake energy modelling in office buildings tends to be less well developed than in the domestic sector, and the interactions are generally more complex, the following are useful guiding principles:

- use cost-effective, simple energy technology which can be upgraded later;
- keep floor plates as shallow as possible to avoid air conditioning;
- introduce naturally ventilated atria where deep plans are unavoidable;
- maintain high rather than low ceiling heights;
- alternate atria with internal courts to aid air flows;
- protect south and west elevations from excessive solar gain and glare;
- use steel rather than concrete construction for flexibility;
- place blinds and solar screens under the control of occupants;
- insulate to levels well above minimum standards;
- build in existing urban areas to take advantage of public transport and other infrastructure facilities.

Industrial buildings

Of the total energy used in industrial premises about 20 per cent goes towards heating and lighting buildings. As a consequence energy conservation related to the building fabric has tended to have low priority. It is, however, recog-

An overview of energy and building design

nized that up to a third of building energy consumption in the industrial sector could be saved by better insulation, cutting down heat loss by air infiltration, upgrading heating systems and better staff management. Not only would such measures save money and cut CO_2 emissions but by reducing the costs to industry such economies could reduce the price of manufactured products.

Schools, hospitals, universities

A similar picture emerges with regard to public sector buildings such as schools, government offices, hospitals and universities. It has been suggested that energy savings of up to 40 per cent are possible[3] by a combination of:

- improvements to light sources and control systems;
- restricting the use of, and need for, air conditioning;
- upgrading heating systems and introducing new controls;
- enhancing insulation levels to well above regulation standards;
- introducing energy management systems;
- using the potential of solar gain in hostel and student housing accommodation.

In many ways public bodies such as central and local government, health authorities and universities could set an example of good energy housekeeping for the private sector to follow. Being less tied to profit considerations, the sector is in a position to lead public awareness and demonstrate that environmental issues are compatible with resources management. With schools alone the introduction of straightforward and inexpensive energy efficiency measures would, according to the Building Research Establishment, save local councils £60 million per year (at 1993 prices) and a reduction of almost one million tonnes of CO_2 entering the atmosphere. As the Toyne Report noted of the college and university sectors 'if the institution is not seen to be committed to good environmental practice, its attempts to teach students the importance of environmental responsibility will lack credibility.'[4] Public bodies of one kind or another could set an example of how to realize sustainable development within their own estates (see later case studies for examples).

Institutional barriers to energy conservation

One dilemma which has to be faced in the UK construction industry is that of the fragmentation of ownership,

design, construction and use of buildings. Designers do not have to pay the energy bills, nor in most cases do those who own the buildings since it is usually the tenant who pays. There is little incentive, therefore, to put wider questions of global warming at the top of an already complex equation of decision making. As many commercial buildings are constructed as speculations, it is difficult for the designer to know exactly what the energy needs are of the tenant. The resulting compromises lead to heating methods, building orientation, control systems, insulation levels which at best meet only minimum regulatory standards. There is a strong argument that these standards need to rise significantly, particularly if Britain wishes to compete with European expectations of energy efficiency.

Reduced to a question of economics, investment in measures to cut carbon dioxide emissions do not always make sense within the short timescales of government or company decision making. With primary energy costs as low as at present (in 1994), it takes at least eight years to repay the initial investment in low energy lighting systems. With little prospect of a carbon tax materializing from earlier discussions in the European Parliament, Britain will need to raise regulatory standards and persuade its construction professionals to adopt a new ethical stance if the problem of global warming is going to be addressed.

Without an energy labelling scheme the energy efficiency in buildings is not highlighted as a matter of concern to potential tenants or owners. Compared to the purchase of a car where the fuel economy figures are often part of the decision, the heating and lighting bills for a building are quietly ignored by university estates officers, health building administrators and the letting agents of commercial properties. The market does not appear to recognize the value and cost savings of low-energy architecture. With regard to office buildings many are let on the basis of 'being air conditioned' as if this was by itself a desirable characteristic. Some buildings are air conditioned as a sop to market expectations though they could be ventilated and cooled by low-energy means. Full air conditioning is expensive in capital and revenue costs, let alone the damage it causes to carbon dioxide emissions and the thinning of the ozone layer through CFC use. Sustainable development can only be achieved if those who procure, let and design buildings adopt alternative environmental priorities.

CASE STUDIES

Student residences, University of East Anglia

The new student residences, known as Constable Terrace and Nelson Court, at the University of East Anglia, create

---

[3] *Ibid.*, p 40.
[4] *Environmental Responsibilities: An Agenda for Further and Higher Education* (The Toyne Report), HMSO, 1993, p 89.

housing for 800 students in two separate low-energy developments. Designed by Rick Mather, they represent one of the largest energy-conscious designs in the domestic sector in the UK. The designs are based upon the 'radical proposition that even in winter heat input of only 250 W – the equivalent of two light bulbs – is required for each occupant'.[5] Mather's approach is unusual in its basic strategy. Rather than adopt a shallow plan with long southern exposure, he chose a deep, highly sealed building using mechanical ventilation and heat recovery. Windows are relatively small, well sealed, with interior light shelves exploiting scarce daylight and hence saving on lighting energy costs.

The student residences are arranged as ten study bedrooms sharing a living room and kitchen where each 'house' has its own conventional front door. Above each house is a top floor of two-bedroom flats accessed by a central corridor. The long blocks of Constable Terrace and Nelson Court are composed of repeating elements of 'houses' arranged either as a serpentine curve or as an open courtyard. Both sit in largely leafy university grounds and suffer little from overshading or external noise.

The deep plan, heavily insulated buildings with central service cores and windows facing in all directions deliver a commendable U-value of 0.22 W/m² K in walls and 0.15 W/m² K in the roof. This is achieved by a mixture of high insulation levels, double-glazed windows with low-emissivity glass, and particular attention to air-tightness of junctions (roof to wall, and wall to window). Air-pressure tests carried out during construction verified the building details employed. To reduce heat loss window sizes are the minimum permitted under UK building regulations and the openings are splayed to make the most of daylight.

Ventilation, a crucial element in the energy management and health of occupants, is the displacement system which draws in fresh air under the roof canopy and releases it into the study bedrooms at low level, with cool fresh air displacing stale warmed air. Mechanical extractors located at high level in shower rooms in the centre of the block extract the air at the rate of one air-change per hour in the bedroom. A heat recovery system on the top floor reclaims 70 per cent of latent heat from the extracted air and uses it to pre-heat the incoming fresh air.

The system is so efficient that a single 250 W panel heater fitted below the worktop is sufficient to heat each bedroom. Computer modelling suggest that in the relative cold of Norfolk it will be needed for the maximum of six weeks in the year.[6] In the summer windows can be opened to enhance ventilation, many being fitted with external canopies to reduce solar gain. The eaves oversail more than a metre to afford protection for the external walls (the render finish needs to stay dry for effective insulation and good appearance).

The residences work well from many points of view. The compact form allows heat losses to be controlled and the use of deep plans means that external wall areas are small compared to interior volume. The students live in high density communities where contact with the outside climate is carefully controlled. Rick Mather has designed residences which could readily prove a model for wider urban use. The use of mechanical ventilation, made possible by the single metering of the blocks, reduces the heating from 8196 kWh required for a passive system to 333 kWh. However, the energy cost of running the fans is 2000 kWh, thereby evening out the balance of efficiencies. Questions could also be asked of the embodied energy cost compared to the running costs. The use of expanded polystyrene insulation and relatively energy expensive metal and aluminium finishes means the buildings are more expensive in energy costs than conventional construction. Whether these higher embodied energy costs are recovered in the life of the building remains to be seen. Also lighting is a higher percentage of costs here than in conventional residences suggesting that the balance between heating, lighting, ventilation, embodied and running energy costs needs to be monitored. The Energy Efficiency Office is at the time of writing monitoring the buildings through a research contract with BRECSU. That they cost no more to construct than conventional residences suggests that if the monitoring proves the efficacy of Mather's decisions, these residences could have much wider significance.

Energy demonstration projects in Milton Keynes

For all the inconsistency of a new town built around a 1 km grid system of dual-carriageway roads, Milton Keynes has experimented for over a decade with different energy and building initiatives which have at their heart the demonstration of sustainable development principles. A project of about fifty terraced houses known as Pennyland applied solar gain practice to the familiar problem of low to middle income terraced housing. Built in 1984 it was the first in the UK to distinguish the area of windows according to orientation, to link this to construction employing high thermal mass, and to arrange the buildings on the site to maximize a southern aspect. Measurements subsequently taken suggest that the additional costs of construction (then about £2–3000) were recouped in 8–10 years in savings in energy bills.

In 1986 the new town built Energy World, a demonstration project consisting of a solar square with sun- and

---

[5] Mark Swenarton, Warm space, cool aesthetic, *Architecture Today* No 45, March 1994, p 28.
[6] *Ibid.*, p 30.

An overview of energy and building design

wind-driven technologies applied to commercial buildings, and the construction of about forty energy houses. The latter were built mainly by volume house builders, as examples of how their designs could be adapted to low energy design, and by building materials manufacturers such as Pilkington plc, anxious to show off their latest energy technologies. Unlike Pennyland, Energy World with its subsequent off-shoot of factories built to low energy design principles, was open to the public and accompanied by information packs. A year later Milton Keynes developed its own 'Energy Conservation Index' which set minimum standards of efficiency for every building to be constructed in the new town. The index increased construction costs by about 1 per cent but reduced heating bills (and greenhouse gas production) by about 30 per cent.

In a similar spirit Future World, the energy demonstration project of 1994, is based upon the theme of 'designing for a sustainable future in the built environment'. It is similar in spirit to Energy World and suffers from the same weakness of separation between energy used in buildings and energy consumed in transport. Most houses have space for two or three cars in the drive, and though a tram system could be incorporated later, the low density of development and the lack of storage for bicycles suggests a poorly balanced view of sustainability. The houses though are of interest in themselves, particularly the diverse range of solutions proposed. The architect Jonathan Ellis-Miller has designed a house of great transparency using advanced building and glazing technology and much openness of interior space. Another architect David Woods is responsible for a more traditional house which has evolved under the constraint of keeping to a minimum the energy and material resources used during construction and the life of the building. It is also designed to be flexible enough to accommodate changing family sizes over a thirty year period. Futurehouse is the result of the RIBA/Future World Competition to promote 'telecottaging'. Here, in a house with high thermal mass, high levels of insulation and skirts of conservatories on the south side, employees of the future will work from home communicating by modern telecommunications.

In the search for sustainable patterns of building Milton Keynes has set such an admirable example that it is frequently referred to as the UK's 'Energy Efficient City'. Partnerships with energy suppliers, such as British Gas, have allowed the houses built in projects like Pennyland to be separately metered, thereby permitting the monitoring of performance. As many of the developments are prototypes, the systematic recording of energy and consumer satisfaction is important. Putting aside the dilemma of a new town based upon a Los Angeles-type grid of superhighways, the different developments have raised awareness of energy and sustainability issues amongst the public and professionals alike.

Linacre College, Oxford University

The new buildings at Linacre College, Oxford have been designed for low energy and environmental impact in terms of both running costs and capital cost. By examining the energy embodied in the main materials of the building and cross referencing this to the energy consumed in the operation of the College, the architects, ECD Partnership, were able to strike the right balance of efficiencies.

In buildings of this type – four storey accommodation block for student occupation – the embodied energy of 800 kg/m^2 represents about twenty times the annual CO_2 production of 39 kg/m^2.[7] In the life of the building (say fifty years) the embodied energy measured as global warming gas production equals about 40 per cent of total CO_2 emissions. Although running energy costs are of major importance, the capital energy costs are by no means unimportant and have a bearing on the overall equation.

The research into the relative levels of energy embodied in the main materials for the College was undertaken by Davis Langdon and Everest Consultancy Group (DL & E) as part of a wider study for the Building Research Establishment (BRE). By studying the energy used in extracting raw materials, transport to the factory, manufacture and delivery to the site, DL & E was able to compile a working table (see Table 10.1) of embodied energy used in the various building materials and components. From the table, the architect was able to make the following choices based upon reducing energy costs in the construction cycle:

- Structural masonry with timber floors was better than concrete frame and floors.
- Solid concrete blockwork was preferable to solid brickwork for external walls.
- Double glazing pays for its extra embodied energy (over single glazing with wooden frames) in about a year.
- Pitched timber roofs with tiles were lower in embodied energy than steel-framed or flat concrete and asphalt.
- Cellulose fibre insulation from recycled newsprint was better than mineral, glass fibres and polymer foams. The optimum thickness for insulation is 150 mm above which ventilation heating losses take over.
- Natural fibre carpets with hessian backing were better than carpet tiles which have high embodied energy costs due to manufacture and short life.
- Air conditioning and mechanical ventilation use significantly more energy in manufacture than simple electric or gas-fired heating systems.

---

[7]Barry Evans, Counting the global cost *The Architects' Journal* 24 February 1993, p 57.

An overview of energy and building design

These strategic choices led naturally to the design of the building. Putting aside the traditional styling of the College, the compact building beneath a simple pitched roof equates well with low energy in use and manufacture. The building is not, however, exemplary at 8 GJ/m² since some recent structures have achieved a figure of 4 GJ/m². But it does demonstrate the need to consider energy at both the production and use stages in the life of a building.

Other green initiatives taken in the building include:

- the exploitation of passive solar energy by placing study bedrooms on south side with service areas to the north;
- maximizing daylight with simple curtaining for glare control;
- the use of thermal mass to create stable internal temperatures;
- using stack-effect ventilation linked to solar currents and simple opening windows;
- high levels of thermal and acoustic insulation;
- recycling of water;
- recycling of waste (four different waste bins are provided);
- consideration of life-cycle health and environmental impact;
- use of timbers from sustainable sources (only European and American hardwoods considered);
- avoidance of insulation made by using HCFCs in manufacture and expanded polystyrene insulation because of high energy costs;
- use of recycled copper for main pipework.

The various measures bring a coalition of environmental interests together. The predicted reduction in resource use looks impressive: 36 per cent reduction in water use, 20 per cent reduction in gas consumption, 25 per cent reduction in electricity, and 22 per cent reduction in overall CO_2 emissions.[8] These reductions have mainly been achieved by simple inexpensive measures (southern orientation, energy efficient light fittings, etc.). To balance the equation of environmental impacts the architects ECD suggested to Linacre College that they adopt an area of rainforest equal to the extent of CO_2 emissions in the building. Based upon the assumption that 1 m² of rainforest absorbs about 1 kg of CO_2 per year, the cost of adopting the ten acres necessary would have cost the College £265 annually (just over £25 per acre). The reaction of the College was to ask whether the rainforest could be in the Oxford area (rather than Brazil). Putting aside questions of location, the main value of the exercise is in the computation of impacts (capital and revenue) and the recognition that forests as converters of CO_2 to oxygen are as important as buildings in converting oxygen to CO_2.

Table 10.1
Embodied energy in the design of Linacre College, Oxford

Element	Embodied energy (Gj)	Embodied CO_2 (Tonnes)	(%)
Site preparation, spoil disposal	350	29	3.5
Substructure and basement	2141	226	27.1
Frame	8	1	0.1
Upper floors	2212	228	27.4
Roof	254	24	2.9
Stairs	89	10	1.2
External walls	1194	141	16.9
Windows and external doors	97	9	1.1
Internal walls	782	86	10.3
Internal doors	28	3	0.4
Wall finishes	136	13	1.6
Floor finishes	349	39	4.7
Ceiling finishes	237	20	2.4
Sanitary and disposal appliances	39	4	0.5
Total	7918	834	100
Total/m²	8.0	0.8	

Source: The Architects' Journal, 24 February 1993, p 58.

Two Sheffield health centres

In 1989 the Woodhouse Medical Centre in Sheffield designed by Robert and Brenda Vale achieved the remarkable figure for CO_2 emissions of only 28 kg/m²/year. The building achieved this by using three times the recommended levels of insulation and careful attention to window area. The fact that the building was constructed at about the same price as a conventional health centre is one reason why it won the *Independent on Sunday* award for the 'Green Building of the Year' in 1991.

By careful design the Woodhouse Medical Centre saves 80 per cent in space heating demand over a health centre of comparable size.[9] Aesthetically the Centre is by no means exceptional, it achieves energy saving without appearing at all revolutionary. The Birley Health Centre, also in Sheffield, takes the approach a stage further. Here the roof is insulated to a thickness of 400 mm and again

---

[8] *Ibid.*, p 59.

[9] *Architecture Today* 31, p 45.

An overview of energy and building design

Figure 10.8
Woodhouse Medical Centre, Sheffield, designed by Robert and Brenda Vale. (Peter Lathy, University of Sheffield©.)

small triple-glazed windows are used to avoid excess heat loss. A wind turbine is planned to produce all the heat and electrical power needed with surplus being fed into the National Grid. The architects believe that over time the returning of the renewable energy generated electricity to the grid will offset the embodied energy contained within the building materials.[10]

Atlantis Building, London

The Atlantis Building in London docklands by Paul Hyett Architects provides comfortable working conditions at remarkably low energy cost by simple architectural means. By integrating a natural ventilation strategy early into the design process, the architects and engineers were able to manipulate building form and thermal mass to the benefit of energy conservation.[11] The building, combined shop, office and warehouse for a supplier of quality art paper, occupies a south facing site in east London where excessive summer heating was a potential difficulty. The design team overcame this by using a monopitch roof with its lowest point to the south, and deep overhanging eaves on south and west sides. In addition, manually controlled blinds were placed behind the storey-height double-glazed windows, and because of the inclined ceiling, heat was drawn off by the stack effect. Temperature sensors in the building trigger an automatic change in ventilation rates linked to a fan which provides four air changes an hour. Temperature fluctuations, a problem with single storey, highly glazed buildings, is overcome by exploiting the high thermal mass of solid tiled floors and exposed concrete mezzanine floor slabs.

The simple combination of monopitch roof, oversailing eaves and concrete structure (rather than steel) for a single storey structure had the effect of dealing by design with problems normally solved by elaborate building services. The low-tech solution which incorporates 75 mm of prefelted woodwool roof decking, high efficiency modular boilers with perimeter radiators (which double as security grilles alongside the external windows) creates a responsive, low cost, yet highly attractive building. Constructed at about £780 per square metre, it compares well with other headquarters buildings for small companies.

The building form alludes to energy-conscious design. The basic profile and configuration presages an attempt to pursue low-energy building design with a natural ventilation strategy at its centre. The use of appropriate technology, such as opening windows, simple blinds, manual control of heating and ventilation, results in a building which is easy to use, cheap to maintain, flexible in use and appreciated by the building occupants. The emphasis upon high levels of natural lighting and ventilation gives the building its distinctive appearance which allows it to perform its function as a company landmark and point of punctuation alongside Devon's Road Station on the Docklands Light Railway.

Prototype low-energy office, Leeds

British Gas, perhaps the most energy-conscious of the major utility suppliers, commissioned Peter Foggo Associates in 1993 to develop a prototype office design of the future. The objective was to explore the application of low-energy design within the normally high-energy world

---

[10]*Ibid.*

[11]Martin Cook, Atlantis Building – energy comment, *The Architects' Journal* 2 March 1994, p 2.7.

An overview of energy and building design

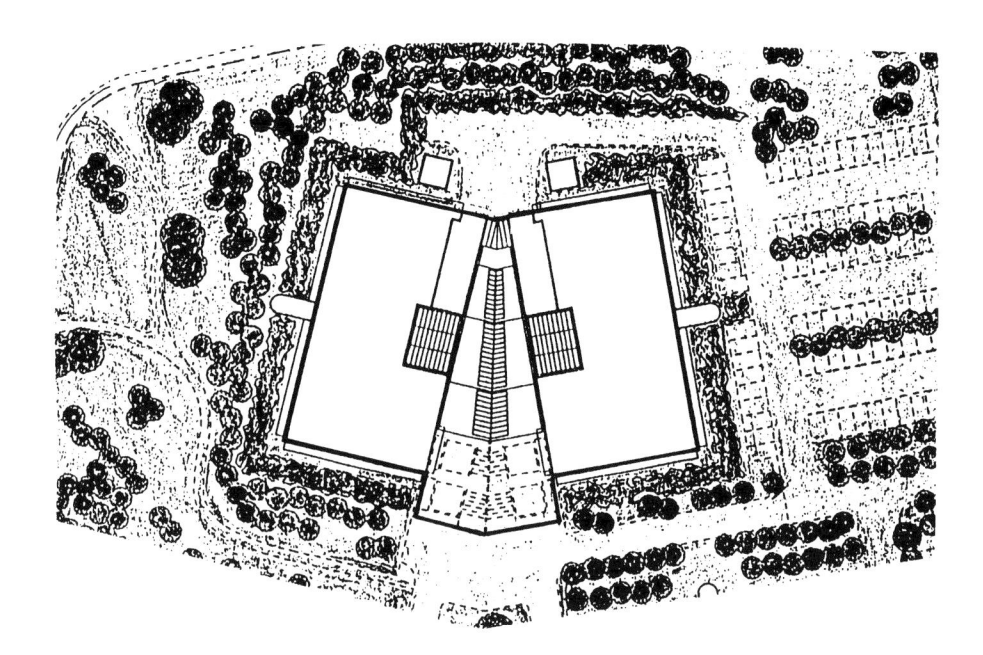

Figure 10.9
By orientating the atrium to the south, stepping its section and angling the office wings, Peter Foggo and Associates have exploited the stack effect to aid natural ventilation. The use of solar powered ventilation is a growing feature in the design of today's office buildings. (Peter Foggo and Associates©.)

of commercial office space. The development of the design was partly public spirited; to show that modern office buildings do not have to rely upon air conditioning and deep plans. British Gas was also keen to evolve a new generation of office buildings for eventual construction on the company's significant holdings of land in the inner city.

The Foggo design, evolved initially for a site in Leeds, involved the architect in the preparation of a masterplan for an area of 3.5 ha near a link road to the M62. Being surrounded by run-down industrial buildings, the strategy was to produce a trio of buildings with a relatively tranquil wedge-shaped space of planting in the centre, each office building also containing a similar, though smaller, wedge-shaped atrium. The exploitation of solar radiation to drive the naturally ventilated atrium in each building led to the geometry of the site layout with its associated wedges. Because the expectation existed that in the foreseeable future office workers would use cars, the masterplan contains large areas of surface parking (as well as parking beneath buildings) set as parallel strips between large banks of tree planting. Conceived like Stockley Park as a green park into which pavilions of buildings are located, the plan puts generous green space back into an urban area for wider public use.

The office buildings themselves, each of about 6000 m², consist of two, three-storey angled wings which meet in a wedge-shaped atrium. The service core (toilets, stairs, etc.) is located at the north end of the wedge with the sunny south side left open to exploit solar gains. Traffic noise and air pollution, assumed normally to be at the north side, result in a marked difference in the architectural treatment of façades. Clean air for ventilation is drawn in at roof level, filtered and delivered via a raised floor 400 mm high to the office areas with circular diffusers in floor tiles providing displacement ventilation.[12] Heated air containing contaminants rises through the offices and is extracted through grilles in the two decks of the atrium roof. The system is driven entirely by the air heated by solar gain plus secondary and incidental sources of heating.

With calculated equipment gains of 15 W/m² and occupancy levels of one person per 13 m², the need is often one of cooling. Cooling is provided by lowering the temperature of the supplied air to 19°C, using fans to force the air against thermal currents. Air supply is normally 2.2 air changes per hour with the potential to more than double this in order to cool the exposed concrete elements, thereby reducing radiant temperatures of the main structure. By boosting night-time ventilation to cool the fabric, Foggo has exploited off-peak electricity tariffs.

Heating is by a diversity of sources and methods, and the balance varies according to the season, orientation of office, and expected levels of occupancy. Heat reclaimed from extracted air, a heater battery in the air supply, perimeter hot-water radiators and solar gains are the main sources. The whole system is driven by the 'stack effect' which is dependent upon the configuration of the wedge layout and stepped profile of roof. Without these geometries and sections, greater use of supplementary fan power

---
[12]Barrie Evans, Low-cost, low-energy offices, *The Architects' Journal* 6 April 1994, p 20.

An overview of energy and building design

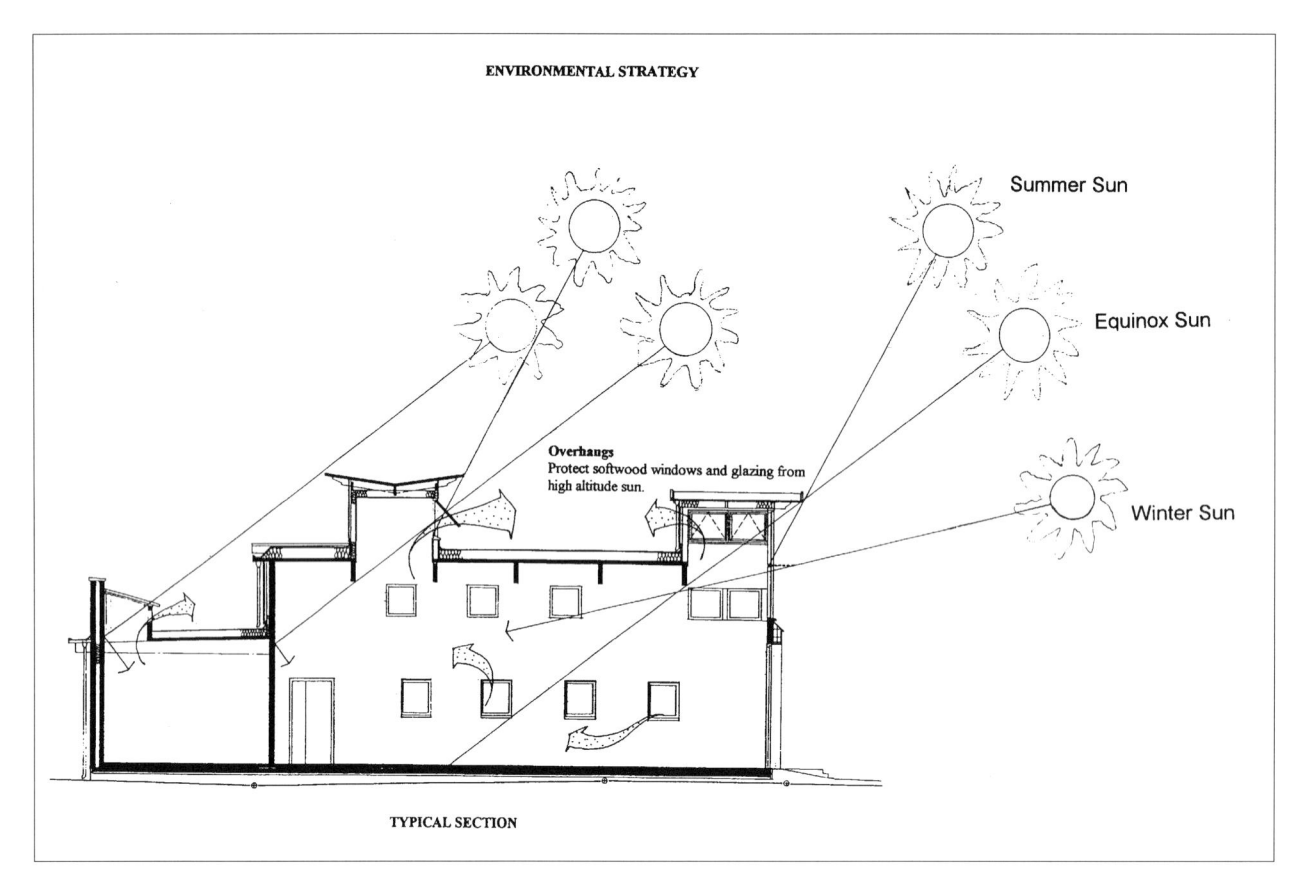

Figure 10.10
Environment strategy at business units in Greenwich designed by Short Ford and Partners. (Short Ford and Partners©.)

would have been needed with consequences of overall energy use. Automatic opening of windows in the atrium roof and different sizes of grilles according to the floor height (the stack effect means that extract pressures are greater on the ground floor than higher floors) ensures that air-flow rates are balanced.[13] Powered blinds in the roof add also to the control of the stack effect by modifying rates of solar gain. Under extreme conditions the atrium can achieve ten air changes per hour in order to control interior temperatures or to dispel CO_2.

Solar gains are controlled in the office areas by a combination of exterior mounted aluminium sunscreens which double up as daylight shelves and maintenance walkways. For this reason they run on all elevations, even those facing north. Interior mounted blinds allow occupants to modify their working environment.

The basic geometry of the building will allow British Gas Properties to let the building in whole, by floor, or by wings, with units down to 930 m². British Gas began construction of the prototype office in Leeds in August 1994 in order to test the building's actual energy usage against predictions, and to measure the response of the property market to the novel layout. Calculations suggest that the building will consume only 30 per cent of the energy of a more orthodox air-conditioned office. Since lighting energy is fairly high in offices (as much as 50 per cent of total energy used), an education scheme for occupants is planned, funded under the EC Thermie Programme, covering building use and light switching.[14] Under the BREEAM environmental labelling scheme, the design achieved an 'excellent' rating. The design is an important step towards the creation of a responsive, sustainable office development of the future, not in terms of prestige commercial space but the everyday environment of letable floorspace.

---

[13] *Ibid.*, p 21.

[14] *Ibid.*

Low-energy business units in Greenwich

In 1994 Greenwich Enterprise Board, an inter-government agency given the task of regenerating the Greenwich Peninsular (a loop of former docklands alongside the river Thames) appointed architects Short Ford & Partners to design low-energy and environmentally friendly small business units. The commission reflects the growing interest amongst clients in green buildings.

The design evolved by the architects is unusual in several respects. Rather than employ a high-tech strategy to reduce environmental impacts, the business units are designed in plan and section to maximize the use of natural daylight, ventilation and the stack effect of passive solar gain. The stepped section and highly indented plan (see Figure 10.11) with its regular sequence of factory units and courtyards, ensure that renewable sources of energy are exploited to the full. By placing the service areas to the north and by employing large areas of glazing to the south, the site layout was largely dictated by energy considerations. The advantage of a southerly orientation in terms of maximizing natural energy sources led also to the placing of the car park to the south, thereby exploiting the summer shading of trees placed between cars and building to protect the factories from excessive solar gain.

If a concern for primary energy use leads directly to the site layout, building plan and section, the same is true of the choice of materials and heating system. Instead of the normal metal cladding system, these business units use timber frame construction and timber boards (cedar) for external cladding because of its low embodied energy. Unusually, insulation thicknesses vary from 100 to 300 mm according to the position in the building and the need to dispel excess heat due to solar or process gains. The differential thickness also encourages the stack effect natural ventilation system which is the primary factor in determining the building section. With only a relatively modest stack height of 6 m, the careful positioning of windows and internal room profiles allows the building to achieve 9 ac/h (air changes per hour) which is over twice the recommended standard for advanced factory units.[15]

The use of timber as the primary building material (justified on environmental grounds) has the weakness of not providing adequate security or not having enough thermal mass to exploit passive solar gain. Hence, the design uses concrete blockwork as the secondary building layer – providing solid external walls to prevent theft and fire risk, and adding to the building's thermal capacity. Thermal modelling suggests that the internal temperatures will be between 16–25°C irrespective of season and outside temperature.[16] Depending upon the heat generated in any manufacturing or light industrial use, the architects anticipate that no space heating will be needed – incidental, process and solar gains will generally provide sufficient background heat. To retain these gains, movement in and out of the building is via glazed lobbies which exploit solar energy (they all face south) or via insulated delivery doors.

Lighting passive solar business units without the glare of direct sunlight is solved here by an ingenious zigzag elevation of glass, and by facing windows onto small courtyards which have much reflected light. Having an even level of lighting inside the factory is important for comfort, work efficiency and safety. Here Short Ford & Associates have also used skylights with overhanging roofs to light the back of the work areas without sunlight penetration, thereby reducing the need for artificial lighting.

Although about 20 per cent more expensive than orthodox business units, they are much cheaper to run and have less energy and environmental impact embodied within the fabric of the building. The estimated energy consumption is less than half of that recommended in BRE's *Good Practice Guide: Energy Efficiency in Advanced Factory Units* (100 kWh/m² as against 230 kWh/m²). This gives a payback period of under ten years based upon building costs of £675/m² in April 1994.

School of Engineering, De Montfort University

The School of Engineering at De Montfort University in Leicester reverses many design principles associated with institutional buildings. These normally consist of buildings based upon a conventional steel and glass envelope, with mechanical plant and automatic controls providing the primary building services. By way of contrast the School of Engineering building combines, within a concrete and brick frame, natural light and ventilation, passive heating and user control.

Buildings such as this which have high levels of internal heat gains from equipment and occupants, need to consider daylight needs rather than space-heating. Lighting from artificial sources is the most critical element of energy consumed, not heating. The building employs a multiple-stepped section to bring as much daylight into the building as possible, exploiting internal light shelves, light shafts and gable glazing. As a result the building is complex in plan and elevation with much top-lighting enlivening the general external appearance.

A similar concern for exploiting natural energy flows is evident in the stack-effect ventilation. Rather than employ mechanical ventilation the architect Short Ford & Associates with engineers Max Fordham & Partners, have created ventilation and summer-time temperature control by linking the stack effect to thermal capacity. By building in concrete and brick the building has high thermal mass

---

[15] Alistair Blyth, Low energy for industry, *The Architects' Journal* 8 September 1994, p 45.
[16] *Ibid*.

An overview of energy and building design

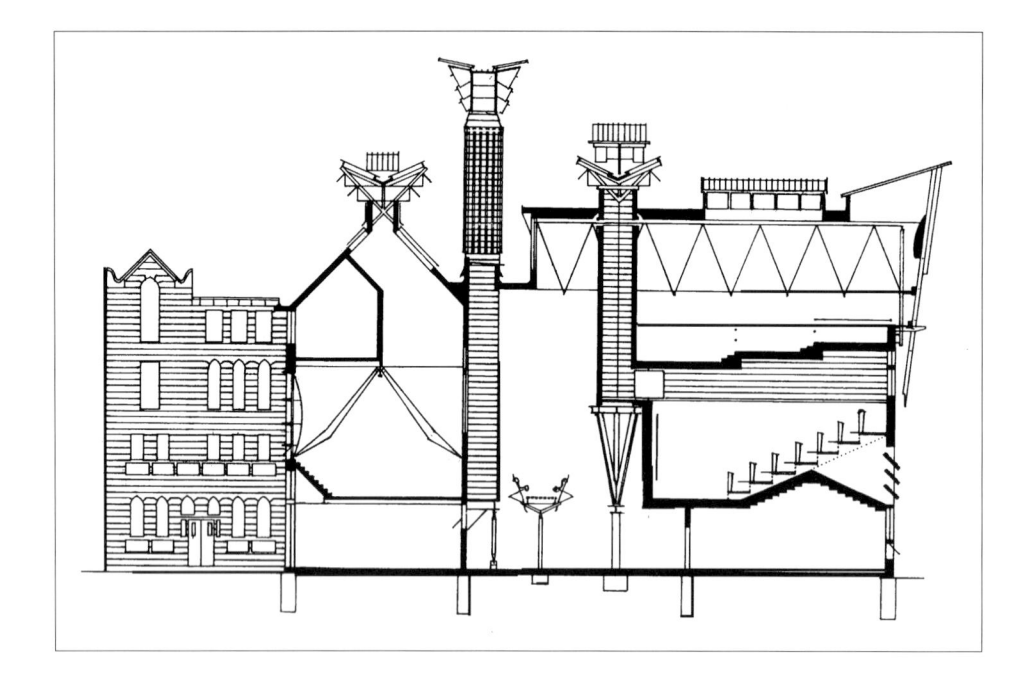

Figure 10.11
This elaborate cross-section of the School of Engineering Building at De Montfort University designed by Short Ford and Partners is driven by the need to maximize natural ventilation whilst minimizing energy consumption. (Short Ford and Partners©.)

which allows local fluctuation in temperature to be absorbed relatively effortlessly. Tall vent flues, evident on the outside roofscape and profiled to accelerate air movement, signal the use of a low technology solution to building services. The system does not eliminate the need for mechanical plant altogether, but it means this can be simple to use, cheap to install and under the control of building users. The latter consideration adds to the user-friendliness of the engineering building, also providing an element of education for the students. The way the building communicates architectural physics in its layout and details is an added bonus of the design.

The effectiveness of such an approach to building depends to a degree upon a reciprocal appreciation of values by building user and designer. The problem with the building to date is that energy awareness is not high amongst technical staff and students in the building. As a result a reviewer of the building for *The Architects' Journal* found lights were on when they were not needed, and rather than have workplace lighting, the preference was for total room illumination.[17] Also it was found that heating controls were too elaborate for users to readily adjust, the natural desire being to open a window rather than reset the radiator valve.

The Toyne Report[18] highlights the importance of greening education, providing all students with an understanding of the environmental problems facing future generations. Toyne argues that the design of buildings used in higher education have a role to play in communicating good energy practice. Here in Leicester, the School of Engineering building takes the view that the university estate itself should not only embody green ideals but should express them in built form. That the building is not being used as planned is itself a useful lesson in the limitations of using a building as a vehicle for expressing values and principles. Toyne reported that it is not only courses which need to give greater attention to green issues, but the policy of those who control the university estates needs to change. This building is part of the change in direction precipitated by the Toyne Report; for all its weaknesses there is much to learn from the experiment at De Montfort University.

---

[17] Dean Hawkes, User control in a passive building, *The Architects' Journal* 9 March 1994, p 28.

[18] *Environmental Responsibilities: An Agenda for Further and Higher Education* (The Toyne Report), HMSO, 1992.

11

Technical factors in the design of sustainable commercial buildings

Lori McElroy

There is no single solution to the design of an environmentally responsible non-domestic building and no easy formula for combating the problem of global warming outlined in Chapter 7. Every building is unique, and in each case, decisions in respect of materials and energy strategy will have an unavoidable environmental impact. There is currently a strong European movement towards a more natural internal environment. This bio-climatic, environmentally responsible approach to architecture demands a holistic approach to design. In order to achieve multiple successes, designers must develop an understanding of the new design philosophies and the relationships between internal and external interfaces: form, fabric and comfort relationships with site, climate and orientation together with the global environmental impact of a building. By developing an inherent sensitivity to these issues, many of the new EC and UK legislative requirements (see Table 30.1) will be met automatically.

Three key factors in providing a comfortable and energy-efficient building

Climate

Awareness of the potential impact of climatic considerations, daylight, solar gain and natural ventilation is playing an increasingly important role in the design of buildings, particularly in relation to their general form. Increasingly, narrow plan buildings with openable windows are replacing the 'high-spec/high-tech' air-conditioned solutions of the 1980s. User control over the internal environment is regarded increasingly as paramount. Some degree of control over the internal environment is necessary, however, in order to ensure comfort is achieved without incurring energy penalties. For example, in terms of solar gain, adequate measures have to be taken to avoid excessive overheating in summer whilst ensuring that the potential of useful winter gains is maximized. The sun has to be designed 'out' as well as 'in'. Control over solar gain is a challenge in itself, however when combined with the provision of year-round natural light the problem is compounded.

Notwithstanding the difficulties, approaching the design process with an energy and climate sensitive objective can provide an opportunity to discard many of the usual design constraints faced by designers, offering a vehicle to explore new territory, and resulting in innovative, far-reaching solutions to old problems. In initial projects, however, extra time and effort will be required.

Energy

When considering 'energy' in isolation, particularly in domestic buildings, certain 'standard' design rules are emerging which will help achieve low-energy solutions. However these do not always apply in non-domestic designs due to varying occupancy levels, heat gains, heat losses and building use variations which cannot be standardized as easily as in domestic buildings. Thus, a solution which produces one successful commercial building cannot generally be applied *ad hoc* to other buildings. The relative heating, cooling, lighting and equipment energy requirements, and potential heat gains from people, equipment, lighting and the sun, for example, have to be examined in relation to a building, its form, orientation, fabrics, occupancy patterns and environmental requirements in order to ensure that the full picture emerges prior to embarking on major design decisions. An overall design strategy is emerging, however, and energy

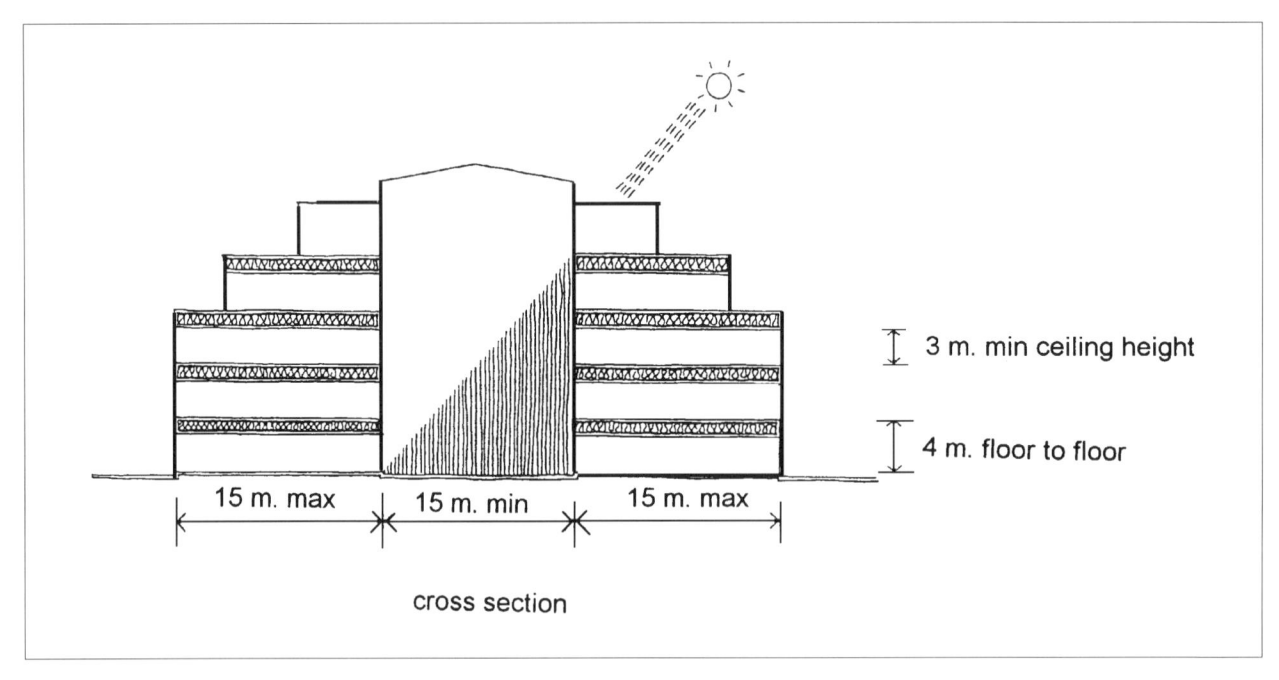

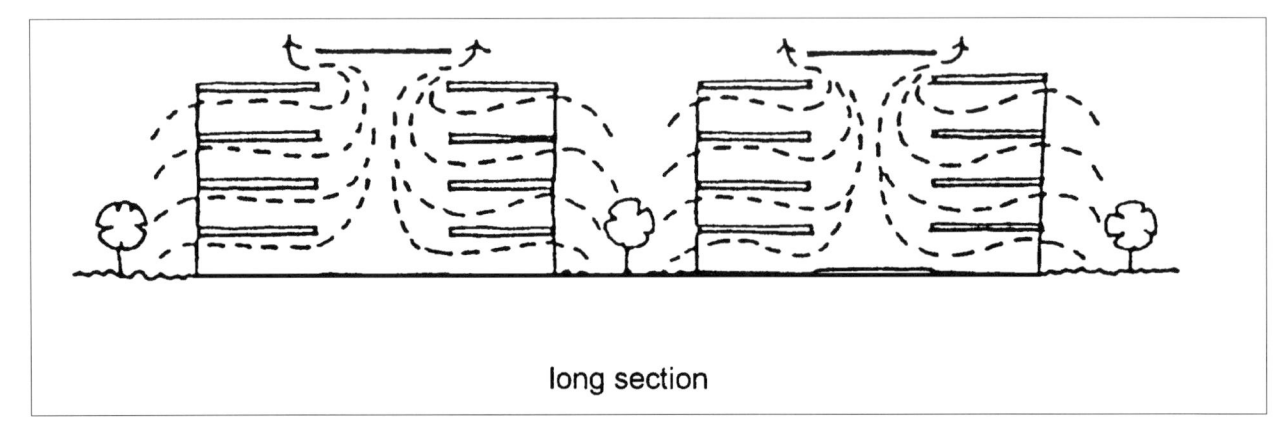

Technical factors in the design of sustainable commercial buildings

Figure 11.1
View of the new Scottish Office – low energy government offices in Leith designed by RMJM, and a diagrammatic section. (RMJM©.)

Technical factors in the design of sustainable commercial buildings

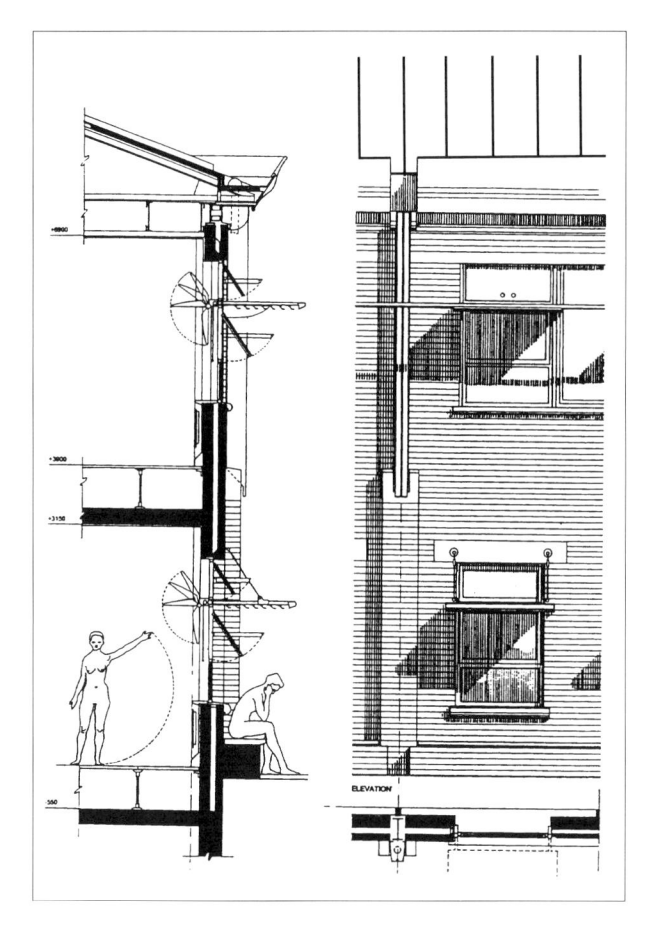

Figure 11.2
Climate-responsive design with natural light and ventilation is replacing the sealed environment buildings of the 1980s. (David Lloyd Jones Associates©.)

conscious commercial buildings are possible without sacrificing aesthetic considerations and at little or no extra capital cost.

Materials

In response to an increasing requirement to address 'caring for the environment', designers now need to understand the embodied energy and life-cycle costs of materials. The concept of 'cradle-to-grave' design responsibility is embodied in measures such as the EC eco-labelling scheme. The most ecologically sound solution in one area of the country will seldom be the best solution in another area. The key to addressing these issues is 'appropriateness'. The BRE's BREEAM initiative advocates consideration of the impact on the environment of buildings in terms of internal, local and global effects. Local and global effects will vary throughout the country from location to location (and throughout areas of Europe) because of the different regional impact of the selection of building materials and components. Architects are faced with a plethora of material alternatives when designing a new or refurbished building. The choices made at this stage are critical to the environment at all levels due to the impact of transport, and 'cost' of production or extraction. Availability of local materials, potential for recycling and impact of production should be considered at all stages. Major material selections should be made on this basis, and provided 'luxury', scarce or high embodied materials are used 'appropriately', the palette should not be too restrictive.

Conflicts and interactions between climate, energy and materials

Considered individually, the criteria 'climate', 'energy' and 'materials', pose interesting challenges. Together, conflicts arise and dilemmas are presented. The following section attempts to set the main factors in context, hopefully providing, in addition, clarification of the complementary areas and contradictions encountered when addressing energy, climate and environmental issues in the design of buildings for the non-domestic sector.

Site and climate

The first decision taken in relation to the position of a building within a site can affect every other decision which follows. Every building site is unique, and therefore exclusive to the design of a building. This immediately places constraints on the ensuing design decisions and every decision will have an energy and environmental impact. When deciding how to make an environmentally responsible intervention with a new building within the site, two major site factors must be addressed:

- the local climate;
- the environmental impact of the building on the site and vice versa.

Local climate considerations should address positive and negative aspects of the site. The building orientation should take advantage of free energy from the sun in terms of both heat and light if appropriate (see Built form below). Local wind conditions, direction and strength should be established and accounted for. Wind effects can be improved by shelter belt planting or permeable walling.[1] By building up a picture of basic microclimatic

---

[1] BRE Digest 350, Parts 1, 2 and 3.

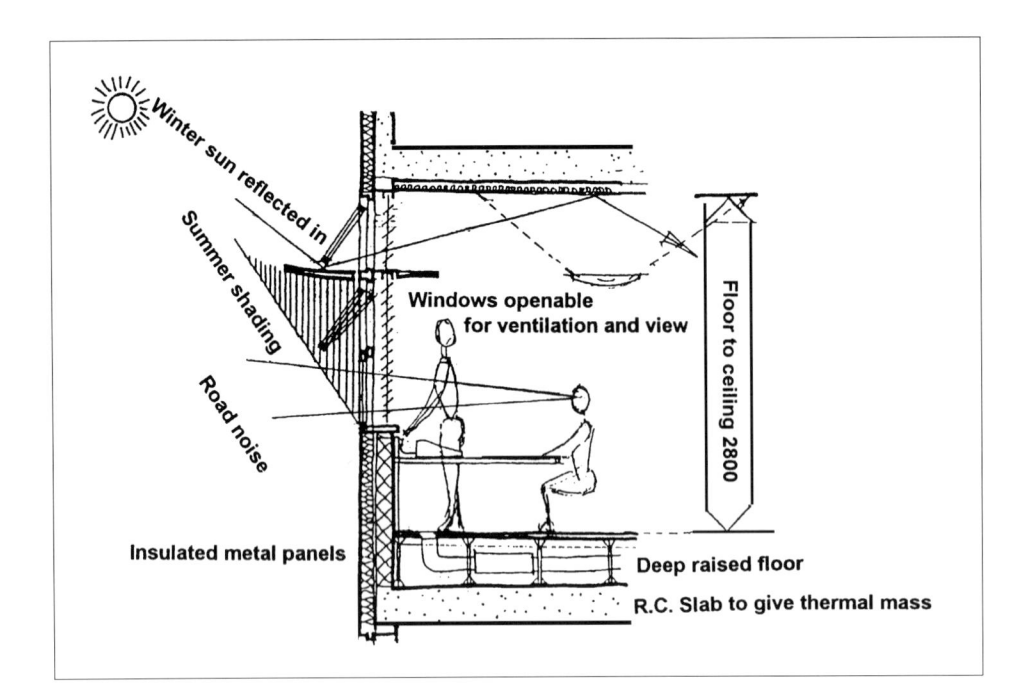

Figure 11.3
The Ionica Building in Cambridge uses environmental factors to determine the façade design. (R. H. Partnership©.)

information such as site orientation, slope/contours, wind direction and pollution effects, it is possible to identify the most suitable location for a building using a process whereby unsuitable (polluted, overshadowed) areas are eliminated and the potential of the remaining sites explored and improved by investigating building form, planting and shelter-belts for example using overlay techniques for clarification. The final design should incorporate adequate fenestration to make use of free solar energy and natural daylight while optimizing heat losses and avoiding glare. This will seldom be achieved by glazing ratios of above 20 per cent but can be checked by manual calculation techniques or computer modelling.

The building should be considered in relation to the site in terms of the impact of the building on the site and its relationship with other buildings on the site. Aspects such as aesthetics, over-shading, self-shading, climate variations, vegetation and pollution should also be examined to avoid negative effects on existing and new buildings. An overall site strategy for energy use and the potential for an integrated energy policy for the site should be evaluated at an early stage – e.g. use of waste heat, potential to generate electricity on site using a combined heat and power scheme, renewable energy, etc. In other words, the site should be considered holistically and not the building in isolation.

Built form

The are two basic strategies in terms of building form to achieve minimum energy impact:

- Minimize surface area to volume ratio, design to high insulation levels and compact building form to minimize heat losses. This strategy helps minimize both the building materials consumed and the direct energy requirement in fuel terms.
- Alternatively, use a shallow plan form to maximize the opportunity to use natural ventilation and daylighting. Provided passive solar energy use is appropriate, and will not result in overheating, site the building to allow for use of solar gains to offset heating requirements. This is likely to be appropriate in buildings with low occupant density where high internal heat gains from equipment will not occur.

Current thinking in new-build low energy building design favours the latter, 'bio-climatic' solution whenever possible, allowing maximum use of natural ventilation, daylight and free solar energy to minimize energy consumption. This approach can be applied even if, on first impressions, the scope appears to be limited. For example, when planning spaces, make sure that rooms without specific environmental requirements which can benefit from natural light and ventilation, such as general offices, are located to make use of the 'free' energy resources available. Conversely, areas with high heat gains (kitchens, computer suites, etc.) should be sited to the north, or in the central core of a deep-plan building if they will require to be fully mechanically treated in any case (e.g. clean rooms and some computer facilities). In other words, make use of free energy in spaces where the gain will be of benefit and avoid solar gains and natural ventilation only if this will exacerbate an existing problem, or if completely inappropriate to the task.

A balance between heat losses from the north and heat gains to the south must be achieved. This can be assisted by careful material selection as well as space planning (see Materials below). For example, heat gains from plantrooms can reduce heating requirements in peripheral zones if plantrooms are sited in the central core. Similarly, circulation spaces, stair wells and corridors can be used to provide buffers between the accommodation and the outside either by siting them on the north to help reduce heat losses, or by reducing excess gain to the south if designed as walkways and galleria for example.

Solar gain will be of benefit in most buildings early in the morning, when the building is cold. This is particularly true in non-domestic buildings where use of solar energy in east and south-east zones in winter can provide free early morning pre-heat to offset heating loads. The associated risk of summer overheating can be addressed by solar shading (see Lighting below). In situations where internal heat gains are high, solar gains to rooms on south-west and west facing aspects of the building may contribute to overheating, for much of the year as sunlight will be incident on these façades later in the day when the interior is already warm. Contrary to current recommendations for domestic buildings, where north facing glass should be minimized, in non-domestic buildings north facing glass should be optimized to make use of daylight while avoiding excessive heat losses. It is important to be aware that artificial lighting can account for up to 50 per cent of the overall electricity costs in a modern office building. Coupled with excess uncontrolled solar heat gain, this can result in unnecessary energy expenditure on air conditioning which could have been avoided by a clearer understanding of the cumulative impact of internal and external factors.

Internal environment: comfort and energy considerations

If the occupants of a non-domestic building treated that building with the same attitude that they have in their homes, energy management would take care of itself. For example, in winter, people are willing to wear more clothes at home to reduce the impact of cold weather on heating bills – there is no reason why they should not do the same at work. A reduction of 1°C in heating set point temperature can have a significant effect on energy consumption and running costs, and can be achieved by encouraging a sensible attitude to weather dressing. Similarly, in summer, light clothing and natural ventilation, achieved by opening windows, is preferable to mechanical ventilation or air conditioning on both health grounds and in terms of energy impact. Many mechanical ventilation systems rely on a degree of recirculation of extracted air and in spite of reducing energy consumption, this can result in malady in the occupants. Recent studies conclude that lack of control over the working environment is a common cause for complaint. Building occupants should, whenever possible, be given some (if limited) control over heating temperatures and ventilation rates to avoid this. Even limited heating control, ±1°C say and openable windows, can help achieve an amicable solution.

Lighting

Studies have shown that access to daylight, sunlight in particular, and views provide a feeling of well being. However, to guarantee a safe, comfortable working environment, occupants should have control over the quantity and quality of light where visual tasks are performed. A mixture of lowered levels of background light from low energy, ceiling mounted fittings and daylight from windows, together with task lighting for close work is often found to provide the most acceptable visual environment.

Artificial light sources should be selected to enhance or match the quality of daylight provided, and also to assist the tasks to be performed. Other aspects of lighting to be considered are avoidance of glare and excess heat gain from sunlight and the balancing of solar gain with comfortable daylighting levels. Centralized control over background lighting levels is the subject of a great deal of current BRE research. Issues being examined include: use of photocell or occupant sensors; time control or user control; central switching or localized. There is no perfect solution. However, guidance is given in BRE Digest 272[2] which gives advice on optimum solutions for various occupancy patterns, levels and building types. This should be read in conjunction with BRE Digest 232[3] – *Energy Conservation in Artificial Lighting* and BRE Information Paper IP 5/87[4] *Lighting Controls: An Essential Part of Energy Efficient Lighting.*

Glare

Glare is a function of contrast and brightness which results when either:

- A bright light source (such as a sunlit window or a bright lamp) is viewed from a surrounding area which is in relative darkness. In this case, glare results from excessive contrast and can be relieved by increasing the brightness of the surroundings. This type of glare causes discomfort to occupants, resulting in poor

---

[2]BRE Digest 272 – *Lighting Controls and Daylight Use.*
[3]BRE Digest 232 – *Energy Conservation in Artificial Lighting.*

visual performance and potential dissatisfaction with the visual environment. Often complaints manifest themselves as more general dissatisfaction with the environment as a whole due to the subjective nature of the problem which is not always obvious.
- If a space is 'over-lit' by a source which is so excessively bright that the eye mechanism becomes saturated, the result is 'disability glare'. This, although less likely to occur, can be debilitating to the performance of a task, or even dangerous. For example, a window in sunlight at the end of a dimly lit corridor can suddenly plunge a pedestrian into relative darkness and could lead to an accident.

Glare can be avoided by careful consideration of window design in relation to the room depth and height, surface attributes of the space and relationship between the window, the exterior and the occupants. A room 3 m high and 6 m deep daylit on one side only should achieve a daylight factor of around 1.5–2 per cent at the back of the room, for around 15–20 per cent glazing/external wall ratio. In terms of the visual environment created by this scenario, these levels are described as 'cheerfully daylit'. A height to depth ratio of 1:2 allows good light penetration for the aforementioned glazing ratios and this can therefore be applied to rooms with higher and lower ceilings/deeper and shallower plans pro rata. The effect of this ratio is to limit the depth of a non-residential building to about 12 m, assuming it is lit on both sides.

Glare problems can be solved by improving or reducing contrasts, for example, by increasing internal surface reflectances. In schools, glare often occurs when light-coloured walls are concealed behind posters or friezes, this could be alleviated by concentrating such material on walls adjacent to the window to allow the wall opposite the window to remain as free as possible of artwork, etc.

Solar protection

Whilst winter and mid-season solar gains can be useful in offsetting heat losses, it is nevertheless important to avoid excessive heat gains in summer, particularly if this will result in a need to provide artificial cooling.

Fixed shading

Fixed horizontal shading devices such as overhangs are very effective for south facing windows but have a disadvantage in that they operate on a 'worst case' basis, depending on sun altitude only and not external temperature. Thus, these shades may block out useful solar gain under certain conditions when heating is required. Horizontal fixed shades are not effective in dealing with sunlight at azimuths outwith 8° of south facing. East and west facing façades will always require some degree of vertical shading.

**Table 11.1
Effect of shading on solar gain**

Shading method	Solar gain factor
No shading	0.72
External louvred blind	0.11
Mid-pane white venetian	0.25
Internal white venetian	0.45

Movable shading

Movable shading has two main advantages:

- It can be adjusted to suit outside conditions to allow maximum benefit from solar gain and sunlight and to provide protection from glare and excessive heat gain.
- In winter, devices can be closed to reduce heat loss from the building by radiation to the night sky.

Fixed devices offer no such protection.

In terms of protection from solar gain, external shading devices are more effective than mid-pane and mid-pane are more effective than internal devices.

External devices prevent sunlight from entering the space, while internal devices allow solar energy to penetrate and then attempt to reflect the sunlight back out through the glass. The process is never 100 per cent efficient, but the most effective solution will be achieved by a light-coloured or reflective finish on blinds or curtains. As a guide, total transmission through double-glazed, clear glass with typical louvred blinds varies approximately as illustrated in Table 11.1.

Green shading

From an environmental viewpoint, an organic approach can often provide the optimum solution. Deciduous plants, trees or vines provide maximum summer protection and by shedding their leaves in winter, allow sunlight through in winter when desired. Some knowledge of varying seasonal growth is required to establish the correct species to suit the problem – for example beech trees do not shed their leaves until late winter/early spring, just before the growth period.[4] Certain trees, such as ash, allow a large amount of light through their canopy whilst effectively screening out sunlight. Beech is often advocated as an effective shade tree but the density of leaves can be excessive with little

---

[4] BRE Information Paper IP 5/87 – *Lighting Controls: An Essential Part of Energy Efficient Lighting*.

Figure 11.4
Façade design has great influence upon the even distribution of daylight and hence internal comfort conditions. (Peter Foggo Associates©.)

light penetrating through, and little growth of other species beneath the canopy. A biological approach to design would place coniferous trees at the site edge to create wind shelter, deciduous trees nearer to the building, vines or creepers at the building edge, and internal planting on the window sill and inside the structure for enhanced air quality and general ambience.

Summary of shading options

In view of the above points, it is advisable to provide external or mid-pane shading in preference to internal shading in situations where heat gain and glare are to be controlled. As movable devices can provide additional protection against heat loss in winter, it is suggested that application of an external device such as movable blinds, or mid-pane protection is preferable to providing fixed shading (particularly on the east and west façades) with internal blinds. By combining energy, amenity and biological considerations, a combination of fixed and movable, solid and planted shading devices becomes attractive and cost effective.

In the past, fixed shading devices have been preferred to movable ones, in part due to simplicity, low cost and minimum maintenance and also partly because limiting human interaction in some ways limits room for error or misuse. However, they are not as effective as movable shades for anything other than to shade buildings facing due south. If it is the intention to employ a fixed solution, this should be borne in mind. In the UK, a horizontal shelf-type screen of (approx.) 0.7 m width will be required to shade each metre height of exposed south facing glass effectively in summer (from mid-May through to early August) at a latitude of around 56°. Various configurations can be considered to achieve the same effect, e.g. shading can be provided at the top of the glass, or a reduced depth of shelf can be installed lower down the pane. Alternatively, the shading device can be located part inside/part outside providing a light shelf to throw light deeper into the space, etc. Careful detailing is important to avoid excess glare or heat gain via an exposed upper pane. Louvred devices allow hot air to pass through, and are not subject to snow or wind loadings. Architecturally, louvres can be used to provide articulation, and less projection is necessary to achieve an equivalent degree of protection compared with a solid shelf arrangement.

Solar control glazing

Heat absorbing glass

Tinted, heat absorbing glass was very popular in the 1970s and 1980s. However, although effective as a shading device it has a number of disadvantages. Heat absorbing glass absorbs shortwave (light) radiation and thus reduces heat gain to the inside of a building. However, depending on coincident internal and external climatic conditions, this

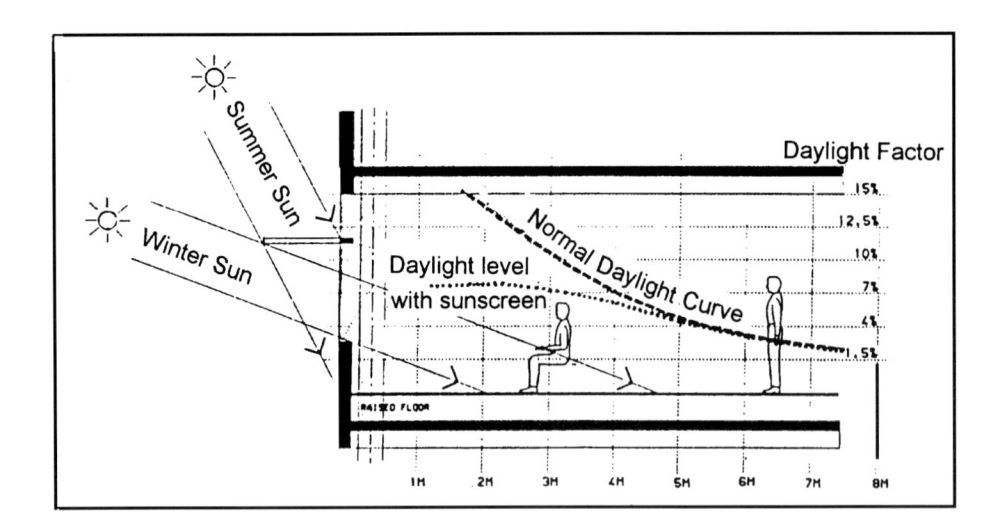

Technical factors in the design of sustainable commercial buildings

Figure 11.5
Questions of environmental health, amenity and energy use are related topics in much building design. (Peter Foggo Associates ©.)

energy stored as heat may be 're-radiated' into the space as the temperature outside begins to fall in the late afternoon. At this time, the internal equipment and casual gains tend to be at a peak. Thus, summer overheating can be more severe than would have occurred otherwise with clear glass and winter heat gain may occur too late in the day to be of any real use. In addition, the chemicals used to achieve this heat absorption cause the glass to be tinted. Studies have shown that the tints used can have two effects:

- longwave (light) transmission is reduced resulting in an increased need for artificial light, and/or larger window areas to achieve the same level of daylight;
- the psychological effect of looking at the world through brown, grey or green glass can be disturbing and has been suggested as a contributory factor in building related health problems.

Reflective glass

Reflective glass can be used to reduce solar penetration without affecting the view to the same extent as heat absorbing glass. However, this solution reduces both shortwave (heat) and longwave (light) transmission which results in reduced useful winter heat gain and year round use of artificial lighting at times when natural light could have been used, in other words heat gain is eliminated at the expense of good quality natural lighting. Reflective glass can however be useful in situations where heat gain is not desired and where the use of external shading is not possible – particularly on west façades.

Low emissivity glass

Low emissivity glass is more discerning than the options discussed above as the film on this glass reduces direct heat gain by transmitting a greater proportion of light than heat. It reduces heat loss by re-reflecting heat back into the space and has an appearance similar to that of clear glass. It is thus useful for situations where daylight is required but solar heat gain should be minimized. It also allows the use of slightly larger windows for daylighting, without necessarily incurring an energy penalty in winter.

New 'intelligent' glazing systems which overcome the problems of differing summer and winter requirements are currently being researched and some are available already – at a price – and the use of photo-chromatics, phase-change materials, holograms, electrically responsive glass, etc. will become more commonplace. In the meantime, the environmentally responsible line tends to encourage the use of clear or low emissivity glass, in high quality double or triple glazed units, wherever possible with shading provided preferably by easily adjusted, external devices to allow occupant control. Failing that, fixed shading is effective on south façades and mid-pane shading is preferable to internal.

Ventilation considerations

Natural ventilation

Use of natural ventilation can result in both capital cost and energy savings and in addition, it is also desirable to minimize the requirement for mechanical ventilation and air-conditioning systems in order to ensure a 'healthy' building. Enclosed central courtyards or atria can be used to save energy by using the space as a means to bring fresh air into the building and to provide natural preheat. In addition, a design incorporating such an atrium space should lend itself to natural ventilation by virtue of the fact that the inclusion of the atrium will modify the building form to one avoiding deep-plan accommodation in favour

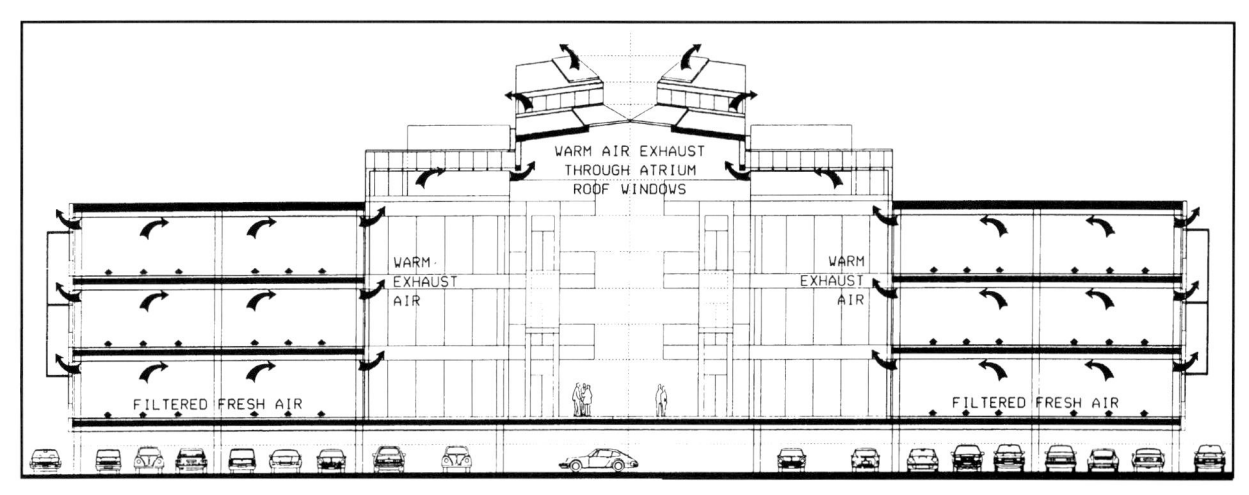

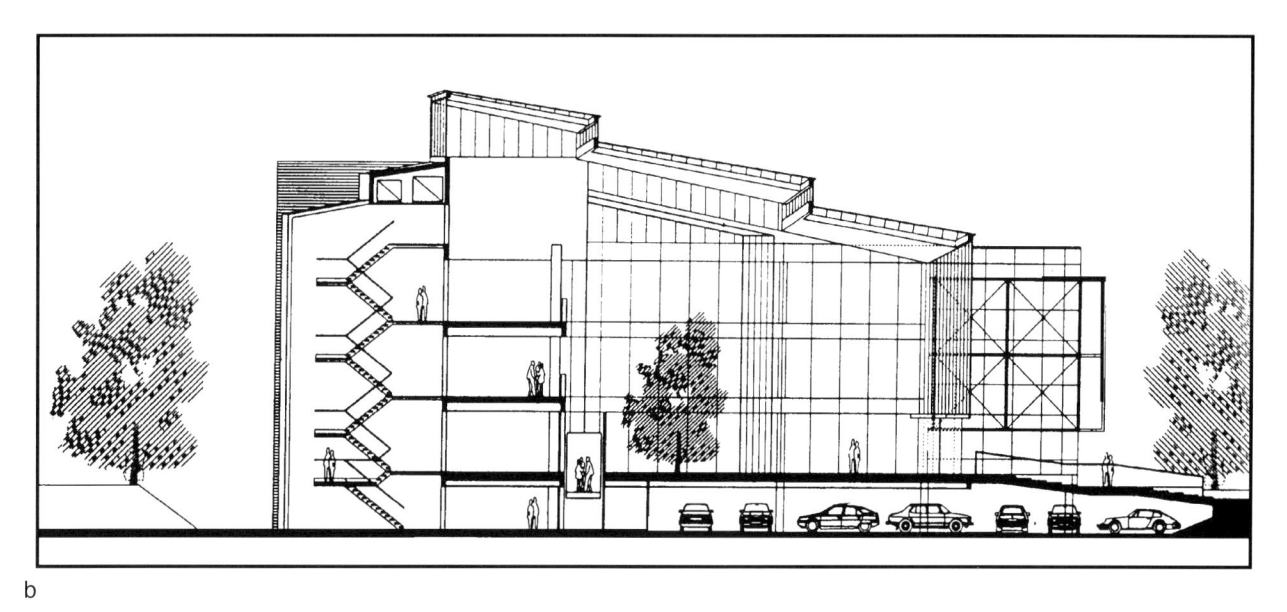

Technical factors in the design of sustainable commercial buildings

Figure 11.6
Long section (a) and cross-section (b) of a building at the Leeds City Office Park developed by British Gas as a green demonstration project and designed by Peter Foggo Associates. (Peter Foggo Associates©.)

of a layout with windows on inner and outer façades allowing facility for good cross ventilation.

Natural ventilation should be employed whenever possible without incurring heating (or cooling) energy penalties. Air movement will be encouraged by temperature and pressure differentials between inside and outside, particularly where temperature differences are enhanced by climate sensitive considerations such as passive solar gains, atrium spaces/glazed courtyards, etc.

However, not all buildings lend themselves to a completely natural approach, and indeed in winter, care must be taken to avoid 'over-ventilation' and consequent energy penalties due to excessive fresh-air cooling. As a result, in larger buildings, 'mixed-mode' and 'displacement' ventilation systems have begun to emerge as a means to conserve energy in winter.

Mixed mode systems

The basic approach encourages natural ventilation in summer and mid-season when outside temperatures are conducive (depending on internal gains, etc.). In winter, energy losses are minimized by a changeover to a mechanical ventilation system, employing some recirculation of extracted air or preferably heat recovery from the extract system. Ventilation air is then supplied tempered to around 2°C below the space set-point temperature and energy saved by virtue of the fact that ingress of cold air via opened windows is virtually eliminated, as this could result in a need to heat the space due to excessive cold air infiltration.

Displacement ventilation

In this case, generally, the system employed introduces air at floor level, tempering only the occupied zone, to around 1.8 m above floor height.

There are 3 main benefits of this:

- Energy is saved by allowing the space above 1.8 m to 'float'. For this reason a higher than normal ceiling height is generally required to gain maximum benefit (a height of the order of 3 metres is usual).
- Contaminants, CO_2, etc. are encouraged to rise towards a high level exhaust zone and incoming clean air travels upwards from low level.
- In summer, if the space temperature rises above the design set-point of say 27°C, air can be introduced at low level at the outside air temperature (which will be slightly cooler). The upward movement of this cooler air should produce a cooling sensation and will improve comfort for the occupants as a result.

In addition, the inertia of the mass of concrete floors/ceiling voids is often used to provide some additional, free cooling, as the slab temperature should be below the room air temperature. This can provide a further degree or so of free cooling which may be critical. The cooling effect can be enhanced by running cold, outside air through the system overnight for a few hours to remove residual slab heat. The effectiveness of this approach depends on the finished ceiling arrangement – suspended ceilings restrict the flow of air up and 'into' the slab.

Air conditioning

The following guidelines should be applied to buildings which are unavoidably fully air conditioned.[5]

- Avoid dual-duct systems and/or fixed volume terminal reheat as both involve cooling air and reheating as required at the point of use.
- Avoid high velocity systems as they consume more energy.
- VAV systems are the most economical way of providing local control.
- Employ heat reclaimed from parts of the building with a heat surplus.
- In terms of building material the amount of space taken up by the air-conditioning plant should be established, as this could have a marked effect on the available useful floor area.
- Avoid any system incorporating CFCs or HCFCs.

Equipment gains

Any process or equipment with high heat gains should be considered separately. However, it is important to note that gains from modern computing equipment such as PCs, laserwriters, etc., have reduced substantially in recent years. Recent studies conducted by various bodies such as BRECSU suggest that heat gain from such machines is often overestimated. In a typical office situation with up to one PC per desk and average occupancy density, an overall equipment load of around 18 W/m^2 is currently typical. However, as equipment evolves, and as the requirement for increased automation increases, these figures may change. For example, installations of one PC per desk are now 'typical' rather than 'hi-tech' and laserwriters, although currently running at one per three people, may be provided on a 'one-to-one' basis rather than shared in the future. The BSRIA Technical Note – Small Power Loads provides an indication of the actual heat output from office equipment compared with that stated on the nameplate.[6]

Insulation, fabric and control in non-domestic buildings

It is often taken for granted that higher insulation levels are the obvious solution to reducing energy use in buildings. However, more insulation is not *necessarily* the answer. The thermal performance of materials has to be considered in conjunction with other factors such as:

Air leakage	Loss of heat through air leakage can begin to dominate 'heat loss' if not addressed simultaneously with insulation levels.
Heating system	Heating systems and components must be designed and selected with effective energy use in mind and must 'match' the building fabric and purpose. A well-insulated building with an inefficient or poorly controlled heating system will probably overheat –

---

[5]*Working in the City* CEC Publication, University College of Dublin.

[6]BSRIA Technical Note (TN8/92) *Small Power Loads*; *ASHRAE Journal* September 1991.

Technical factors in the design of sustainable commercial buildings

Summer and winter strategies

without saving energy. 'Domestic' hot water production may also become a critical factor in the overall energy picture and so a 'holistic' approach is needed. High insulation levels will reduce the rate of heat loss in winter and in summer. They also reduce the potential for heat gain. The thermal performance must be evaluated to optimize heat gains and losses, in both summer and winter, to avoid trapping heat gain from internal sources in summer while avoiding excessive losses in winter. Simultaneously, potentially useful winter gains should not be eliminated by only considering avoidance of summer gains. The optimum solution will be achieved by:
1 Optimizing insulation levels.
2 Designing heating systems appropriately and for high operating efficiency.
3 Providing solar protection in summer without compromising useful winter solar gains.

The above does not discount the potential benefits of high insulation standards but seeks to highlight the fact that the solution should be carefully thought through. It is possible to achieve insulation values of well above the statutory requirements at little additional cost, using modern techniques and materials, and this approach should be adopted.

Materials

The above design principles should be integrated with and complemented by an equally responsible approach to selecting materials for construction. When detailing a building from a bio-climatic and environmental standpoint, it is also crucial to consider the energy and environmental impact of selecting a particular material. This is not always a straightforward exercise (as outlined below); however, with reference to earlier discussion, if designers take responsibility for their actions by adopting 'appropriate' as a criteria for the selection of materials and if they avoid both arbitrary and extravagant decisions, the problem will, to an extent, take care of itself – particularly if an effort is made to become familiar with locally available and locally manufactured products which exploit the natural resources of the region (see Chapter 18).

Much of the information available on energy 'contained' within building materials relates to mass rather than commonly used areas of wall to floor construction. This can be misleading – for example how does one compare a kilogram of glass with a kilogram of brick, or aluminium, or lead? Davis Langdon and Everest who are leaders in the field of evaluating the energy embodied in buildings attempt to address this by comparing square metres of alternative construction methods (including transportation energy where appropriate) in terms of energy consumed to achieve a built result. In an article in *Architecture Today*[7] they advocate:

- Substitution of materials with known high embodied energy with materials of lower embodied energy.
- Recycling of materials where possible.
- Design to minimize the *quantity* of materials used.
- Design new buildings for long life and reduce the need to refurbish.

By comparing the materials used to construct a house by different construction methods it was shown that timber frame construction can be up to 20 per cent less energy intensive than traditional construction and that it can take two years for polymer based insulation to 'pay for' the energy consumed in manufacture. In a three-bedroomed house, the energy consumed to produce the main building components is equivalent to between two and five years of energy consumed by heating, light and power.

Capital and revenue energy costs of construction materials

Another method advocated for coming to grips with the energy embodied in construction materials is to distinguish between the energy capital and the energy revenue of a building.[8] Such a distinction allows designers to understand how much energy is locked away in common building products (concrete blocks, tiles, steel beams, etc.) and what the relationship is between energy costs (capital) in construction and energy costs (revenue) in use. The equation is a complex one and poorly researched and too little understood. However, if the production of sustainable buildings, largely benign in their energy and environmental impacts, is to be society's prime objective, then designers and engineers will need to develop a methodology to suit.

The construction phase of building consists largely of putting together building products previously manufactured at some distance and transported mainly by road to the site. Assembly on site is labour rather than energy intensive. Generally speaking the capital energy costs are divided between 70 per cent used in the manufacture of

---

[7]*Architecture Today*, July 1991 p 83.
[8]Brenda and Robert Vale, Building the sustainable environment, in Andrew Blowers (ed.) *Planning for a Sustainable Environment* TCPA, 1993, p 95.

products and 30 per cent in transport and erection.[9] For more high-tech buildings such as offices the balance is likely to be 80 per cent to 20 per cent. Even with simple low-tech materials such as bricks it is important to appreciate the often invisible energy costs of poor choice and specification. For example, bricks delivered to a building site from over 250 miles away have effectively doubled their capital energy cost. The transportation energy costs for that distance have been computed at 1250 kWh per 1000 bricks whilst the manufacture of the bricks (clay extraction, moulding and firing) would require 1400 kWh.[10]

Capital energy embodied in construction amounts to 10–20 per cent of the total energy cost within the life of a building. The more toilet pods manufactured in Belgium, marble cladding panels in Italy and glazing systems from Germany are employed, the greater the percentage of capital energy to revenue energy costs. However, the equation is not always a simple one. Sometimes a higher investment initially in energy saving technologies (even if they are transported some distance) can result in lower revenue energy costs. The conservation of process energy and the conservation of building-in energy are both desirable targets. If a distinction was drawn more frequently between capital and revenue costs, designers would be able to make the necessary adjustments between material choice, built form and energy management systems. Commercial buildings with their shorter life spans (thirty years with major refurbishment every decade or so) have a more critical relationship between capital and revenue energy costs than in the domestic sector. In fact, it has been suggested that the embodied energy may equal the energy in use over the duration of short-life buildings. Here the equation begins to approach the levels of unsustainability witnessed in the automobile industry.

Choosing materials for use in the construction of commercial buildings

As an extension of the above, all materials should be selected on environmental grounds (see Chapter 18). The environmental impact of selecting a particular material should be considered from growth or extraction through manufacture and transport to building, use and demolition. A full life-cycle assessment is required as outlined in Chapter 25. The following provides guidance in the choices relevant to commercial buildings.

Glass

Although glass is very energy intensive to manufacture, so are the alternatives. In addition, glass is generally used in thin sheets and compared with the alternative mass of concrete to fill the space, may not be more energy intensive. Glass can also provide solar gain and hence reduce heating needs and aid natural ventilation through the stack effect. As material it can also be recycled in whole or part.

Insulation materials

There is a potential risk to occupants due to off-gassing from materials such as urea-formaldehyde foam for example, and as a result, environmentally conscious designers should avoid the use of such materials. Although 100 times less damaging than CFCs, HCFCs still contribute to the greenhouse effect, and the insulation materials thus produced are oil-based – a debatable use of precious fossil-fuel reserves.

The environments in which glasswool and mineral wool are produced are considered to be unhealthy for people directly involved (this should be improved by the growing awareness of and adherence to the COSHH Regulations) and the process is fairly energy intensive. However, overall, glass and mineral wool insulation materials are preferred in terms of 'greenness', although the most responsible approach of all is arguably recycled paper/cellulose insulation. This material is currently available to be 'blown' *in situ* only, and in addition its use requires some, if limited, understanding of thermal and moisture migration in construction.

Steel or aluminium?

In the UK, steel is almost 100 per cent recycled. However, steel production is extremely energy intensive, and steel has to be 'treated' to avoid corrosion:

- the treatment often involves polymeric paints;
- the treatment has to be repeated, i.e. maintenance implications.

Aluminium is extracted from bauxite; the process is highly energy intensive and only 10 per cent of the extracted material is used. If waste is a serious environmental problem, aluminium production is also chemical intensive and potentially environmentally very damaging to air quality. However, aluminium production has much lower maintenance requirements than steel as it does not corrode. Aluminium also weighs less than steel and this results in reduced transport costs. Putting aside embodied energy, designers should seek to use structural materials locally produced. In Scotland, for instance, aluminium is produced on a large scale using relatively clean hydro-electricity. With no steel industry left in Scotland, architects would naturally look to aluminium as the more appropriate choice. Aluminium production uses 26 times as much energy as timber production, but most softwood

---

[9] *Ibid.*, p 96.
[10] *Ibid.*

used in Britain is imported thus adding to the complexity of the choice faced by designers endeavouring to adopt green principles.

General guidelines for material selection

- Where possible substitute timber for plasterboard, brick or concrete, plasterboard for brick or concrete.
- Substitute timber for metal or plastic unless required for strength/lightness, and use only as much as required.
- Use just enough glass to achieve good daylighting. Use double or triple glazing if economics allow. Avoid use of tinted or reflective glass as both cut down light transmission – thus requiring a greater area for the same light levels and also because of the potentially adverse psychological impact of viewing the outside through dark glass. Tinted glass also produces an unfriendly environment when looking in from the street.
- Look for the potential to use recycled material on the site without incurring additional transport energy expenditure, e.g. hardcore or recycled steel.
- Specify and design with recycling in mind so that materials chosen today can be used in tomorrow's buildings.

Internal finishes

For a healthy internal environment opt for organic paint to avoid formaldehyde and other solvent pollution. Floor coverings should be natural rather than synthetic, e.g. wool based/hessian backed carpets or linoleum. Furniture and fittings should be of natural materials preferably using timber, unstained and unpainted and from managed, renewable sources.

Pollution

Pollution can be roughly divided into four categories:

- atmosphere;
- water;
- noise;
- waste.

The impact of the building on the site and the potential effects of the site on a new building have to be considered simultaneously. The interaction in both directions is important, especially when contaminated land is being employed (see Chapter 24).

Noise and atmospheric pollution have to be controlled to avoid effects on occupants of new and existing buildings. Much legislation from the EC and new codes of conduct in the UK focus on the effects of pollution of various kinds upon the health and safety of building users. This is discussed further in Chapter 19. Pollution in the form of CO_2 is also a problem which the introduction of a carbon tax, sometimes mooted within the EC, may seek to reduce. A carbon tax introduced at some stage in the future would apply to the fossil fuels consumed within buildings currently on the drawing board. In the light of the prospect (in 1995) of an expanding Europe with its legislative given additional powers, it is clearly prudent to design for maximum energy efficiency. The 'polluter pays' principle has yet to be extended to a situation where a developer is required to plant sufficient trees to absorb the carbon released within the building. Such solutions, though fraught with bureaucratic difficulties, may appear one day on the EC's legislative horizon.

FOUR ENERGY EVALUATION CASE STUDIES

The complexities of choice underpinning the design of a sustainable non-domestic building are demonstrated through the following four case studies evaluated at the project design stage. Each was researched by the author of this chapter in her capacity as Technical Director of the Energy Design Advice Scheme (EDAS) at the University of Strathclyde. In each only revenue energy (not capital) costs were considered.

Scottish Office – Victoria Quay

EDAS was approached by RMJM Scotland, on behalf of Victoria Quay Ltd, to give advice on a proposed low energy office development on Victoria Quay, Edinburgh. The object of the study was to look at the thermal performance and energy consumption of the building and to predict the internal environmental conditions to establish whether imposed targets on the building design would be satisfied. No area of the building should exceed 26°C for more than 105 hours per annum. In addition to this the study had an overall objective of providing a building which would, as far as possible, use natural light and ventilation. RMJM Scotland had drawn on lessons learned from the design of a sister building for the NFU building at Stratford upon Avon, and proposed to exploit building mass as part of the strategy. After initial discussions ABACUS Simulations Ltd were commissioned to undertake a thermal analysis of the proposed development.

The building comprised a number of individual office buildings connected by an internal street, or galleria, one of which was selected for analysis. The individual block consisted of shallow plan office accommodation grouped around a central courtyard or atrium. This central space was analysed to determine its optimum configuration as:

Technical factors in the design of sustainable commercial buildings

Table 11.2
Fact file: Victoria Quay, Edinburgh

Title	Victoria Quay	Client	RMJM Scotland
Type	Offices: New Build	Enquiry	Low Energy Building, Environmental Performance
Area	45 000 m²	Energy Saving	Up to 4.5 million kWh/annum £170 000 pa
Location	Edinburgh	Benefits	Internal environmental strategy combining mechanical and natural ventilation achieving economic and comfort optimum

- an open courtyard;
- a covered atrium;
- an atrium with north light only.

A number of simulations were conducted using climate data for east Scotland to establish the optimum configuration of the courtyard to minimize energy consumption and to ensure comfort conditions within the offices.

The final simulation of the building incorporated the client's requirements for the building. This included an external wall with an inner leaf of heavy weight construction and reversed low-E glazing systems with blinds to all façades.

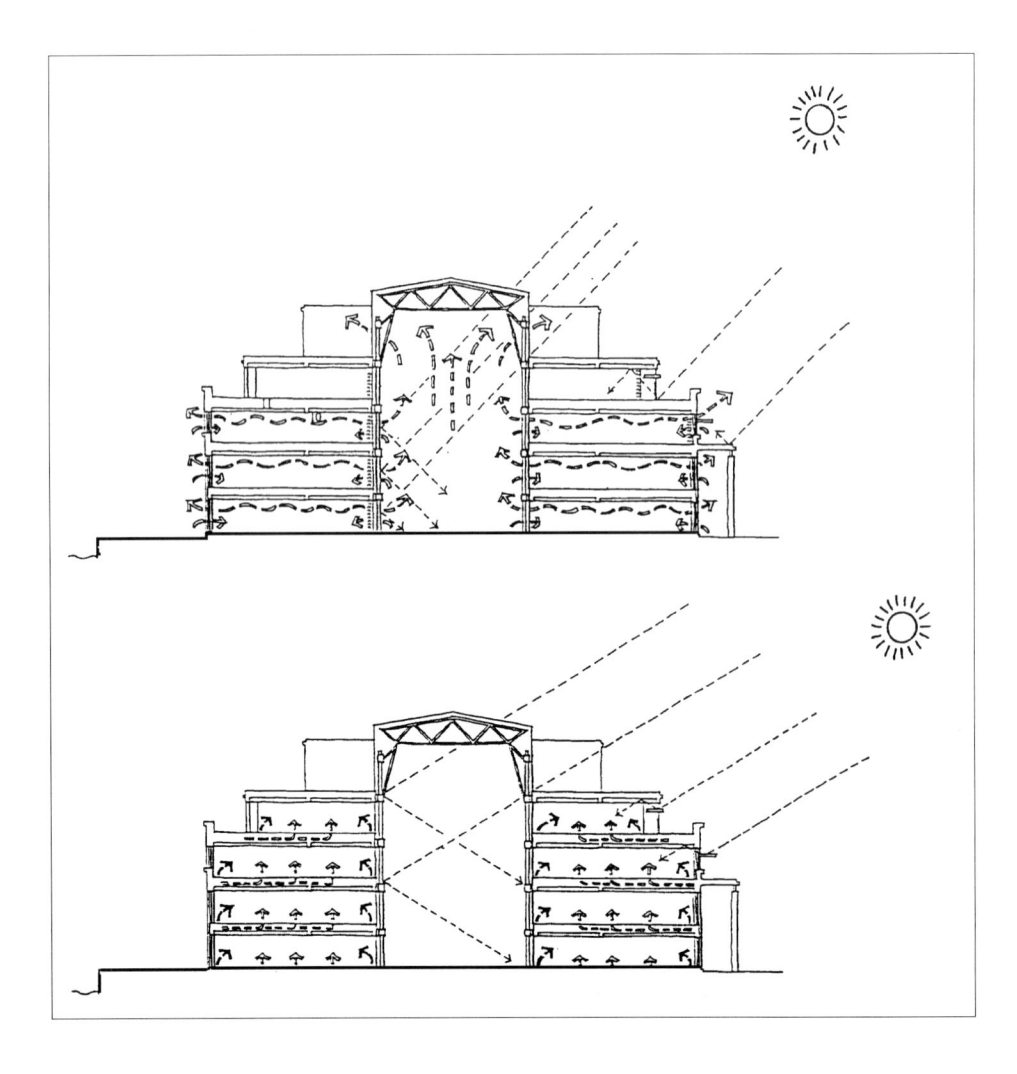

Figure 11.7
Buildings perform differently in the summer and winter. Design needs to respond to both conditions if energy use is to be reduced. (RMJM©.)

Results

The initial studies established that a central covered atrium achieved a significant energy saving over the winter period and did not affect the natural ventilation of the building during the summer. It was concluded that the building should adopt a mixed mode ventilation system (natural and mechanical) to suit the seasonal variations:

Winter: the building would be mechanically ventilated, with recirculated air and a minimum fresh-air intake, to reduce energy consumption. A perimeter heating system would be provided, although results indicated that general casual gains from electrical equipment might eliminate this need beyond a certain level of provision.

Summer: the building would be naturally ventilated during the daytime. At night the ventilation system would be used to purge the lower temperature night-time air through the building, cooling the structure. On the hottest days, mechanical ventilation would be required to supplement natural ventilation.

It could be seen from the results that the high thermal mass of the structure and the passive shading devices had a considerable influence on moderating the internal climate. The building was predicted to perform satisfactorily as a non-air-conditioned building, with no area exceeding 26°C for more than 52 hours.

1 Castle Street, Edinburgh, office development

The Palace Hotel, which was situated on the corner of Princes Street and Castle Street in Edinburgh, was destroyed by fire in 1991 leaving a prime and prominent gap site for development. Due to the sensitive location of the site any proposed building would be subject to severe planning constraints. Trafalgar House acquired the site with the intention of developing it as an office block, with retail uses on the ground floor.

EDAS was approached by Blyth & Blyth Associates Ltd., on behalf of Trafalgar House, with a request for assistance to assess the potential of displacement ventilation within the office block and to predict the internal environmental performance by means of computer modelling. The design conditions require a minimum temperature of 21°C and incorporate a perimeter heating system. No refrigerated cooling was proposed (and hence no CFC used), therefore the maximum room temperature profile would be determined by the external ambient temperature and the inertia of the building. It was also intended to run the system overnight in summer to cool the floor slab in order to assist by precooling the offices. EDAS recommended that the Energy Simulation Research Unit (ESRU) in Strathclyde University be commissioned to carry out the study using Environmental Systems Performance (ESP) software. Blyth and Blyth wanted to assess the potential of positive displacement ventilation through floor mounted diffusers and extracting through the light fittings at high level within the new office as opposed to using air conditioning. The project had necessarily to include investigation into the glazing and shading considerations due to sensitive site considerations and strict planning constraints limiting the type and style of fenestration to the elevations.

The proposed building has eight levels, including a basement, with a central glazed atrium to optimize the provision of natural light and ventilation. The external façade of the building was to be constructed of two leaves. The first was in effect a glass skin, supported by lightweight construction, that enclosed the entire façade, producing the required aesthetic demanded by planning constraints. The second was a glazed unit embedded within heavy-weight construction. The intention of this leaf was to control the internal climate. Access walkways were situated in between the two leaves.

Through computer simulations, ESRU looked at the predicted environmental performance of the proposed building both under summer and winter conditions. Two clear glazing options were considered, each using a proprietary project.

- Okalux – Okasolar: a clear glass which incorporates a fixed reflective louvre system.
- Hunter Douglas – Luxaclair – sealed glass blind. Manually adjustable venetian blinds within a sealed glass unit.

Results

It was found that extreme summer conditions demanded additional shading or cooling measures. Automatic window blinds were investigated and it was found that when operated during the extreme conditions the amount of shortwave solar penetration into the building could be reduced by 12–13.5 per cent, lowering the air temperature by 1–2°C. The result of this was to reduce the temperature difference between the core and perimeter of the building. In addition the inclusion of floor slab mass into the ventilation scheme and the use of night purge cooling resulted in the predicted reductions to peak temperatures during the summer period. The predominant contribution to the thermal loads in the summer was found to be the equipment which was to be used in the offices. This suggested a strong case for occupants to consider using much more energy economical equipment.

Technical factors in the design of sustainable commercial buildings

Table 11.3
Fact file: 1 Castle Street, Edinburgh

Title	1 Castle Street, Edinburgh	Client	Blyth & Blyth Associates
Type	Offices: New Build	Enquiry	Potential of displacement ventilation
Area	3500 m²	Energy Saving	35 000 kWh/annum
			£8750 pa
Location	Edinburgh	Benefits	Improved running costs and capital savings without loss of comfort

EED Offices for Scottish Power: Hillington, near Glasgow

EDAS was approached by Scottish Power to give advice on the energy performance and management of their proposed Energy Efficient Design for one of the office building units at the proposed Hillington Business Park. Scottish Power wished to assess the merits of the proposal in comparison to the standard Building Regulation requirements. The philosophy was to increase the fabric insulation and air tightness of the building above those of current Building Regulation Standards, in order to reduce heat losses. Further reduction in annual energy consumption is made by using an all electric direct acting panel heater system utilizing off-peak electricity with daytime top-up. The proposed building at Hillington Business Park encompassed all the concepts of EED as well as additional energy saving features such as mechanical ventilation with heat recovery, increased fabric mass to reduce internal temperature swings (and therefore the effect of solar gains) and the facility to precool the building structure to reduce the risk of summertime overheating.

The study was undertaken in two phases, the first phase consisted of studies to investigate the effects of fabric thermal mass and glazing type on energy performance and internal comfort conditions, as well as a solar shading study of the building to assess the effects of structure in reducing the risk of summertime overheating. The second phase consisted of a series of annual energy simulations to assess the comparative running costs for two heating systems respectively, a gas-fired boiler and an all-electric storage system, against a 'traditional' heating design.

Results

Fabric option five was adopted as the preferred design for the EED building due to its ability to reduce the peak summertime internal temperature by approximately 3°C. The results of the annual running cost simulations show that due to the increased levels of insulation and fabric mass:

Table 11.4 Fabric and heating options for offices for Scottish Power, near Glasgow

Fabric options
Building Regulations:
- 100 mm brick
- 0.45 W/m²°C

One:
- Lightweight external wall construction: 100 mm brick, 50 mm airgap
- 0.32 W/m²°C
- Low 'E' double glazing

Two:
- Lightweight external wall construction: 100 mm brick, 150 mm concrete block
- 0.36 W/m²°C
- Low 'E' double glazing

Three:
- Heavyweight external wall construction: 100 mm brick
- 0.36 W/m²°C
- Low 'E' double glazing

Four:
- Heavyweight external wall construction: 100 mm brick
- 0.36 W/m²°C
- Low 'E' Antisun double glazing

Five:
- Heavyweight external wall construction: 100 mm brick
- 0.36 W/m²°C
- Low 'E' Antisun double glazing + internal louvres

Heating system options
One:
- Building insulated to current Building Regulation standards utilizing an electric storage heating system

Two:
- Building insulated to current Building Regulation standards utilizing a conventional gas boiler central heating system

Three:
- Proposed EED building incorporating increased levels of insulation and fabric mass, utilizing electric panel heaters to supply off-peak heating to the fabric mass and daytime 'top-up' when required

Four:
- As system 3 above but with plant de-activated between the hours of 1630 and 1830

Table 11.5
Fact file: Hillington, Glasgow

Title	Hillington Business Park	Client	Scottish Power
Type	Offices: New Build	Enquiry	Energy Performance and Management
Area	1500 m²	Energy Saving	£549–939 p.a.
Location	Hillington, Glasgow	Benefits	Low running costs achievable by electric system at low capital cost

Table 11.6
Fact file: Bonnington Bond, Edinburgh

Title	Bonnington Bond (Phase 2)	Client	Mountglen Development Company
Type	Refurbishment	Enquiry	Mixed mode displacement ventilation
Area	11 000 m²	Energy Saving	£66 000 pa
Location	Edinburgh	Benefits	Lower running costs with no additional capital costs due to avoidance of air conditioning

- Heating system three has the lowest annual operating costs of £2152.
- System two cost £2542 and system one cost £3091.
- System four uses slightly less heating energy than three so would have the lowest annual operating costs if it were to be compared on cost terms.

Bonnington Bond (Phase 2), Edinburgh

This project entailed the conversion of an existing whisky bond into a prestigious office complex. EDAS was approached by the project engineers M & E Engineers RSP Consultants on behalf of Mountglen Development Company Ltd with a view to establishing the effectiveness of a mixed mode displacement ventilation system together with assessing the performance of various glazing and solar control options. The design proposal included the creation of a south facing glazed courtyard, achieved by cutting into the existing building which is of heavy mass construction. Control over temperature swings across the building is paramount and therefore fabric finishes were also considered.

The simulation study predicted that space temperatures could be maintained below 26°C by using an advanced glazing system with mid-pane blinds, and use of overnight purging to cool the floor slab was recommended to delay peak internal temperatures by up to two hours.

Results

The study therefore concluded that the installation of a displacement, mixed mode system was viable in terms of occupant comfort and that full air conditioning could therefore be avoided.

12

Renewable energy

Global warming gas production can be addressed by looking at the supply rather than demand side of the energy equation. Although engineers and designers are mostly concerned with improving the energy performance of buildings through better design, there are tangible benefits also in increasing the supply of energy by less damaging environmental means. Here, too, the Maastricht Treaty, European legislation, energy policy plans and much EC funded research is directed. If sustainable development is to be achieved (see Chapter 28) then the 'supply' and 'demand' sides of energy need to be addressed. Architects are well placed to take advantage of new technologies relating to both how energy is consumed and produced.

Of the potential sources of renewable energy in Europe – wind, wave and tidal power – the British Isles are the best endowed. However, because of the abundance of fossil-fuel reserves in the North Sea and a UK Government more committed to nuclear energy than benign sources, Britain has probably been the most backward country in Europe in exploiting these national reserves. As with CHP, Denmark, Norway, Sweden and the Netherlands have set the lead with France and Germany not far behind. Specific clauses of the Maastricht Treaty encourage the development of renewable energy, thereby favouring further the energy technologies of more progressive Member States.

Under the electricity privatization legislation of 1989 the UK Government gave a limited boost to the development of renewable energy by requiring supply companies to buy a percentage of their electricity (usually up to 10 per cent) from non-fossil fuel sources. Under the Non-Fossil Fuel Obligation (NFFO) both the nuclear electricity industry and the embryonic alternative energy technologies have benefitted. In *This Common Inheritance* (1990) the UK Government, alarmed by predictions of global warming, accelerated the development of energy from renewable sources hoping to reach a capacity of 1000 MW by the end of the century. Before its demise in 1992, the Department of Energy estimated that by 2025 renewables would be providing 20 per cent of Britain's energy demand, mainly from wind.[1]

Although renewable sources are the only clean energy supplies, they carry local environmental impacts. Wind farms lead to ecological disturbance, visual impact and noise: tidal power threatens the wildlife of estuaries (discussions over the Severn Barrage highlight the complexity and strength of feelings involved), and wave power can disturb local fisheries and tourist interests.

Figure 12.1
Wind farms will increasingly become part of the rural scene in the UK as Britain conforms with EC policy on expanding the exploitation of renewable sources of energy. (South West Electricity Board©.)

[1] Adrian Webb and Chris Gossop, Towards a sustainable energy policy, Andrew Blowers (ed.) *Planning for a Sustainable Environment* TCPA 1993, p 59.

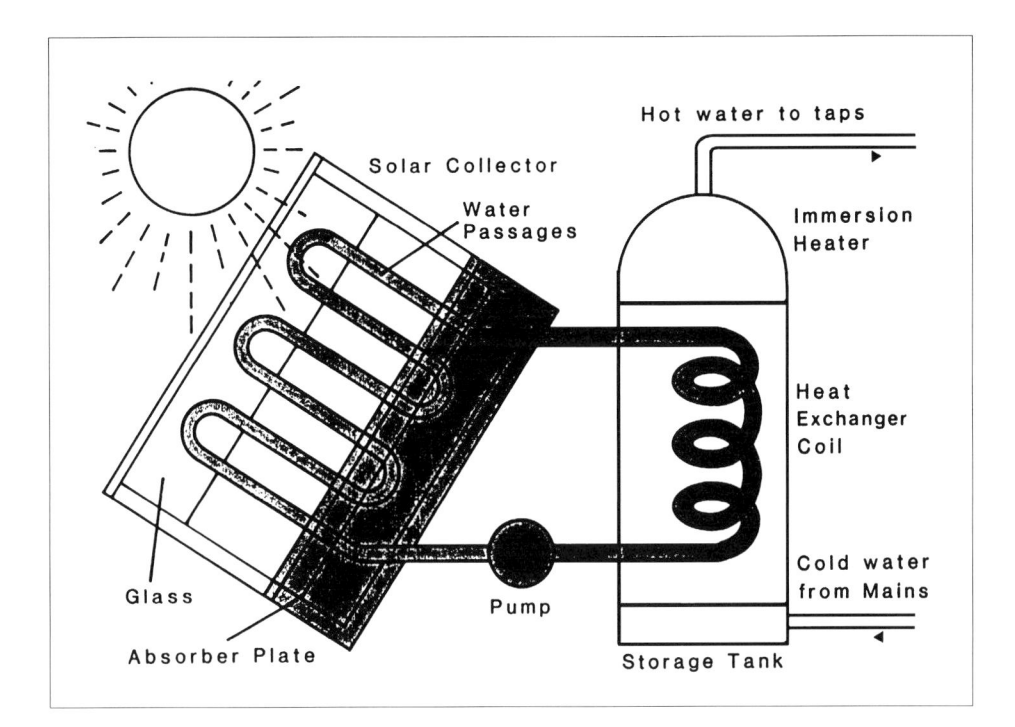

Figure 12.2
Diagram showing how a domestic solar water heater works. (Lothian Energy Group©.)

These local impacts of concern to people nearby are, however, minor compared to the global problems faced by society at large.

Of the three main sources of renewable energy, wind is the most abundant, usable and economic to develop. Wave power has potential, especially for remote coastal areas where mains supplies do not exist, but its wider development has recently been stopped in the UK by a government which believes benefits lie in developing other renewable sources. Tidal power is also at present considered less cost effective than electricity generated from the wind, and in spite of one or two well-published projects, looks set to be wound down. If the UK Government is withdrawing research funding for renewables except wind, the same is not true of the EU which is taking greater interest than ever in exploiting renewable sources of energy.

Biomass

Biomass is the production of energy by burning renewable biological products – timber, straw, grass, etc. The combustion of these materials does produce CO_2 but as long as the crop is replanted immediately the carbon dioxide emitted is taken up again by the new crop. In different parts of the world a variety of energy producing crops can be grown – willows in the north, rape methyl ester (RME) and miscanthus grass in the temperate areas, and sugar cane in hotter regions. Energy is produced usually via gasification reactors producing electricity to the national grid or as with RME, diesel fuels are distilled for internal combustion engines. In Brazil a third of the country's 12 million cars are run on ethanol produced from sugar cane.[2]

Since fertilizers are used in the growing of many of the new energy crops, a full life-cycle assessment of impacts is required. Short-term crops, such as annual harvesting of RME, contrast with five yearly coppicing of fast growing willows in Scotland or Ireland. As a timber crop, climate modifier and amenity, energy forests contain benefits over a broad front and provide one of the justifications for urban forests planted on derelict city land.

Combined heat and power (CHP)

Power stations based upon CHP generate electricity to the grid and utilize the waste heat (either steam or hot water) for district heating. Whereas conventional power stations release the waste heat to the atmosphere (where it adds to the 'heat island' effect), CHP power stations benefit local neighbourhoods and sometimes industry by providing much of their space heating needs. It has been suggested that CHP schemes are 80 per cent more efficient than conventional power stations, as long as the total energy benefits are equated.

---

[2]*Ibid.*, p 60.

Renewable energy

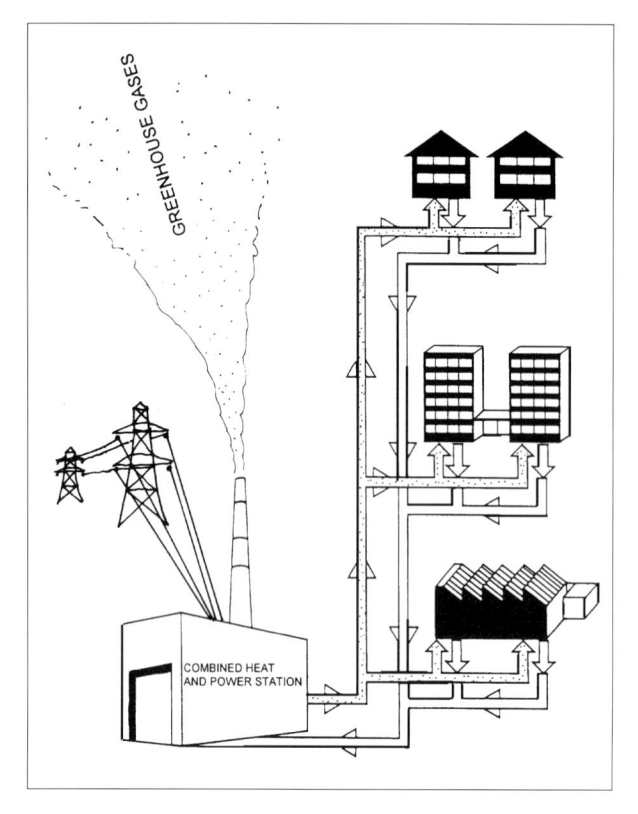

Figure 12.3
Principles behind Combined Heat and Power (CHP) Schemes. Hot water, used in generating electricity is distributed to surrounding buildings and then returns to be preheated. (Adapted from Lothian Energy Group©.)

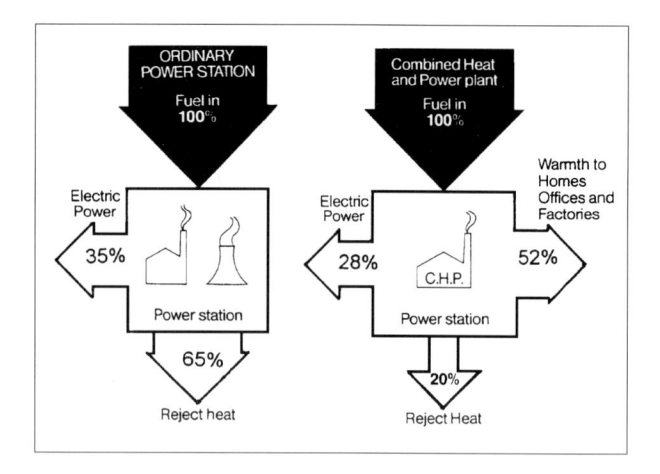

Figure 12.4
Comparison between ordinary power station and CHP station. (Lothian Energy Group©.)

CHP plants are particularly prevalent in Scandinavia. In Odense in Denmark 95 per cent of homes are directly heated through the city's CHP power station.[3] In Sweden about 30 per cent of the country's space heating needs are met by CHP, most fired by coal or refuse. In terms of global warming gas production CHP is a considerable improvement over conventional power stations since some of the losses in energy conversion are eliminated by utilizing the secondary energy sources. However, to be effective CHP plants and local neighbourhoods need to be close together. The waste heat or steam cools as it passes through underground pipes, limiting the radius of benefit to about 500 metres. One experimental scheme funded by ICI at Teesside in Britain currently under construction will provide power (up to 1800 MW) to the national grid and process steam for an adjoining chemical works. In CHP schemes supply and demand are necessarily physically adjacent to each other.

Such proximity requires urban form to be compact with clear servicing corridors for the passage of heating pipes. The *EC Green Paper on the Urban Environment* sought to encourage CHP schemes, highlighting their benefit not just for energy production but in terms of tackling wider urban problems. The inner cities where poverty and blight are concentrated provide ample sites for CHP plants whose benefits in terms of cheaper energy will flow to the people of greatest need. As the Green Paper remarked, the move towards sustainable energy policies could be linked to environmental improvement in the worn-out cities of Europe, as well as job creation in the construction of CHP plants. Urban compaction is a prerequisite for the wider introduction of CHP. So also is the management of waste upon which many plants depend for their primary source of fuel. Small to medium sized CHP schemes powered by household refuse, constructed by developers who sell the electricity generators to the national grid and the waste heat to local houses, require the guiding hand of local authorities. In Sheffield and Nottingham, town councils have taken the lead in developing CHP schemes in partnership with electricity generators utilizing UK government grants, such as City Challenge. As concerns for global warming grow the momentum for CHP will increase, especially with the EC seeking to 'prevent all the residual heat from conventional power stations being simply released to the environment'.[4]

The new breed of power station will be smaller than in the past and, as they generally generate less power per metre of land area than fossil-fuel competitors, there will be more of them. Over the next decade large isolated

---

[3]*Ibid.*, p 56.

[4]*Ibid.*, p 57.

power stations will be replaced by a new breed of small community power plants. Such a change will mean planners facing an increase in the number of applications with, no doubt, environment impact assessments required of each. As with changes in the design of buildings and the settlement patterns of cities which stem from global warming concerns, new energy policy will create new employment opportunities for those with environmental skills.

The creation of a sustainable environment based upon environmentally benign principles of development will lead to new urban patterns, where power plants are integrated with housing and industry. Under the new powerful forces of environmental change, towns and their buildings and public spaces will be shaped by fresh factors. CHP is likely to be as important over the next generation as the construction of conventional coal-fired power stations was to the last. Where the latter were mainly constructed away from towns, the new more environmentally friendly power plants will be within cities, perhaps even within some of the larger public buildings themselves.

The European Union 'Action Plan' for renewable energy

In 1994 the European Union announced an 'Action Plan' to promote renewable sources of energy in order to replace 15 per cent of primary energy by various forms of renewables by the year 2010. The need for an Action Plan, signed in Madrid on 18 March 1994, highlights the lack of a coherent strategy in Europe for the use of renewable sources of energy. In the UK in 1994 only 3 per cent of energy comes from renewable sources. Various institutional barriers to the development in the UK and elsewhere of energy generation from wind, solar, tide, wave and other sources exist. The main impediments to progress identified by the European Union (EU) are:[5]

- *Legislative and administrative* – The lack of a regulatory framework for renewable energy across Europe and in Member States results in renewable energy being discriminated against at a political level. As a result third party generators cannot gain access to the grid and there is little transparency in the field of energy charging.
- *Financial and fiscal* – Distorted competition results in renewable energy technologies being considered uncompetitive and unreliable in terms of end-user price. The monopoly enjoyed by many primary energy suppliers has the effect of favouring conventional energy sources. As a result the Action Plan recommends that taxation policy should take into account the distortions in the energy market and deliberately favour, through mechanisms such as the European Investment Bank, the development of renewable energy sources.
- *Technological* – Renewable energy technologies need not only to be developed but also demonstrated at a practical level with the results more widely disseminated. As a result the EU decided in 1994 to fund further R & D programmes with an emphasis on practical demonstration and information dissemination. The Action Plan believes that the 15 per cent target for energy generation from renewable sources, will only be met by direct European action to support technological development.
- *Information, education and training* – The lack of public awareness of the potential of renewable energy hinders development at a political, social and technological level.

The Action Plan, supported by the EU after MEP Carlos Robles Piquér intervened on behalf of a sizeable lobby of advocates for renewable energy, recognizes the importance of energy to European society. Politicians have begun to realize that a substantial increase in world energy needs over the next century could have unacceptable consequences for the economy, employment and the environment. Renewable energy is part of a Community-wide energy strategy which contains three guiding principles for energy research and development:[6]

- Energy security in the broadest sense, i.e. providing reliable energy services at acceptable costs and under acceptable conditions.
- Environmental concerns, and in particular the strategic objectives relating to the reduction of CO_2 emissions, constitute the main driving force for change.
- To be effective and consistent, energy research must consider the entire technological process embracing research, development, demonstration, dissemination and the deployment of technologies by the market.

These priorities are balanced by energy policies which seek, on the one hand, the improvement of energy production from conventional energy sources and the rational use of energy and, on the other hand, the development of renewable energy sources and their introduction into Europe's energy balance.[7]

---

[5]European Report No 1936, 23 March 1994, Chapter IV, Internal Market, pp 5–6.

[6]EU Programmes Summaries, Fourth Framework Programme, Clean efficient energy technologies, April 1994, p 17.
[7]*Ibid.*, p 18.

Renewable energy

Figure 12.5
The Eye Power Station designed by Lifschutz Davidson converts half of Suffolk's chicken manure waste into electricity using Danish technology. (Lifschutz Davidson©.)

The renewable energy programme of the EU comprises the development of a substantial range of new technologies: biomass conversion using numerous innovative thermodynamic cycles; photovoltaic systems using sophisticated solid-state physics techniques; windmills involving leading edge engineering sciences; solar architecture combining optical and electro-optical technologies. Preliminary projects are also proposed for tidal energy, wave energy, solar hydrogen, liquid hydrogen powered vehicles, etc., seeking to demonstrate the benefits of renewable energy.[8] These projects are considered of strategic importance for the introduction of renewable energy sources on a significant scale in the different Member States. The EU acknowledges that it has a role in demonstrating the practicality of new energy technologies in the face of often sceptical EC governments.

---

[8]*Ibid.*

Renewable energy

CASE STUDY OF RENEWABLE ENERGY

Photovoltaic electricity generation

Turning light into electricity, known as photovoltaics, promises in the longer term to become a viable method of generating power directly from sunlight. At present it costs about ten times as much as electricity generation from more conventional means, but the costs are falling. Energy companies such as BP are at the forefront of research and development, believing photovoltaics to be a good investment for when fossil fuels begin to run out in 30–50 years time.

For the price of photovoltaics to fall, the world market will need to expand to bring costs of production significantly down. A larger world market would allow the introduction of mass production which, as with computer chips, makes an expensive product relatively cheap. The main use for photovoltaics at present is in servicing remote rural communities, in providing energy for satellites, and where power needs are very small, as in pocket calculators.

One problem with photovoltaics is the high life-cycle costing of environmental impacts. For the energy created a great deal is needed to produce the aluminium, glass and steel of a typical photovoltaic panel. It may take as long as 120 years for the embodied cost to be recovered by the electrical energy generated. This compares with about 15–20 years for glass used in passive solar space heating. The main advantage, however, of photovoltaic panels for the construction industry is the opportunity to combine them with cladding systems. The Seville Expo Pavilion designed by Nicholas Grimshaw in 1992 used photovoltaic panels as sunshading – thereby combining solar protection with electricity generation.

The Non-Fossil Fuel Obligation of the UK's 1990 Electricity Act gave some encouragement to those such as BP and Colt International who have invested in the development of photovoltaics. The EC's Altener Programme of 1993 has a similar objective with the specific target of trebling electricity generated from renewable sources (other than hydro) by 2005.[9] Under Annex 2 of this programme, the EC has made a commitment to fund pilot actions aimed at introducing a measure of guarantee in the 'market for solar collectors and solar water heaters'.[10] Such policy initiatives have encouraged experimentation from Sir Norman Foster's Business Promotion Centre at Duisburg, which uses rooftop photovoltaics to help power the cooling system, to the use of photovoltaics incorporated into an overcladding system for the upgrading of a 1960s teaching building at the University of Northumbria

---

[9]*Official Journal of the European Communities* 18 September 1993, L235/44.
[10]*Ibid.*, Annex II.

Figure 12.6
Photovoltaic panels developed by BP Solar used as a façade recladding at the University of Northumbria. (University of Northumbria ©.)

in Newcastle (funded under the EU Thermie Scheme). The latter example which costs nearly £500 per square metre has been developed by Arup's Facade Engineering Group and BP Solar. It generates an anticipated 50 per cent of electricity needs in the summer from the south facing overcladding and 10 per cent in the winter.[11] Surplus generation at the weekends is fed into the national grid.

---

[11]*The Architects' Journal* 16 March 1994, p 26.

Renewable energy

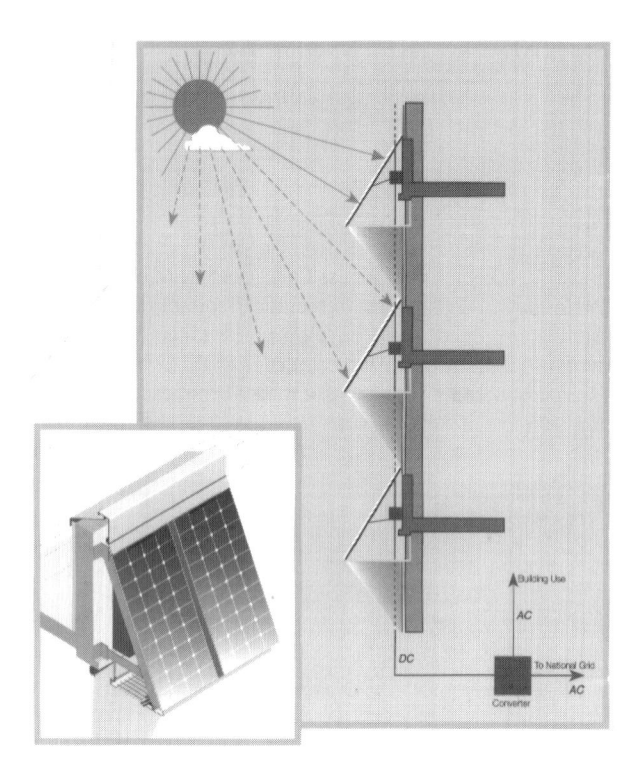

Figure 12.7
Diagram showing how photovoltaic panels work. (Ove Arup and Partners©.)

Since they are lightweight, photovoltaic panels can rotate to follow the angle of the sun. Colt International has developed a system (installed at Digital's headquarters building in Geneva) which combines motorized sun-shading louvres with photovoltaic cells. On grey days the louvres can be inverted so that they reflect external light inwards via light shelves, thereby reducing the need for internal illumination.[12] By setting the louvres on horizontal and vertical moving motors, they can track the sun through the day and the seasons. The result of such technology is to produce an architecture of movable external parts. Buildings will respond to external conditions just as much of the natural world does. The potential of photovoltaics is enormous, only capital cost and embodied energy in the components is impeding the wider application of this new technology to the construction industry. Although Britain is not well placed for the development of solar energy compared to much of Europe, it has the advantage of relative coolness. Photovoltaic cells perform less well above 25°C so the ideal application is in climatic zones which are both sunny and cool.

Photovoltaics in use: the example of the Business Promotion Centre, Duisburg, Germany

Sir Norman Foster and Partners' Business Promotion Centre at Duisburg in the Ruhr area of Germany embodies a wide range of energy, environmental, health and comfort initiatives. It is a key building within a business park set out to achieve the following masterplanning objectives.[13]

- reflect in a direct and optimistic fashion economic structural change;
- social and ecological compatibility with the environment;
- harmony of living and working;
- most up-to-date working conditions;
- energy usage as low as possible and low pollution;
- applications of micro-electronics to building technology.

The Business Promotion Centre seeks to combine economical and ecological efficiency within a building whose landmarking qualities (essential as an information and innovation centre on the estate) grow directly from environmental and energy considerations. Standing at the entrance to the business park, the elegantly curved profile of Foster's building signals a new approach to office development.

The building places particular emphasis upon incorporating photovoltaics and giving the user the ability to

Figure 12.8
Photovoltaic panels incorporated into an overcladding system at the University of Northumbria. (BP Solar©.)

[12]*Ibid.*
[13]The list is adapted from the brochure *Micro-electronic Park, Duisburg*. Business Promotion Centre, Duisburg, no author, no date.

Renewable energy

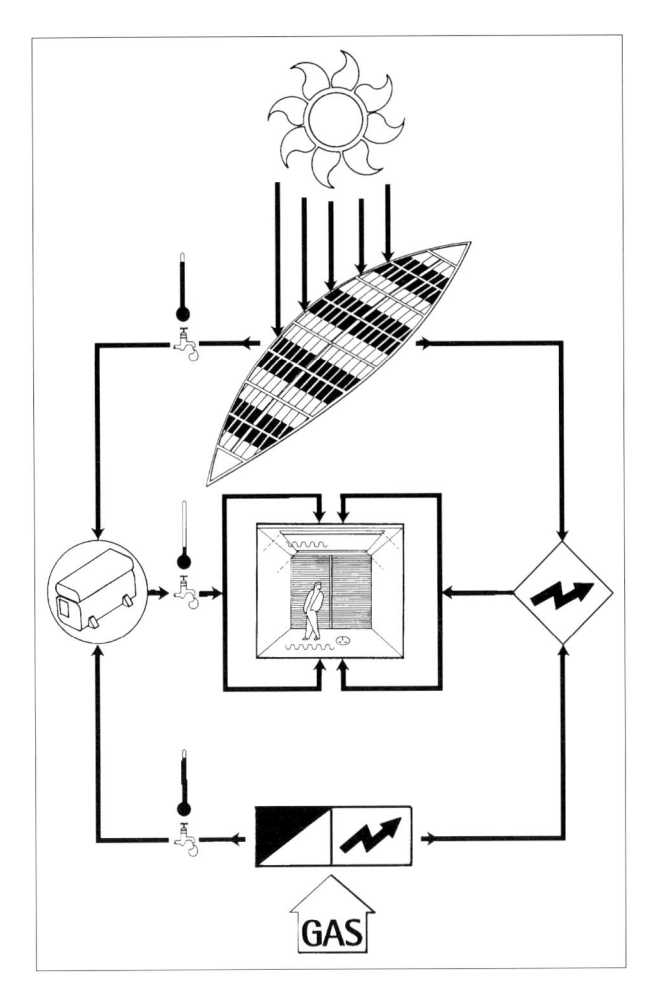

Figure 12.9
Solar powered heating and cooling system used at Duisburg by Sir Norman Foster and Partners. (Sir Norman Foster and Partners©.)

modify the local environment within the office. Each room or work space has its own control panel regulating thermal and visual comfort linked directly to sensitive shading systems in the external cladding. Each local control panel is connected to a central building management system which governs total energy use in the building. Hence user, external environmental conditions and internal energy sources are engaged in a perpetual three-way dialogue. Added to this each room is naturally air conditioned using thermal flows generated purely by the thermal capacity of the human beings and equipment in the room. Without mechanical air conditioning there is no fan noise and little justification for the use of deep suspended ceilings. Excess heat (which occurs on sunny days) is absorbed by water pipes in the ceiling and radiation cooling is achieved via solar powered Absorption Cooling Machines (Figure 12.10).

The primary energy is provided by a gas generator which provides power, heat and cooling. The exhaust is used for heating in the winter and in the summer for absorption cooling. Photovoltaic cells embodied in the façade glazing (Figure 12.9) assist in the energy production, as does transparent insulation in the roof.

Elsewhere at the Business Park, Sir Norman Foster and Partners and their German technical collaborators Kaiser Bautechnik, have been developing buildings based upon 'climatic halls' which allow internal walls to better act as energy collectors and environmental moderators. Again transparent insulation and photovoltaics provide the means whereby roof and façade (both elegantly curved for aerodynamic and thermal reasons) contribute to the broader environmental strategy. The EC's Joule II Programme provided the means to undertake the energy R & D research with the EC's Thermie Programme giving additional assistance to test the application in the building.

Foster's innovations at Duisburg reflect a move from questions of energy usage to concerns regarding wider environmental management. Here biology, ecology, human health and comfort combine with strategies for energy usage to produce buildings which are visually distinctive. The involvement of Kaiser Bautechnik has brought a technological edge to the different building projects. These buildings at Duisburg, under construction at the time of writing, represent the high-tech philosophy followed by many designers to creating an architecture of benign environmental impacts. They are useful experiments in the evolving of new methods and strategies for the 'green' age. Whether the high environmental and energy costs of the materials employed is retrieved during the life of the building is perhaps worthy of further investigation.

Daylight and energy conservation: new glazing technology

The EC's Thermie renewable energy research programme has highlighted new developments in glazing materials technology which have the potential of saving energy by creating a glass which responds to external conditions. Daylight is normally provided by windows which, as they face in all directions, allow different levels of light and solar energy to enter a building. Since they are generally made of thin, poorly insulated materials (i.e. glass), windows let in light and allow heat to escape. The balance between daylight, solar gain and thermal insulation is an important consideration for building designers. Normally a crucial part of the equation is the window area and which direction it faces. Today, however, new developments in types of glass have provided greater choice and climatic responsive-

Renewable energy

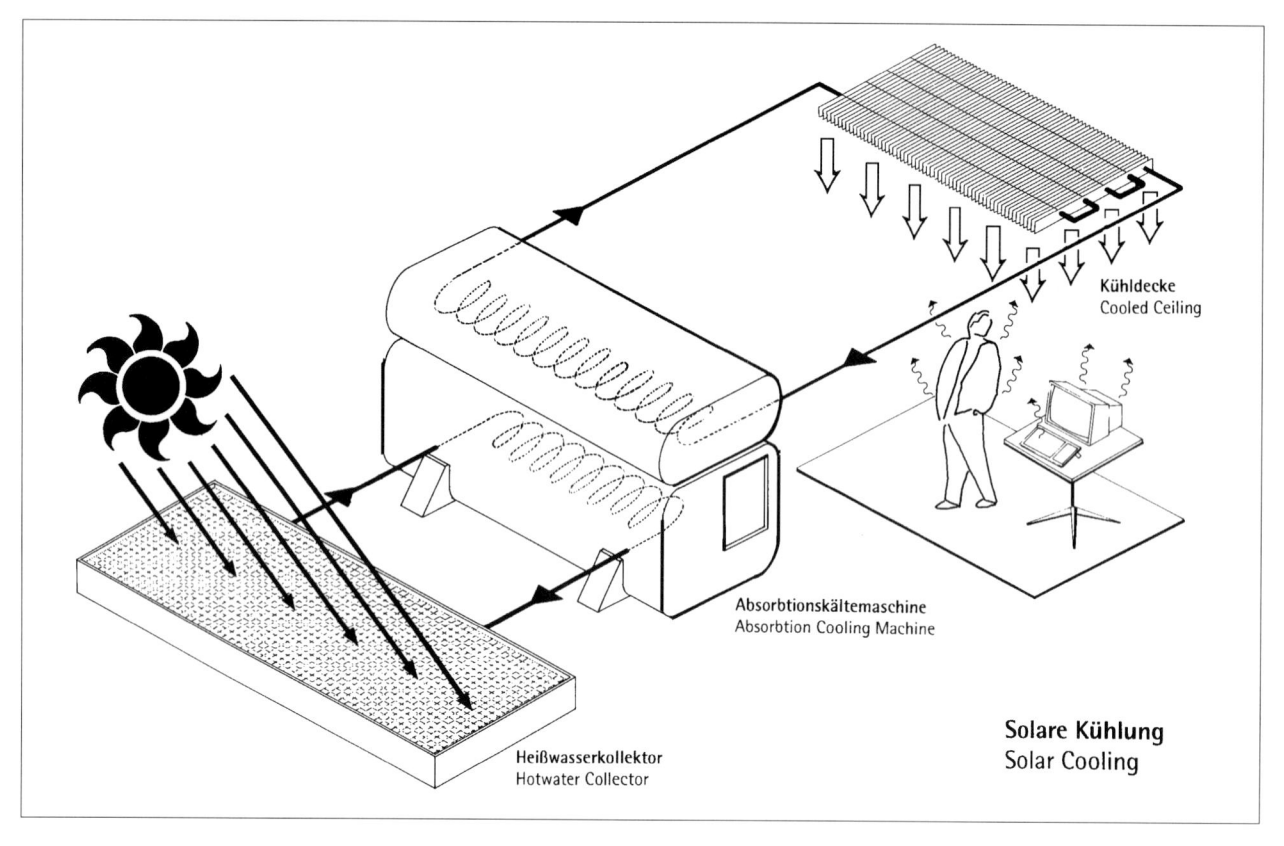

Figure 12.10
Solar-powered cooling as employed in new office development in Germany designed by Sir Norman Foster and Partners. (Sir Norman Foster and Partners©.)

ness for the architect and engineer. The report *Daylighting in Buildings* produced by the Energy Research Group at Dublin School of Architecture for the European Commission Directorate-General for Energy in 1994 highlights the following recent developments in glazing.

- *Electrochromic glass* which responds to an electric field to become dark or cloudy. With the push of a switch such glass will shade the interior from excess solar radiation.
- *Thermochromic glass* which responds to changes in external temperature to either transmit heat or reflect heat. The selected temperature for the switch can be engineered into the glass.
- *Photochromic glass* which darkens gradually as light intensity increases.
- *Holographic glass* which has the ability to reflect high level sunlight or redirect light onto a specific surface. By applying holographic patterns to the glass, the glass responds in different ways and at different times to external lighting conditions.
- *Transparent insulation* which allows light into a building (though not view since it is translucent) whilst providing thermal insulation. It is available in honeycomb, fibre or foam.

These various developments in glazing technology have the potential of reducing energy use – either in space heating, by reducing the need for cooling, or by allowing the inside levels of lighting to take maximum advantage of natural daylight. In a full life-cycle assessment of energy and material costs, the potential saving is likely to be recovered in 5–10 years in terms of embodied energy and a little longer in terms of capital costs. Case studies in the report for the EC suggest an energy saving of approximately 20 per cent by the incorporation of better lighting design and the more appropriate selection of glass type.[14]

---

[14]*Daylighting in Buildings* European Commission Directorate-General for Energy, 1994.

Figure 12.11
This biodrier at Avonmouth designed by architects Whicheloe Macfarlane for Wessex Water extracts methane gas which fires a power plant in the building. Norman Whicheloe©.)

Power from sewage sludge

Britain produces 30 million tonnes of sewage a year which is used either to enhance farm soil fertility or dumped at sea. Sewage sludge is, however, a source of energy which, with EC Directive 76/464 banning the dumping of sludge at sea after 1998, can provide a useful substitute fuel for use in power stations. The EC Directive means that in future sewage sludge is either to be spread on agricultural land or put in land-fill sites (where methane release adds to global warming) or recycled as a source of power.

Wessex Water has constructed a biodrier at its Avonmouth sewage works to dry, sieve and mill the 30 per cent of sewage sludge which was previously dumped at sea. The biodrier is Swiss-made and produces 'biogram' – grey, colourless granules which have potential use as a fuel and methane-free fertilizer. The plant produces 30–40 million tonnes a day, exploiting in the recycling process the production of methane gas, water and heat which is used to power a small generator to produce the energy to run the building.[15]

The ecological sewage plant, designed by architects Whicheloe Macfarlane, exploits low energy design principles in the building fabric and services (such as low-energy lighting). Wessex Water claims it is the biggest biodrier plant in Europe and is proving a source of attraction for other companies considering meeting the Directive in a similar fashion, and for local school groups who use the building and its processes for environmental education. The simple hangar-like design with high-tech industrial finishes reflects the role of advanced technology in meeting the environmental dictates of the future.

---

[15]Deborah Singmaster, Clean container for an ecological sewage plant, *The Architects' Journal* 28 July 1993, pp 26–7.

13

The potential of wind power

Lawrie O'Connor

The nature of wind

Wind is probably, after muscle, the oldest exploited source of motive power. Primitive man, on the crudest of boats, would have quickly become aware of the strength of the wind. It was the harnessing of this power, refined over thousands of years, which drove exploration and international commerce until it reached a pinnacle in the last century with the clipper ships. Windmills also have a long history, traceable to the ancient Chinese and Sumerians. These used vertical axis machines for irrigation and milling. The Chinese design was a particularly ingenious junk-rigged system with flapping 'sails'.

Wind is caused primarily by the temperature differentials between the ground and the high atmosphere and also between the equator and the poles. The basic patterns set up are distorted on the global scale by the rotation of the earth. There are also transient variations due to topography and localized pressure and temperature changes. Europe, and particularly the British Isles, is well supplied with wind energy. The latitude is one with prevailing south-westerly winds which arrive unchecked after crossing the Atlantic. These winds are very reliable on an annual basis and, although occasionally reaching gale force, almost never have the destructive power of tornadoes or hurricanes.

Figure 13.1
Wind farms such as this at Ovenden Moor near Halifax in Yorkshire provide the opportunity to diversify upland land uses. (Lawrie O'Connor©.)

The potential of wind power

Figure 13.2
Wind distorted trees provide a useful guide to where wind farms could potentially be located. (Lawrie O'Connor©.)

Extraction of power from the wind

Modern windmills are, at present, almost invariably used for electricity generation and are thus generally referred to as 'wind turbines'. They have efficiencies in the order of 40–50 per cent, much greater than the conventional 'Dutch' drainage windmill which operated at around 5 per cent. Wind turbines also compare well with conventional steam-cycle electricity generation, which has a practical limit of around 42 per cent efficiency. It should be noted that there is a maximum theoretical windmill efficiency, which cannot be exceeded, of 59.3 per cent. Some manufacturers have in the past quoted efficiencies of 70 per cent, by which they mean 70 per cent of the theoretical maximum, i.e. around 42 per cent actual. It is quite likely that the practical limit for windmill efficiencies especially for electricity generation is in the order of 50 per cent.

The power available from the wind is proportional to the cube of its speed, i.e. a doubling of the wind speed produces eight times the power. It follows from this that the siting of the turbine is more critical than a design improvement of 1 or 2 per cent. A slightly different location, less sheltered say, which has a 1 per cent higher wind speed produces almost 6 per cent more power. Readings taken after the erection of an 80 kW turbine in Yorkshire have shown that a site within 200 metres of the one chosen has 15 per cent more available power. Such differentials mean that not all upland areas are equally suitable for the siting of wind farms and that any Environmental Statement needs to acknowledge the relative advantage of the chosen site.

Wind turbines are designed around two basic wind speeds. The lower is the 'cut-in' speed, i.e. the speed above which the blades will turn and produce useful power. The higher is the 'rated' speed, at which the generator operates at maximum efficiency. Because of the cube law, winds above the rated speed produce a rapidly rising power curve which could overload the unit. For this reason it is necessary to limit the power extracted from winds above the rated speed, usually by fitting some form of 'spoiler' to reduce the mill efficiency at high wind speeds.

Site conditions

The ideal wind turbine site is near the crest of a high, smoothly rising ridge on the downwind side of a large flat plain (Figure 13.2). Proximity to the crest will depend on the steepness of the slope and the degree of turbulence caused. Failing this ideal the position chosen should be free from obstructions in all directions, not just in the direction of the prevailing wind, in order to avoid sheltering and turbulence. The wind turbine and generator must be selected to match the characteristics of the site if electricity is to be produced economically. The usual procedure is to determine the 'mean wind speed', that speed which is equalled or exceeded for 50 per cent of the time. The system might then be designed to begin to produce power at a 'cut-in speed' slightly below mean

The potential of wind power

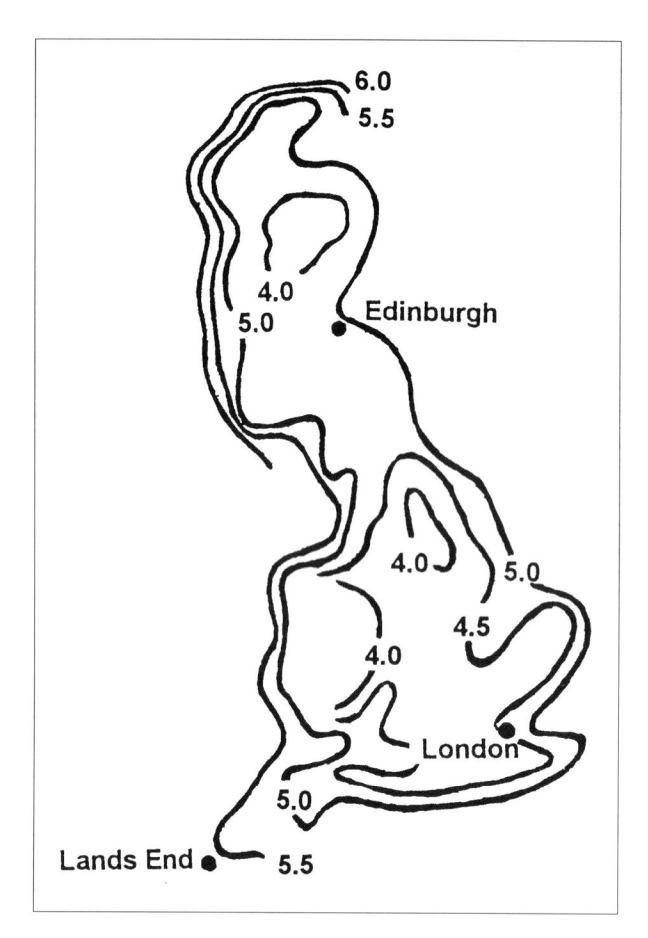

Figure 13.3
Mean wind speed contours in mainland Britain. Both coastal and upland areas are viable for wind generation of electricity. (Lawrie O'Connor©.)

Figure 13.3 shows mainland Britain illustrated as wind speed contours based on Meteorological Office data. It should be noted that these values relate to a height of 10 m above ground level and they are not necessarily a good guide to the actual conditions at a particular site. A superficial reading would indicate that mean wind speed falls rapidly with distance inland and this is generally true. If however the inland site is in an elevated position the local wind speed may be much greater than that suggested by the map; the siting of wind farms on the moors of the Yorkshire/Lancashire border being a case in point. The variation will be less for low lying coastal sites with average exposure and the map indicates a value of between 5 and 6 m/s applicable to the majority of the UK coastline. These values straddle wind speeds Nos 3 and 4 on the Beaufort Scale. Speeds between 3 m/s and 6 m/s produce a 'gentle breeze' (extends light flag) and a 'moderate breeze' exists between 6 m/s and 8 m/s (raises dust and loose paper). A site with a mean wind-speed of 6 m/s and a load such that all electricity may be used directly, is probably worthy of detailed analysis. Denmark currently produces 3.2 per cent of its electricity from wind energy, (the highest proportion of any country in the EC), from mean speeds of about 5 m/s. It should however be noted that Denmark has a deliberate fiscal policy of encouraging local wind projects of around 50 kW or so. The economics obviously improve not just with increasing wind speed but the guarantee of a market for wind energy products.

Wind readings should be taken on site for a full year if possible, preferably at the proposed hub height. Data from nearby weather stations must be used with care unless they are very close and match the site in altitude, exposure and orientation. Initial assessments of a site's potential can sometimes be gauged from the degree of wind distortion in surrounding trees and bushes. It can also, however, simply show that a site is exposed in one direction and unacceptably sheltered from another. From an Environment Impact point of view, exposed sites are also visible ones, and besides the visual impact of the windmills, there are also access roads, maintenance buildings and overhead lines to consider (see Chapter 14).

Design principles

Windmill design has been refined since the 1920s and can be broadly classified as either horizontal or vertical axis. The horizontal axis unit, the standard 'fan' design, most commonly uses either a two or three blade rotor with an aerofoil cross section. These are high speed units with the highest efficiency of all the windmill designs. Power output at high wind speeds is controlled by adjusting the blade pitch, or by the use of 'spoilers', or simply by restricting the rotational speed. Vertical axis machines have a much

speed and full power a little above, at the 'rated speed'. The effect is that for something over 50 per cent of the time the power produced is less than the design output, and for the remaining time excess wind energy is not utilized.

The 'obvious' alternative, of using a larger generator rated against a higher wind speed, is not economic. This approach would inflate the capital cost whilst simultaneously increasing the time during which the plant ran at low efficiency. It can thus be seen that the proper selection and design of a wind system is a careful balance of capital cost, electricity demand and wind regime; with an accurate estimate of mean wind speed the critical factor. Such considerations need to figure in any Environmental Statement in order to provide the justification for a chosen site, or to allow a thorough appreciation of the relative energy and environmental costs of different designs.

wider variety of designs and applications. At the most trivial level they are used for extract ventilation on delivery vans and for advertising. This type of unit has a low efficiency since the 'returning' element has a negative power contribution. The more modern designs are claimed to have efficiencies approaching 50 per cent.

The largest windmills so far produced have all been horizontal axis machines although vertical axis wind turbines with outputs in excess of 100 kW have been commissioned. The horizontal axis type has the highest potential efficiency and is probably now close to its design limit. Significant improvements are likely to be restricted to developments in materials technology applicable to the blades and tower. Vertical axis machines have only received scientific study since the 1920s and are still evolving. However, even though theory predicts that they can never match horizontal axis efficiencies, useful comparisons may still be made.

Power output

Power is a function of efficiency and effective area. For a 'fan' machine the effective, 'swept' area is a circle whereas for many, although not all, vertical units the area is rectangular. The much greater 'swept' area of the vertical design can often more than compensate for its lower efficiency.

'Tracking' the wind

A vertical axis unit can instantly accept winds from any direction whereas the more conventional design must 'track' the wind. The latest horizontal axis turbines do not have tail fins to keep the rotor facing into the wind but use sensors and electric motors to achieve this. The control system is designed to ignore short-term fluctuations in wind direction, such as would occur in gusty conditions. Trials have been carried out on self-tracking units with the rotor downwind of the tower but this arrangement is now considered to impose undue stresses on the blades as they pass through the 'wind shadow' from the mast. Some blade stresses are inevitable in large machines due to the constant reversal between the upward and downward motions.

The principal operating stresses on vertical axis designs are on the tower, rather than the blades. The force acting on an individual blade changes during each revolution as it moves; at first with, then across and finally into, the wind. These changing forces are transmitted to the tower, which in some smaller units is also the drive shaft, as side to side oscillations.

Assisted starting

Almost any type of 'fan' design will start to spin in a strong enough wind. This is not the case with all vertical units, particularly some of the latest high efficiency models. However, with large machines of any design, the inertia is normally so great that the wind speed required to cause a stationary mill to rotate is much higher than the 'cut-in' speed. It is normal practice to fit large units with wind speed sensors and an auxiliary electric motor to initiate rotation. Once started the mill produces useful power and the motor cuts out.

Matching the supply to the load

Because of the controls built into a modern wind turbine it is not possible for it to produce more than its rated power. There may, however, be times when the output exceeds the demand and, where this is the case, the options available to the operator are to store or to sell the excess.

Store the excess

This is only practical for fairly small installations, due to the expense, size and weight of batteries. Small installations where this is used have normally been designed to be totally self-sufficient, and must rely on battery back-up during calm periods.

Sell the excess

This is common practice and at present all surplus power is sold to the national utilities. Under the current regulations they must buy any surplus power offered but the purchase price is generally less than their own prevailing unit generating costs. Each of the regional utilities is able to set its own purchasing tariffs and these must be considered at the design stage. Their effect is to limit the penetration of wind generated electricity into the market.

It is also possible, technically and legally, to sell to another consumer, although this has not yet been attempted. Producer and consumer would negotiate an acceptable rate and the consumer's normal bill from the utility would be credited with the units supplied to the grid by the producer. The utility would then charge the producer a rental fee for the use of mains cables between the two sites.

Both these options require the exported electricity to be compatible with that available on the grid and stringent safety features must be incorporated.

Create an 'artificial' load

The number of sites where this can be done to a significant degree will be limited by environmental factors. If, for example, a site has a heavy hot water demand and large storage capacity it may be possible to use the surplus

The potential of wind power

electricity to increase the storage temperature. The reverse could be the case where the main load is due to a refrigeration plant serving cold stores. Surplus power may then be used to lower the store temperature to below its normal operating value. Surplus energy could also be used to pump water uphill, it then being released later to drive a water turbine.

The most common mis-match between load and output will be in periods of calm when the turbine output is zero. Again there are three possibilities open to the site operator: meeting the shortfall from a utility, from storage or from a standby generator.

Shortfall met by the utility

This is the simplest and most common solution. However, it is inconvenient for the utilities to have a large load which is only 'on line' at infrequent and unpredictable intervals. The site owner is therefore likely to be penalized for this by way of a higher than normal tariff for any electricity supplied from the mains.

Shortfall met from storage

This option is limited to those installations small enough to be designed to be totally self-sufficient. An adequately sized battery store will be required, as previously discussed with regard to problems of excess supply. Since batteries pose particular environmental problems (in manufacture and disposal), this solution is far from ideal.

Standby generation plant

Standby generators, usually diesel powered, are expensive items. In general they are normally used:

- for essential services, e.g. operating theatres;
- in remote sites, e.g. islands, lighthouses;
- for 'peak lopping', e.g. where a large consumer wishes to avoid prohibitive Maximum Demand charges.

The last two examples are closest to a conventional wind turbine installation. Factors which must be considered include:

- capital cost of generator;
- utility's tariffs and probable annual charges;
- are any loads non-essential?
- what are the likely running hours and fuel costs?
- global warming gas production in burning fossil fuels.

Environmental impact

Good wind turbine sites are, by definition, exposed, and thus windmills cannot be hidden or disguised. Whether a single unit is an eyesore or a thing of beauty is a matter of opinion but wind farms with hundreds, perhaps even thousands, of units are a major visual intrusion (Figure 13.1). Sites currently being developed in the UK are being vigorously opposed by local pressure groups while simultaneously attracting sightseers on family outings. In comparison the Danish wind turbine programme has broad public approval, due in large part to a financing strategy which directly involves the local population. There is also the Danish awareness that all their fossil fuel must be imported whereas the British economy is 'energy rich'. Denmark also has a population educated in energy matters, and hence the broader environmental benefits of wind farms are more likely to override local objections.

Noise is a significant factor in the opposition argument, with decibel levels well above permitted industrial limits frequently quoted. The sound produced by an operational turbine has two principle components, wind noise across the blades and gearbox noise. In truth the levels measured, under rated wind speed conditions on an exposed hillside, are similar either with or without a wind farm. The differences lie in the nature of the sound. On the one hand a natural gusty buffeting on the other hand the same background noise combined with a regular beat. There are statutory regulations designed to minimize possible noise problems, relating to the design of turbines and the layout of sites. One of the most significant regulations prohibits the erection of large units within 400 m of any dwelling.

There are minimum design spacing limits between turbines, to avoid downwind units being affected by turbulence, which leads to farms of large size. The advantage is that the land is in multiple use and can be farmed in the normal way while simultaneously producing an energy 'crop'. There are also no restrictions on existing footpaths and rights-of-way, as would be the case with conventional power stations. Just as environmentally sound buildings are mixed use with various activities taking place within them, so too wind farms have the effect of diversifying the productive use of land.

Inevitably there is considerable disturbance of the moorland soil during the construction phase and the mast foundations, underground cables and essential service roads are permanent structures. Fears have been expressed that this could have a detrimental effect on the natural drainage of large areas, resulting in ecological damage. This argument is superficially plausible but difficult to sustain. Whilst it is possible that a once boggy area may dry out, and vice versa, such variation is natural on peat and heather uplands. There will be little change in the proportions of dry to wet areas or large-scale alterations in the nature of the soil. There is also the view that present day moorland is no more *natural* than a field of wheat and is simply the product of centuries of deforestation, sheep farming and grouse shooting. Wind farms have also been accused of disturbing wildlife and causing the deaths of birds of prey who have been known to fly into blades in stormy weather. Such factors, although a problem in sensitive locations such as Orkney, are rarely a problem in more populated regions.

A planning framework

The conflict between amenity and the development of wind farms has thwarted the exploitation in the UK of this important energy source. Since many suitable sites for wind generation are in sensitive upland or coastal locations, those who wish to construct large-scale wind generators find themselves seeking to develop land in areas designated for their natural beauty or wildlife interest. These collisions of interest are not well handled via the British planning system with its adversarial politics and resolution of conflict via the mechanism of public inquiries. Instead what is needed is guidance from government on the type and location suitable for the construction of wind farms. Such guidance would help local planning authorities in compiling local plans with an indication of preferred sites for wind farms and in determining planning applications. If guidance is needed on large, multi-generator wind farms, the same is true of small-scale stand alone wind generators serving isolated rural communities. Architects who wish to incorporate wind generators into their designs for buildings in the countryside find planning authorities increasingly an obstacle to their plans for contributing towards the realization of sustainable development.

The EU Action Plan for renewable energy mentioned earlier requires both national and local policies for smooth implementation on the ground. Denmark has exploited wind and reduced in the process the production of greenhouse gases by providing fiscal incentives, education and support for alternative energy technologies. If Environmental Statements provide a consistent framework for evaluating the ecological costs of wind farms, no comparable directive provides an incentive to grasp the opportunities of the wind. The Action Plan of 1994 is a start, but it is by no means an adequate measure to persuade reluctant, fossil-fuel rich countries, such as the UK, to move wholesale towards a renewable energy culture.

CASE STUDY

Yorkshire Windpower

Yorkshire Windpower is a Yorkshire Water and Yorkshire Electricity joint venture company. The pairing of the two parent companies is particularly fortuitous as they can, in combination, provide good wind turbine sites and easy access to the electricity grid. Yorkshire Water owns large tracts of Pennine moorland which act as catchment areas for numerous reservoirs. Yorkshire is one of the prime UK wind regime locations and, while being a remote and at times beautiful region, is principally outside major National Parks. However, most potential sites inevitably have 'Green Belt' designation which places development within Annex 2 projects of the EC Directive on Environmental Assessment.

A total of thirty-six wind turbines are currently operated by Yorkshire Windpower on two separate sites, one at Ovenden Moor near Halifax with twenty-three units and the remaining thirteen at Royd Moor near Sheffield. Both wind farms became operational in 1993 and have similar design and planning considerations. The following comments are specific to Ovenden Moor but, in general engineering terms, may be taken to refer to either site.

The wind turbines, i.e. the blades, gearbox and generator, are Vestas Windane 34 units, manufactured in Denmark. They each have three blades, in fibreglass reinforced polyester, with a total diameter of 34 m. They are mounted on 32 m tall, 2.2 m diameter, tubular steel towers. The towers are manufactured in Leeds and are painted off-white to reduce visibility when viewed against a cloudy sky.

The blades rotate at a constant 35 rpm, the output being regulated by adjustment of the blade pitch angle between 0° and 90°. Generation does not occur until the wind speed reaches 5 m/s, slightly below the site average of 7.5 m/s. The output expands with increasing windspeed until the design maximum of 400 kW is produced at 11 m/s. This maximum is then maintained for all speeds between 11 m/s and 25 m/s. This is in line with current practice to maximize power production within the limits of safe operation. Above 25 m/s (i.e. about wind force 6 on the Beaufort Scale) the units are shut down and the brakes applied. The generator output is a constant 690 V. This is passed to a transformer at the base of each tower and converted to 1000 V for compatibility with the local grid. Connection to the grid is made at the nearby substation at Denholm and all cables between site and substation are underground, this having been a condition of planning permission.

Peak output is 9.2 MW but this will only occur at speeds of 11 m/s and above. A more useful measure of the wind farm's benefit is its expected annual production. For Ovenden Moor it is estimated that the average annual output will be equivalent to the electricity consumption of 7500 dwellings (a town about the size of Skipton). The anticipated life of the wind farm is 20–25 years, with the main factors being cumulative stresses and wear in moving parts, rather than corrosion or weather damage. Each unit is provided with a grounded lightning rod.

Relationship between the windmills on any site is always a critical consideration. There will inevitably be times when the wind is from a direction such that some units are 'downstream' of other turbines and therefore suffer reduced output. There is also the problem of adopting a compact layout which will both minimize site access roads and reduce visual impact. The solution at Ovenden was the adoption of two lines of turbines, on a slightly curved plan layout, served by two permanent access roads. The alignment of turbines and their proximity to ridges is clearly of consequence in terms of visual impact.

The proposal to locate a wind farm at Ovenden Moor was opposed in some quarters, even though it had approval and financial backing from the EC under the Thermie programme. Additionally, the Town and Country Planning (Assessment of Environmental Effects) Regulations 1988 required an Environmental Statement to assess the impact of the wind farm development. Submission of the formal planning application was therefore preceded by a comprehensive investigative and consultative programme which formed the basis of the environmental statement required under Schedule 3 of these regulations.

At this altitude (420 m) the growing season is 209 days (from mid-April to early November). This, combined with the predominantly peat soil, limits the land use to sheep and grouse rearing and water catchment. Electricity generation is thus a significant extension of the economic options, provided that it can be achieved without interference to the environmental and leisure aspects of the area.

Studies of the flora and fauna (as part of the Environmental Statement) showed that the site did not contain any species which were rare but, even so, the construction techniques used were designed to allow the site to re-establish without loss of vegetation or bird life. The access roads, for initial construction and for maintenance, were recognized to be the single largest potential threat to wildlife. Tracks were 'floated' on the surface wherever possible using geotextile support and these were then re-established using hydroseeding techniques. Where foundations were required, sandstone, rather than the more alkaline limestone, was used to preserve the acidity of the soil. Disturbance was also limited by laying cables using mole ploughing, rather than conventional trenching.

Information provided by The Nature Conservancy Council listed six bird species breeding on Ovenden Moor. These were golden plover, dunlin, curlew, lapwing, snipe and wheatear. Research on other sites has shown that birds quickly become accustomed to wind turbines within their breeding territories and learn to avoid them. Although there is a danger of migrating birds striking a blade at night, or in poor weather, there is almost no detrimental effect when visibility is good. Added to this, the tendency is for migrating birds to use river valleys and they will thus be steered away from the turbine site. Hence its impact is largely benign in terms of biodiversity.

Part 4
Environmental Impact

14

Environmental impact assessment

Although environmental protection has been an implied objective in the town and country planning system of the UK since its inception, its importance rose considerably after the EC Directive 85/337 on Environmental Impact Assessment. The Directive stated that:

> Member States shall adopt all measures necessary to ensure that, before consent is given, projects likely to have significant effects on the environment by virtue 'inter alia' of the nature, size or location are made subject to an assessment with regard to their effects[1]

For the British planning system this Directive of 1985 brought certain types of project under control which would previously have been 'permitted development'. Of these forestation, harbours, electricity power lines and major highways were the most significant. Hence, the Directive extended the scope and influence of the UK planning system, particularly as far as large-scale infrastructure projects were concerned. For architects, engineers and developers the Directive has had the effect of introducing a further hurdle at the project design and planning stage. The justification for such assessments was to readily predict the likely impact a major development would have upon the environment at both local, regional and perhaps international level. The 1985 Directive introduced two project categories: Annex 1 projects where environmental assessment (EA) was obligatory and Annex 2 where EA was needed if Member States considered that the characteristics of development so required. Annex 1 projects could be considered as having impacts of wider than national concern such as with the erection of a thermal or nuclear power station, whilst Annex 2 projects were mainly of local or national interest. The main problem with the Directive concerns the lack of consistency between Member States in implementing the controls over Annex 2 projects. Since the definition of works under Annex 2 is loosely worded, different European countries have adopted varying standards. In 1995 there is talk in the community of a new Environmental Assessment Directive with a more consistent screening process, greater access and exchange of information, and a more rigorous methodology of carrying out the appraisal. Under these changes not only will the ambiguities of Annex 2 projects be removed, but additional categories of development (such as the temporary storage of nuclear waste) will be placed in Annex 1.

Under the current EC Directive[2] guidance was issued with regard to categories of assessment and how the assessment was to be undertaken.

The Town and Country Planning (Assessment of Environmental Effects) Regulations 1988 and Circulars 15/88 and 24/88 which incorporated the Directive into the UK planning acts considered three main criteria of 'significance' in terms of the environmental impact of Annex 2 projects. First, whether the project has more than local

---

Table 14.1 Annex 1: Developments which require EA

- Crude oil refinery
- Thermal power station (heat output over 300 MW)
- Nuclear power station
- Installation for storage or disposal of nuclear waste
- Iron or steel works
- Asbestos extraction or processing
- Asbestos cement factory
- Integrated chemical installation
- Major infrastructure project such as road, railway line or trading port
- Waste disposal for incineration or treatment of special waste
- Major landfill site

---

[1] 1985, Directive on Environment Assessment (1985), *Official Journal of the EC* L175/40-8. See also 85/337/EEC.

[2] *Ibid.*

Environmental impact assessment

Table 14.2 Annex 2: Typical developments which may require EA

- Certain agricultural projects such as the installation of a salmon hatchery, or land reclamation from the sea
- Certain projects associated with the extractive industry such as open-cast mining, marble quarrying, peat extraction
- Small-scale non-nuclear power station, or the erection of overhead power lines
- Small ironworks, forge or foundry
- Installation for glass making
- Plant for producing pesticides or pharmaceutical products
- Factory for manufacture of vegetable products, fish meal, brewing
- Textile factories such as bleaching or fibre-dyeing
- Factory for the manufacture of rubber
- Infrastructure projects such as certain types of urban development, yacht marina, industrial estate, etc.
- Major holiday village or hotel project
- Waste water treatment plant or site for disposal of sewage sludge

importance, principally in terms of physical scale. Second, whether the project was intended for a particularly sensitive location such as a National Park, Site of Special Scientific Interest (SSSI) or Conservation Area, and hence would have consequences which may be significant even though the project was not of major scale. Third, whether the project was likely to give rise to particularly complex or adverse effects by, for example, the discharge of water-borne or air-borne pollutants. The Regulation also translated the Annex 1 and 2 projects of the EC Directive 85/337 into Schedule projects in UK law.

It is clear, therefore, that the question of environmental impact is not merely a matter of scale of development but sensitivity of site. Hence, a small development (such as a coastal holiday village) could be considered as coming under Schedule 2 because of the characteristics of the location, not the size of the development. The power to decide on EA rests not with the developer but the local planning authority and if a dispute arises whether the development comes within the Directive's terms of reference, the Secretary of State for the Environment has the final say. A distinction is drawn between the obligations placed upon the developer to furnish an Environmental Statement (ES) and that of the local planning authority to undertake the Environmental Assessment (EA). Circular 15/88 states that in

> determining the planning application, the local planning authority is required to have regard to all the environmental information, that is information contained in the Environmental Statement.[3]

Figure 14.1
Upland landscapes on the edge of cities face change as renewable sources of energy are used more widely under the EC commitment to sustainable development. Development to exploit water and windpower would come under Annex 2 projects of the EC Directive on Environmental Impact Assessment. (Brian Edwards©.)

A duty is placed upon the local planning authority to determine whether the ES is adequate in terms of scope and quality, and can delay determining the planning application until all the relevant environmental information is provided. Both the EC Directive and subsequent UK circulars employ the term 'significant' in terms of environmental impact. However, the word is not defined, and it is argued that it is not sensibly capable of definition within the various contexts in which development exists.

---

[3]Circular 15/88. The circular embodies EC Annex 1 and 2 projects as Schedule 1 and 2 projects.

However, the reluctance to define terms and to leave much to the discretionary powers of planning authorities and UK ministers, has reduced the worth of environmental assessment at least as far as Schedule 2 (i.e. Annex 2 of the EC Directive) development is concerned. In fact in the first five years only some thirty developments were formally considered under EA procedures in England and Wales.

Not only does the local planning authority have to decide if a development comes within Schedule 1 or 2 but whether the ES is adequate. It must then determine the application in accordance with the EA procedures laid down in Directive 85/337/EEC and Circulars 15/88 and 24/88. A failure of the local planning authority to require an adequate ES (on which it could base its decision) could lead to a challenge in the courts as a failure to comply with EC law.[4] The implications for the architect or engineer are also considerable: he or she has the task of advising the client that such development comes into either Schedule 1 or 2 and that a great deal of extra time, cost in compiling the Statement, and possible redesign of the proposals may be required.

The project planning and design process

A large amount of information will need to be compiled to satisfy ES procedures. Although this may be viewed by the developer as an unnecessary additional burden, an astute professional adviser will use the information systematically gathered to help ensure the project proposals are compatible with sensible environmental management. A distinction here is drawn between the minimum standards required under EC law and a professional person's wider responsibilities to the environment and society. A clever architect will use the ES information to redesign aspects of the project to reduce its adverse impact, thereby not only diffusing local authority objections at an early stage, but reducing potential conflict with bodies such as Friends of the Earth.

The architect needs to ask what information he or she requires to gather together at the early stages of the project. Specifically, there may be a need to collect information on potential environmental impacts under the following headings:

- visual aspects of the design;
- effects on health and safety;
- pollution management;
- land take and its agricultural capacity;
- impact management and public relations.

Not all the information required comes readily into the professional domain of the architect, surveyor and engineer, and hence a new generation of specialist environmental social and natural scientists have grown to satisfy EA procedures.[5] Increasingly in continental Europe, though to a lesser extent as yet in the UK, social and economic impacts of major development are being embraced within EC development law.

The first task the architect or engineer leading the development team needs to carry out is to ask is what are the likely significant impacts. This is usually carried out under 'scoping' and 'screening'.[6] 'Scoping' consists of making a preliminary assessment to decide which environmental impacts should be pursued and 'screening' consists of deciding which issues should be addressed with regard to the likely concern of the public. Hence, a question such as road access may be identified under 'screening' whilst the impact of the new road upon an SSSI under 'scoping'.

Clearly the scope of effects cannot be predicted in qualitative or quantitative terms unless the profile of the existing environment is well understood at the outset. An early task of those compiling an ES is adequately to record and understand the environment to be affected by the development proposals. This may entail systematic data gathering on the natural, man-made, social, community, economic, cultural, atmospheric, hydrological, etc. profile of the area. An estimate will then need to be made of the likely effects on these various subjects. Such effects could be categorized under:

- size (large, medium or small impacts);
- duration (long, medium or short term);
- characteristics (direct, indirect, reversible, irreversible);
- timing (before construction, during operation, after decommissioning).

Whilst the local planning authority is likely to offer advice on subjects it considers of importance, the developer's professional advisers have a role in explaining the potential impacts so that the parameters of the ES can be established at the outset. A prudent authority or developer would also seek the advice of the Government's own experts such as the Countryside Commission, Ministry of Agriculture, Health and Safety Executive, English Heritage, etc. Whilst the legislation requires consultation with such bodies in reaching an EA judgement, there are obvious benefits in early pre-submission discussions.

Many applicants voluntarily provide an ES even though the development does not readily fall into Schedules 1 or 2. This is partly because of the lack of definition of

---

[4]*Environmental Auditing: A Management Guide* Vol 1, McKenna and Co, Intelex Press Ltd, London, 1993, p 108.

[5]The integration of environmental assessment with development planning, Natheniel Lichfield, *Project Appraisal*, Vol 7, No 2, (June 1992).
[6]*Ibid.*

'significant' and because small developments can have a large impact upon particularly sensitive issues or locations. For example, a hotel built alongside Lincoln Cathedral may be construed as having an environmental impact upon a heritage site of European importance even though the building elsewhere would not have required an ES. The discretionary power vested with the local planning authority provides the opportunity for informal discussion so that developers, objectors and the local authority can resolve certain problems before formal submission even if it is finally decided that an ES is inappropriate. For the architect, such discussions can help win public support or, alternatively, provide the justification needed to modify the proposals in the light of the views expressed.

When adverse impacts are predicted by the ES, the developer can still go ahead and fight the local authority or appeal to the Secretary of State arguing that the proposals carry public or economic benefit of sufficient importance to outweigh environmental objections. Such appeals, however, usually fail as they are contrary to the spirit of the EC Directive. Alternatively, the developer can ameliorate the proposals by instructing the architect to reduce the adverse environmental impacts by:

- better design;
- improved energy management;
- using cleaner technologies;
- building on a different site;
- reducing the scale of development.

Making the environmental assessment

The regulations specify that an ES must contain:

- a description of the development proposal including information about the site, design, size and scale of development;
- the data necessary to identify and assess the main impacts likely on the environment;
- a description of the 'significant' effects, direct and indirect on the environment with reference to:
  - human beings, flora, fauna, soil, water, air, climate and the landscape,
  - the interaction between any of the foregoing,
  - material assets and the cultural heritage;
- where significant adverse effects are identified, a description of the measures envisaged in order to avoid, reduce or remedy these effects;
- a summary in non-technical language of the information provided.

These regulations, reduced here for brevity, place a duty upon the developer not only to systematically identify likely impacts but show how they are to be ameliorated. It is clear that the duty of environmental care extends beyond that of simply measuring impacts to one of reduction and avoidance. Such new duties broaden the definition of professional responsibility for the architect and engineer, changing the nature of his or her relationship with the client and society at large. The philosophical or ethical shift introduced by the EC Directive to the professional person's responsibility to society should not be underestimated.

The local planning authority has the task of determining the Environmental Assessment (EA) on the basis of the ES provided by the developer. Clearly, the first task is to determine whether the ES is adequate and if any further information needs to be provided. It is worth noting that in deciding upon effects the term Environmental Assessment (EA) is used in British legislation, not the more familiar term Environmental Impact Assessment (EIA) common in America since its introduction under the US National Environmental Policy Act 1969. The adoption of ES and EA as titles as against EIS and EIA allows the European System to be identified from that adopted generally in the world. Such tinkering with names has more than symbolic importance: the different titles employed represent differing methodologies and points of emphasis.

The merit of EA lies in its comprehensiveness. The importance of third parties should not be overlooked in maintaining a comprehensive view. Besides the statutory duties placed upon the local planning authority to consult with specific advisers (such as the Pollution Inspectorate) many voluntary bodies such as local civic or natural conservation organizations can have much to offer. The participatory aim of EA established under Article 6 of the EC Directive places a particular duty of consultation upon the local authority.

The regulations ensure that better consideration is given to the environmental impacts of development. The clear structure of ES documents allows the local planning authority not only to understand more fully the complex impacts of major development, but can encourage authorities to take effective action to mitigate the environmental consequences at source. The integration of planning, energy management and pollution control becomes possible with EA procedures. Town planning by itself has become over concerned with land-use matters to the detriment, some would argue, of energy planning, pollution control and hazard management. EA provides an opportunity not only to make the British Town Planning system more sensitive to environmental and consumer needs, but helps focus the attentions of architects, surveyors and engineers upon the environmental costs of development.

The management of an ES

If the developer is advised that the proposal requires the submission of an ES, a team needs to be assembled to submit the relevant statement. Normally the local planning

Environmental impact assessment

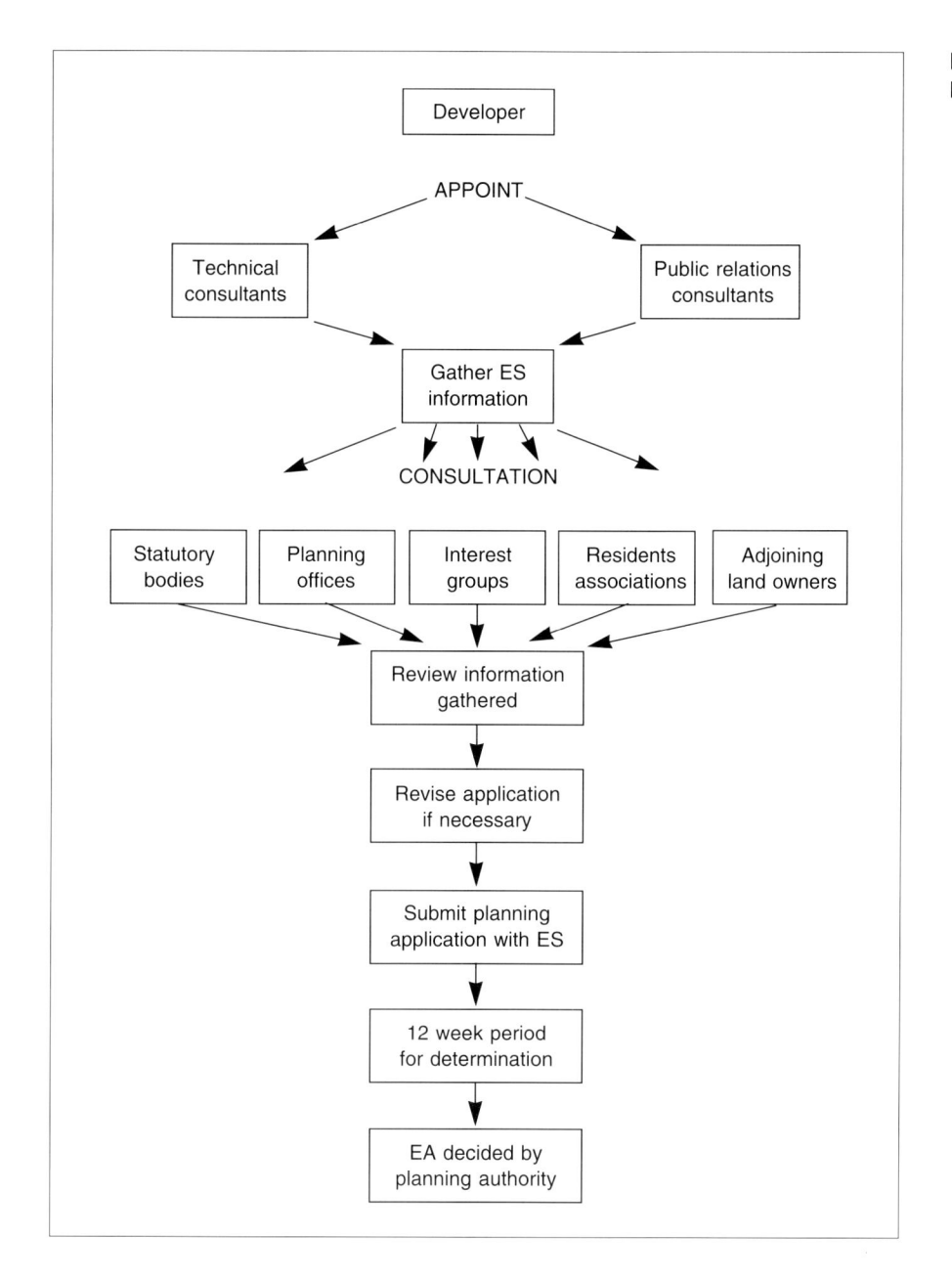

Figure 14.2
Large project ES flowchart

authority has three weeks after receipt of the planning application to notify the developer that an ES is needed, and in turn the applicant has three weeks in which to appeal to the Secretary of State over the decision. A prudent applicant would accept the planning authority's decision and use the reasons given for an ES to help establish the parameters for the exercise. If the developer takes no action, either to appeal against the decision or acknowledge that an ES will subsequently be lodged, the planning application is deemed to be refused. It may console some developers to realize that the Directive also requires local authorities to lodge an ES for the major developments it proposes to undertake.

Once the ES has been lodged the local planning authority has sixteen weeks (as against the usual eight) to determine the application. The additional period of time is acknowledgement that the ES forms the basis for wider ranging consultation (with community groups, highway authorities, nature conservation bodies, etc.) than with normal applications. Whilst the planning authority is required to take into account the views obtained, the EA procedure does highlight the importance of a well-formulated ES.

Environmental impact assessment

As the compilation of the ES is likely to take several months, the decision to require an ES subjects the developer to considerable extra cost and time delays. The environmental statement (ES) contains often complex information gleaned from various sources. Three main bodies of information are usually covered:

- details of the development itself;
- environmental information provided by statutory consultees;
- environmental information provided by third parties.

The information lodged should cover both the existing environmental conditions and how they are likely to be altered by the development. Such matters deal with measurable impacts (such as air pollution) and subjective impacts such as risks to health, injury to eco-systems, and visual intrusion.

Irrespective of the difficulties inherent in the ES system, it removes some of the secrecy and suspicion common under former planning procedures. The old system of deciding applications after appeal meant that conflict and confrontation usually accompanied planning decision makers. In theory at least ES makes pre-submission consultation obligatory with the scale and likely impact in the open at the outset of development planning, not mid-way through the process.

The successful steering of an ES through the planning process requires that consensus is the best strategy. The developer has to gather and present the information on a full range of environmental, social, economic and cultural factors as part of the ES. It is a task beyond the normal duties of an architect, town planner or surveyor and often requires the appointment of public relations consultants to work alongside the technical team. Whatever the final combination of professional advisers, it is clear that the developer has everything to gain by openness and reflective communication.[7] A likely flow chart of duties and liaison procedures is shown in Figure 14.2.

As Figure 14.2 shows, if consultation is to be effective and two-way, the developer should be willing to revise his proposals before the scale and magnitude of the plans become too fixed. Consultation may, for instance, lead to better waste management, a reduction in the height of the building, or the use of another part of the site to protect biodiversity. It is important that the technical team maintains flexibility so that tactical changes in the application can be engineered during the application process.

Use of CAD in EA

The question of 'significant' impact mentioned earlier embraces the issue of visual effects. The Directive talks of assessing the 'effects of certain public and private projects on the environment' and the best environmental policy 'consists of preventing the creation of pollution or nuisance at source'. Computer aided design (CAD) is a useful method of predicting the likely visual effects of major development before planning content has been granted. It gives developers and public bodies vested with the powers to determine the EA a chance to measure the visual impact and take action if necessary to reduce the problem of visual pollution or aesthetic nuisance.

The Department of Environment (DOE) has defined Environmental Assessment as a:

> technique for drawing together, in a systematic way, expert quantitative analysis and qualitative assessment of a project's environmental effects, and presenting the results in a way which enables the importance of the predicted effects, and the scope for modifying or mitigating them, to be properly evaluated.[8]

Such prediction, evaluation and presentation can be effectively undertaken with the aid of computer graphics (see case study in Chapter 15). Remembering that Annex 2 projects embraced smaller development within sensitive sites such as conservation areas or national parks, the use of CAD allows the development to be modelled within its landscape or urban context. It also permits the design to be modified so that the appearance of the development is less damaging in visual terms. Hence CAD is a useful predictive tool when visual matters are at stake, and also one which allows interaction between designer, public administrator (exercising EA powers) and third parties such as amenity or conservation groups.

Recently, the Ministry of Defence has used CAD to predict the visual impact of an office building in the centre of Bristol subject to an EA, and in Nottingham the Inland Revenue employed a similar CAD system to model its new offices. In both cases questions of visual detriment and nuisance were accurately predicted using modern computer graphics and submitted as part of the ES.

The use of digital mapping data from Ordnance Survey, photographic studies from various viewpoints and 3D modelling of the design proposals can, in combination, be used to compile visual images from critical viewpoints. These can be employed as a basis for discussion with residents groups, civic societies, planning authority and adjoining owners. Any weaknesses in the design, or excessive impacts can be addressed by remodelling the proposals. Potentially

---

[7]Environmental assessment: the quiet planning revolution, Adrian Salt, *Estates Gazette*, January 28, 1989.

[8]Circular 15/88.

CAD has considerable benefit particularly for people inexperienced in reading plans or lacking the ability to visualize the proposals themselves. Also as CAD tends to be user friendly, there are obvious advantages for those who as third parties are affected by proposals and who can now make their views known more effectively.

The main problem with CAD, however, is that although the quantitative impacts can be measured and predicted graphically, the qualitative basis for judgement tends to be missing. There are few agreed criteria for assessing quality in the urban or rural environment. The work of Kevin Lynch in *The Image of the City*, Gordon Cullen in *Townscape* and Robert Krier in *Urban Space* provides useful starting points for the visual analysis of urban areas. In terms of the aesthetics of the countryside, land form and ecological richness tend to be the most important elements contributing towards the visual experience. Whatever method is employed the analysis of zones of visual intrusion or corridors of impact (with overhead power lines or road proposals) is more effectively and dispassionately described through computer graphics than through more traditional means such as hand rendered prospective drawing or photo-montage.

The bringing together of quantitative and qualitative visual data by CAD is more cost effective and accurate than other means. Once the database has been collected it remains of value to others when further impacts are to be predicted. Some city centres such as Glasgow and the Old Town of Edinburgh have been modelled to relatively fine levels so that changes to the fabric and appearance of the towns (in both cases within conservation areas) can be monitored. These programmes provide a database whereby the planning authority can exercise its duties with regard to visual impact assessment. Once development is mooted the authority can require that the ES contains visual modelling of the proposal within the city database, perhaps presented as a video display for elected members and the general public.

The introduction by the DOE in 1993 of the guide 'Environmental Appraisal of Development Plans' reinforces the importance of visual criteria in shaping regional and local plans, and in determining planning permission. The guide establishes three sets of environmental priorities for the UK planning system – global sustainability, natural resource management and local environmental quality. The latter category embraces the importance of visual, aesthetic and cultural considerations. The advice to planning authorities is to compile a database of environmental resources (based upon environmental stock, environmental capital and environmental capacity) against which development will be tested. Within these categories CAD has a role in measuring and recording prime visual corridors and the like against which development proposals can be tested. Any ES can, therefore, grow from an appreciation of visual resources as they exist, moving the use of CAD in ES from a role which is usually reactive to one where the emphasis is proactive.

15

Predicting visual impacts by computer aided visual impact analysis

Professor Thomas W. Maver and Dr Jelena Petric

The natural and man-made environments of Europe are under increasing stress. We are entering a phase when the exploitation of energy resources is likely to cause a dramatic acceleration in our rate of impact on the natural environment; in particular, there is cause for serious concern regarding the damaging visual impact of energy related developments – oil terminals, dams, power stations, electricity transmission lines, open-cast mining – on remaining areas of relatively unspoilt rural landscape. EC Directive 85/337 provides a framework across European frontiers whereby the environmental impact of such development needs to be clearly stated and assessed before consent for such work is granted.

In European countries, the urban environment is presenting architects, planners and development agencies with some of the most significant and intractable problems in the last decade of the twentieth century. The problems, listed in the EC's Green Paper on the Urban Environment (see Chapter 1), are most chronic in those cities which rose to greatness at the height of the industrial revolution. Here as heavy industry has declined, manufacturing sites have become derelict, the working population has drifted away, and housing has fallen below tolerable standards. Yet in most cases, much evidence of urban greatness remains – in the grandeur of the public buildings, in the scale of the cityscape, and in the spirit of those who still have their homes and their cultural roots in the inner city.

In 1988 – European Year of the Environment – the EC Directive on Environmental Impact Assessment came into force in the UK requiring architects, planners and developers to make explicit the impact which their schemes will have on the environment. Compliance with the legislation with regard to visual impact is constrained, however, by the underdeveloped state of objective visual appraisal, particularly in the clear presentation of the harmful and beneficial effects of interventions in the rural and urban landscape. This chapter is intended to give cause for optimism. It illustrates a selection of computer-based facilities already in use by architects and planners to predict, appraise and compare the visual impact of proposed interventions in the landscape objectively, economically and, above all, meaningfully. Such information will necessarily form an important element of an Environmental Statement (ES) required in support of development coming within an Annex 1 or 2 project as defined within the Directive (see Chapter 14).

Principles of computer aided visual impact analysis

The two related questions which need to be answered in any visual impact analysis are:

- what will be the degree of visibility of the proposed intervention in the urban or rural landscape;
- what will the intervention actually look like in the context of the landscape from any particular viewpoint.

The modelling of geometry

Central to any computer aided visual impact analysis which attempts to answer these questions is the modelling of geometry; the geometry of terrain, the geometry of vegetation and the geometry of the constructions which already exist and which are proposed.

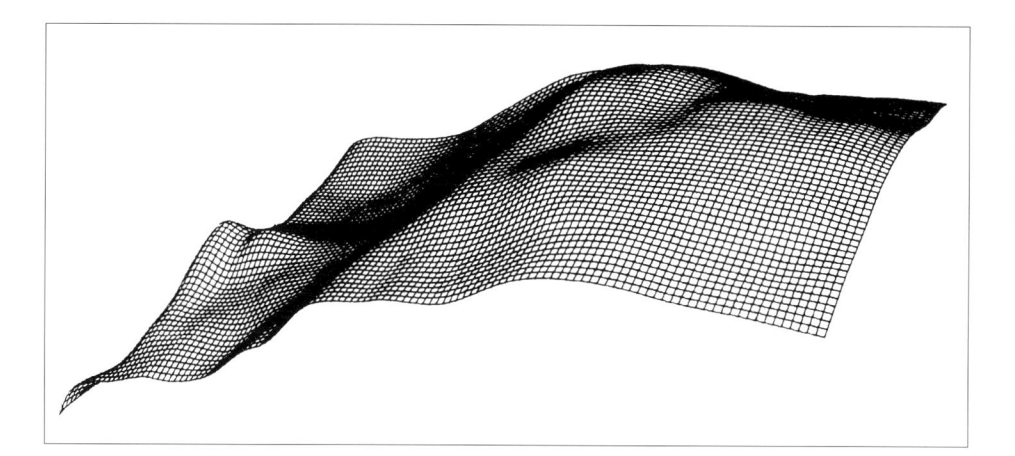

Figure 15.1
Computer generated perspective view of terrain represented as a rectangular planar mesh. (Abacus, University of Strathclyde©.)

Terrain models
The data acquisition for computer based models of terrain is important as it affects the fidelity and the degree of realism which can be obtained in any computer generated visualizations of land form. There are four main sources of data:

- *Field surveying techniques* using electronic tachometers and data collectors; this demanding procedure is appropriate where high accuracy within a limited area is required.
- *Digitization of Ordinance Survey contour maps*, carried out manually or automatically, either by line-following or raster-scan algorithms; this approach offers an economical compromise between accuracy and large-scale application.
- *Aerial photogrammetry* which utilizes either analytical stereo plotters or instruments for orthographic projection; this approach is suitable only for relatively large-scale applications.
- *Satellite remote sensing* which analyses reflected and emitted radiation from the earth's surface; this technology has the potential to generate reasonably accurate data over very large areas.

Whatever the origin of the data, it is eventually stored in the computer, for the purposes of a digital terrain model (DTM), as x, y and z co-ordinates, i.e. easting, northing and level, either on a regular rectangular (x, y) grid, or randomly located. There are many DTM software packages which can convert such data into three-dimensional perspective views of the landscape, represented either as connected planer triangles or rectangles. The scale at which the vertices of the triangles/rectangles is set, coupled with the reliability of the source of the data, obviously determines the accuracy of the visual image created.

The impression of visual accuracy can be enhanced by the 'texturing' of the planer geometry through the application of fractal generation. Natural terrain exhibits the property that, as one views its surface at greater magnification, more and more structure is revealed; fractal sets exhibit exactly this property. It is possible, therefore, through simple mathematical intervention, to 'roughen' the planer geometry generated from the DTM data to provide a spurious but helpful 'realism' to the DTM.

Rather more importantly, available DTM software packages can carry out geometric operations which are crucial to the analyses of visual impact. These include one based largely on the principle of intervisibility, i.e. if an observer at position A can see an object at position B, then an object at position B can be seen by observers at positions A i–j. Sophisticated software packages are now available which will generate 'contours of visibility' from digital terrain models. The user identifies the position within the DTM of the proposed object (e.g. a chimney stack) together with its height above the DTM surface; the software 'looks out' radially from the top of the object and 'sees' all visible points on the surrounding landscape. The 'visibility contours' thus generated can be plotted as a 'visibility map' which informs the architect/planner as to which viewpoints, i.e. those habitations, sections of roadway, etc., which may be worthy of further investigation and from which computer generated views of the object(s) might be produced.

Vegetation models
The geometry of vegetation is exceedingly complex in its variety and its seasonal and temporal variation. The current approach is to operate a mathematical model which is faithful to the botanical nature of trees and recognizes their branching and growth. This requires the mathematical models to incorporate the following features:

- Integration of the botanical knowledge of the tree-architecture: how they grow, how they occupy space, where and how leaves and flowers are located.

- Integration of time which enables viewing the ageing of a tree. It includes the possibility of getting different pictures of the same tree at different ages, and simulating seasonal variation.
- Integration of physical parameters such as gravity, wind, plantation density, etc.

The perceived realism of advanced models is extremely high, as are the computational overheads. In most visual impact analyses, however, the primary concern is how mass planting, e.g. by the Forestry Commission, will impact on visibility (or invisibility) of distant landscape scenes and horizons; in such cases a crude 3-D model of forestry blocks is sufficient to communicate to landscape architects the primary impacts on the rural environment. Such a technique can obviously be employed to test the degree of planting, its density and geographical spread to screen a development, such as a holiday village, at various stages into the future.

Construction models

The buildings and structures which we place in the natural environment are, understandably, easier to model in a computer environment; they are, largely speaking, composed simplistically of plane geometry arranged, often, rectilinearly. There are a number of different ways of representing the constructions which people propose to impose on the landscape.

Wire-line representation: In 'wire-line' models, the construction is represented only by a set of vertices some of which are connected to others by lines. Computer algorithms which generate perspective views of 3-D objects have been in existence for nearly twenty years; they accept as data the Cartesian co-ordinates of the vertices of the object together with a list of those vertices which are jointed. The algorithm is thus able to deduce the geometry of the planes which bound the object.

The user can then specify the viewing parameters – eyepoint, focus point, cone of vision – and the algorithm computes the mathematics of perspective geometry and displays, on a screen or on a pen plotter, the resulting 'view' of the object. Given additional information on which planes in the object are transparent and which are opaque, the smarter algorithms, by sorting the places in terms of their distance from the viewer, can suppress the hidden lines thus reducing the possibility of misinterpreting the shape of the object and enhancing the realism of the image. There are occasions however (as with 'Image Mixing') when there is an advantage in representing the object only as a set of lines rather than a set of surfaces.

Surface representation: Wire-line images, with or without hidden line removal, represent plane surfaces only by the lines which bound the surface. In more sophisticated computer models, the user can attach attributes – colour, transparency, reflectivity, texture – to each surface to allow, on an appropriate screen or hard-copy device, a rendered image of the object. Many computer programs for surface representation have a lighting algorithm which allows the user to illuminate the object with one or more light sources. The software can then cast shadows and render each surface in response to the angle it makes to the 'eye' and to each and every one of the light sources. The degree of realism attained by these models is quite remarkable.

Solid modelling: Solid modelling, perhaps better termed volume modelling, allows the user to construct the geometry of the object by performing set operations (union difference, intersection) on a range of parameterized primitive volumes, e.g. cube, sphere, pyramid. The images obtained from solid model representation are similar to those obtained from surface representation.

Image mixing

Visual impact analysis is often concerned with the relationship between the existing landscape or townscape and the object which it is proposed to place within it. It is necessary, therefore, to conflate, onto one image, the geometry of what exists and what does not yet exist. The proper appreciation of both the landscape in its current state and the degree to which it will be altered is central to any systematic analysis of environmental impact. If a computer model of the terrain or townscape exists, the computer model of the proposed construction can be recalibrated to the same co-ordinate origin and scale and thereby merged with the terrain or townscape into one geometrical model. This single model can then be analysed, as described previously, to identify contours of visibility which may suggest the most important places from which perspective views should be constructed. It may be relevant also to superimpose a vegetation model which allows analysis of how, over time, particular planting strategies can mitigate visual impact. The advantage of merging computer-based data of terrain, vegetation and construction is the complete flexibility which the user has in choice of viewpoint. The disadvantage lies in the relative crudeness of computer generated images of terrain and vegetation; this may not be a serious disadvantage to professionals, but could prove problematic for the general public.

Where a limited number of realistic images are to be put to the public, the process of photomontage is appropriate. This involves careful photography of the site from each of the critical viewing positions, noting in each case the exact position of the camera, the direction of view and the focal length of the camera lens. These parameters can then be used to generate a computer perspective of the proposed construction which is scaled and positioned correctly in relation to the photographic image. The conflation of the photographic image and the computer generated image can then be done in two different ways:

Figure 15.2
Computer aided visual impact analysis of the Torness electricity transmission line: site photograph (a); computer generated perspective from the camera position (b); electronic merging of site with computer generated perspective of the line and computer generated vegetation (c); the line as built (d). (Abacus, University of Strathclyde©.)

- by obtaining a hard copy of the computer image, cutting round it and pasting it directly on to the photographic print of the site;
- by scanning the photograph of the site into the computer and composing, on the screen, the scanned image and the computer generated image of the proposed construction.

Verisimilitude

If computer based visual impact analysis is to be cost effective, it is vitally important to make good decisions on the degree of visual realism which is necessary and sufficient. The question of level and felicity of detail will normally be dictated by the development under examination. The choice of image modelling, the level of detail, etc. will need to be appropriate for the task. In terrain modelling the size of the triangular or rectangular grid mesh must be chosen in relation to the 'roughness' of the terrain, the scale of the proposed intervention and the distance of the viewpoints from the object. Too large a grid scale may misrepresent the degree of visibility and therefore the visual impact; too fine a grid will entail unnecessary processing time and cost.

The same issues of geometric 'granularity' are relevant to the modelling of the construction itself; whether or not to represent a building, say, as a simple 'shoe-box' or to model the fine detail of form and façade. This decision, together with those concerning the choice between wire-

Predicting visual impacts by computer aided visual impact analysis

a

b

Figure 15.3
Computer generated perspective of proposed transmission line to Stansted Airport (a), resulting photomontage (b), and line as constructed (c). (Abacus, University of Strathclyde©.)

c

line, grey-scale or fully coloured, shadowed and rendered images is intimately bound up with the nature of the subjective value judgements on visual impact which the professional or the lay-person is being asked to make. Clearly, if a development was proposed in a Conservation Area or National Park, the detailed representation of the construction would be greater.

CASE STUDY

Electricity transmission line to Stansted Airport

This case study describes a computer based visual impact study in a highly sensitive rural area of two 33 kV wood pole overhead transmission lines to provide electricity to the expanded Stansted Airport. As the proposed works came within the definition of Annex 2 projects under EC Directive 85/337 an Environmental Impact Assessment was undertaken for which the following pages describe the visual element of the Environmental Statement (ES).

Background

In 1985, the Government gave the final go-ahead for a third London airport which was to be built at Stansted in Essex. The BAA (formerly the British Airports Authority), initially requested an 8 MW supply at 11 kV. This was subsequently increased to 12 MW and required in time for the scheduled opening of the new airport terminal in August 1990. The existing 11 kV system in the area, which also supplies the present airport, is a typical rural overhead distribution system and was in need of some reinforcement.

From system loss and reliability studies, it was clear that the optimum supply for the new airport and reinforcement of the existing system could be achieved from the west by erecting two single 33 kV wood pole overhead lines from the Bishop's Stortford grid to a new 33/11 kV primary substation on the perimeter of the airport. The decision to use overhead lines was one of economics and convention. The additional cost for undergrounding the supply would have been £1.25 million.

The environmental challenge

Having established the most economic way of providing the supply, it was necessary to assess the impact this supply would be seen to create on the natural environment. To give some idea of the extent of local feeling towards the airport, it is necessary to go back to the 1960s, when a government study of airport usage and future requirements reported that a third airport located at Stansted should be built. A public inquiry was held in 1965 and following some very well presented opposition from local people on environmental grounds and from other objectors, the BAA's application was turned down.

The Stansted story was reopened in 1979, when the BAA again applied for permission to develop a third London airport. Another public inquiry began on 15 September 1981, and took twelve months to hear. The Inspector dismissed the objections and approved the BAA's application. The Government gave its final blessing in June 1985.

It had taken some twenty-five years to overcome the objections which had been led by the Hertfordshire and Essex County Councils, the Uttlesford and East Hertfordshire District Councils, and several influential landowners. The objections had been based on economic, social, financial and environmental issues. Nevertheless, the BAA's case was finally accepted. The challenge to Eastern Electricity was very clear. With this background in mind, it was necessary that proposals were carefully prepared in the knowledge that even after the decision for the go-ahead had been made, the anti-Stansted lobby would still raise its head.

The first indications were that the objectors would base their case on the statement of the government minister of the time:

> The Government does not intend to betray its obligations to such an attractive part of the English countryside and will resist any airport-related development outside the new airport boundary.

This raised fundamental problems for Eastern Electricity as the overhead line was part of a much wider development plan. It was recognized that the application was the first in an area which was not within the designated boundary of the new airport and raised questions of visual impact of sufficient scope to come within the parameters of the EC Directive. The local residents perceived the overhead lines as a forest of towers to be built on their doorstep. It had to be demonstrated to the local planning authorities, the landowners, the environmentalists as well as local residents, that the proposals would have minimal impact on the local environment. It was at this point that the Department of Architecture and Building Science at the University of Strathclyde was approached for assistance.

Computer simulation

The University was already carrying out work on the development of computer programs for visual impact analysis comprising three-dimensional perspective viewing from any required viewpoint. These programs were used for large-scale, terrain level modelling and appeared ideally suited to support planning submissions on the Stansted line. Some of the earlier work at Strathclyde had been applied successfully to the planning and visual impact assessment of a double circuit CEGB 400 kV line in the Scottish Borders. This included the production of computer projections of towers and lines superimposed onto a computer model of the terrain. Validation studies, conducted after this line had been built, demonstrated the high level of accuracy of the modelling techniques.

The aim of the Stansted project was to analyse the visual impact of two 33 kV wood pole overhead lines by superimposing computer images of the planned line onto photographs of the routes. These photographs were to be taken from visually or emotionally critical viewpoints. The photomontages thus produced would give a true visual impact of the proposed line in terms that were readily understandable to both planners and public.

The basic data

The information the University required from Eastern Electricity was relatively straightforward:

- A 1:10 000 OS map of the Stansted Mountfitchet area.
- The position of the lines of poles marked with pole positions to the nearest metre.
- Drawings of two wood pole types scaled 1:20. Single pole and 'H' pole.
- Conductor cages for 200 mm^2 ACSR.
- A set of photographs, enlarged to approximately A3 and taken with a level camera and compass. The actual viewpoints were seen as critical and they were chosen and discussed with professional local authority planners and those employed by the BAA.
- A table of correct viewing parameters. For the accuracy of computer photomontage it is essential to establish the accurate location of camera and target point. In addition, the camera height above ground, the focal length of the camera lens and enlarging factors from negatives to print, were also supplied.

Computer modelling

The computer modelling study of the new overhead line and its route was carried out in six stages.

Terrain

A segment of the terrain (6.5 × 2.5) from Bishop's Stortford to Burton End was modelled on the computer. The contours with 5 m height intervals were digitized from 1:10 000 OS maps. A polygon mesh with 50 m grid intervals was used to represent site features. Perspectives were subsequently generated. This stage was used to eliminate poles which were partly hidden by landform.

Poles

The modelling of two intermediate and angle poles was the first step taken, the variation in height of the poles (10–12 m) being incorporated into the geometric data.

Catenaries

Overhead cable catenaries were modelled to give a more realistic representation of the proposed overhead line. The method adopted was to model catenaries in accordance with the distance from the camera, for each specified view. Most of the catenaries were single conductors and only those close to the observer were modelled on three separate conductors. An average sag of 1.5 m was used for all the spans.

Lines of poles

Two proposed lines were modelled, one with 57 poles and the other with 54. The two main types of poles were copied, sited and rotated along a vertical axis relative to the selected datum point to generate a view of the proposed lines. The cable catenaries were then added to the data files for each of the views.

Computer generated perspectives

A series of perspectives were generated from the six selected viewpoints. These contained landforms and lines of poles with catenaries and were used as working plots to establish the degree of clipping by a particular landform.

Computer photomontage

The computer photomontage technique was used as the most appropriate to communicate the visual information. Views were generated of pole lines which were then plotted onto the transparent overlays and then merged with the photographs.

Conclusion

The computer based visual impact analysis yielded a series of highly accurate and economical images (at a cost of £500/view at 1990 prices) which could be readily appreciated by all the interested parties involved in the planning process. The comprehensive modelling of the line allowed questions of visual impact to be set within the Environmental Statement. The techniques outlined provided a better guide to likely impacts than would have been available with non-computer modelling methods. The visual impact analysis jigsawed into a wider review of the effects of the line on the environment. Two benefits followed: first, the line was modified to improve its design on the basis of the visual predictions made, second, the clarity and reliability of the computer images reassured the local planning authority and placated objections. The project was successful: planning permission, wayleaves and ministerial consents were granted on the basis of the images presented and the line has since been constructed.

16

Environmental audits

In parallel with the Environmental Assessment of development projects, companies are increasingly undertaking audits of their own environmental performance. The Institute of Business Ethics (IBE) report of 1992 *Towards Good Environmental Practice*,[1] produced partly in response to expanding EC legislation, recommends elements of an environmental checklist which industry should follow. Since construction products manufacturers have a major ecological impact, the IBE report is relevant to their needs and contains case studies within this field. Jointly sponsored by the UK Department of the Environment (DOE) and the Department of Trade and Industry (DTI), it follows an earlier IBE report on *Ethics, Environment and the Company* produced in 1990.

Environmental management is also encouraged in the EC by Regulation 1836/93/EEC which introduces an Eco-Management and Audit Scheme. The Regulation is designed to urge industrial firms to behave in an environmentally responsible manner. Although the scheme is at present voluntary, the reward for firms is that they can exhibit the EC's Eco-Management and Audit logo. Architects and engineers wishing to specify green products may well look for the presence of the logo as a guarantee of good environmental practice. Firms which participate in the scheme are required to submit their activities and an environmental audit for scrutiny by independent assessors. Such scrutiny ensures that both the industrial community and general public are kept informed of the processes undertaken and their ecological impact.

The Regulation is required to be in operation by Member States by May of 1995. In the UK, the British Standard on Environmental Systems (BS 7750) satisfies the criteria within the European scheme insofar as the BS covers the formulation and use of environmental and ecological management systems. Hence, firms in the UK wishing to display the logo should, in the first instance, ensure that their activities satisfy BS 7750. Any further work to fulfil the needs of the EC Regulation will be outlined by the independent assessors.

The main purpose of the IBE report of 1992 is to provide a methodology which provides a 'systematic and comprehensive review of the interaction between companies' activities and the environment'.[2] Although there is some confusion in the use of the terms 'environmental audit' and 'environmental assessment', the report dismisses debate over terminology preferring to concentrate upon what should be measured. Understanding environmental implications for a manufacturing company (usually called an Environmental Audit) consists of:

- looking at what results from a process in terms of waste, emissions and impacts of various kinds;
- looking at the environmental impact of the final product in full life-cycle terms.

To achieve these objectives the term 'inventory' is used – the quantified and systematic recording of all wastes and impacts. Frequently the term 'environmental or ecological baseline' is employed to provide a description of environmental standards against which changes can be measured before, during and after operations. This implies some monitoring whilst the manufacturing process is taking place and can be used as a predictive tool to assess likely impacts before they occur. The terms 'environmental review' is usually used to denote a limited form of environmental audit sometimes targeted at specific concerns (such as toxic releases).

Within the expanding field of environmental audits there is the need for greater consistency in terminology not just between Britain and its European partners but between Europe and international competitors such as the USA. Life-cycle analysis, for instance, is known also as Eco-profiling, Eco-labelling (in EC legislation) and Resource and Environmental Profile Analysis in North America. Consistent standards of environmental protection in international agreements such as GATT and the Rio Summit Protocol can only be effective with consistent terminology related to standard methodologies.

---

[1] Julie Hill *Towards Good Environmental Practice* The Institute of Business Ethics, London, 1992.

[2] *Ibid.*, p 3.

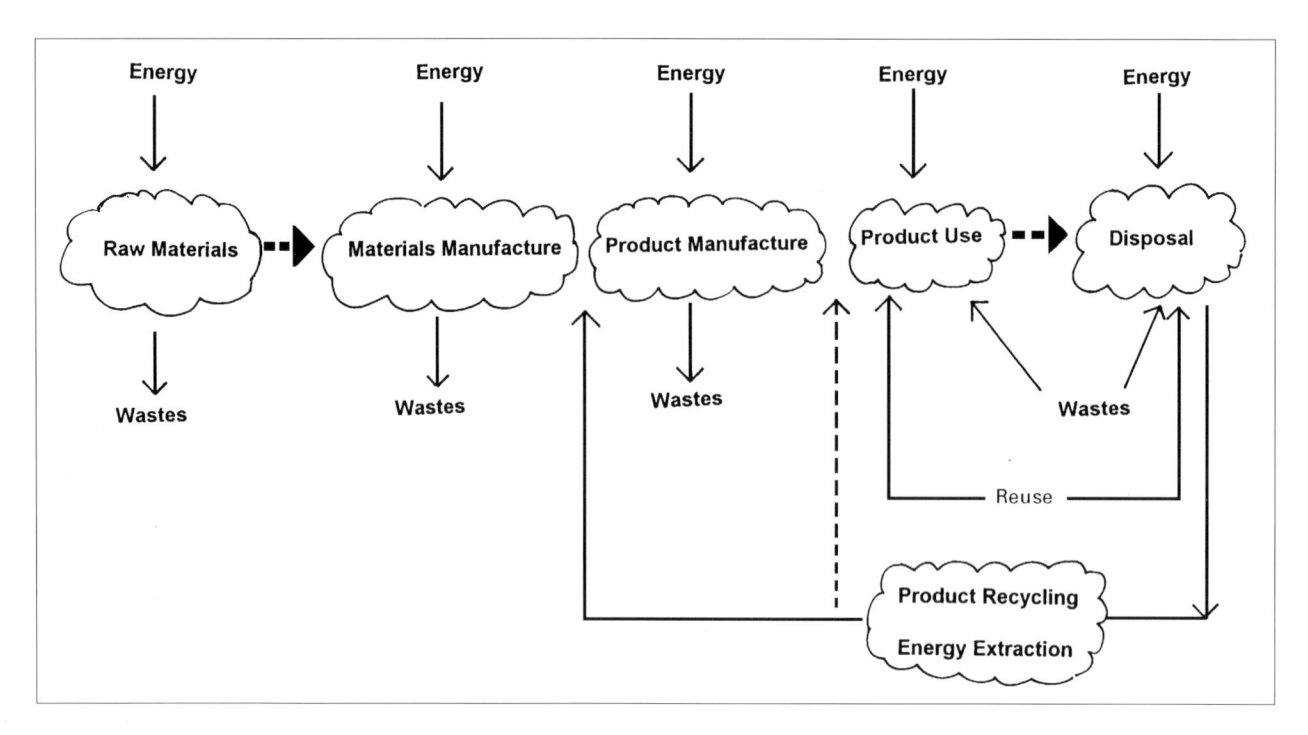

Environmental audits

Figure 16.1
The progression of energy and environmental impacts involved in the life-cycle from manufacture to disposal of building products.

LIFE-CYCLE IMPACTS OF A BRICK

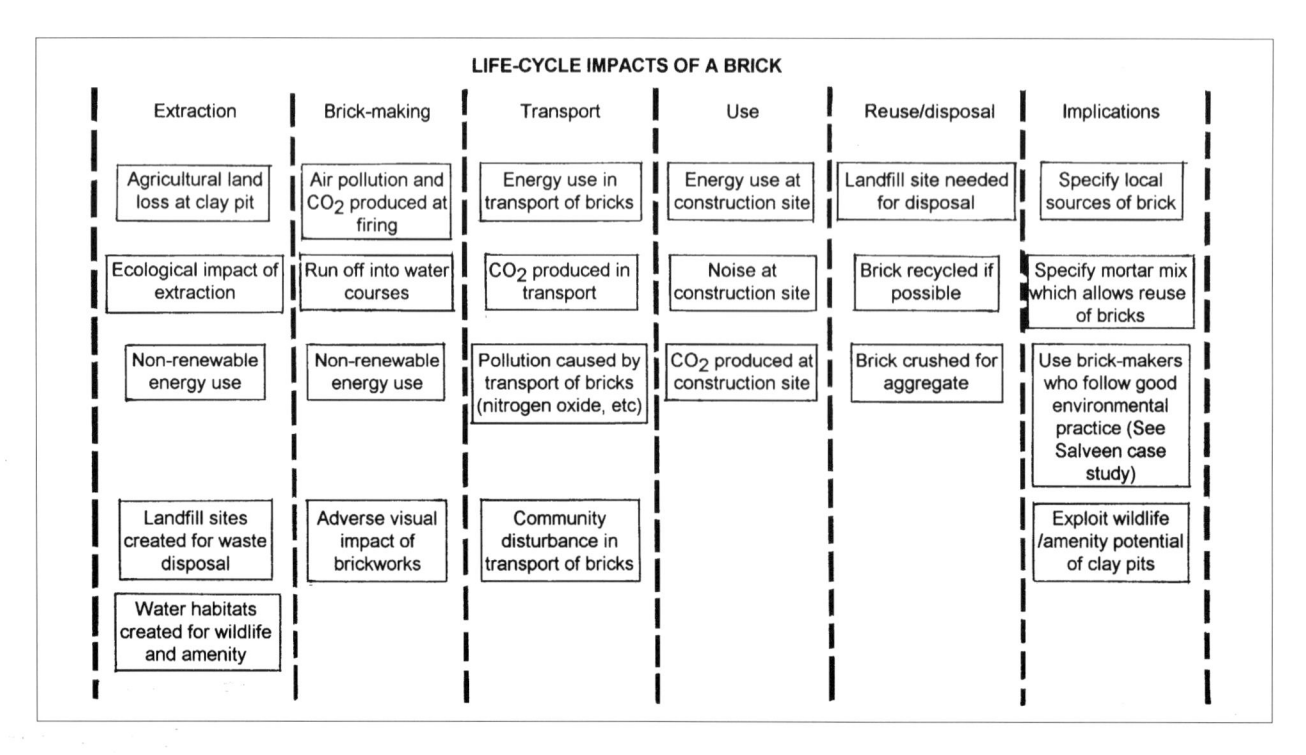

Extraction	Brick-making	Transport	Use	Reuse/disposal	Implications
Agricultural land loss at clay pit	Air pollution and CO_2 produced at firing	Energy use in transport of bricks	Energy use at construction site	Landfill site needed for disposal	Specify local sources of brick
Ecological impact of extraction	Run off into water courses	CO_2 produced in transport	Noise at construction site	Brick recycled if possible	Specify mortar mix which allows reuse of bricks
Non-renewable energy use	Non-renewable energy use	Pollution caused by transport of bricks (nitrogen oxide, etc)	CO_2 produced at construction site	Brick crushed for aggregate	Use brick-makers who follow good environmental practice (See Salveen case study)
Landfill sites created for waste disposal	Adverse visual impact of brickworks	Community disturbance in transport of bricks			Exploit wildlife /amenity potential of clay pits
Water habitats created for wildlife and amenity					

Figure 16.2
Life-cycle impacts of a brick. (Brian Edwards©.)

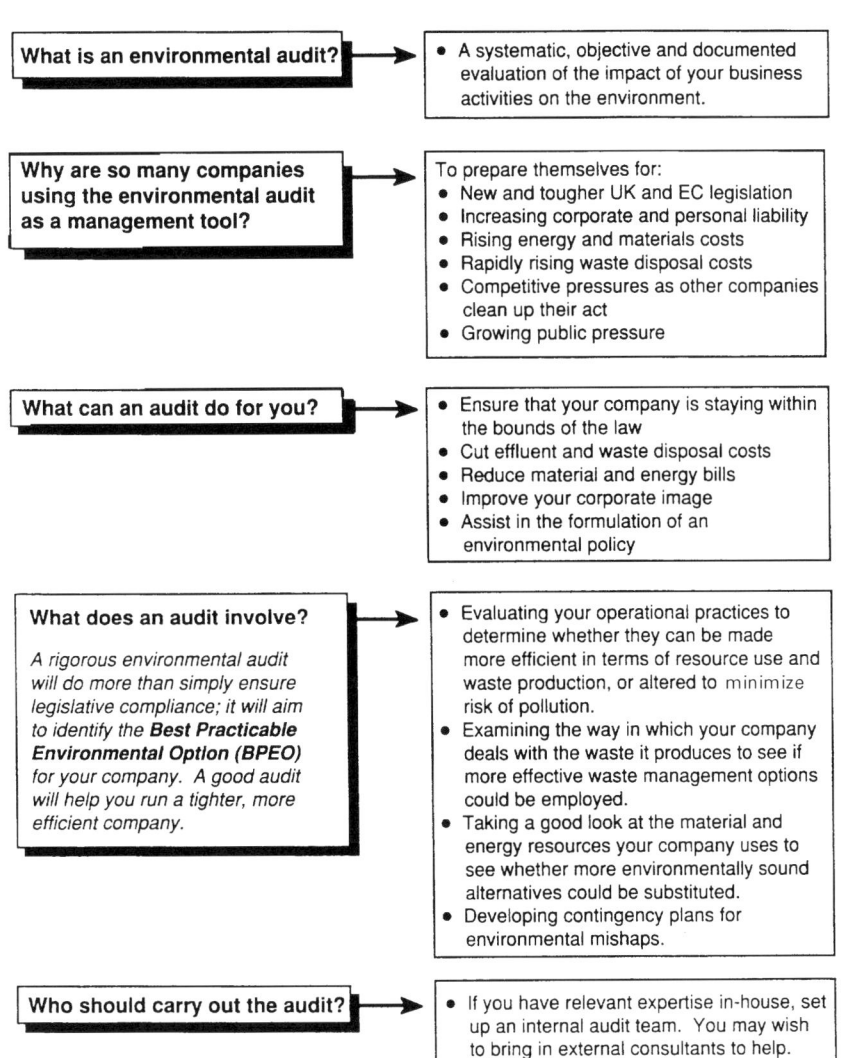

Figure 16.3
Elements of an Environmental Audit. (CEBIS©.)

What is an environmental audit?	• A systematic, objective and documented evaluation of the impact of your business activities on the environment.
Why are so many companies using the environmental audit as a management tool?	To prepare themselves for: • New and tougher UK and EC legislation • Increasing corporate and personal liability • Rising energy and materials costs • Rapidly rising waste disposal costs • Competitive pressures as other companies clean up their act • Growing public pressure
What can an audit do for you?	• Ensure that your company is staying within the bounds of the law • Cut effluent and waste disposal costs • Reduce material and energy bills • Improve your corporate image • Assist in the formulation of an environmental policy
What does an audit involve? *A rigorous environmental audit will do more than simply ensure legislative compliance; it will aim to identify the **Best Practicable Environmental Option (BPEO)** for your company. A good audit will help you run a tighter, more efficient company.*	• Evaluating your operational practices to determine whether they can be made more efficient in terms of resource use and waste production, or altered to minimize risk of pollution. • Examining the way in which your company deals with the waste it produces to see if more effective waste management options could be employed. • Taking a good look at the material and energy resources your company uses to see whether more environmentally sound alternatives could be substituted. • Developing contingency plans for environmental mishaps.
Who should carry out the audit?	• If you have relevant expertise in-house, set up an internal audit team. You may wish to bring in external consultants to help.

Environmental auditing is a new field and finding the right combination of expertise to suit a company's needs is not always easy. External consultants do not always fully understand the culture of a company, and senior company staff are not always familiar with the language and methods of outside consultants. As far as possible the two cultures need to coalesce if auditing is to be effective. Another problem is knowing where to draw the line in terms of impacts. Does, for example, a brickworks need to assess the noise and air pollution caused by lorries which deliver the bricks to building sites or the manufacture of dyes made by another company used to produce different colours of brick? Following through every link of the chain beyond the factory gate is expensive but with big companies it is essential if they are to have environmental credibility. To help firms undertake an environmental audit the CBI published in October 1994 an *Environment Business Forum Handbook* which outlines the steps necessary, the expertise required, and a range of model methodologies to follow.

Once the audit has been undertaken a company or public body such as a health authority may wish to issue a 'statement of policy' regarding environmental matters. This, as ICI can testify, has the benefit of letting staff know what the company is 'setting out to do regarding the environment and thus help to create a sense of direction and purpose',[3] and provides a measure against which the company wishes to have its environmental performance assessed. Such a statement of environmental policy allows everybody concerned from chief executive downwards to monitor, report and review performance. In terms of

---

[3] *Ibid.*, p 4.

Environmental audits

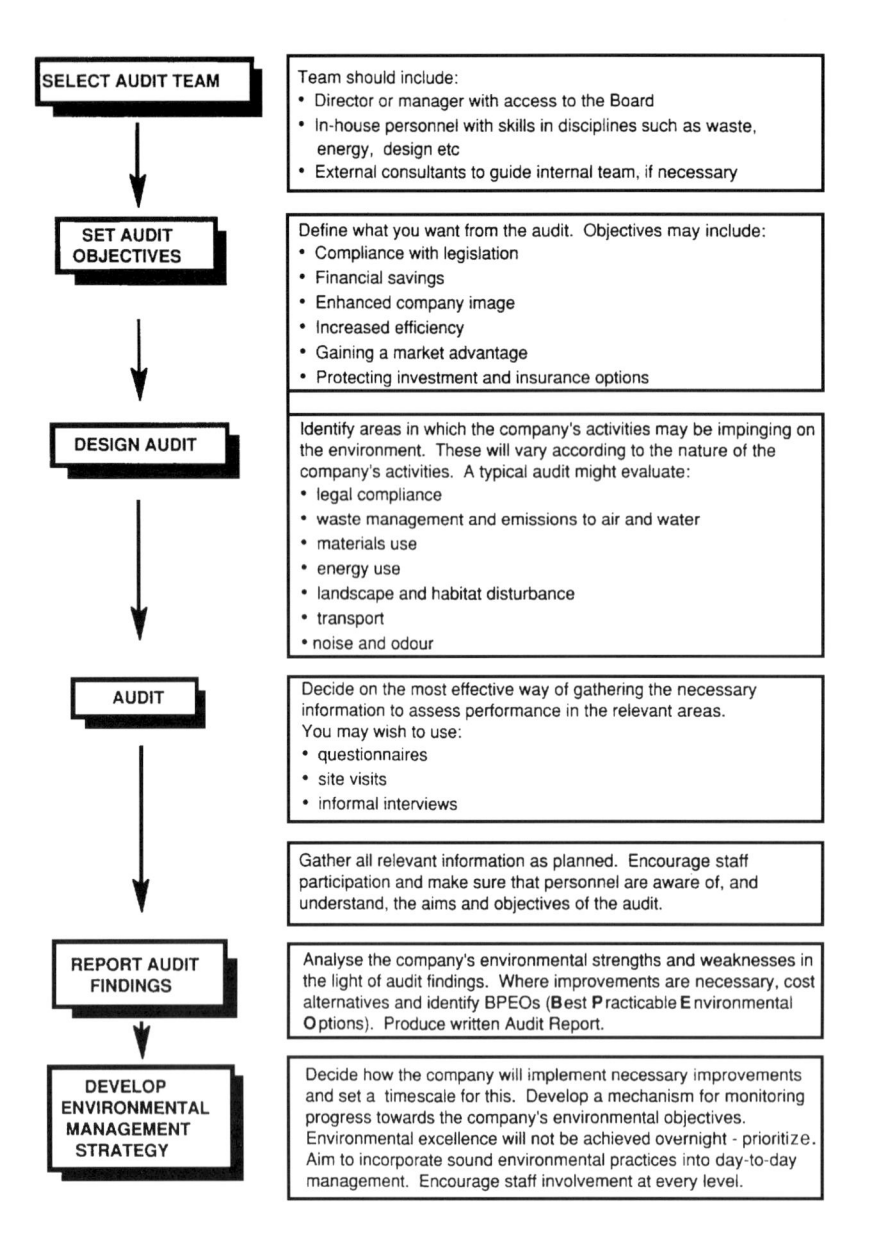

Figure 16.4
Undertaking an Environmental Audit. (CEBIS©.)

SELECT AUDIT TEAM
Team should include:
- Director or manager with access to the Board
- In-house personnel with skills in disciplines such as waste, energy, design etc
- External consultants to guide internal team, if necessary

SET AUDIT OBJECTIVES
Define what you want from the audit. Objectives may include:
- Compliance with legislation
- Financial savings
- Enhanced company image
- Increased efficiency
- Gaining a market advantage
- Protecting investment and insurance options

DESIGN AUDIT
Identify areas in which the company's activities may be impinging on the environment. These will vary according to the nature of the company's activities. A typical audit might evaluate:
- legal compliance
- waste management and emissions to air and water
- materials use
- energy use
- landscape and habitat disturbance
- transport
- noise and odour

AUDIT
Decide on the most effective way of gathering the necessary information to assess performance in the relevant areas.
You may wish to use:
- questionnaires
- site visits
- informal interviews

Gather all relevant information as planned. Encourage staff participation and make sure that personnel are aware of, and understand, the aims and objectives of the audit.

REPORT AUDIT FINDINGS
Analyse the company's environmental strengths and weaknesses in the light of audit findings. Where improvements are necessary, cost alternatives and identify BPEOs (**B**est **P**racticable **E**nvironmental **O**ptions). Produce written Audit Report.

DEVELOP ENVIRONMENTAL MANAGEMENT STRATEGY
Decide how the company will implement necessary improvements and set a timescale for this. Develop a mechanism for monitoring progress towards the company's environmental objectives. Environmental excellence will not be achieved overnight - prioritize. Aim to incorporate sound environmental practices into day-to-day management. Encourage staff involvement at every level.

gaining development consent for new projects, such statements can provide an air of reassurance to planning officers concerned with likely environmental impacts. BS 5750 on quality assurance provides a framework for such statements and the more recently introduced standard BS 7750 on environmental management sets out best practice guidelines. The latter, effective as an auditing tool, meets new EC regulations on the monitoring of environmental performance.

Besides companies setting up formal audits of their environmental impacts, other institutions such as universities are also exploring how they can reduce their impact upon the environment. Liverpool John Moores University adopted early in 1995 a comprehensive policy statement aimed at minimizing its environmental and ecological impacts. The statement addressed a wide range of subjects from waste, transport policy to energy use and the procurement of buildings. Inspired by the 1992 report 'Environmental Responsibility: An Agenda for Higher Education' the policy statement deals with both general issues and charts an 'Action Plan' for implementation. Amongst the measures are the introduction of regular audits of energy consumption, a shift from car to cycle use to the campus by staff and students, the purchasing of materials and professional services from those with green standards or credentials, the use of local and regional

Figure 16.5
Key assessment factors in Environmental Auditing. (CEBIS©.)

LEGAL COMPLIANCE
- Do you know how UK and EC regulations and standards affect your business?
- Do your current practices comply with these?
- Do you take future environmental standards into consideration when planning new projects?
- Are you aware of, and where possible do you implement, the best available technology?
- Do you keep up with the latest regulatory requirements?

WASTE
- What waste does your company produce and how do you dispose of it?
- Could your waste be minimised, recycled or eliminated?
- Could you participate in waste-exchange schemes (ie. selling your waste to other businesses to use as raw materials or buying waste in for your own use)?
- Could you recycle office waste?
- Do you have adequate emergency procedures for accidental spillages and emissions?

TRANSPORT
- Do you transport your goods efficiently (eg avoid empty vehicles)?
- What special precautions do you take in the transport of dangerous goods and wastes?
- Do you regularly maintain vehicles and plant to minimise noxious emissions?
- Could you switch to vehicles with smaller engines?
- Could you develop a strategy that minimised use of staff transport? Could you encourage car pooling or offer a 'bicycle allowance', for example?

MATERIALS
- Could you cut down on use of materials? eg: Can products be reduced in size or reshaped to minimise materials and packaging? Is packaging excessive? Are you recycling materials within processes where possible?
- Could you use more environmentally friendly materials? eg: Do your materials come from renewable resources? Could you replace toxic materials with less toxic ones? Could you replace non-recyclable materials and components with recyclable ones?

ENERGY USE
- How much energy is used in each area of your business and do you regularly review energy use?
- Could waste energy be usefully redirected?
- Could you use combined heat and power?
- Is there potential for energy saving in your business? For example, could better insulation and heat controls, more energy-efficient lighting and plant, cut your fuel bills?

LANDSCAPES & HABITATS
- Do any of your activities (eg. the development of new sites) damage landscapes and habitats?
- Are your sites as tidy, quiet and dust-free as they could be?
- Are your sites landscaped to make them look attractive?
- Do you preserve natural habitats around your sites where possible?

supplies of consumables, minimum packaging of products, and waste recycling schemes. Such a culture change has clear implications for the procurement of buildings and the choice of professional designers.

CASE STUDIES OF CONSTRUCTION PRODUCTS

ICI

As the UK's main producer of CFCs (50 per cent of which are used in the construction industry), the company has been under pressure to reduce the environmental impact of both its processes and products. Concerned that the profile of ICI was being undermined by the heavy pollution which accompanied its plants and its reputation for being one of the world's biggest manufacturers of ozone depleting chemicals, the company in 1989 decided to undertake an environmental audit. The task was not inconsiderable in time and cost. With 150 manufacturing plants to assess each at a cost of between £70 000 and £300 000,[4] the undertaking was a major commitment.

The problem encountered by ICI was also a technical one. Tracking wastes and assessing their impacts proved by no means easy and at the Billingham plant in Teesside six to ten key substances were used for monitoring. By

---
[4]*Ibid.*, p 22.

Table 16.1 Environmental effects, Salvesen Brick's Checklist

In all cases the relevant register of environmental effects must contain information relating to:

- controlled and uncontrolled emissions to the atmosphere
- controlled and uncontrolled discharges to water
- waste and discharges to land
- land use and potential for contamination
- use of water, fuel, energy, raw materials and other natural resources
- potential for noise, odour, dust, vibration and visual impact
- effects on areas of nature conservation or ecological value

Such assessment must include situations of normal operation and also an evaluation of effects arising from potential incidents, accidents and emergency situations

Reproduced from Julie Hill *Towards Good Environmental Practice*, IBE, 1992, London. Extract from Salvesen Brick's Environmental Management Procedures Manual.

---

checking their levels against base standards, managers and scientists were able to review the complex system as a whole. By using ecological filters (reedbeds at the edge of the plant) they have also tried to measure the relative damage caused to the wider environment by their discharges. In parallel with these measures ICI has identified energy use as a priority. Although the company has halved its energy use per volume of output over the preceding seventeen years, it has set a target of a 5 per cent reduction use per year over the next fifteen years.[5]

Each ICI plant adopted in 1993 an 'Environmental Improvement Plan' to allow the general targets set above to be implemented at a local level. The Environmental Audit established a baseline against which targets could be set within the company as a whole and at local level. Within the company environmental matters now take higher priority, though whether this is in response to leadership from the top or ICI having to respond quickly to new legislative controls on waste emissions and global impact (such as the US Toxic Release Inventory regulations and the EC Large Combustion Plants Directive) is a moot point.

The Montreal Protocol of 1992 to phase out CFCs led the company to be the first to develop (and patent) the less damaging substitute material HCFC. Whether ICI would have moved as quickly or at all without the international agreement is debatable. Regulatory pressure has traditionally been the motor for environmental protection in the chemical industry rather than corporate ambition. However, by moving speedily into the manufacture of HCFC the company has seized a market opportunity during the phasing out period of CFCs. By being more in tune with growing ecological and global concerns than its competitors, ICI has shown that environmental sensitivity can be compatible with business success. The architecture of the sealed environment, heavily glazed building which depended upon CFCs in the past for refrigeration efficiencies now has an extended life with the use of HCFCs. Whether such buildings are compatible with green philosophy is questionable: thanks largely to ICI they promise at least to be less damaging to the ozone layer.

Salvesen Brick

Salvesen Brick (part of the Scottish-based Christian Salvesen Group) has four brickworks in the UK employing 260 people. It produced its first policy statement on the environment in 1991 (using BS 5750) listing eight objectives. From 1992 the managers of each brickworks were given linked financial and environmental targets to meet, rather than merely financial ones as in the past.

Unlike ICI, Salvesen Brick did not have relatively unlimited resources upon which to draw in compiling an environmental strategy. It was aware that its impacts upon air quality, land, agriculture and energy use were considerable but lacked a sense of how these could be measured. The first task, therefore, was to decide which issues were priorities and hence worthy of going into in greater detail. The National Federation of Clay Industries (NFCI) provided some advice, as did the Coopers and Lybrand Deloitte report 'Business in the Environment'. With the cost of undertaking an environmental statement of a single plant at about £100 000 (at 1990 levels) and the study of air pollution alone £30 000, the company decided to use one brickworks as a test bed to help develop general environmental targets for the others.

---

[5] *Ibid.*, p 23.

Armed with the general appreciation and the detailed knowledge of the environmental impacts of one brickworks, Salvesen Brick developed the first certified environmental management system for a UK brickworks. Adapting BS 5750 on quality assurance systems and working to what were then the draft standards of BS 7750 (Environmental Management) the company produced a manual on the environment setting out general policy, defining targets and establishing environmental responsibilities of staff. Since management systems can lead to inertia, Salvesen Brick also introduced 'environmental awareness' into its criteria for recruitment of managers.

In some ways the need to upgrade procedures and plant in response to fresh legislation (UK and EC) provided the impetus for changes at Salvesen Brick. The 'duty of care' responsibilities entwined in the 1990 Environmental Protection Act and the expectation of the widening of the EC Eco-labelling Directive to construction products, encouraged the company to become more proactive in environmental matters. The initiative by Salvesen Brick has led to the parent company Christian Salvesen adopting an environmental policy statement which it thinks is important in 'the long-term relationship with customers'.[6]

---

[6]*Ibid.*, p 38.

17

Protecting Europe's cultural heritage

The protection of Europe's cultural heritage has been a recurring topic for resolutions and declarations since 1982 when the European Parliament established the protection of the architectural heritage as a worthy ambition of Member States. This resolution of 14 September 1982 was followed on 19 June 1983 by the 'Solemn Declaration on European Union' which contained a paragraph on 'the advisability of undertaking joint action to protect, promote and safeguard the cultural heritage'.[1] Joint action did not, however, entail any modification of the powers of the Community or impose any requirements on the Member States regarding the level of legal protection afforded to the architectural or cultural heritage of Europe. Rather action under the resolution was one of making grants available for restoring selected monuments in Member States and providing scholarships for the study of conservation in appropriate training institutions such as the Conservation Centres in Rome and Edinburgh.

A fresh resolution adopted by Ministers with responsibility for Cultural Affairs on 13 November 1986 extended the range of initiatives taken to protect Europe's architectural heritage. Under the new resolution the Community agreed to:

- develop effective co-operation on aspects of Europe's architectural heritage between Member States and other European countries where appropriate;
- encourage the exchange of experience and the transfer of information on the architectural heritage by standardizing terminology and establishing databases across Europe;
- promote awareness of the economic, social and cultural aspects of Europe's architectural heritage, especially amongst public, intergovernmental and private organizations;

Figure 17.1
Europe's architectural heritage spans national boundaries, hence EC policies to conserve monuments such as castles and cathedrals are increasingly international in outlook. (Brian Edwards©.)

- encourage public institutions and others specializing in conservation of buildings to enhance the interest of sites to the wider public by the means of visual and other measures.[2]

The Commission set aside grants under the 'Pilots Projects' and 'Fourth Framework Environment Programme' to ensure these initiatives were achieved. For example, early in 1995 the EC announced grants for the conservation of European religious monuments, including their interiors but only if still in ecclesiastical use and regularly open to the public. The policy of the Commission in the past has been to accept the legal powers of protection afforded by Member States to their aspect of

---

[1] *Official Journal of the European Communities* No C 320/1.

[2] Council Resolution 86/C/320/01.

Figure 17.2
Buildings are one of the prime embodiments of Europe's cultural identity. (Brian Edwards©.)

Figure 17.3
Supporting training programmes to maintain craft skills is an important strand of EC heritage policies.

Europe's architectural heritage, seeking instead to influence public and professional opinion by education programmes and grant assistance. Rather than require the standardization of legal protection measures, as was the case with ecological sites, with the man-made heritage more peripheral interests have been targeted. This reflects the feeling within the Community that all Member States had an adequate statutory framework for preservation based upon fairly consistent criteria for protecting archaeological sites, historic buildings, and areas of character within towns.

The 'Green Paper on the Urban Environment' of 1990 gave further emphasis to the importance of Europe's architectural heritage. The historic quarters of towns and cities were seen as establishing a distinctive European character to places. Rather than concentrate upon individual monuments, the Green Paper describes how the street patterns, squares and historic buildings establish an identity which is distinctively European. The cities as a whole are seen as important symbols of the Community's rich cultural diversity. The Green Paper suggests that the uniqueness of European character resides in the distinctiveness of European towns and cities and that interest in protecting them is not restricted to 'that city's own citizens'. The wider interest that is alluded to hints at the adoption in the future of stronger measures, perhaps in the form of a directive, to ensure greater consistency for the protection of urban character (rather than merely individual buildings) across European frontiers.

The Green Paper also raises the spectacle of grant assistance to help with the preservation of areas 'of European significance'. There is the suggestion here of a classification of areas and buildings of European, rather than national or regional, importance. Were this to be adopted as a concrete measure, the necessary directive or regulation would need to define standards and criteria. Many Member States, such as the UK, already have historic areas and monuments classified according to their relative importance. In England a building listed as grade 1 is of national or international rather than local importance and a conservation area designated as 'outstanding' carries similar overtones. It is quite conceivable that a schedule of sites and areas of European importance could readily be compiled from information currently available, with grant assistance provided to ensure that the methods of restoration and area enhancement were of the highest standards.

If the richness and diversity of European cities and individual sites is to be preserved across national boundaries, then some kind of European standards is needed. Much of the best of European architecture spans national boundaries. The cathedrals of the Norman period, the castles of the twelfth century, the palaces of the Renaissance and early sites of the industrial revolution are not confined by the frontiers of countries. Member States may have to play their part in European measures to identify, protect, conserve, interpret and present a particular period of Europe's cultural development. The Green Paper suggests that such measures may not be far beyond the horizon. Quite how a 'Community system of recognition of the historic and cultural significance' of buildings and areas is to be compiled is not proposed. The idea remains in 1994 an ambition and one which the tide of subsidiarity may thwart.

---

[3]*Ibid.*

Figure 17.4
Europe's cultural identity and distinctive urban character is of growing concern to European legislators. (Brian Edwards ©.)

18

An A–Z of environmental impacts of commonly used building products, processes and services and related design issues

Buildings have a large impact upon the environment in a number of ways. They are responsible for about half the energy consumption in the UK and about 45 per cent of global warming gas production amounting to 300 million tonnes in 1993. They affect the health and sometimes safety of occupants, their spatial distribution influences the amount of energy used in transportation, and they are major occupiers of land which could otherwise be used for agriculture.

The materials and products which are used to make buildings are also large users of energy in manufacture, energy in transportation, and land to derive the raw materials. Decisions affecting the design, layout, density, methods of heating and lighting, the employment of different materials, etc. have a great potential impact upon the environment both directly and indirectly. Architects and engineers are increasingly aware that the decisions they make can affect the well being of both the local and global environment, the resources available to future generations, and the realization of balanced, sustainable communities. Poor judgements today can lead to future action being directed not so much towards environmental protection, but environmental repair and rehabilitation. Good judgements can also help reduce the £20 billion spent annually in the UK on heating, cooling, lighting and ventilating buildings.

The report researched by Ove Arup and Partners *Going Green*[1] provides a useful checklist of commonly used building products and their environmental impacts. It has been augmented here by other issues concerning resources, thereby providing a more comprehensive gazetteer. In any such checklist the effects can only be the merest summary, yet taken together the full impact of buildings become clear. The checklist is arranged alphabetically and cross-referenced where appropriate to EC directives.

Adhesives. Most are based on non-renewable resources but have a useful contribution to make in the efficient use of other materials such as structural timber. Some raise health risks in certain applications but have a beneficial use in the repair and refurbishment of timber and concrete structures. If possible specify resins from renewable sources and use water-based as against oil-based products.

Aggregate. Normally obtained by quarrying or dredging, the use of aggregates in construction has large environmental impacts both in terms of land lost to agriculture, disturbance to communities, energy use in transportation, and adverse visual impacts. It is possible to use recycled aggregates (from crushed concrete), colliery waste and pulverized fuel ask (pfa) from power stations. Greater use should be made of recycled materials, and the need for concrete reduced by more frequent reuse of old buildings and the employment of steel rather than concrete framing because of its flexibility.

Air conditioning. Air conditioning should be avoided in all new design. The inclusion of atria and lighting wells in large, deep-planned office buildings, thereby utilizing the stack effect for natural ventilation, should avoid the use of mechanical forms of air conditioning. As air conditioning is usually based upon CFCs in refrigeration, the arguments are both about reduced energy consumption and ozone

---

[1] *Going Green* guide by Ove Arup & Partners commissioned and published by J T Design & Build, 1993.

protection. In terms of comfort, divide large offices into small spaces with individual controls and try to reduce the internal equipment and lighting loads.

Aluminium. This is a useful but high energy producing material. It has good strength to weight qualities, admirable stiffness, corrosion resistance and low maintenance costs. Its lightness tends to lead to low transport costs, encouraging its use as a self-build material and permits ready reuse. Greater use should be made of recycled aluminium and designers could design for reuse by avoiding coated finishes and by specifying to standard dimensions.

Asbestos. A dangerous substance when inhaled and controlled by a specific EC Directive (87/217/EC). Rarely used in new construction products, operatives are often exposed when rehabilitating or demolishing buildings of the 1950s and 60s. Asbestos exists in both the building and wider environment and should be avoided even when used in a binding matrix as in some floor coverings.

Asphalt. A by-product of petroleum production, this material is generally produced synthetically though it does occur naturally in the form of lakes. A useful material with good waterproof qualities though it is a non-renewable resource and is increasingly recycled particularly for road surfacings. Has a particular use as a waterproofing layer in turf roofs – the soil and vegetation providing useful protection against sunlight and thermal insulation.

Blocks. Concrete blocks consume large amounts of energy in production and are major users of aggregates and cement. They offer good structural and insulation qualities, and the energy consumed in manufacture may be balanced by energy conserved in use, especially with better insulating lightweight blocks. They offer good durability, and provide low maintenance walling although it is of poor visual quality unless given a special finish. Lightweight blocks are easier to handle, cheaper to transport and may be partly made from recycled materials. Try and specify local sources of manufacture and lime mortar mixes for subsequent reuse of the blocks.

Boards. Organic boards utilize parts of the tree not used for structural timber but avoid resin or concrete binders and boards made from tropical hardwoods. Inorganic boards are generally derived from non-renewable sources and can pose health risks in the release of dust or fibres. Both types of board can also pose health and environmental risks through Formaldehyde release. Often the energy used in production is offset by energy saved in use as insulation materials.

Bricks. Bricks have major environmental impacts (Figure 16.1). The raw material for production involves large land losses to agriculture (though the clay pits are often utilized for leisure purposes and provide useful wildlife habitats), the baking of bricks consumes large amounts of energy, and transportation to the building site takes further fossil fuels. They offer advantages as an attractive and durable low maintenance finish. Designers should specify locally made bricks, those bricks which require less energy in manufacture, and the use of lime-based mortars for eventual recycling of the brick. Recycled bricks have potential use in new housing (providing a patina of ageing in sympathy with some consumer tastes), in conservation work, and in ground surfacing such as estate roads, footpaths and cycleways.

Cement. Cement production is a major resource depleting and energy consuming process. There are also health risks in its manufacture and use. Improvements can be engineered by reducing the portland cement element by the use of admixtures, by using industrial by-products, and by producing new concrete made from recycled concrete aggregates. In terms of the total energy equation of a building, concrete has high thermal mass and hence is beneficial when used in conjunction with passive solar design. *In situ* concrete is inherently inflexible and pre-cast concrete offers greater potential for recycling of structural members and framing elements.

Ceramics. Similar in basic qualities to bricks, ceramic tiles are about to be covered in the UK under the EC eco-labelling scheme (EEC/880/92). It is a versatile and durable material with good decorative qualities and it is possible to reuse ceramics in certain situations.

Conservation. Sustainable development is only possible if the conservation of buildings, land, energy and resources becomes commonplace. Recycling is part of the equation, but good, energy-efficient and socially responsible architecture is also important. Designers should seek 'minimum footprint' not maximum impact buildings.

Cycling. An energy efficient, health promoting means of local transport often ignored by designers. Cycling is frequently constrained by lack of cycleways, shortage of cycle storage space in the home or office, and the danger posed by unsegregated road space. Greater facilities for the cyclist could make significant savings in transport energy use, particularly if linked to dense patterns of development.

Electric power. Electricity production is a major source of global warming gases and until the recent shift from coal to gas use at power stations, the source of much acid rain. Designers should avoid wasting electricity by not using it as a source of heating, by placing lighting on control systems, providing local monitoring of consumption, and encouraging combined heat and power systems. Also electricity use can be reduced by using renewable sources of power such as hydroelectric, wind, wave, solar. The use of low-energy lighting has obvious benefits.

Energy. Buildings are major consumers of energy directly and indirectly. Decisions over the type of development, its location, density and land-use diversity all have profound effects upon the amount of energy used. The use of high levels of insulation, the employment of compact forms of development in self-sheltering layouts, the avoidance of high-rise or widely spaced development of single land use, the adoption where possible of renewable energy sources are all essential starting points. Each building type has its own preferred low energy typology. With domestic buildings mid-floor apartments in four storey flats consume only a third of the energy of a detached house of equal size, and a terraced house less than half of the energy. Consequently, designers must couple their strategy for technology with an appreciation of the physics of the building type as a whole.

Environmental impacts. Designers should investigate impacts at source, in manufacture, use and disposal. Certain schemes are available to help determine the benign nature of products (such as eco-labelling) but many full life-cycle impacts have yet to be evaluated. Impacts vary according to situation. The loss of land, visual intrusion, health risks, damage to eco-systems, loss of biodiversity are as legitimate as concerns over fossil-fuel use.

Fibres. Most fibres employed in building are derived from non-renewable sources and often involve energy-intensive manufacture. However, their use can be beneficial with, for instance, glass fibre quilt paying for itself in six to eight years in terms of energy consumption in the home. Most fibres pose risks to health in manufacture or installation due to dust and fibre particles being inhaled or irritating the skin.

Floor finishes. These are either derived from renewable sources such as linoleum, cork, wood block or timber boarded floors, or from non-renewable sources such as plastic-based synthetic fibre finishes, ceramic tiles or non-wool carpeted finishes. Consider the energy used in manufacture, atmospheric pollution at the factory, solvent release in the building. Ask whether floor finishes are required or whether the structural floor (as in timber) can also be the decorative finish.

Glass. Glass has many benefits in passive solar gain and as the material through which daylight normally enters a building, but it is expensive to produce in terms of non-renewable resources and energy. The manufacturing process is particularly energy intensive and because plants for the manufacture of glass are few and far between (85 per cent of the UK's glass comes from Pilkington plc in St Helens), transport energy costs are also high. Glass is, however, a flexible material capable of being recycled and in different thicknesses, layers and subject to treatment, can offer some insulation (see Chapter 10). Used wisely glass can save some of the energy used in manufacture by its ability to deliver natural light and solar gain. Glazing design needs to strike a balance between heat gain in summer, heat loss in winter and natural daylight. The nature of the balance varies according to building type, to latitude and to orientation. Modern coatings and treatments, such as K glass from Pilkington, significantly improve the solar control or insulation properties of glass.

Heating. The heating of buildings is a major user of energy (about 50 per cent of all energy in the UK) and contributes a corresponding proportion of CO_2 production. Designers have a key role in alleviating environmental problems, both local and global, by placing energy conservation near the top of design priorities. Simple measures can reap benefits for client, user and society at large. For example, maximizing passive solar gain can save significant amounts of fossil-fuel use (10–20 per cent is quite attainable without much effort). Primary energy sources should be selected on the basis of efficiency and environmental cleanliness. Clients should be persuaded not to overheat buildings and to provide users with the means to control their own environment. Heating systems should be designed for minimum losses, maximum efficiency, and operational flexibility.

Insulation. Well-insulated buildings conserve energy and are more comfortable. However, most insulation products are petroleum-based and some use CFCs or HCFCs in their manufacture. Man-made mineral fibres (such as glass fibre quilt insulation) are considered to be more 'green' but pose problems during installation with the inhalation of airborne fibres. Insulation products poorly specified can lead to Sick Building Syndrome (see Chapter 19) but generally the energy saving benefits outweigh the disadvantages of insulation. Where possible use natural insulating materials (such as cork) or those made from recycled waste paper (see Chapter 29: Findhorn).

Lead. Lead is a seriously cumulative poison and affects mental and physical performance. Health risks occur with inhalation, ingestion (mainly through lead water pipes) and from skin contact. Lead is more likely to be encountered in an existing building than specified in a new one. However, it is a useful material when properly specified and is frequently employed in conservation work.

Lighting. Artificial lighting is a major user of energy and adds to the incidental heating of many non-domestic buildings. Increasing evidence suggests that poorly specified lighting has adverse health effects for building users. Two guiding rules should be followed: maximize the use of natural light, and employ task lighting. Automatic switching has obvious benefits for energy conservation, as does the use of modern efficient fittings. Use high-frequency control gear to minimize health risks, and avoid deep plan buildings unless lit by atria.

Organic solvents. Many building products, from paints and adhesives to some laminates, contain organic solvents which are a health and environmental hazard in application, use and disposal. Whenever possible, designers should specify water-based, solvent-free materials, and maintenance staff should avoid solvent-based cleaning agents.

Paint. Many paints contain damaging environmental materials such as organic solvents, chromium, lead and cadmium compounds (the latter often ending as heavy metals in rivers). Although lead-free paints are readily available, they are often encountered in rehabilitation work where the removal of old lead paint poses health threats. Water-based paints are preferable. Synthetic resin paints can cause skin and respiratory difficulties. Good design can eliminate the use of paints to a degree, and many natural finishes are less harmful than painted finishes. The disposal of paints poses environmental problems.

Plasters. Plastering and rendering use non-renewable materials, involve energy-intensive manufacturing processes, and the extraction and transportation of their raw material has big environmental impact. Plastering and rendering is a durable finish, helps to keep walls dry (and hence perform better as insulators) and can be used with simple water-based coatings.

Plastics. The building industry is a large user of plastics (perhaps as much as 40 per cent of all plastics produced are used in construction). Plastics are a complex group of materials with high strength-to-weight ratios, good chemical and thermal resistance, and low toxicity. Plastics are generally produced from non-renewable materials (mainly oil products) though renewable sources are currently being developed. Plastics are difficult to dispose of except by land-fill site. In Germany attempts are being made to recycle plastic and in Denmark it is used as a fuel in a new breed of power station.

Preservatives. These are dangerous and highly toxic materials used to resist fungal or insect attack in softwoods. Good design and specification will normally eliminate the need for timber preservatives, either by using hardwoods (from sustainable sources) in vulnerable situations, or by ensuring the construction is dry and well ventilated. A difficult choice has sometimes to be made between softwood plus preservative and hardwood from non-renewable sources.

Radon. This naturally occurring gas causes lung cancer if inhaled at fairly high concentrations over a long period. Its geographic distribution means that people in buildings in Devon, Cornwall, Derbyshire and parts of Scotland are at greatest risk. Here the gas is sucked from the ground into the building via openings in floors or cracks in masonry. Good construction detailing, particularly thorough sealing and controlled ventilation, can reduce the problem. Standard details are available to help designers overcome the problem.

Steel. This commonly occurring material uses finite resources (iron ore and energy) in its production, often leading to air pollution and severe environmental impact. However, it has exceptional structural qualities, can readily be recycled or reused. There are health risks with welding in confined spaces. Unlike aluminium which requires four times more energy per unit of structural member to produce, steel in non-durable in moist conditions and requires regular painting.

Stone. The energy required to produce natural stone was generated in geological time and hence the only energy costs today are for quarrying, working the stone and transportation. Of these transportation is the largest component. Stone should therefore be used close to its point of supply. Quarrying activities have significant environmental impacts and the working of stone creates health risks from the siliceous dust. Stone is, however, a green material if used locally, it is highly durable, can be recycled, has high thermal capacity and creates employment for skilled craftspeople.

Structure and construction. Of the commonly used structural members, only timber is derived from renewable sources. Although most structural timber is kiln dried, it uses far less energy in manufacture than steel, concrete or aluminium. Modern methods of structural design have enhanced the potential of timber to span large distances and to be used in multi-storey construction. Timber is the only green structural material available, and has the benefit of taking up CO_2 in its growth cycle. Hardwoods such as oak and beech have added strength and durability and offer further advantages if cropped from renewable forests. Concrete has the advantage of having high thermal mass and hence gives passive solar benefits. Life-cycle analysis of energy and material costs, health and environmental problems is essential if the correct choice is to be made between timber, steel, concrete, brick or aluminium structures.

Sustainable design. This is a component of sustainable development (see Chapter 29) and entails the design of buildings which are *resourceful* in the use of energy, *robust* in use, *appropriate* in the choice of materials and services and *durable*. These four characteristics should ensure that the buildings of our generation add to the stock of man-made structures which later societies can use profitably, and which adapt readily to changing environmental needs.

Timber. The loss of tropical rainforests is one of the biggest environmental problems (see Rio Summit commitment: Chapter 29) of our age. The construction industry is a major user of tropical hardwoods, most of which come from non-renewable sources. The rainforests contain the main reservoirs of biodiversity and maintain the global balance of oxygen and carbon dioxide. Softwoods come from non-renewable sources (in Canada and USA) and renewable sources (Sweden, Russia, etc.). Only a small percentage of UK grown softwood is used in construction. Specify timber from sustainable forests (using a reliable tag system) and diversify the use of hardwoods to save vulnerable species (teak, etc.). Design with recycling of timber in mind.

Water. There are increasing economic and energy pressures to conserve water by better design and specification. Water conservation requires designers to question the demand for water, to reuse waste water and to collect rainwater.

Zinc. Although the manufacture of zinc entails high levels of energy use and is resource depleting, zinc

Figure 18.1
Timber construction using indigenous species is emerging as one of the more environmentally benign forms of construction. (White House Studio©.)

provides useful corrosion protection for steel when used in construction. There are problems of toxic waste which is produced in manufacture, possible adverse impacts on the environment and health, but generally these are not as severe as other metals.

CASE STUDY

Reducing environmental impacts: An education centre, Dyfed, Wales

The education centre at Castell Henllys in Dyfed is a simple 'green' building constructed of mainly locally obtained materials alongside an important Iron Age fort. Designed by Niall Phillips Architects, the building aims to:

- use timber from local ecologically managed woodlands;
- allow visitors to understand building structures and construction;
- sit well within its beautiful natural landscape;
- demonstrate 'green' principles of design;
- provide an environment which introduces the construction and atmosphere of the Iron Age.[2]

These general principles have been interpreted in a building which is set into a hillside with a shallow angle turf roof and central rooflight forming the most conspicuous elements. As such the visual impact is kept to a minimum and what one does see is a continuation of local grasslands onto a roof whose simple timber-framing alludes to the forest edge nearby. By keeping the materials as simple and natural as possible, the impression is one of a building which grows out of its site. Such environmental felicity also

---

[2] *The Architects' Journal* 6 July 1994, p 29.

allows the education centre to refer to the attitudes and craft skills of the reconstructed Iron Age dwellings a few yards away.

If visual impact is kept to a minimum so too are the ecological and environmental impacts. The timber used comes from woodland managed by the Pembrokeshire Coast National Park Authority and has not been treated with chemicals but left to breathe either externally or through well-ventilated internal spaces. By using oak rather than softwoods for the main structure, the timber was considered more durable in its natural state. Walls or partitions are formed either of cross-cut oak boards or lime plaster on wattle frames. The stonework of the building is constructed of local boulders gathered from a nearby hillside with joints left deliberately open to encourage the colonization by mosses, wild flowers and lichen. Such plants not only allow the new structure to be more readily absorbed into the local scene but improve the visitor centre's thermal performance and resistance to driving rain. A curving stone wall screens visitors' buses and runs from the car park to the building defining the path and forming the rear wall of the visitor centre. Capped with turf, the wall continues a local Pembrokeshire tradition and leads naturally to the main turf roof of the centre.

The turf roof, laid on a long curving monopitch, has been cut from local fields rich in wild flowers. Like the wall, the roof is part of the strategy of visual absorption into the local environment. The use of a local source for the turf ensures that nearby meadows and roof share the same habitat of plants and insects. To protect the timber below, the roof extends forward over a metre with stone walls forming a rampart at the building edge as a protection against driving rain.

Such an approach to structure and construction has required the employment of many local skills. The sense of craftsmanship and the quality of being hand-made gives the building a particular charm. Built at the relatively cheap cost of £114 per m^2 it demonstrates that 'green' building can be cost effective. It also employed a large number of people in an area where jobs outside towns are scarce. The social benefits supported by a grant from the government initiative, the West Wales Task Force, helped to lead to a valuable coalition of environmental and economic interests whose lessons could be applied in other remote rural areas.

Part 5
Environmental Health and Safety

19
Environmental health and pollution problems with buildings

Health and pollution are of growing concern to European legislators and, as buildings become more complex, the liability and responsibilities upon the shoulders of designers, and to some extent the constructors of buildings, also increase. Health and safety in buildings are matters covered in whole or part by EC Directives 76/579, 79/343, 79/640, 80/1107, 88/642, 83/477, 86/188 87/217, 91/382 and pollution is covered by various Directives including 80/779, 84/360, 85/203, 91/692 and Regulations 880/92 and 2157/92. The main areas where health and pollution risks occur are:

- in the construction process, especially when dangerous substances are handled;
- in the demolition process, including burning of waste materials;
- air quality risks for users of buildings;
- ground water pollution;
- ground gas pollution;
- construction work on contaminated land;
- dust and noise pollution associated with construction sites.

Although designers, promoters of building and construction managers have a growing basket of controls with which to contend, those covering health and pollution carry the most heavy penalties and expose building professionals to particularly high liability risks. Environmental management to reduce the risks is aided to some extent by EC and British Standard regulations, particularly the growing introduction of eco-audit procedures.

Information on hazardous substances varies in quality and usefulness, especially with secondary pollution problems such as contaminated sites disturbed by construction work where gases such as methane are released to the atmosphere and leachate flows contaminate groundwater. Environmental Impact Assessment should identify these potential hazards, but too often the development is too minor in scale to have come under the mandatory requirements of EA. It has only recently become apparent that certain building materials can have an impact upon the health of occupiers. The problems of asbestos are well known, but increasingly other products such as man-made mineral fibres and the dust and vapours of other substances are causing concern. These problems are not usually identified in EAs and they are not easily quantified in eco-labelling or BREEAM assessment schemes. The problem at present is that eco-labelling tends to be based on contestable value judgements about the relative significance of difficult-to-compare environmental impacts.[1]

In seeking to discover the health and pollution risks, designers and specifiers should seek comprehensive information from material manufacturers and suppliers. The risks and hazards need to be known by those who carry liability as professional advisors, contractors or building managers. Many materials used on site, though safe and stable in themselves, become less so when cut, drilled or altered in some way. Construction changes the local environment, and taken together collections of building projects modify the regional and, to a lesser extent, the international environment. As many occupiers of buildings also realize, construction affects the health and safety of users of structures. The outward impacts of a building span noise, air-borne pollution, water pollution, visual disturbance, community disruption, and the inward ones, health, safety and psychological problems such as stress.

The designer and specifier have the duty to ensure that material-related hazards are not introduced to the building or to the construction site. Risks should be identified at the design stage and appropriate action taken to minimize environmental damage. Successful risk reduction requires co-operation between the client, designer, specifier, material manufacturer, contractor and building manager. No single professional group has

---

[1] Barrie Evans, Rating environmental impact, *The Architects' Journal* 19 May 1993, p 46.

Figure 19.1
People spend 90 per cent of their time indoors, hence buildings have a big impact upon personal health. (Brian Edwards ©.)

sole responsibility: good environmental practice relies heavily upon a shared culture of risk reduction. Designing in a benign fashion to cut down on pollution, health and other environmental problems should be part of a union of interests across the building and development industries.

Pollution hazards and health problems occur in construction in a variety of ways:[2]

- when materials are installed or erected;
- when they are worked on site;
- as they decay or mature in use, including emissions to the atmosphere;
- when they are disposed of or recycled.

Generally speaking the hazards consist of dusts (from cement, gypsum, wood, etc.), fumes (from welding, cutting, fossil-fuel use, etc.), liquid and solid chemicals (paints, glues, coatings, resins, fungicides, etc.). Less tangible, though still important hazards, occur away from the building site, such as risks to health at manufacturing plants, in transportation, and to peoples and habitats on a global scale (as with rainforest destruction to create the products for the two million hardwood doors and window systems used in the UK annually).

The internal environment

Once the building is occupied the problems of health, pollution and hazard control do not cease to exist, in fact they continue throughout the life-span of the structure. The main hazards to avoid and possible action at this stage in the building's life are:[3]

---

[2]Derived from CIRIA Special Publication 94, p 83.

[3]This summary is derived from CIRIA Special Publication 94, pp 97–115.

- risk of Legionnaire's disease;
- avoidance of Sick Building Syndrome (SBS);
- ventilation to avoid gaseous pollutants, especially volatile organic compounds (VOCs);
- Radon control;
- control of microbial contamination;
- control of passive smoking;
- control of dust and fine fibres;
- psychological factors.

Legionnaires' disease

Legionnaires' disease is a form of pneumonia which is associated with water and which can be contracted within buildings by inhaling contaminated water spray (as part of the operation of evaporative cooling systems) or through shower sprays. In both cases the water has to have become contaminated with high concentrations of Legionellae bacteria which can occur in buildings if precautions are not taken. The young and elderly are particularly at risk and death at the rate of 1 in 10 can occur if the illness is not recognized and treated properly.[4]

It is important for the designer to avoid the conditions which lead to growth of Legionellae bacteria such as water stored in stagnant conditions between 30 and 40°C and allowed to become contaminated by organic sources. Air conditioning based upon the evaporative cooling system has been responsible for outbreaks in hospitals and office buildings. Recirculating water which becomes contaminated by contact with dust, insects, spores, etc. also poses a particular risk. Water poorly stored in hot water cylinders is another potential source of bacteriological contamination. 'Dead' lengths of pipe and the bottoms of cylinders are likely places to find concentrations of the bacteria.

With Legionnaires' disease both designers, specifiers and maintenance managers need to be vigilant. Disease prevention needs to be co-ordinated across professional boundaries. Extensive literature and guidelines are available to help prevent the disease[5] but as a general rule:

- avoid storing water between 30 and 40°C;
- maintain water temperature at outlets above 50°C;
- prevent external environmental contaminants reaching the water system, particularly with evaporative cooling systems;
- fit lids to cold water tanks (to keep out contamination and prevent algae growth);
- distance air intake for ventilation from extract from cooling towers;
- flush out water systems regularly;
- avoid pipe lengths with stagnant water;
- provide easy access for maintenance staff to water systems.

If reasonable precautions are not taken the designer, engineer or specifier may be open to litigation. Guidelines for disease prevention within buildings are becoming more comprehensive and elaborate. As health concerns rise, the internal environment needs to be designed and maintained with disease prevention in mind. As with growing concerns over particulate pollution, health and safety are issues taking a higher priority in the parameters which shape modern buildings.

---

[4]*Environmental Handbook for Building and Civil Engineering Projects: Designer Specification* CIRIA Special Publication 97, p 116.

[5]See for example *Minimising the risk of Legionnaires' Disease* Chartered Institute of Building Services Engineers, 1987, and *The Control of Legionellosis including Legionnaires' Disease* Health & Safety Executive, 1991.

20
Environmental health and building occupation

All of us occupy buildings of one kind or another for 90 per cent of our lives. The growing use of synthetic materials, solvents and mechanical systems of environmental control within buildings carry threats to health and personal well being. About a decade ago the term sick building syndrome (SBS) was coined to describe the condition where people became ill simply by occupying a particular building. The symptoms of SBS – headache, nausea, stress, sore throats, asthma attacks, etc. – can cause genuine distress in some, and mild discomfort in others.

SBS is generally seen as a problem caused by a combination of factors such as poor thermal, visual and aural comfort conditions, the presence of gaseous pollutants, microbiological contamination, dust and fibres, and tobacco smoke. SBS is exacerbated when occupants of buildings lack the ability to perceive natural conditions (daylight) and are unable to control their own internal environment conditions. Work related stress is both a symptom of SBS and a cause of some of its conditions. EC Directives 80/1107, 88/642, 89/391, 89/654, 90/270 and 91/382 extend the provisions of the Health and Safety at

Figure 20.1
Since we spend 90 per cent of our lives inside buildings of various kinds, they have a big impact upon our health. (Peter Foggo Associates ©.)

Work Act 1974 with regard to worker health rights or safeguards in buildings. Various HSE guidelines are also available (though not all carry statutory authority) and a number of papers published by the World Health Organization (WHO) set further standards of internal environmental quality.

Effective control of SBS requires a full appreciation of the toxicology of all materials, finishes and decorative veneers employed in building, furnishings and furniture. In addition, the quality of the internal environment may be affected by external pollutants finding their way inside, e.g. traffic fumes, radon, landfill gases. As much indoor air quality control is dependent upon using outside air for dilution and displacement of pollutants, the interior environmental quality relies upon clean exterior air. In some town centre sites the outside air may be more contaminated than that on the inside. Often SBS problems are dependent upon a combination of factors and the mixing of pollutants and low level toxicity from many sources. As psychological factors play their part, it has been observed that sealed air-conditioned buildings are more prone to complaints of SBS than buildings ventilated and lit by natural means.

As people spend the majority of their lives indoors the quality of the internal environment greatly affects their health. The emergence of deep planned, relatively small windowed office buildings and shops in the 1970s onwards coincided with a growth in health problems. As energy conservation has become more important, buildings have tended to become more highly sealed to control unwanted air filtration. With reduced ventilation rates, the low level toxicity inside becomes more critical to the well being of building occupants. The period 1970–94 also saw a big increase in synthetic carpeting, the use of adhesives, plywoods and particle boards which are known to give off gaseous pollutants. At the same time the growth in service industries led to greater use of office machines of various kinds which became another source of background pollution through dust and electromagnetic radiation.

These changes to the office environment have been paralleled in the home where wall-to-wall carpeting (usually incorporating man-made fibres), sealed window systems and the replacement of open fires by central heating, has led to concern over SBS in the domestic sector. This background provides the clues to how a healthier internal environment may be created. Generally SBS would be reduced if buildings were:

- constructed, finished and furnished using natural rather than man-made materials;
- lit and ventilated by natural means;
- managed so that the cleanliness of air-conditioning and mechanical ventilation systems are maintained;
- managed so that cleanliness of the interior is maintained (with particular regard to dust mites);

Figure 20.2
Indoor air quality is determined partly by external conditions. Planting and car restraint improve conditions indoors as well as outdoors. (Elder & Cannon©.)

- designed to give occupants control over their interior environment;
- located where external air quality is high;
- designed to avoid interior condensation.

Unfortunately for the designer and specifier, the rate at which pollution is given off by certain materials is not readily available. The lack of necessary judgemental data means that well-intentioned architects remain in the dark. The concentration of air-borne pollutants from inside buildings may be a hundred times that in the outside air but little is known of their precise origin (whether in paints, cleaning solvents, particle board, pesticide applications, halogens, etc.) and hence the task of designing SBS-free buildings is particularly difficult. Some pollutants are certainly the result of design decisions, others stem from the nature of maintenance or management contracts, and others are introduced by the occupants themselves.

The Construction Products Directive 89/106/EEC seeks to harmonize standards across Europe to ensure that building products do not give off toxic gases or are a source of particulate contamination or radiation. EC law tends to be stricter than UK legislation in the field of building health and safety. The Construction Products Directive is leading to pressure on manufacturers to produce emission data for their products via European Standards Committees.

Radon is a colourless, odourless pollutant which can pose a serious health risk within buildings. It is produced by the natural decay of uranium present in many soils and masonry products. Radon reaches the building through the ground and via the products from which it is made. There is a marked geographical concentration of buildings where radon is a particular problem. In granite areas

Environmental health and building occupation

(Derbyshire, parts of Devon, Aberdeenshire, etc.) radon levels are high, sometimes dangerously so especially in homes with poor ventilation, and particularly in the underfloor. As more evidence becomes available the scale of risk to health from radon pollution increases. It is now widely accepted that people exposed to radon stand a greater chance of contracting lung cancer, especially if they smoke. Radon can enter the building fabric relatively easily and stand undetected for long periods, thereby having lethal potential. Advice on those areas of the country most at risk, methods of construction to employ, and safe levels of exposure, can be obtained from the National Radiological Protection Board (NRPB) and the Department of the Environment.[1] Statutory regulations are administered through the HSE and the matter comes under EC Regulation 880/92 (R), and indirectly under Directives 80/836 and 84/467 which provide protection for the general public from ionizing radiation.

Microbial pollution caused by the presence of dust mites leads to asthma attacks in some people and allergic reaction in others. Dampness tends to lead to an increase in the population of dust mites and in the growth of moulds, which through the release of spores, can lead to hay fever attacks. It is thought that 10–15 per cent of the population are subject to such attacks. If other contaminants are present, such as gaseous pollution given off by particle board, such attacks are more severe and can lead to complicated secondary illnesses.

Indoor air quality is also affected by passive smoking. Tobacco smoke is a major source of particulate and gaseous contamination and passive smoking poses direct health risks through contracting lung cancer and secondary risks by increasing susceptibility to respiratory conditions caused by other sources of indoor pollution. The issue is of concern to designers since they have the task of providing buildings which can be effectively zoned into smoking and smoking-free areas, and provided with ventilation systems which keep contaminated air away from non-smokers. As with the mixing of other pollutants, the cocktail of contamination caused by building fabric gaseous leakage, dust, moulds and toxic smoke introduced by people themselves can lead to damaging combinations of inhaled material.

Display screens and the internal environment

To solve the problem of stress and eye strain associated with VDUs and other office machines, the EC introduced Directives 90/270 'Display Screen Equipment' and 89/654 'Workplace'. Both have been enacted into UK law by new Health and Safety regulations with effect from January 1996. The main principles of interest to designers are that:[2]

- room lighting shall ensue an appropriate contrast between the screen and the background environment;
- disturbing glare and reflections on the screen shall be prevented by co-ordinating workplace and workstation layout with particular regard to artificial light sources;
- workstations shall be designed so that sources of light such as windows, and brightly coloured fixtures cause no direct glare and, as far as possible, no reflections on the screen;
- windows shall be fitted with adjustable covering (blinds, curtains, etc.) to attenuate the daylight that falls on the workstation;
- the lighting at each workstation shall be individually controlled.

The Directives address the balance between general internal environmental standards and the specific standards at the workstation. In the process they put the control of the lighting environment more in the hands of the office worker by providing curtains and individual lamps. A Gallup report in 1990 'Productivity Loss in the Office' found that companies are losing 15 per cent of productivity every year due to light-induced stresses and illnesses.[3] This amounts to more that £2000 per employee per year, a sum more than adequate for the cost of adapting most working environments to the new standards.

There are dangers, however, in the Directives from an energy point of view. The need to fit blinds on every office window will lead to higher levels of artificial lighting in the core of the building. As lighting in offices is often the major source of heat, this will add to the pressure to mechanically ventilate the building (with increased energy costs). A naturally ventilated office with opening windows is to some extent undermined by having to pull blinds and curtains. Also the screening of daylight at windows will inevitably block views with the possibility of adverse psychological effects.

The Directives may deal with display screen eye stress but they could lead to stresses elsewhere. The design of the contemporary office is moving towards greater use of natural light and ventilation with more contact between the internal and external environments. The case studies in Chapters 10 and 11 show how the balances can be struck particularly with regard to the design of windows as a mediator between the inside and outside. The Directives seek in their way to make offices consist of less amorphous open space and have more individual workstations whose total environment can be controlled by the office worker. This laudable aim carries wide implications for energy use in the next generation of office buildings.

---

[1] See for instance *The Householders' Guide to Radon* Department of the Environment ENVI J0539 NE 1990.

[2] The list is derived from Carl Gardner, Rulings that do little to illuminate, *The Architects' Journal* 11 August 1994.

[3] *Ibid.*

21

Environmental health and safety on building sites

A number of directives, not specifically aimed at environmental protection have, all the same, environmental implications for the construction professions. The main directives are:

Health and Safety:	Directives 86/188/EEC, 89/391/EEC, 89/654/EEC, 89/655/EEC, 89/656/EEC, 90/270/EEC, 90/269/EEC, 91/382/EEC
Public Procurement:	Directives 89/440/EEC, 90/380/EEC, 90/531/EEC
Professional Services:	Directives 85/384/EEC, 90/658/EEC, 92/50/EEC
Construction Standards:	Directives 89/106/EEC, 93/5068/EEC

Health and environmental safety are key aspects of the single European Act. Although it includes only 7 per cent of the Community workforce, construction accounts for 30 per cent of the workplace fatalities.[1] Various directives are concerned with ensuring the harmonization of conditions of the working environment so that Europe can enjoy a common approach to safety and health at work. Such provisions encourage cross-border work and allow contractors to tender on an equal safety basis. To some extent the provisions duplicate the work of the UK Health and Safety Executive which is currently amending national legislation to embrace the provision of the various directives.[2] Since many of the risks encountered in the field of Health and Safety have their origins in poor environmental practice, they are included here.

Directive 89/391 EEC on the safety and health of workers at work (as against on construction sites) established the following practices:

- risks at work should be avoided;
- risks that cannot be avoided should be evaluated and combated at source;
- dangerous practices should be replaced by less dangerous ones;
- measures which protect groups of workers should be given priority over those which protect only individuals;
- first aid, fire precautions and emergency arrangements should be provided at work;
- consultation with workers' representatives should be undertaken;
- workers have the right to information and safety training.

Directive 89/654 introduced standards on structural stability at the workplace, emergency escape routes, levels of ventilation, toilets, rest rooms, lifts, escalators and loading bays. Directive 89/655/EEC places a duty upon employers to ensure equipment at work is safe and that risks of accidents or ill health are reduced through the control of emissions of gas, dust, liquid and other substances. Directive 89/656/EEC deals with the assessment of risks, training in the use of dangerous equipment at work, the provision of personal protective equipment, and what equipment is needed for specific risks. Directive 90/270/EEC has provisions on the design of display screen equipment, the entitlement of workers to eye tests and spectacles. Directive 90/269/EEC establishes the principle that manual lifting should be avoided in the workplace, or if unavoidable should be safe and healthy.

---

[1] N F Spencer Chapman and C Grandjean *The Construction Industry and the European Community* London, 1991, p 126.
[2] *Ibid.*

Health and safety on construction sites

The Temporary or Mobile Sites Directive (89/391/EEC) and the Construction Sites Directive (92/57/EEC) apply to the building site. They extend the scope of safety and health requirements at construction sites with the appointment of a project safety supervisor to ensure that health and safety concerns are incorporated at the project design stage. The Directives remain subject to further consultation with construction organizations and the Health and Safety Executive (HSE) which carries out certain parallel functions in the UK but crucial elements have been implemented.

The Directives place a duty upon architects to design buildings so that they can be constructed and maintained without risks to health and safety. The contractor will no longer be solely responsible for health and safety on the building site: both designers and clients are also liable. The 'planning supervisor', appointed before construction work begins, has the statutory duty to ensure risks are minimized.

Under the Directives and associated UK Construction Design and Management (CDM) regulations nearly all construction work is embraced, including excavation, demolition, drainage, refurbishment and more conventional building activity. Work to gas, electricity and telecommunications services is also included as long as such activity is related to structural alterations. Designers are broadly defined and include all those who specify materials or products and prepare building designs. The designer's task is to 'ensure, so far as reasonably practicable, that the design he or she prepares is such that ... persons at work ... will not be exposed to risks to their health or safety.'[3] Under the CDM regulations designers are also under an obligation to co-operate with planning supervisors.

The term 'planning supervisor' is somewhat misleading as it suggests some affinity with council officers dealing with planning permission under town and country planning acts. Within the framework of these CDM regulations the planning supervisor has to plan and co-ordinate health and safety precautions. Normally, the client will appoint a planning supervisor from within the professional design team. Architects are likely to be asked to take on this duty by clients for which they will no doubt be able to charge an additional fee. Under UK regulations the Health and Safety Executive will need to be notified of the name and address of the planning supervisor.

One of the inadvertent effects of the regulations may be to stifle innovation in the building industry. The risks of using new products or untried constructional systems will be too great for many planning supervisors to condone. Building high, or employing wide span structures, may also entail risks to the health and safety of construction workers which architects and clients may no longer feel to be appropriate. The legislation may have the effect of encouraging the re-employment of well-proven technologies and structural systems, rather than the use of more experimental constructional or servicing systems. Hence, one can predict a move to more conservative practices within the building industries as Europe feels the effects of the Directive.

The 'Health and Safety' plan is a document which under the regulations needs to accompany each project. It identifies residual hazards (environmental, health and

Table 21.1 Duties of the planning supervisor under the Temporary or Mobile Sites Directive 89/391/EEC and CDM regulations

- Prepare pre-tender 'Health and Safety Plan' and notify HSE of the project
- Assess health and safety implications of tenders submitted
- Advise client of health and safety profile of main contractor
- Develop 'Health and Safety Plan' with main contractor appointed
- Prepare 'Health and Safety File' for those with task of maintaining building

Table 21.2 Design implications of the Temporary or Mobile Sites Directive 89/391/EEC and CDM regulations

- Design to avoid foreseeable risks to health and safety
- Combat risks at source by better design and specification
- Provide general protection as well as measures targeted at specific problems
- Include adequate information in drawings and contract documents of risks to health and safety
- Co-operate with the appointed 'planning officer' and adopt a philosophy of environmental health and safety from masterplanning to detailed design
- Carry out risk assessment as part of design development, whether on a new construction project or rehabilitation scheme
- Since many risks to health and safety have their origin in poor environmental standards, design with benign environmental impact in mind

---

[3] *The Architects' Journal* 18 August 1993, p 24.

[4] Sylvester Bone and John Loring, How to be a planning supervisor, *The Architects' Journal* 13 July 1994, p 34.

safety) and includes precautions that should be taken during construction.[4] Although most hazards are meant to be designed out at an early stage, residual hazards are those lesser dangers which remain but which require to be notified to construction workers.

The various directives listed have potential impacts upon how buildings are designed, constructed or operated. The avoidance of dangerous substances in the workplace or on the construction site, the proposed reduction in manual handling, changes in the environmental conditions of factories and offices, etc. all have a profound effect upon workplace design. There are also wider implications with regard to environmental discharges or the reduction of workplace noise to surrounding neighbourhoods.

The directives seek not only to reduce problems but to introduce the assessment of risk where danger in unavoidable. For the building designer risk assessment applies at the design and construction stage, and when the workplace is in operation. Risks of damage to health can be overcome by relatively simple measures such as the provision of better levels of artificial or natural lighting, enhanced levels of ventilation, better control of dangerous emissions. The assumption that the health and safety of the worker or the environmental health of the neighbourhood can be sacrificed for economic advantage is finally outlawed by these directives.

The designer and engineer have an important role to play in introducing more health and safety-friendly workplaces. The duty of care extends from the designer to the factory or office owner down to the worker. Although each has a duty to reduce the potential risk to health and safety at work, the designer faces a greatly expanded portfolio of responsibilities under the Directive. These extend from conceptual design to the periodic upgrading of working environments to meet the new standards. Rather than bemoan the excessive bureaucracy stemming from Brussels, the EC design professional should take advantage of the extra work generated by such measures.

22

An overview of environmental safety and the architect

Dr Paul Yaneske

Environmental safety is used here to encompass not only those harmful effects which the built environment may have on people but also those effects of immediate, proven and serious hazard potential related to the process of building which people may have on the environment. It therefore encompasses both environmental and health and safety issues and requires an integrated approach.

Overview of environmental safety

Environmental legislation has undergone a steep change in volume and complexity over the past decade. It is also changing fast with, for example, the EC continuing to adopt a very large number of measures in addition to those already adopted under its environmental policy.[1] The increasing range and complexity of environmental legislation, coupled with different levels and agencies of policy making and future uncertainty, presents a considerable challenge to understanding.[2] It becomes all the more necessary to keep in mind some of the main concepts underlying this profusion in order to see the wood for the trees.

The EC arose out of the Treaty of Rome which contained no specific provisions for the introduction of environmental legislation so such legislation was introduced under the general provisions of the Treaty. This changed when the Single European Act 1986 came into force in 1987 amending the Treaty to provide specific powers to implement EC environmental policy (see Chapters 3 and 4). The objectives of EC environmental policy and the principles on which it is to be based are set out in Article 130r of the amended Treaty. The objectives are to:

- preserve, protect and improve the quality of the environment;
- contribute towards protecting human health;
- ensure a prudent and rational utilization of natural resources.

The principles can be summarized as:

- prevention is better than cure;
- environmental damage should be rectified at source;
- the polluter should pay.

Between 1973 and 1992, the EC successively adopted four Action Programmes on the Environment. A fifth has now been adopted on the theme of 'sustainable development' setting out the EC policy objectives until the end of the decade.[3] Specific environmental issues identified in the fifth Action Plan include climate change, air quality, nature protection, water protection, the urban environment, waste management and the management of health and safety. However, this Action Programme differs from the previous ones in recognizing that, in addition to legislative instruments from the EC and national bodies, several levels of society will have a role to play from the general public through professional institutes to private enterprises and public authorities.

With regard to national legislation, three concepts typically embodied within environmental legislation are as follows:

---

[1] *European Environmental Law Guide* Clifford Chance Publication, London, September 1992.
[2] J Garbutt *Environmental Law – A Practical Handbook* Chancery Law Publishing, London, 1992.

[3] *Towards Sustainability* OJC 138, Vol 36, 17 May 1993.

Pollution. Pollution refers to the release of certain substances into air, water or land. The aim of pollution control is to protect these environmental media.

Nuisance. Nuisance refers to an act or omission that affects the material comfort and quality of life of an individual, a group of people or the public generally.

Some specific nuisances have been included within statute law. Most have now been brought together under the Environmental Protection Act 1990.

Duty of care. As the term implies, the duty of care is about taking sufficient care not to cause injury to a neighbour. The Environmental Protection Act 1990 requires a person to take all such measures as are reasonable with regard to the circumstances although, in the case of waste, the duty of care has become a statutory duty for all parties concerned in the waste production, carriage and disposal chain.

It is interesting to note that the EC's environmental strategy as given in its fifth Environment Action Programme is broadening the extent of responsibility for the environment to placing a duty of care for the environment on us all.

The Construction Products Directive

As part of the progress to a common market within the EC, one aim of the Construction Products Directive (89/106/EEC) is to remove barriers to free trade within the EC by making it illegal to discriminate against construction products which are deemed fit for their intended use. Consequently, it is then necessary to define the nature of that fitness (See Chapter 6 for a full account).

The Directive is based on the idea that products will be fit for their intended use if they enable the construction works in which they are permanently incorporated to satisfy six essential requirements under the following headings:

1 Mechanical resistance and stability
2 Safety in case of fire
3 Hygiene, health and environment
4 Safety in use
5 Protection against noise
6 Energy economy and heat retention

The Directive has been implemented in the UK through the Construction Products Regulations 1991 (SI 1991/1620). The details of the essential requirements are set out in Schedule 2 of the Regulations. The interpretation of works to which the Regulations apply include both buildings and civil engineering works.

Each of the essential requirements will be covered by interpretative documents making the link between the requirements and the technical specifications. These will form the basis for the development of new European products standards by the European Committee for Standardisation.

Products or product control processes which satisfy the requirements of the Regulations may be issued with an EC certificate of conformity allowing the EC mark of conformity to be placed on or to accompany the products (e.g. packaging, documents). In relation to the EC mark of conformity, there are two points the designer should note. First, while the mark of conformity is intended to signify that the product must have free access to markets within the Member States, it does not signify that the product meets some general quality standard. Second, the mark signifies a product is fit for its intended purpose only insofar as the works in which it is employed is properly designed and built. Accordingly, 'specifiers must continue to consider whether the product used in the way they intend will satisfy and identify performance requirements'.[4]

Contaminated land

In the sense that there can hardly be a square metre of the planet that has not been contaminated by man's activities to some extent or other, the question of what constitutes officially contaminated land is a matter of degree. In general, contaminated land refers to land where certain substances are present in sufficient concentrations to cause harm to people, animals and plants and/or to building services and structures.

Some substances are particularly harmful. Schedule 6 of the Environmental Protection (Prescribed Process and Substances) Regulations 1991 (IS 1991/472) lists a number of substances whose release onto land is controlled.

Contamination is not simply a matter of site history, such as its previous industrial use, which is a particular issue in the UK. Nearly twice the area of land may be contaminated and in current use (such as housing) as compared to that which is derelict and brought, for instance, within the scope of the Derelict Land Act 1982.

A main emphasis in current environmental policy is on the restoration of contaminated land for reuse in connection with urban renewal and inner city regeneration. In addition, there are former waste disposal sites in rural and semi-rural locations to be redeveloped. Reuse of such land often owned by public agencies of one kind or another makes an important contribution to the protection of green areas.

Dealing with past contamination

Under section 143 of the Environmental Protection Act 1990, the Secretary of State is empowered to establish

---

[4]*Practice* Issue 76; Practice Department, Royal Institute of British Architects, June 1991.

regulations requiring local authorities to keep registers of contaminated land which will be open to public inspection. Proposals issued in August 1992 by the Department of the Environment were withdrawn in favour of a period of wide consultation with interested parties.[5,6]

This reflects the complexity of the problems raised in dealing with such contamination. Among the crucial questions to be resolved are:

- At what level of contamination should action be triggered?
- Who will bear the cost of clean-up?

With reference to the first question, contamination is not just a matter of risk to the people, building materials, animals or plants on site. Contaminants may spread, particularly through the movement of leachates and ground water, to pose a threat elsewhere.

In relation to the second question, it is likely that the two most commonly used methods of reclamation in the UK, namely either leaving the untreated toxic substances in place and capping them, or removing the contaminated material and dumping it elsewhere will become increasingly untenable in favour of methods of *in situ* treatment.[7] Pressure for such change will come both from the harmonization of environmental legislation within the EC and from tightening UK waste disposal legislation.

While there may be no legal obligation to provide information on such contamination in an initial planning application, the local authority may well refuse the application where significant contamination is suspected under the Town and Country Planning Act 1971, the Building Act 1984 and Building Regulations 1992 (SI 1991/2768). Where an element of doubt exists, it is sensible to try to volunteer sufficient information (as Sainsbury's does – see case study) to satisfy the planning authority.

The Confederation of British Industry has published guidelines on dealing with contaminated land which provide a general perspective of the problem.[8] More detailed guidance on the sale and transfer of contaminated land is available through the Construction and Research Information Association.[9]

---

[5]*Paying for our Past* A Consultation Paper from the Department of the Environment (England) and the Welsh Office, March 1994.
[6]*Contaminated Land Clean-up and Control* A Consultation Paper, Scottish Office Environment Department, March 1994.
[7]*Croner's Environmental Management* Section 3, Croner Publications Ltd, Kingston upon Thames, 1992/93.
[8]*Tackling Contamination: Guidelines for Business to deal with Contaminated Land* Confederation of British Industry, London, May 1994.
[9]*Guidance on the Sale and Transfer of Land which may be affected by Contamination* Construction Industry Research and Information Association, 1994.

Preventing future contamination

Contamination from processes which produce polluting emissions, effluents or waste are already coming under the control of legislation and are reasonably easy to foresee. However, there are other sources of pollution which may occur which are less immediately obvious but where the designer has a part to play.

A potentially important source is where contamination is washed into the drainage system to end up in natural waters. If there are to be storage tanks for and/or deliveries of fuel or chemicals on site, what happens in the case of spillages? If there are grounds and gardens, what happens to the leachates off these areas? Similarly, what happens to the fuel and heavy metal contamination from parking areas?

A large hospital (see later case study) is an example of where all these factors may be encountered. There may be storage tanks of oil for fuel and of bleach for laundry purposes. There may be areas of grounds and gardens. While the use of fertilizers and pesticides is an obvious source of potential contamination, the accumulation of organic matter acidified by acid rain, such as the fall of leaves from deciduous trees is a less obvious contaminant. There may be very large areas for parking with considerable lengths of access roadway within the site.

The provision of a water-tight container in the form of low level walled compartment around a tank is not a sure control for spillage. Breaches of a tank, through accident or vandalism, may well occur at a level high enough to allow fluid to flow above and over the containment. In fact, unless there is a regular programme of emptying rainwater from the containment, it will simply fill and allow any spillage to flow out and away. In addition to attempts to alleviate contamination at source, attention should be paid to ensuring relevant drainage systems contain interceptors to stop the outflow of contamination. With reference to drainage systems, it may well be the case that new buildings are connected to older drainage systems.

Hospital sites again provide such examples. Contamination may occur not only because of the poor condition of drains leading to contamination of land through uncontrolled leakage, but also because of unappreciated connectivities, e.g. between surface water drains and sewers. Appropriate knowledge of such drainage systems may prevent future damage to the environment and consequent liability.

Integrated pollution control and building materials

The specification and choice of building materials by an architect has environmental consequences. In particular, the industrial processes used in the production of these materials involves the risk of environmental pollution to a greater or lesser degree. Clearly, it is of concern to know which materials are associated with the highest risk.

A Framework Directive on Integrated Pollution Prevention and Control (IPPC) is under preparation (in 1994) by the European Commission. It will have the aim of achieving as high a level of protection as possible for the environment in general and human health in particular by minimizing emissions from certain installations. The IPPC Directive would gradually replace Directive 84/360 (Combating of Air Pollution from Industrial Plants).

A model is provided by the Environmental Protection Act 1990 which introduced into the UK a system of Integrated Pollution Control (IPC) for those industrial processes with most potential to inflict harm on the environment. IPC is enforced by Her Majesty's Inspectorate of Pollution (HMIP) or the regional equivalent.

Prescribed processes coming under IPC are set out in Part A of Schedule 1 of the Environmental Protection (Prescribed Processes and Substances) Regulations 1991 (SI 1991/472) as amended by the Environmental Protection (Prescribed Processes and Substances) (Amendment) Regulations of 1992 (1992/614), 1993 (SI 1993/1749 and SI 1993/2405) and 1994 (SI 1994/1271). The Part A listed processes have been identified within certain categories by HMIP, namely fuel and power, waste disposal industry, mineral industry, chemical industry, metal industry and other industry, e.g. timber treatment.

Prescribed processes coming under local authority air pollution control are set out in Part B of Schedule 2 of the Regulations. A simple summary of prescribed processes directly relevant to building materials is given below in Table 22.1.

It is immediately obvious from Table 22.1 that many common building materials are associated with industrial process having the most serious potential for environmental pollution. This raises the question of balance between utility and risk of environmental damage.

A situation in which the materials produced by these processes are effectively used once and thrown away to be replaced by further materials is weighted more towards risk than a situation where the materials and products are recovered for reuse. Given that many of the materials are potentially very durable, if reused, the disbenefits of their manufacture could be balanced by their longer useful lives (see Chapter 24).

In the spirit of 'duty of care' towards the environment, the architect has a responsibility to design buildings which reduce the worst aspects of pollution associated with their materials of construction. Such duties have been expanded by the Environment Act 1995.

Ozone layer depletion

Until the discovery of the 'hole' in the ozone layer and the principal role played by chlorofluorocarbons (CFCs) and halons in atmospheric ozone depletion, such chemicals were regarded as safe, non-toxic and as having useful properties. Because of the potentially devastating consequences to life in the event of increased ultraviolet light reaching the Earth's surface as a consequence of the destruction of the ozone layer, there has been international agreement between the major consumers and producers of CFCs to phase these substances out.

The Montreal Protocol, to which the UK was a signatory, came into force in 1989 and imposed a ban on CFCs and halons by the year 2000. Within the EC, the protocol was implemented through Regulation EEC/88/3322.

However, recognition of the growing urgency of the situation led to a tightening of controls at the first review meeting of the Protocol in 1990. The original EC Regulation was superseded by Regulation 91/594 and control was tightened even further at the Protocol meeting in 1992 in Copenhagen (Regulation EEC/92/3952). CFCs will now be phased out by January 1996 and halons by January 1994.

Table 22.1 Prescribed processes associated directly with building and construction

Industry	Process
Mineral	Cement
	Asbestos
	Fibre
	Glass
	Ceramic
Metal	Iron and Steel
	Non-ferrous
Other	Paper manufacturing
	Tar and Bitumen
	Timber treatment

Table 22.2 The main uses of CFCs in buildings

Material	Application
Polurethane/polyisocyanurate	Roofs
	Walls
	Floors
Expanded extruded polystyrene	Flat roofs
	Pitched roofs
	Terraces and balconies
	Wall linings and cavities
Phenolic	Building panels
	Dry linings

A significant proportion (at least half) of the use of CFCs and halons is associated with buildings. CFCs have found use as refrigerants in air-conditioning systems and as blowing agents for plastic foamed insulations. Halons have been used as fire extinguishing agents.

With respect to CFC blown insulation materials, their main building uses can be summarized as shown in Table 22.2.

Substitution of other materials is difficult in the cases of inverted flat roofing, applications below grounds, laminated panels and external insulation of existing buildings where a waterproof board of high vapour resistance is important. Some 60 per cent of the use of such materials is accounted for as an essential structural element in claddings.[10]

The search for a substitute for CFCs is underway but there are many questions to answer regarding performance in the various applications.[11] The architect can respond to this situation by designing out any need for air conditioning or by using alternative insulation materials wherever possible. The architect will also have a responsibility to gain an understanding of the implications of changes in performance, such as decreased durability, that may result from using alternative foaming agents.

Nuisance

While nuisance has a long history within civil law, some specific nuisances have been included within statute law. Most of the statutory nuisances have now been drawn together, with some amendment of definitions, under the Environmental Protection Act 1990.

Among the statutory nuisances listed in the Act in terms of being prejudicial to health or a nuisance are:

- the state of premises;
- the emission of smoke, fumes, gases or noise from premises;
- dust, steam, smell, or other effluvia arising on industrial, trade or business premises;
- any accumulation or deposit.

Equipment is a potent instrument of environmental policy. Careful purchasing, if it gives full weight to environmental considerations in the selection of products, can help improve environmental standards by reducing pollution and waste. It can also influence purchasers and suppliers in their pricing policies and products.[12]

Eco-labelling schemes such as that introduced into the UK under SI 1992/2383 in response to EC Regulation 92/880, and the eco-labelling of building materials and building products in particular, is of interest here. Unfortunately, the underlying issues of life-cycle assessment are complex and will take time to resolve.[13]

In the absence of such eco-labels, it falls to the purchaser of goods and services to interrogate individual suppliers about their environmental performance. Although there are a large number of questions that could be asked, the concern here is to limit the worst excesses of environmental impact and damage. In this context, the following questions are of generic significance to suppliers of both products and services including those related to buildings.

- Can the supplier provide evidence of compliance with policy and/or of environmental improvement?
- Is there any independent verification; can the supplier provide an environmental policy statement?
- Is there any independent verification of the environmental credentials of the product (e.g. eco-label) or organization (e.g. certificated under the CBI Business Environment Forum)?
- Does the supplier publicly report on environmental performance?
- Has the supplier or any of its directors, officers, employees or persons working on behalf of it been the subject of litigation under environmental legislation?
- In the case of environmental claims in any advertising by the supplier, do they conform to a recognized code of practice?[14]
- Does the supplier ask such questions of its own supply network?

Where the architect has a purchasing role or an influence on purchasing decisions, these or similar questions can be used to determine environmental priorities in procurement from competing sources. As a provider of services,

---

[10]S R Curwell, R C Fox and C G March *Use of CFCs in Buildings* Friends of the Earth, London, December 1988.
[11] S Halliday *Building Services and Environmental Issues – The Background; Interim Report* The Building Services Research and Information Association, Bracknell, April 1992; *CFCs in Buildings* BRE Digest 358; Building Research Establishment, Watford, October 1992.

[12]*Environmental Action Guide: For Building and Purchasing Managers* Department of the Environment, HMSO, London, 1991.
[13]C J Atkinson and R N Butlin *Ecolabelling of Building Materials and Building Products* BRE Information Paper IP 11/93, Building Research Establishment, Watford, May 1993; *The LCA Sourcebook: A European Business Guide to Life-Cycle Assessment* Sustainability Ltd, London, 1993.
[14]*Environmental Claims in Advertising: A Single Guide to all the Applicable Advertising Codes* The Incorporated Society of British Advertisers Ltd, London, January 1992.

An overview of environmental safety and the architect

Figure 22.1
Hospitals have larger environmental impacts than most building types. Designing for environmental health and safety are increasing concerns of architects and engineers. (Sir Basil Spence & Partners©.)

the architect will not be exempt from such questioning from clients. The complexity of the environmental problem is encouraging many client bodies to come together in self-help groups to effectively generate environmental codes of practice.

The formation of the Estates Environment Forum for the NHS in Scotland and Northern Ireland is one example with direct significance to buildings in the healthcare sector.[15] Supported by individual Trusts and Health Boards, the mission of the Forum is to generate a Greencode (crown copyright) which will include environmental codes of practice for the whole life cycle of healthcare buildings. Increasingly, the architect and engineer will be working within the framework of such codes.

CASE STUDY

Environment Forum for the National Health Service in Scotland and Northern Ireland – the Greencode initiative

In March 1993, by open invitation, a meeting of interested estate professionals from within the NHS in Scotland took place to discuss how to respond to the issuing of the document 'A strategic guide to environment policy for General Managers and Chief Executives'. Key recommendations from the meeting were that a common approach should be taken to enable both purchasers and providers of healthcare to take a consistent line and that some form of award scheme should be put in place to focus attention on environmental issues.

These ideas were developed by the author in a report to the second meeting in June 1993 where it was decided to proceed to set up a formal 'Estates Environment Forum'. Subsequent meetings in July and August agreed the 'bottom-up' principle that the Forum would be owned by the membership, which would be restricted to subscribing members of the NHS and prepared the way for an official launch. During this preparatory period, the Northern Ireland Management Executive joined the 'shadow' Forum and six working subgroups were set up to begin work and build up momentum prior to the launch.

The inaugural meeting of the Estates Environment Forum for the NHS in Scotland and Northern Ireland took place on 5 November 1993. The Articles of Association of the Forum state that:

> The Aim of the Environment Forum for the NHS Estate is to create a cost effective means to provide guidance which would enable Trusts and Directly Managed Units etc, to meet their own and the government's strategic claims by introducing pro-environmental regimes within their organisations.

Working together, members of the Forum would assist one another and an Executive Team, attached to the Forum to establish the best practice and explore new initiatives in the field of Environmental Management.

The Forum will also administer an accreditation award system or rating system, issued by the Forum to Hospitals achieving high environmental standards.

The aim of the Forum is to provide a unified response to the environmental agenda which is not only affordable but also credible. It is based on collaborative effort, common guidelines and methods of performance appraisal and a recognition of the need to involve people at all levels if environmental initiatives are to succeed.

A majority of Health Boards, NHS Trusts and Directly Managed Units in Scotland and the Northern Ireland Management Executive have already invested funds and staff time in the work of the Forum. The aim is to develop a 'Greencode' of environmental performance with an associated award scheme. The business plan agreed by the Forum set priorities on certain outcomes as follows:

- A protocol for the production of Environmental Policy Statements to an appropriate standard acceptable to the Management Executive.
- A training course to introduce Forum members to the concepts in environmental management and to assist

---

[15] P P Yaneske The Estates Environment Forum for the NHS in Scotland and Northern Ireland *Health Estate Journal* Vol 48, No 6, July 1994.

them in the preparation or completion of credible Environmental Policy Statements.
- A review of best current technical practice leading to specific operational guidance.
- Initial guidance documentation on the creation of a register of significant environmental effects.

The Forum largely achieved these outcomes by the end of March 1994. An additional outcome under development is the production of awareness material centred around a concept video for which sponsorship is being sought. Sponsorship is also being sought for other areas of work.

The Articles of Association require the Forum to meet in full session a minimum of three times per year in order to review and direct the work of its subgroups and, in the democratic spirit of its formation, to vote on matters relevant to the achievement objectives.

The engine of the Forum is the work of the subgroups of which there are currently six: Energy, Waste, Pollution, Natural Resources, Procurement and External Relations. The latter subgroup reflects the recognition that the environment requires a broad perspective encompassing both technical and social issues. The Forum is, therefore, in sympathy with the direction of the current EC Fifth Environment Programme and with the recent Mason Report.[16]

Whilst EC Regulation EEC/1836/93 and BS 7750 on Environmental Management Systems is seen as an informative framework, the Forum is taking a measured approach to the implementation of environmental management. This is reflected in the conceptual structure of the award scheme which allows for a phased implementation going no further than needed to address the needs of individual Trusts.

The business plan programme for the year to 31 March 1995 anticipates further progress on a number of fronts including:

- The carrying out of a number of subgroup related pilot studies to generate guidance and criteria for the award scheme.
- The creation of guidance material and procedures supporting the award scheme.
- The development of databases to support environmental management including developing the environmental component of the SAFECODE database.
- The production of awareness materials for use by Forum members within their own organizations.
- Further training opportunities for members (which are already linked to university certification for professional development and higher degree purposes).

Although the Forum members are clearly concerned to have practical and affordable outcomes to their efforts, they do share a vision – a kind of environmental holy grail. This has become known as Greencode, which is a system of regulation and assessment based on co-operating and collaborating organizations. The essential requirements of such a system can be set out as follows:

- An environment award scheme that rates performance against set criteria and encourages improvement.
- A register of significant environmental effects (based on a common language approach to prioritization).
- Environmental performance measures and indicators.
- Informative databases.
- Audit systems for monitoring both individual Trust/DMU performance and overall NHS in Scotland/Northern Ireland performance.
- A mechanism for producing an annual report for the NHS in Scotland/Northern Ireland setting out environmental policy, performance standards, objectives and targets.
- Supporting software.
- Training support.
- Appropriate guidance on how to improve environmental performance.
- An environmental incident reporting system.

The content of Greencode can therefore be defined in terms of supporting the above requirements. It is intended that the award scheme will form an integral part of the future Environmental Management System (under EEC/1836/93).

The Forum builds on the strengths of professionals from within the NHS and higher education who share a common concern for the environment. As such, it seeks to pool constructively environmental knowledge at a time of decentralization of information and control, and to achieve environmental improvement in a practical and affordable way.

Acknowledgement

The author is indebted to the Executive Team of the Estates Environment Forum of the NHS in Scotland and Northern Ireland for their support and kind permission to publish this article. It is abridged from 'The Estates Environment Forum for the NHS in Scotland and Northern Ireland' by Dr Paul Yaneske published in *Health Estate Journal* July 1994, pp 10–11.

---

[16]*The UK Environment Foresight Project* HMSO, 1993.

Part 6
Recycling

23

Waste management and recycling

The EC through Directives 75/442/EEC and 91/156/EEC is keen to encourage reuse or recycling of materials which would otherwise be thrown away, and to recover energy from the waste which cannot readily be recycled. Broadly speaking recycling:

- conserves natural resources;
- saves energy in production and transport (by reusing a product rather than making a new one);
- reduces the risk of pollution;
- reduces the demand for landfill sites;
- enables goods to be produced more cheaply by embodying recycled material or by using energy from waste.

A successful recycling scheme must ensure that the energy and resources saved are greater than those needed to make a fresh product. The costs and benefits of recycling vary from one material or component to another. Certain industries such as paper and textiles have a tradition of recycling, others do not. Government action at EC, national and local level seeks to encourage the supply of recycled materials and create the demand for them.

If consumers are to recycle more effectively, they need to have space in the home to store the different rubbish containers to allow them to separate out paper, glass, cans, plastic and compost. Designers need not only to design with recycling of products in mind, but to create a convenient mechanism in the home or office which allows waste to be treated as a potential resource. Some building products such as bricks can readily be reused (as long as soft mortar is specified), others less so. Designing for reuse requires a new holistic way of seeing the building process. It also requires manufacturers to take a broader environmental view of their responsibilities. An example is a Yorkshire based brick manufacturer which extracts methane gas from the landfill sites it leases to the local authority for the disposal of household waste. These sites, initially created to extract the clay for brick making, then provide about 50 per cent of the energy to fire the bricks. Instead of seeing brick making in isolation, this brick manufacturer comprehends brick making as a flow of environmental and energy impacts, and benefits from the knowledge.

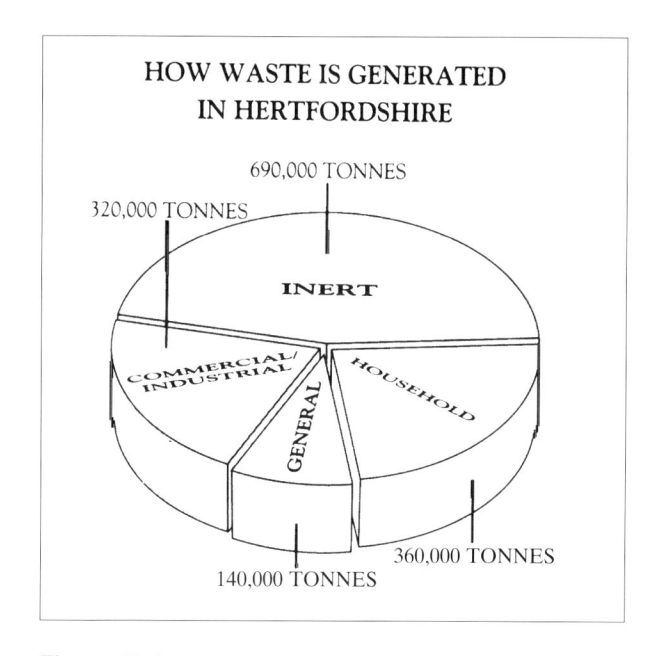

Figure 23.1
The volume of waste generated per year in Hertfordshire. Waste is a resource which offers many secondary uses – heat, materials, chemicals. (Hertfordshire County Council©.)

Waste management is also a matter of public health. Under the Environment Protection Act 1990 a duty of care is placed upon everyone (excluding householders) who handles waste (including at the building site) to ensure it is disposed of legally and does not cause pollution or harm to health. This Act, in response to EC Directives 75/442 and 91/156 and Recommendation 81/972, introduced several new measures to encourage recycling. Every local authority in the UK is now required to have a 'Recycling Plan' and can enforce the use of

Waste management and recycling

special recycling containers if they want to collect recyclable waste from householders. They can also insist upon better standards of skips and other measures to minimize environmental pollution and maximize recycling opportunities.

The tightening or extension of UK legislation has often been in response to EC laws. It took nearly ten years for the EC Recommendation on Recycling (81/972) to be embodied in British national law. The same was true of safeguards on the disposal of hazardous wastes, PCBs and the international trade in waste, all areas where the UK was behind sensibilities in Europe.

Recycling measures and waste management in the construction industry

The EC Directive 75/442 and Recommendation 81/972 encourages Member States to introduce recycling measures largely in order to conserve the world's diminishing supply of resources. Recycling, however, is not only a matter of resource conservation: it is also a question of good waste management which could well save money by allowing a construction company to maximize the hidden potential within waste products. Such hidden potential released by recycling may entail aggregate production, the extraction of metals, the re-burning of waste for energy (as in cement manufacture), and the rescue of components or products such as panel doors, windows and bricks.

Besides fossil-fuel energy, the primary mineral and natural resources employed in the UK construction industry are stone, sand, gravel, clay and timber. The main environmental impacts are in extraction (habitat loss, agricultural land take, landscape damage, methane release), in transportation (noise, dust, carbon dioxide emissions, air pollution) and in construction (energy use, noise, community disturbance). The production of a bag of cement highlights the problem. First, land is lost for the extraction of clay and chalk, large amounts of energy are used in the burning of materials to make cement (enough fossil-fuel energy to drive a family car for 80 miles), further energy is consumed and pollution created in transportation, and finally more energy is used in concrete making equipment on the building site. This cycle of landscape impact, energy use in manufacture and transportation is typical of building products from plasterboard to roofing tiles. Although the environmental impact of timber products is less acute, there are significant costs here too, especially with the application of timber preservatives, paints and solvents.

Measuring environmental impact is a complex business. There may be environmental benefits as well as losses, as with timber production and also mineral extraction where wildlife habitats are created around former gravel or clay pits. As a general rule, however, environmental impacts

Figure 23.2
Recycling the components of buildings has little tradition in UK. Here a dovecote has been built on waste land by pigeon fanciers using discarded building materials. (Brian Edwards©.)

should be kept to a minimum and to allow this to happen the construction industry is encouraged by EC directives to adopt recycling measures.

Recycled products reduce the demands made for new materials and components. The main construction materials capable of being recycled are:

- aggregates produced from crushed concrete;
- structural members such as steel girders, timber beams and joists;
- small components such as bricks, roofing tiles, slates and concrete blocks;
- decorative elements such as sash windows, panelled doors, window shutters, architraves, etc.

Figure 23.3
Recycling buildings is as important as recycling bottles, plastics and glass. The environmental costs of existing building have already largely been paid. These warehouses by the Thames in London have been converted to offices and apartments. (Brian Edwards©.)

Recycling has three main benefits: it reduces the demand upon new resources, it cuts down on transport and production energy costs, and it uses waste which would otherwise be lost to landfill sites. Construction generates about 40 million tonnes of carbon dioxide and lesser quantities of acid gas and nitrous oxide.[1] Recycling, though it will not prevent these adverse environmental impacts, will at least reduce them. At the end of a structure's life, large quantities of waste material are produced, adding to the 24 million tonnes of construction waste per year. Although the UK construction industry recycles about 11 million tonnes of this, it is thought there is the potential for 70 per cent of all construction waste to be recycled.[2] A major impediment to recycling is the lack of foresight shown by designers in anticipating the reuse of structural members such as steel beams and smaller components such as bricks. Another impediment is the lack of facilities for recycling, especially for more dangerous construction substances. Recently, however ICI, ISC/Rhône Poulenc and Du Pont have offered a free recycling service for CFCs, and a few local authorities recycle CFC refrigerants. Those involved in specifying such materials could use clauses which facilitate easy dismantling and hence encourage recycling.

As discussed earlier in this book, eco-labelling has the potential to identify recycling possibilities. Once the ecological and environmental costs of a component or even a whole building have been identified, consumers and the professionals they employ will be encouraged to consider recycled materials when new construction is in hand, and how to reuse elements of a building when refur-

---

[1] *Environmental Issues in Construction* CIRIA Special Publications No 94, 1993, p 55.
[2] *Ibid.*

Figure 23.4
Engineering structures such as this Winter Garden in Glasgow pose particular difficulties in finding acceptable new uses. It was demolished in 1990. (Glasgow City Council©.)

bishment or demolition are under consideration. The current lack of legislation to demand eco-labelling in the building industry has the effect of failing to bring energy costs, environmental costs and ecological impacts to public notice.

Other countries are more keen to recycle their construction waste than in the UK. This is party because countries such as Holland and Germany do not have Britain's aggregate or energy resources, and because of greater public awareness of the environmental benefits of recycling. In Germany plastics are readily recovered for reuse or reburnt in power stations for electricity production. Glass, steel, bricks and structural timber are also collected in Germany often through recycling schemes promoted by regional councils. In Britain, bricks are beginning to appear as a recycled material often in conjunction with house building where the patina of second-hand bricks has a particular appearance. It is thought that 2 per cent of brick consumption in the UK consists of recycled bricks, making a total of 75–100 million bricks per year from recovered sources.[3]

Recycled buildings

The benefits of recycling building materials apply equally well to the reuse of whole structures. The conservation of buildings not only saves resources and energy, but ensures

---

[3]*Ibid.*, p 65.

Figure 23.5
Conserving buildings creates many useful jobs and helps promote heritage-led tourism, one of Europe's fastest growing economic sectors. (Brian Edwards©.)

that the infrastructure of our towns continues to be used. Existing buildings tend to be located in central areas where public transport links are strong, and the network of social, health and educational facilities exist. To retain such buildings maintains the physical, social, aesthetic and energy resources of towns.

Demolition should only be a last resort. It has frequently in the past been the first decision made by the developer or the architect. Whilst many older buildings are poorly insulated and suffer from inefficient heating systems, it is generally more cost effective, and certainly more resource conscious, to recycle than demolish and bear the heavy construction and energy costs of rebuilding. The process of constructing buildings consumes about 4 1/2 per cent of Britain's total energy consumption and contributes to a wide range of other adverse environmental impacts.

Where recycling is possible, adaptation and refurbishment should be undertaken with environmental considerations in mind. The high thermal mass of many existing buildings should encourage the use of passive solar principles, and the shallow floor plans and relative lack of height of older structures means that movement through the building, lighting and ventilation can all be achieved by non-mechanical means. Whilst existing buildings are often aesthetically pleasing, they also offer cheaper floor space than new buildings, thereby maintaining the social and economic mix of urban areas. They often provide exemplars of energy-efficient design since many were constructed when energy and building materials were relatively expensive. The vernacular tradition of many older buildings embodies 'green' principles of value today such as centrally placed hearths, orientation which takes advantage of solar gain by placing living or public rooms on the southern aspect, and large sheltering roofs often providing living or storage accommodation within the roof space.

Demolition in the UK is not controlled under planning law except in conservation areas and with listed buildings. Though planning consent is needed to undertake development, it is not required for demolition. This anomaly allows many structurally fine and socially useful buildings to be demolished every year in spite of the obvious benefits. If energy and environmental costs were considered part of town planning responsibilities then more existing buildings would be recycled.

The need to consider the recycling of buildings as a whole places a new responsibility upon the shoulders of those who design them. Certain building types are more conducive to reuse than others. Those with simple forms, well constructed, and flexible in use have greater robustness in terms of the demands likely to be made by future generations. The adage 'long life, low energy, loose fit' applies equally well today as it did when it was coined over twenty years ago.

CASE STUDIES

Eye Power Station, Suffolk

Eye Power Station in Suffolk is Britain's first electricity generating station powered by poultry litter. Built in 1993 by the Danish energy company Aalborg Ciserv International for Fibrepower, the local business established to run the plant, it has a capacity of 12.5 MW – sufficient to supply 12 500 homes. The power station burns 125 000 tonnes of poultry litter per year, which is about half of Suffolk's annual poultry litter waste.[4]

---

[4]*Architecture Today* 31, p 49.

Waste management and recycling

The benefit of the power station is twofold. First, it saves on fossil-fuel consumption thereby reducing emissions of CO_2 which add to acid rain problems and second it reduces pollution which results from high concentrations of poultry manure. The greenhouse gas methane is released into the air by poultry waste and nitrates are released into local water courses. Fibrepower claim that the plant will produce a saving of 70 per cent in greenhouse gas emissions compared to a coal-fired power station.[5] A further benefit is the production for sale of nitrate-free fertilizer which is a by-product of the generation of electricity at the plant.

The power station was designed by architects Lifschutz Davidson Design with energy consultants Foster Wheeler Energy. The design is compact yet elegant and with its high level of landscaping is intended to be an exemplar project for the 'green' community-based power station of the future. Built on a disused airfield with a few other business units nearby, the Eye Power Station was jointly funded by the UK Department of Energy and the EC under the Jourle programme. As a demonstration project the design of the power station puts particular emphasis upon reducing visual impact. The bulk of the plant is broken up into separate units, each expressed in a different profile of cladding, and structural elements are exploited (rather than hidden) to break up the planes of wall and roof. Square and curved sections are also employed and a simple geometry unites each part. To reduce the visual impact further a high grass bank surrounds the site with dense planting of deciduous trees on its outer slope. Attention to detail has helped reduce the apparent scale of the building – an important consideration if such power stations are to be built in residential areas. A single stack deals with the emission of waste air and gases.

Recycling of waste, demolition of IBM laboratories

IBM has a general recycling policy which seeks to reuse or recycle about 50 per cent of the non-hazardous waste produced by the company.[6] When in 1993 the company decided to demolish an office block in the heart of an estate of computer laboratories at Hursley near Winchester, it decided to demolish the 1960s building subject to the following criteria:

- as many building materials as possible to be recycled;
- demolition to be safe for site users and those occupying adjoining buildings;

---

[5] *Ibid.*
[6] Barrie Evans, Demolishing an office block safely, *The Architects' Journal* 28 July 1993 p 33.

Figure 23.6
Demolition of IBM offices at Hursley was undertaken with the objective of recycling as much construction waste as possible. (IBM©.)

- noise levels to be kept as low as possible;
- damage to adjoining buildings to be avoided.

The emphasis upon recycling, though part of IBM philosophy, resulted in a demolition contract where 90–95 per cent of materials were recycled, either in whole or as a usable waste. This was achieved in a contract only two weeks longer than a conventional demolition contract. Demolition was let as a separate contract to the construction of a new conference centre which the company planned on this and an adjoining site.

The demolition contract was let on the basis of dismantling the eight storey office block floor by floor, rather than demolishing the building in conventional fashion using the basement to catch falling rubble, glass and concrete. Not only was dismantling more friendly environmentally (with the opportunity of salvaging many of the building components) it allowed IBM to carry on operations in adjacent buildings.

The contractors who tendered for the demolition contract were aware of IBM's policy on recycling through discussions with Buro Happold, the consulting structural engineer. The selected contractor Griffiths McGee used skips at the site to segregate demolished material so that the different building elements and components could be recycled. The contractor had first to produce a statement for IBM indicating where the recycled materials were to go to ensure that recycling was not a hollow gesture. Daily records were kept of the movement off site of skips and some were followed to ensure that fly-tipping was not taking place.[7]

Of the materials recycled only sanitary ware, doors, carpets and blinds were directly reused, the remainder was rendered down to more basic material. Glass, a major component in the building was recycled to a plant in West Yorkshire, concrete was transported to be crushed to hardcore, steel was melted down and CFCs recycled by ICI. Dismantling the office block floor by floor allowed conventional skips to be used for storage, each being transported by an externally mounted crane to waiting lorries. Materials which could not readily be reused, such as plasterboard, were taken by skip to approved landfill sites.

IBM monitored proceedings from beginning to end, seeing this demolition contract as highlighting green needs for the future. It is one thing to have a company policy on recycling, quite another to apply it to the difficult and dangerous task of demolishing eight storey office blocks. The documentation of the contract held by IBM records the history of the destination of the materials.

Under the contract Griffiths McGee was able to sell the waste materials, thereby reducing their costs. Unfortunately, some recycling plants (such as Berrymans Cullet Glass Recycling Plant in Yorkshire) were some distance from the site adding to the contractor's costs and upsetting the energy equation of the whole operation. The value of the waste was often less than the cost of energy to transport it. Had there been more local recycling plants the environmental benefits would have been considerably greater.

Recycling allows the embodied energy in building materials (which account for 8 per cent of UK CO_2 production) to be reused. However, demolition by disassembly is not always as simple as with the 1960s office block at Hursley. The trend today is to use laminated components and composites where the materials cannot easily be separated into predictable elements. Modern synthetic materials and some jointing (such as glueing and welding) make disconnecting building components difficult and expensive. In Europe only 5 per cent of building materials are recycled though it is said the potential exists to increase this to 75 per cent.[8] Designing and specifying for reuse is essential if this figure is to be reached.

---

[7]*Ibid.* p 35.

[8]*The Architects' Journal* 22 June 1994, p 26.

24

Contaminated land use

The EC Directives (75/442/EEC and 92/43/EEC) which encourage recycling and the use of brown field rather than green field site development carry implicit, if inadvertent, risks to health and safety. Many brown field sites are contaminated with often hazardous pollutants (see Chapter 22) and buildings which are to be reused may contain dangerous substances in their fabric such as asbestos. The designer, engineer and specifier will need to pay particular regard to the health and environmental safety implications both in the demolition, construction and occupation stages of building works.

The first problem is to identify the risk, its extent, and the implications. This is not always straightforward: a site may be contaminated by a fractured oil storage tank. Whereas pollution should have been restricted to one area, in reality the contamination may have spread with the help of underground water courses to much of the site. Land with high sulphate levels may not be harmful to humans but is likely to restrict how and where concrete is employed. Risks may also occur from outside the site either by water- or air-borne pollution. If the risks are not properly investigated, a great deal of money may be

Figure 24.1
The reuse of brown field sites is more environmentally sound than the development of green field land.

wasted on inappropriate design or selecting the wrong part of the site for development.

Demolition or building work can release hazardous substances to the atmosphere or water courses affecting the health of site operators and those living or working in the vicinity. Hazards can occur also as a consequence of the materials once stored in the building or in the manufacturing processes once carried out. Dust disturbed by construction work on existing buildings or whilst under demolition can be damaging to health. Buildings and sites once used in the chemical or textile industries pose particular threats, as do former landfill sites of which it is estimated that 1000 in England and Wales require treatment.[1]

As more brown field sites are redeveloped and more existing buildings, recycled, the nature and scale of the threats to health, safety, the durability of construction materials and wider pollution control need to be understood. It is one thing to quantify the complex environmental impacts of the design of a new building where the properties of materials and their risks can be predicted in advance, quite the contrary with buildings already in existence or preused sites where the nature of the construction and extent of pollution is more poorly understood. In this case the designer needs to ask:

- How was the building constructed and are there any specific hazards present (e.g. asbestos, heavy metals)?
- How was the building or the site used and does this pose further threats (e.g. radiation)?
- How can the building be dismantled or refurbished safely or the site redeveloped, bearing in mind the hazardous substances present?
- Do any pollutants on the site or nearby pose particular risks to health or safety, or threaten constructional processes?

One of the problems often encountered is that the quickest and cheapest form of demolition or redevelopment of contaminated sites is often the most dangerous. Health and safety are frequently sacrificed by the need to keep costs down and to speed up the development process. Sometimes underground stores of highly hazardous substances are discovered during site works and it is often tempting to dispose of it illegally or to compromise the health of site workers in improper handling. Sometimes leakage into the soil or water courses poses problems, other times discharges can be into the fabric of the structure itself. When industrial processes have taken place on the site, the materials stored may have changed their molecular structure or become mixed with other substances thereby enhancing their toxicity.

Much training in the UK construction industry does not prepare designers, contractors or site operators for the problems which may be encountered in dealing with existing buildings or brown field sites. To counter this the Building Research Establishment (BRE) introduced a new service in 1994 to provide advice on contaminated land, and to test the effectiveness of companies offering remedial systems for treating heavily polluted land. Health and safety expertise may also exist in local authorities, and the help of public services and utility companies (such as water authorities and the fire brigade) may well prove beneficial. An architect's liability is likely to be increased if expert advice was not sought when a hazard was discovered. Under EC law it is the polluter who pays and liability may end up at the door of the building professional or contractor who sanctioned work which subsequently proved to be damaging, even if the source of the pollution or hazard was not of the architect or builder's making.

A great deal of research and survey work is often needed to discover the nature of the problem. Old maps may relay information on the former uses made of the site and earlier building plans may provide details of the materials employed in the fabric of the structure. When a brown field site or building is purchased, the new owner becomes responsible for any pollution it may contain. Acquisition audits[2] have been introduced into the property industry as a means of providing information to potential purchasers. The survey may discover that the site had earlier been used for landfill purposes. If so, designers need to realize that the rate of decomposition and the production of gases is partly determined by site characteristics – a wet site will have a fast rate of methane production, and a dry site a slower rate of emission of both methane and carbon dioxide.

With EC directives and wider urban policy seeking to encourage brown field site use rather than green field, attention will be increasingly focused upon inner city land. Under Section 143 of the UK Environmental Protection Act (1990) local authorities were required to keep a register of contaminated land partly to help developers faced with acquisition audits. Unfortunately, in 1993 the registers were temporarily abandoned whilst a review of their effectiveness was undertaken (see Chapter 22). There is little sense in a multitude of surveys being undertaken on the same parcel of land when a central register could satisfy most needs. At present, however, the UK Government shows little enthusiasm for entrusting the wider task of environmental auditing to planning authorities and in 1995 is establishing an Environmental Agency to rationalize the current multiple inspectorate approach. It would seem sensible to have some kind of public co-ordination of land potential and pollution particularly if

---

[1] *BRE News* December 1994.

[2] CIRIA Special Publication No 94, 1993, p 80.

Table 24.1 Site types and likely contamination

Site types	Possible pollutants or contaminants
Alkali and paintworks, dyeworks, fertilizer plants and chemical works	Acids, alkalis, metals, solvents, phenols, benzene
Oil or tar refineries, fuel storage areas	Hydrocarbons, phenols, alkalis, acids, asbestos
Iron and steel works, electroplating, shipbuilding, engineering plants, scrap yards	Various metals including zinc, copper, lead, etc. and asbestos
Power stations and gas works	Coal dust, phenols, cyanides, sulphur compounds, asbestos, radiation
Railway depots, docklands	Combustible substances, metals, asbestos
Mines, pits and filled sites	Metals, leachates, methane
Old housing areas	Metals, asbestos, micro-organisms

the information was tied to the opportunities offered by the site as expressed in local planning documents.

In the UK certain companies such as the retailer Sainsbury and construction company AMEC have accumulated particular expertise in developing contaminated sites. The skills and techniques they have employed in the past decade have allowed both companies to utilize sites other developers have avoided. Their exploitation of brown field urban land has often provided well-located sites at less cost than comparable land further afield, even allowing for remedial work to combat pollution.

Impact of construction upon environment

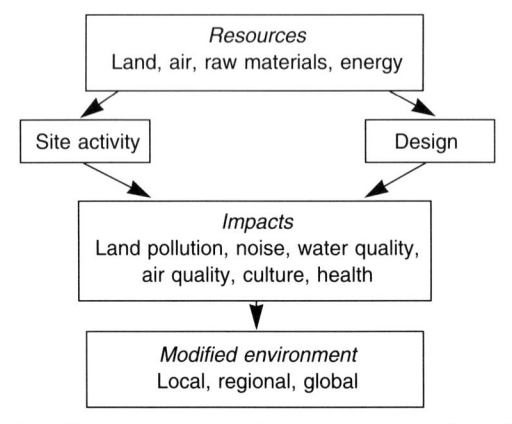

Resources
Land, air, raw materials, energy
↓
Site activity — Design
↓
Impacts
Land pollution, noise, water quality, air quality, culture, health
↓
Modified environment
Local, regional, global

Pre-demolition surveys and acquisition audits allow environmental conditions to be predicted prior to construction work. Unfortunately, the full nature of the problems sometimes unfolds as construction or demolition work is in progress. Occasionally also, environmental disruption leads to conflicts with local communities especially over questions of noise and dust. The site works on former docklands at Canary Wharf were subject to time limits, imposed after surrounding communities effectively lobbied the London Docklands Development Corporation (LDDC) over disturbance caused both on and off site. For many communities affected by operations on brown field land, the Environmental Protection Act gives certain safeguards. The 'duty of care' provisions under the Act place a responsibility on those who handle waste to deal with it properly. Designers and specifiers need to ensure that the Act's provisions are built into contract specifications.

Contaminated sites can often be dealt with effectively by a combination of biological, chemical, physical solidification and thermal processes.[3] Though the techniques are relatively new and some remain untested over a long period, they are of increasing benefit to the developer of brown field sites. The former practice of simply removing the contaminated soil is no longer accepted since it merely transfers the problem to others. Simply stated current remedial processes consist of:

- *Biological restoration* – the removal of contamination by enhancing the activities of soil micro-organisms, employing soil-based water recirculating systems, or by using trees, shrubs or grasses which absorb the pollutants and can be cut down or mown and removed to other sites.
- *Chemical restoration* – the use of soil slurry treatment to enhance oxidation and dehalogenation.
- *Physical restoration* – direct soil treatment by washing, vapour extraction or electro-reclamation. The approach consists of removing the contaminants or bringing them to the surface of the soil where they can be collected and treated off site. PCBs and heavy metals can be removed by such means but the contaminated water used in soil washing requires careful treatment to avoid reaching water courses.

---

[3] *Ibid.*, p 83.

Contaminated land use

Figure 24.2
Before (a), during (b) and after (c) clearing industrial derelict land in Kirklees, Yorkshire. Landscape design is used in combination with ecological principles to create a small urban fringe park. (Helen Stuffins, Kirklees Metropolitan Council©.)

- *Solidification restoration* – thermal or chemical based systems which trap contaminants in soil heated to a point where it vitrifies. Organic pollutants and metals are effectively dealt with by this method which is particularly applicable to sandy soils.
- *Thermal restoration* – a simple, if crude, method of removing contamination by burning. The method is used to deal with soil-based oil pollution or to dispose of dangerous vapours. Often the pollution is dispersed to the atmosphere by such means, thereby transferring the problem off site where it can cause damage or inconvenience to others.
- *Containment* – physical barriers which contain contamination into one part of the site, allowing other areas to be built upon. The method, commonly used in the past at places like Stockley Park, is dependent upon the durability and performance of the containing materials employed.

The recycling of buildings and of land conserves the resources of the world but is fraught with difficulties. Designers, engineers and those who procure buildings have to acquire new skills in building and land restoration to satisfy society's needs. The EC directives and UK initiatives mentioned earlier place fresh responsibilities upon the shoulders not only of architects but those who control development such as planning and building control officers. The whole concept of recycling taken at its simplest level implies a shift of awareness of the nature of materials from that which is new to that which already exists. This awareness applies to the resource of land as well as the fabric of buildings. New skills and ethical stances are required to fulfil these new duties; skills which are currently in short supply in an industry which traditionally occupied new sites in preference to existing ones and which specified products from manufacturers' catalogues with greater enthusiasm than it sought to

Contaminated land use

Figure 24.3
This Sainsbury Superstore was on a site of a former quarry used for landfill. It reuses contaminated urban land effectively by a combination of methane venting and breaking down pollutants by natural means. (Allan Forbes for Reiach & Hall Architects©.)

exploit the potential of building materials already in existence. To help appreciate the environmental cost of building, some kind of construction audit needs to be introduced at a scale below that of a full Environmental Assessment. Such audits if applied to both existing and new buildings could provide a comparative framework between the benefit of recycling an older structure or constructing a new one.

CASE STUDY

The use of contaminated land: the example of Sainsbury

Over half of the new supermarkets built by Sainsbury in the past five years have been constructed on derelict or run-down urban sites. The company deliberately searches out and develops sites, often on heavily contaminated land, which other developers avoid. It prides itself upon supporting green belt policy by setting an example of how to use brown field sites effectively. In the process it has developed expertise in the effective treatment of sites previously used for landfill or heavy industry. For example, the new Sainsbury store built at Craigleith in Edinburgh is on the location of a quarry which had provided much of the building stone for the city in the nineteenth century and had since been used as a landfill site. According to Sainsbury's *Environment Policy Statement* brown field sites afford better access for those using public transport, and provide a stronger case for the supermarkets to be regarded 'by the community as a valuable asset in both retailing and environmental terms'.[4]

---

[4]*Sainsbury's Environment Policy*, October 1993, London.

Figure 24.4
Redeveloping brown field sites requires a broader range of environmental expertise than in building on green field sites. (J. Sainsbury plc©.)

The targeting by Sainsbury of brown field sites for development has created a market in environmental services of one kind or another. Discovering what pollutants exist, how to deal with them, how to build on such land healthily, and what to plant has encouraged the consultants appointed to build up a body of expertise which society at large can benefit from. Other developers have begun to follow Sainsbury's lead, finding run-down urban sites generally cheaper to acquire than scarce green belt land, and on the whole better located in terms of transport and servicing infrastructure.

In parallel to this policy, the company attaches particular importance to the landscaping of its supermarkets by a mixture of tree planting in solid belts, hedges and specimen trees. The objective is to provide shelter, scale and biological richness on land which was once degraded. To some extent planting is used to deal with low level pollutants in the soil by the leaching effect, to improve air quality, reduce levels of noise, and help with the engineering of surface water run-off. The dual policy of derelict site selection and a green approach to remedial treatment of polluted land gives credence to Sainsbury's claim to be a company committed to sound environmental practice.

In parallel with these policies, the company in 1993 banned the use of CFCs and tropical hardwoods in its buildings. Sainsbury also sponsored the UK's Building Research Establishment (BRE) 'green label' scheme for the environmental assessment of commercial buildings. Introduced in 1993, the 'green label' is awarded once minimum standards on CO_2 emissions, CFCs in building materials and air-conditioning plant, air quality, and the use of hazardous materials have been met.

Specifically, Sainsbury's Environment Policy adopted in October 1993 is to:

- Quantify and monitor all environmental impacts – including new projects – of the business. Set specific targets, and seek continuous improvement.
- Influence suppliers of services and own brand goods to reduce their impact on the environment.
- Comply with the current legislation and, where practical, seek to meet future legislation ahead of relevant deadlines.
- Integrate environment considerations and objectives into relevant business decisions in a cost efficient manner.
- Ensure all employees address their environmental

responsibilities within the framework of their normal operating procedures.
- Enhance awareness of relevant issues amongst customers, staff and other stakeholders.
- Publish information on environmental performance.

In practical terms this means that line managers in the company have responsibility for:

- Use of energy, particularly from non-renewable resources.
- Minimization of use of resources.
- Avoidance of generation of waste.
- Management, reuse and recycling of waste.
- Avoidance of environmentally damaging materials.
- The development of alternatives to ozone depletants and the replacement of CFCs and HCFCs within Sainsbury.
- Encouragement of recycling through the use of recycled materials.
- Minimization of the impact of Sainsbury's products on the environment through improvements in design, manufacture, distribution, use and disposal.
- Promotion of an understanding of environment issues relevant to Sainsbury among staff, suppliers and customers.

Given these environmental duties and priorities any architect or engineer engaged by the company needs to be conversant with current environmental knowledge and equipped with relevant skills. What Sainsbury is doing in the mid 1990s could well be commonplace by the end of the decade, at least for major UK retail companies.

Targeting brown field sites for new store development is therefore only one aspect of Sainsbury's increasing focus upon 'environment friendly' operations. It is, however, a more conspicuous manifestation of green responsibility than less visible measures such as the use of recycled heat from refrigeration plants for warming stores. There have been market benefits in becoming greener more quickly than competitors – financial rewards which the company is using to replace (and recycle) CFCs by HCFC22 in its cold stores. Putting aside the transport pollution and energy costs of supermarkets, Sainsbury has demonstrated that there are opportunities for environmental action which major retailers can take.

Part 7
Ecology

25

The EC eco-labelling scheme

The European eco-labelling proposals embodied in Directive 94/2/EEC are as yet poorly understood and unevenly introduced by Member States. Eco-labelling of products varies considerably between different industries and progress via the Eco-labelling Boards of separate Member States (the competent bodies under EC Regulation EEC/880/92) has been patchy. The principle of eco-labelling, to give consumers advice on the environmental effects of the products they buy, is fraught with difficulties. Products affect the environment at all stages in their life-cycle from raw material extraction, to manufacture, use and disposal. The extent of environmental impacts depends upon the nature of the materials employed, how, where and when they are obtained, what combinations are used in manufacture, how energy is used, how the product is transported, the use to which it is put, how it is disposed of, and whether it can be recycled in whole or part. The eco-labelling scheme is meant to present all the environmental information in a systematic way and provide a basis for grading the efficacy of products, and to allow consumers to choose between one product and another. It is, however, a voluntary scheme and hence of limited value at present, though plans exist to phase in different sectors and products over time. A parallel scheme on eco-management (Regulation 1836/93/EEC) provides for the formulation and use of environmental management systems, linked in the UK to BS 7750.

The EC's terms of reference for its eco-label scheme show the shift in policy making from environmental protection to ensuring products are clean and have largely benign effects. The Council resolution states:

> Whereas the objectives and principles of the Community's environment policy, as set out in the European Community's action programme on the environment aim, in particular, at preventing, reducing and as far as possible eliminating pollution, as a priority at source, and ensuring sound management of raw materials resources, on the basis also of the 'polluter pays' principle; whereas the Fourth European Community action programme on the environment (1987 to 1992) highlights the importance of developing a policy towards clean products.[1]

Figure 25.1
Eco-label logo for use on approved products.

The concept of an agreed measure of cradle to grave assessment of the main products in use in the EC has a utopian air. Yet architects need to know what the full environmental costs are of products such as a brick or bag of cement. Moreover objects which are regularly replaced in the home, such as light bulbs, carry huge environmental consequences which consumer groups have long been pressing should be made available at the point of sale. The

---

[1] Community Eco-label Award Scheme OJ (EC) 1.99/1 1992.

163

The EC eco-labelling scheme

Figure 25.2
Being amongst the largest structures which mankind produces, buildings have huge ecological impacts in the manufacture of materials, the construction process, and in use. (LDDC©.)

UK Eco-labelling Board (set up in November 1992) has spent much of its time to date in developing assessment criteria for product groups. Its terms of reference under Article 1 of the Regulation are to:

- promote the design, production and marketing of products which have a reduced environmental impact during their entire life-cycle;
- provide consumers with better information on the environmental impacts of products.

Architects, specifiers and engineers have a particular interest in the first objective, yet to date (1995) few construction products carry the EC eco-label logo (Figure 25.1). The priority of the UK Board is to develop eco-labelling standards for construction products in the field of insulation, paints, varnishes and ceramic tiles[2] since these are the materials most likely to be bought by consumers off the DIY supermarket shelf. Anybody familiar with buildings will quickly realize that, although important, this list does not embrace the more significant impacts construction products have upon the environment. What it does, however, is to concentrate upon products whose impacts can be readily measured thereby allowing the labelling scheme to make some progress in the building field. The product list also contains materials where more eco-

---

[2] *Eco-labelling of building materials and building products* BRE Information Paper 1P 11/93, May 1993.

The EC eco-labelling scheme

Table 25.1 Building products in non EC eco-labelling schemes

Scheme	Building product category
Blue Angel (Germany)	Materials made from waste paper
	Materials made from recycled glass
	Materials made from recycled gypsum
	Low-pollutant varnishes
	Asbestos-free floor coverings
	Paints low in lead and chromates
	Low-formaldehyde wooden products
Environmental Choice (Canada)	Insulation from recycled wood-based cellulose
	Heat recovery ventilators
	Products from recycled plastic
	Water-based paints
Ecomark (Japan)	Thermal insulation
	Cement containing 50% blastfurnace slag

Source: BRE Information Paper 1P 11/93

Figure 25.3
Eco-labelling directives will encourage the use of more natural materials, and a proper assessment of life-cycle impacts. Here the timber, tiles and glass could all be recycled at the end of the building's life. (Brian Edwards©.)

friendly substances are currently available or under development (e.g. lead-free paints) and the effect of the scheme is seen as accelerating the move toward environmentally benign building products. For all its faults, the EC eco-labelling scheme carries the potential of making architects, contractors and consumers more discriminating in their choice of materials or products.

Outside the EC framework, Germany, Canada and Japan have introduced an eco-labelling scheme covering certain building products (see Table 25.1).

Eco-labelling is a complex subject. The assessment of impacts depends upon the parameters adopted, the assumptions made, the state of knowledge and the timescale of damage. Two phases of impact can be identified, the short-term description of effects and the long-term, more interpretative, analysis of environmental consequences. The experience of chlorofluorocarbons (CFCs) is a warning that products considered environmentally benign today may be shown to be environmentally harmful tomorrow.[3]

The eco-labelling of building materials and products requires the use of studies such as life-cycle analysis, impact assessments, energy modelling and environmental auditing to reach a full measure of the ecological impacts. The use of all four, in varying combinations, provides the Eco-labelling Board with a reliable methodology for arriving at assessment judgements. However, as the BRE points out 'none of these study methods is comprehensive'[4] and neither do they help much in studying building products in use. Most consumers and also architects are less concerned with the brick than with how the building as a whole impacts upon the environment. Here it is the interactions which are important, not the individual building components themselves.

As a broad guide the ecological impact of buildings can be divided into:

• *Raw materials production* – the land needs, energy consumption, transport costs and renewable or non-

[3]*Ibid.*

[4]*Ibid.*

Figure 25.4
Houses of the Arts and Crafts period employ locally-made, generally ecologically benign materials. (Brian Edwards©.)

renewable sources of supply (as in timber as against steel) are important factors.
- *Manufacture* – the energy costs (as in cement), waste produced, community disturbance, pollution, etc. are considered important, but some building products are made from waste produced in other industries and hence there are recycling benefits.
- *Design and construction* – reducing energy needs through good design, the employment of natural means of lighting and ventilation, the use of the 'stack effect' to avoid air conditioning, the use of craft-based labour as against machine production at the building site, good packaging to avoid waste at the construction site, are all considerations.
- *Building use* – the employment of energy management systems, high levels of insulation, janitorial training to save energy and waste, good maintenance programmes to preserve components and improve durability, measures to limit damage by vandals, are all part of the impact judgement.
- *Demolition* – the recycling or reuse of materials and components, the letting of demolition contracts subject to recycling clauses, the health risks in dust from demolition, the careful design of new to reuse

rather than demolish existing buildings on site, are important factors.

The complexity of buildings means that separate components rather than the whole are embraced by the EC eco-labelling scheme. Life-cycle studies of building materials is only just emerging as a legitimate activity and still has some way to go to develop a consistent approach across products. In time models may emerge which will help designers produce buildings which are environmentally benign. As with washing machines, the eco-labelling scheme is arguably better at grading the ecological impacts of different types of hoses or wash powders, rather than dealing with washing machines or the washing process as a whole. However, recently the UK Eco-labelling Board has extended the scheme to washing machines using the criteria of energy use, water consumption and detergent use as the main measures of impact. Assuming an average life of twelve years for the machine, these impacts are of greater ecological importance than the making and disposal of the machine itself. Unfortunately, the same cannot be said of buildings where the impact of construction tends to be more significant as a percentage of energy or water consumption.

26
Biodiversity

In June 1992 the UK Government signed the Convention on Biodiversity at the Rio Summit. The Convention obliged each government to 'develop national strategies, plans or programmes for the conservation and sustainable use of biological diversity'.[1] In parallel EC Directive 92/43/EEC on the Conservation of Natural Habitats and the EC's Fifth Environmental Action Programme of 1994 sets the strategic framework for the Community's environmental policy till the year 2000. Both the Rio agreement, the Directive and the EC Fifth Programme commit the UK to more wide-ranging environmental responsibilities than at any time in the past.

It is generally accepted that biodiversity has interests at three levels:

- diversity between and within ecosystems and habitats;
- diversity of species;
- genetic variation within individual species.

To balance development with these responsibilities the UK Government has adopted six underlying principles, three of which are of particular interest:

- where biological resources are used, such use should be sustainable;
- wise use should be ensured for non-renewable resources (such as fossil fuels);
- the conservation of biodiversity requires the care and involvement of individuals and communities.[2]

Although there are practical and scientific reasons why governments are now committed to maintaining biodiversity, the moral and aesthetic benefits should not be overlooked. Beauty and visual diversity are qualities architects seek in the built environment; biodiversity is a way of ensuring that these are also to be found in the natural environment. Since towns are increasingly seen as part of the wider eco-system they have a part to play in meeting these responsibilities. Hence decisions made by architects and engineers can complement those made by ecologists and landscape architects. The culture of a nation – whether British or European – resides in both the built and rural environment. The landscapes and cities of Europe enrich our lives and provide part of the moral justification for the recognition of the importance of biodiversity.

Biodiversity spans national interests: the concept does not recognize state or regional boundaries. Consequently, Britain's role is to contribute to the conservation of natural richness within Europe as a whole. As the world's biodiversity declines (perhaps as much as by 150 species losses per year), action is necessary across national and international boundaries. Many bird species, including those endangered, migrate, passing through regions where laws and cultures of protection are more lax. Britain is host to many internationally important species, and provides habitats for large wintering populations of wildfowl and waders who use the UK's estuaries. Similarly, the migration of most of Europe's surviving storks passes through Greece where conservation laws are particularly relaxed. Action is therefore needed on a European scale (hence the Birds Directive 79/409) to prevent both economic and spiritual loss. The decisions, for instance, to utilize the tidal power of the Severn Estuary was taken before the EC had introduced its wildlife directives. Had they been in place the planning consent would more likely not have been granted without a challenge to the European Court.

As the EC adopts different directives to meet international agreements (including those made at the Rio Summit) UK legislation is forced to adapt. The statutory bedrock of the Wildlife and Countryside Act 1981 has had to expand its provisions (not always with great enthusiasm, since UK ministers have tended to argue that the Act already meets EC laws) to meet European perceptions. Planning Policy Guidance Note number 9 'Nature Conservation' helps interpret EC directives and relate them to UK laws. The new levels of protection afforded by Europe are related to provisions in the 1981 Act (not always satisfactorily) and the Directive's (92/43/EEC)

---

[1] *Biodiversity: The UK Action Plan* HMSO, 1994, p 2.
[2] *Ibid.*, p 3.

re-examination of unimplemented planning permission explained. The 6000 Sites of Special Scientific Interest (SSSIs) in the UK which cover almost 2000 million hectares remain the main protective basis for the conservation of the UK's wildlife.

The EU's Common Agricultural Policy (CAP) has expanded the opportunities for encouraging the management of agricultural land in ways which are more sensitive to maintaining wildlife habitats. In both upland and lowland areas of Britain, such measures are having an increasing impact upon the visual character of the landscape. The Countryside Commission's National Forest Initiative aims to create a forest of 200 square miles in the heart of England near Leicester, and a parallel scheme of community forests is planned to bring benefits to those who live on the urban fringes of other cities. Such measures promise to impinge upon the development of land more widely than in the past where a commitment to set land aside for urban forestry is often a condition of planning consent. The new interest in biomass sources of energy parallels these measures by encouraging the planting of quick growing timber crops (willow, alder, birch). Collectively these activities promise to bring greater biodiversity to the rural and urban scene. Future energy needs, the relaxation of CAP, and international agreements on biodiversity, hold the prospect of a richer and more diversified landscape created by a new order of professionals.

Biodiversity and development

European environment legislation is increasingly concerned with the need to maintain biodiversity: the diversity of living things – habitats, species and genes. Without biodiversity the future of crop production and the development of new medicines will be jeopardized, and the quality of life greatly reduced. The loss of biodiversity which has characterized the twentieth century means a reduction in the planet's ability to adapt to changing conditions. Although biodiversity encompasses a broad spectrum of biological interest, for the construction industry the main issues are:

- the use of hardwood timbers from renewable sources to help protect the rainforests;
- ensuring that building products and servicing systems do not damage the climate or ozone layer indirectly, thereby altering the global balance of nature;
- maintaining habitat richness at the level of the development site;
- providing the opportunity for the colonization of the building and landscape by suitable wildlife species;
- protecting wildlife when encountered in buildings or their grounds (e.g. badgers, bats, owls).

Biodiversity is both a question of human survival and of the richness and quality of life. The growing human population of about 100 million extra mouths to feed a year requires reservoirs of ecological diversity to provide the species and genetic complexity necessary to sustain human populations. The trend has been to rely upon fewer species for our food supply and less diversity in our landscapes. This trend is inherently dangerous and today the human race relies upon about 30 plant species for 95 per cent of its food needs.[3] Architects and designers, though not central to questions of biological diversity, still have a role to play particularly where the activities impinge upon the rainforests (in Britain in 1992 two million hardwood doors were imported, most based upon tropical hardwoods from non-renewable sources). Habitat richness is also a question of amenity. Here decisions about how to build, the relationship between the building and its landscape, and whether the building structure can also encourage colonization by relatively scarce species such as bats and owls, have an impact upon biological diversity. Some notable architects in the past such as Edwin Lutyens created owl boxes in the gables of their houses, and in other cultures wildlife is encouraged into the structure of buildings as a decorative or practical benefit.

European legislation recognizes the importance of biodiversity. Directive 92/43/EEC on the Conservation of Natural Habitats and of Wild Fauna and Flora talks of the 'preservation, protection and improvement of the quality of the environment, including the conservation of natural habitats' as an essential objective of the Community.[4] The provisions are to 'promote the maintenance of biodiversity ... through the encouragement of certain human activities' such as the restoration of 'natural habitats' and 'support for priority species'.[5] It is in the support for endangered species that architects, engineers and developers could play a part. Proactive environment action, such as the erection of bat boxes on buildings, could help deliver the wider biodiversity objective of the Directive. In areas of Europe where certain species of bat are endangered or where owls which characteristically nest in buildings are in decline (such as barn owls in England) action by the owners and designers of buildings could have significant impact upon population levels. In other situations the provision of wildlife areas in the grounds of buildings could help maintain rare species of plants or help support pockets of ecological richness.

It is important to maintain the diversity and abundance of plant life even if it is not required immediately for human needs. Only 12 000 of the 220 000 differing flower-

---

[3] *The Guardian* 22 February 1994, p 16.
[4] Council Directive 92/94/EEC. OJ no L.206/7.
[5] *Ibid.*

Figure 26.1
Industrial firms such as British Gas can set an example not only by conserving but also by creating wildlife habitats on its land. (British Gas©.)

ing plants which grow on the planet are used for human needs, and of these only 150 are grown commercially. Of the 150, however, three species (wheat, rice and maize) provide 60 per cent of our global food requirements.[6] The need to maintain these supplies in a disease free state and to have sufficient genetic variety for unknown future demands is clearly of great importance. The pockets of wild grasses left at the edge of a business park, or the wildlife ponds created, help maintain this diversity. It is also important for designers to realize that untidy corners may be beneficial and that fungus infested trees, and hollow branches are just the conditions many of Europe's scarce species of bird, bat and insect require. Pockets of wildlife diversity, particularly if extended into ecological corridors, provide the means of sustaining Europe's richness of species without jeopardizing the need to accommodate economic growth.

Biodiversity and building design: encouraging wildlife colonization of buildings

As we have seen the concept of biodiversity has emerged as one of the guiding principles of the ecological movement. For architects biodiversity tends to be discussed within the

---

[6] *The Guardian* 22 February 1994, p 16.

Table 26.1 Species of bird and bat to attract onto buildings

Species	Breeding need	Habitat and area of country	Wider benefits
Peregrine falcon	High level ledge on face of building	Urban areas, coastal areas	Pigeon, gull and starling control: amenity species
Kestrel	Ledge or shallow box on face of building	Most areas	Rodent control, small bird control: amenity species
Barn owl	Box or opening in wall	Rural areas	Rodent control: declining UK numbers and amenity species
Swift	Holes and crevices in buildings, entered usually underneath	Villages and towns	Amenity species?
Swallow	On ledges or rafters in roofs and sheds	Rural areas, villages	Amenity species
House martin	On wall under eaves	Rural areas, villages	Amenity species?
Pied wagtail	Holes in walls, ledges (uses nest boxes)	Rural areas, villages, town parks	Amenity species
Black redstart	Holes in walls, ledges	Urban areas, derelict sites, railway yards. Mostly SE England	Rare breeding bird colonizing Britain
Spotted flycatcher	Holes in walls, ledges (uses nest boxes)	Rural areas, parkland	Amenity species: insect control in gardens
Long-eared bat	Roof space of older houses	Villages, rural areas, mostly near woodland	Declining species
Pipistrelle bat	Confined spaces in cavity walls and behind tiles (uses bat boxes)	Rural areas, often near water	Easiest bat to attract to buildings
Daubenton's bat	Under roofs of open barns, bridges	Rural areas, often near water	Declining species
Natterer's bat	Under bridges and other large structures	Town and rural areas, near deciduous trees	Declining species
Whiskered bat	Cracks in masonry, house roofs, under ivy	Near trees in villages	
Lesser horseshoe bat	Roofs and cellars	Mainly wooded country	Elegant bat in flight, often somersaults

context of ensuring that hardwood timbers are from renewable species. Biodiversity means taking an interest in promoting natural diversity at all levels. Many decisions made by architects affect diversity also at a local level and it is to this that legislators are beginning to turn their attention. The Wildlife and Countryside Act, 1981, places a duty on architects to protect specified sites and to notify English Nature if species such as bats are suspected in a building about to be refurbished. Such duties are increasing, partly under the influence of European legislation such as Directives 92/43/EEC on the Conservation of Natural Habitats and of Flora and Fauna, 79/409 on the Conservation of Wild Birds, and also in response to a broader social switch from protecting the environment to taking positive action to maintain richness and diversity in the environment. EC Environment Commissioner Ken Collins thinks that proactive environmental action is important in helping to solve the problem of the loss of biodiversity in Europe. The main objective of the Habitats Directive is 'to promote the maintenance of biodiversity' which may entail the 'encouragement of human activities' to help wildlife.

Architects can do much to maintain and improve the level of biodiversity at local level. Although global action is necessary, responsibilities do not cease at the edge of the rainforest. Buildings have traditionally been the home of a wide range of species beyond human beings and do not have to be the sterile single species environments normally created. Man-made structures provide almost all the nesting sites in the UK for swallows, house martins and swifts, as well as the safest breeding sites for most of Britain's bats. Without buildings the level of biodiversity would shrink enormously. Some architects in the past deliberately created nesting sites in their buildings for owls and hawks, partly as in Lutyens' case as an amenity for wealthy householders but also in earlier times as a form of rodent control around farms. The owl boxes created by Lutyens are integral with the structure, forming secure nesting areas high in the roof space. On many big estates in the eighteenth century, as at Holkham Hall in Norfolk, agricultural improvement recognized the benefit of working with nature by encouraging barn owls to colonize the new farm buildings.

Biodiversity

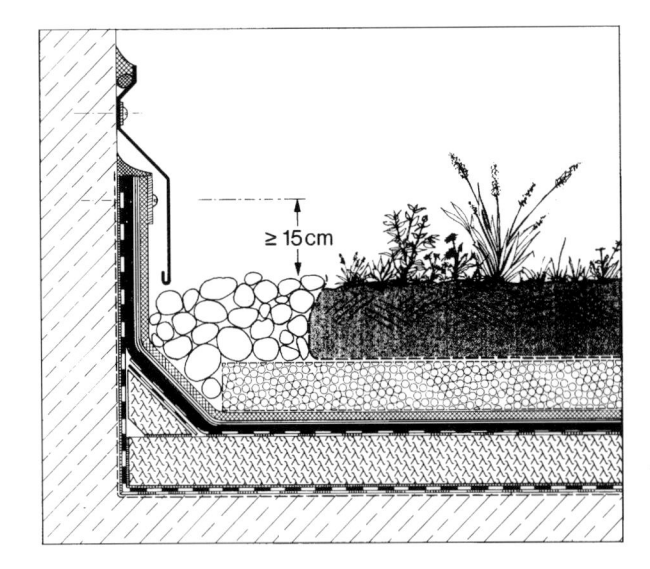

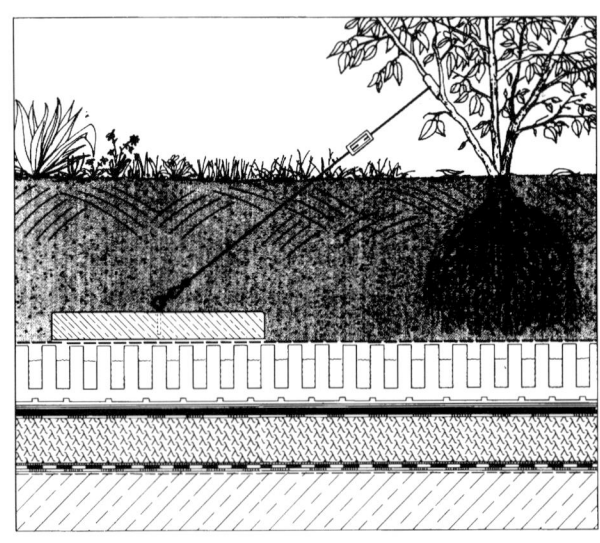

Figure 26.2
Typical construction details for creating planting or wildlife areas on roofs. (Erisco Bauder©.)

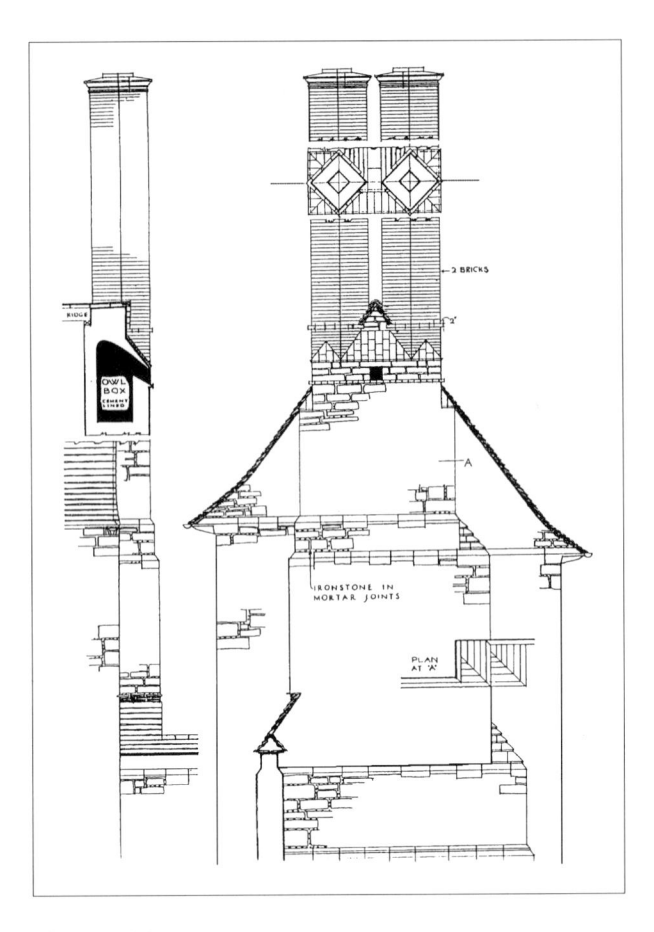

Figure 26.3
Edwin Lutyens' design for an owl box in a house at Little Thakeham. (Country Life©.)

Many species of bird, bat and insect take advantage of the nooks and crannies in older buildings. Swifts nesting beneath the tiles of the irregular roofs of cities like York and Canterbury are a familiar sight, yet their numbers have declined recently as building refurbishment has removed nesting opportunities. Bats, such as the pipistrelle are almost totally dependent upon man-made structures for breeding. Although bats over-winter in large colonies in caves, tunnels and mines, they rely heavily upon buildings for maternity roost sites. A survey of 285 church porches in Northamptonshire found evidence of bats in about a third.

Architects can do much to maintain biodiversity by creating the opportunities for colonization of their buildings by birds and bats. A large amount of guidance is available from groups like the Hawk and Owl Trust and the Bat Conservation Trust. There are four useful principles to follow:

- Create the habitat first as a stepping stone for the colonization by wildlife of buildings. For example, form an insect-rich area in the garden if you wish to attract bats or flycatchers into the nest sites provided in the building. Remember also that ancient trees are potentially more beneficial than younger ones since they provide holes and cavities for nest sites.
- Design and specify carefully to prevent your owl box being colonized by stock doves or jackdaws, the swift box by starlings or the bat box by sparrows. Proprietary tit, bat, owl and swift boxes are manufactured by companies such as Marley and ACO or can be readily made up on site to standard designs.

Figure 26.4
In the past buildings were constructed to accommodate species besides man. Here at Rothesay Castle a wall was lined with nesting boxes for doves. (Brian Edwards©.)

- Use wildlife to help with pest control. For instance in city areas try to encourage nesting kestrels to deter roosting starlings and peregrine falcons to control pigeon populations. Providing nesting ledges for birds of prey high on the sides of buildings is an effective and cheap method of pest management. Bats are also beneficial since they eat midges, woodworm beetles and other undesirable insects.
- When refurbishing old buildings maintain the nesting opportunities for breeding wildlife (especially swifts and bats) and ensure that chemical sprays used in timber preservation are non-toxic to wildlife. Less toxic alternatives have recently been introduced onto the market in response to pressure from English Nature and bat conservation bodies. Learn how to recognize bat droppings from those of mice and rats.

There are pitfalls in wildlife management which need to be avoided. Not all of Lutyens' owl boxes are occupied by owls, and a programme of introducing pole-mounted owl boxes around the Wash for the Crown Commissioners resulted in jackdaws gradually ousting half the barn owls. Even with partial success such measures help with fulfilling responsibilities towards biodiversity and often create considerable amenity. A recent residential conversion of farm buildings, for instance, was advertised by estate agents as containing nesting barn owls, though whether all purchasers would be happy with the night-time screeches is a moot point. The loss of nesting sites following nation-wide barn conversions is why measures are now needed to help declining owl and bat populations.

Birds carry many diseases, and their droppings pose a health and amenity risk. The standard eaves details of the 1960s have proved popular to thousands of house martins whose droppings can be seen down the face of countless suburban house walls. Not all householders see their property as a wildlife haven and take elaborate measures to deter nesting. Less visible are pipistrelle bats which are partial to the cavities within cavity walls. The majority of the British population breeds within houses under thirty years old, often gaining entry to the cavity at gaps in the eaves or where pipes have been taken through the outer wall. These bats can pass through a hole as small as 20 mm by 15 mm. Where gaps do not exist bat boxes can be erected in the outer leaf of brickwork or bat slates in the roof.

The British Trust for Ornithology provides guidance on how, when and where to locate wall-mounted boxes for birds. In certain areas of the country quite rare birds such as the black redstart would expand its range if building designers were more sensitive to its needs. Open-fronted nest boxes, or sheltered ledges high up the building are what this attractive bird needs. In parts of the north of England peregrine falcons have been encouraged to nest on the sides of cooling towers by placing ledges at some distance from the ground. Such measures are helping to bring these dashing hawks to the city where urban pigeons and starlings provide a good food supply.

Flat roofs provide nesting sites for less desirable birds. The lesser black-backed gull is rapidly colonizing cities from Bristol to Glasgow where it scavenges for scraps around the back of fast food restaurants. This noisy gull summers in Britain and winters as far south as the Atlantic seaboard of West Africa. The post-war fashion for flat roofs high off the ground has allowed it to exploit a habitat niche and become the equivalent of the medieval kites.

In this 'green' age architects should not be surprised to discover that their clients are willing to invest in measures to encourage wildlife to colonize their buildings. With membership of the RSPB now nearly a million, the public is increasingly informed and probably sympathetic to such action. Biodiversity is an issue which should begin at the building, extend into the landscape and outwards to the wider problems of global species richness. It is no good thinking that by using hardwoods from renewable sources architects have fulfilled their sole responsibility towards specifying in a green manner.

27

Ecology energy and building: the importance of landscape

Mention has been made of the role of tree planting at the perimeter of a building to improve its energy performance and comfort level. Landscape planning with an emphasis upon planting can improve the quality and enjoyment of external spaces, reduce urban wind tunnels, shelter the edges of development, provide solar protection, and modify rainwater discharges. Planting can also take up some of the CO_2 generated by vehicles and buildings. At the National Remote Sensing Centre at Farnborough in Hampshire, the car park tree planting

Figure 27.1
Trees in proximity to buildings can provide important solar protection in the summer and improve the microclimate in the winter. (Brian Edwards©.)

absorbs more CO_2 than is generated by staff cars used in travelling to work.[1]

Good environmental design entails using landscape and building design in a co-operative and self-supporting fashion. Some of the problems of overheating and chill factor associated with buildings can be remedied not within the building envelope itself but in the spaces outside the architectural skin. A protective outer screen of landscape gives added environmental control: providing a sieve to modify the inflow or outflow of energy. Vertical plant cover (such as vines) on exposed surfaces improves the energy efficiency of the wall by up to 8 per cent, partly by the pockets of air trapped and partly by preventing driving rain from filling the air voids in bricks and blocks with water (a wet wall is a poor insulator compared to a dry one). Screen walls, hedges, shelter belts, planted sun filters and trees in streets, gardens and squares all improve the energy performance of urban areas. From this perspective landscape design is properly seen as much as a part of energy management as site development.

Landscape design is also an important element in the move towards 'liveability' in cities. As an amenity and provider of comfort in urban spaces trees, plants and sometimes water are valuable assets. Where wind is a problem at the city edge or around high buildings, trees can provide valuable shelter. By improving the quality of life outdoors people will be less tempted to sit inside (where they usually consume energy in one form or another, e.g. lights, TV) or travel to the countryside in search of solace. High environmental standards within towns usually depend upon proximity to planting and green space. Social activities can only thrive outdoors where the spaces are conducive to conversation and sitting. Where shelter and enclosure are achieved by a combination of building and planting, the visual complexity and spatial richness which usually follows itself generates use by the wider population.

The design of urban areas is, therefore, more than a question of space for daylighting and access. It has an important role to play in energy management, in creating an amenity upon which the success of cities depend, and through tree planting in absorbing CO_2. The selection of planting for energy conservation needs to consider the daylight transmitted through tree canopies, the shelter afforded, the difference in performance between summer and winter, the way pruning can enhance the density of shade, and questions of distance and height from the building edge. Coniferous trees provide useful winter shelter (especially when planted in blocks) but screen out low angle sun in the winter which could provide useful solar gain. Being of dark canopy, they also increase energy use

Figure 27.2
Planted roofs offer energy, wildlife and amenity benefits. They are in increasing use throughout Europe. (Erisco Bauder©.)

---

[1] Jeremy Dodd, The protective landscape *The Architects' Journal* 7 July 1993 p 42.

Ecology energy and building: the importance of landscape

Figure 27.3
Building and landscape design are related entities in this business park near Edinburgh, masterplanned by Richard Meier and Partners. (Richard Meier and Partners©.)

when used near to a building by obstructing daylight. Deciduous trees, on the other hand, provide useful summer solar screening and do not much obstruct daylight in winter when their leaves have fallen. Large-leaved deciduous trees pruned to form a grid whose height reflects the wind or solar shelter needed for an east, south or west elevation, have benefits also in worker satisfaction and screening out air pollutants. The shape, height, thickness of planting and density of canopy are all important considerations in conserving energy by planting design. At Stockley Park, various types of planting and water have been deliberately employed to improve environmental conditions around office buildings.

Planted walls or screens can also save on the energy costs of more traditional construction materials such as bricks. A biological wall (planting on a wire frame or with soil-retaining elements) can be both cheaper to build than a conventional wall, more attractive to look at, and provide wildlife sites in urban areas. The use of bioengineering combines low energy cost in construction (though sometimes higher energy costs in maintenance), and provides valuable reservoirs of top soil which can remove one tonne of CO_2 per hectare per year from the atmosphere.[2] Similarly planting can help deal with the biodigestion of organic wastes, thereby saving on the engineering and energy costs of sewage disposal. Waste water also can be treated through reed and goatwillow beds until it is suitable for discharge in water courses.

As older urban areas decline the opportunity grows of creating city forests on the wastelands of former industry. Forestry can provide employment, amenity, an improvement to microclimate and reduce air pollution. The timber crop can also provide fuel for small community-based power stations which burn tree wood mass (chipped down to combustible sizes and kiln dried before burning). Planting back urban forests also helps with CO_2 absorption. Urban forests are planned for large areas of the UK (e.g. the National Forest of 240 km² between Burton Upon Trent and Leicester) but development is being thwarted by acid rain pollution which is stunting tree growth.

---

[2]*Ibid.*, p 43.

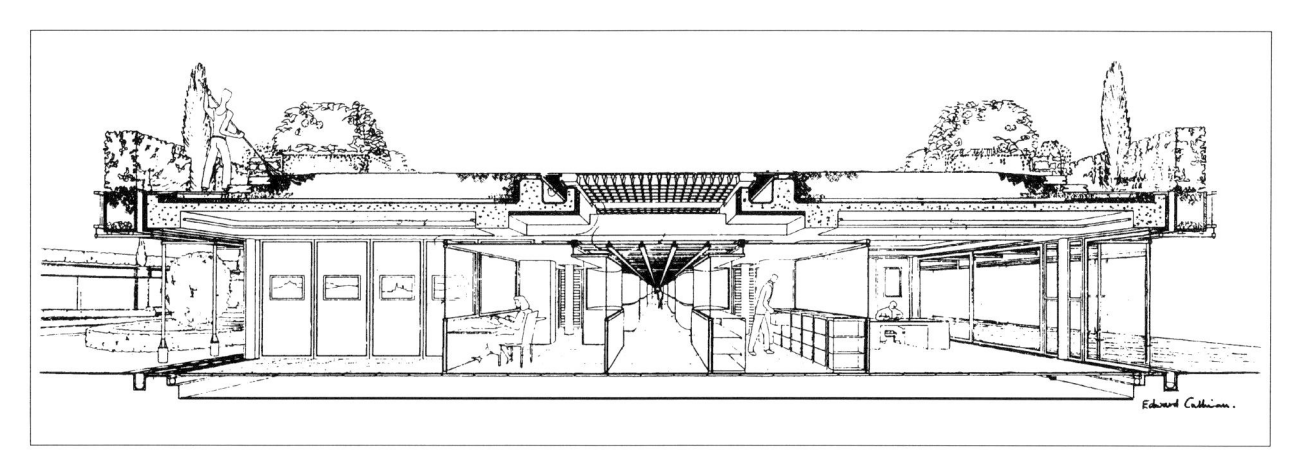

Ecology energy and building: the importance of landscape

Figure 27.4
This planted roof designed by Edward Cullinan provides energy conservation and reduces the building's visual impact. (Edward Cullinan©.)

Figure 27.5
Shelter is particularly important when developing in exposed locations. (Aviemore Photographic©.)

177

Potentially urban forestry brings multiple benefits which address local and global duties. Because of the wider advantages of creating forests as an amenity, energy crop and climate improver, attention is being directed to using agricultural land in set-aside schemes for four or five yearly timber crop rotations, and utilizing more derelict or marginal land for forestry. Once the preserve of amenity and paper production, the UK's forestry industry is moving towards planting trees as an energy crop. The UK has only 10 per cent of its land area under forest cover (compared to 25 per cent in France) yet it has one of the best timber growing climates in Europe. Energy farming provides, by biomass production, 15 per cent of the energy needs of Sweden and Finland.[3] Potentially, Britain could match this figure with significant saving of fossil fuels by substitution, improved biodiversity and ecological richness, better shelter for urban areas, and the absorption of much of the CO_2 emitted by urban activities. It is one of most cost effective ways in which the EC's drive for sustainable development can be realized.

---

[3] *Ibid.*, p 44.

Part 8
Sustainable Development

28

Sustainable development: EC and UK policy and international agreements

One of the key principles adopted under the Maastricht Treaty was that 'sustainable and non-inflationary growth respecting the environment' was to be a cornerstone of European Union (EU) ambition.[1] The same year the UK Government accepted the recommendations of the UN Conference on Environment and Development (The Earth Summit) held in Rio de Janeiro in 1992. The main product of the Earth Summit was a commitment by 160 world governments, including Britain, to adopting four measures on aspects of sustainable development. They were:

- *Agenda 21*: a comprehensive programme of action needed throughout the world to achieve a more sustainable pattern of development for the next century;
- *The Climate Change Convention*: an agreement between countries establishing a framework for action to reduce the risks of global warming by limiting the emission of so-called 'greenhouse gases';
- *The Biodiversity Convention*: an agreement between countries about how to protect the diversity of species and habitats in the world;
- *A statement of principles*: for the management, conservation and sustainable development of all the world's forests.

The Rio summit not only led to a commitment to the principles of sustainable development by the EC, various Member States including the UK, but importantly in the longer term to a new UN agency being established. Known as the UN Commission on Sustainable Development (CSD), it has the task of monitoring progress on the four measures listed above. The CSD has the mandate to review action by governments including America, Japan, Brazil and India against commitments made, to organize international conferences on environmental matters, and to recommend further action by the UN. To date the CSD has concentrated upon monitoring the adoption of sustainability policies by governments and upon the particular problem of rainforest conservation. The EC, mainly through its Environment Commission, also monitors action by Member States to ensure that the Maastricht Treaty agreement on 'sustainable growth' is enshrined in local legislation and policy. The Dutch are arguably at the forefront here with their 'National Environment Policy Plan' adopted in 1991 which is the most effective and comprehensive environment strategy in Europe.

Under the dual imperatives of the Earth Summit and the Maastricht Treaty European governments have begun to prepare strategies and action plans to implement their agreements. It is now accepted that environmental problems affect the whole world and that policies need to address local, national and international issues to be effective across a broad front. This too is the view of the EC whose directives and regulations ensure that environmental protection and energy policies are consistent within the legislative systems of the Member States. Ken Collins, Chairman of the European Parliament's Committee on the Environment, is convinced that what he calls the 'horizontal measures' of European law will lead to sustainable principles of comparative weight in the 'vertical' laws of the ten Member States (see p. viii). Since sustainable growth compatible with environmental systems is effectively a brake upon unbridled exploitation of world resources, the EC is keen to introduce consistent standards within Europe and to influence through the UN the environment and economic policies of other major trading

---

[1] David Wilkinson, Maastricht and the environment, *Journal of Environment Law* Vol 4, No 2, 1992, p 223.

blocks. That the 1994 GATT talks failed to address environmental concerns was rather more the fault of American and Japanese governments than European. The EC trade commissioner Leon Britton sought in vain to insinuate environmental clauses into the agreement on world trade.

UK strategy for sustainable development

If the world community at large is not ready for a global view on environmental policy, both the EC and UK governments have adopted policies which move in a sustainable direction.[2] In its report on Sustainable Development published in 1994 Britain has adopted the following guiding principles (based on the Brundtland Report of 1987) to take into account in pursuing a balance between development and environmental protection:

- Decisions should be based on the best possible scientific information and analysis of risks.
- Where there is uncertainty and potentially serious risks exist, precautionary action may be necessary.
- Ecological impacts must be considered, particularly where resources are non-renewable or effects may be irreversible.
- Cost implications should be brought home directly to the people responsible adopting the 'polluter pays' principle.[3]

Although it is accepted that environmental costs may have to be tolerated as the price for economic development, under the UK strategy for sustainable development there will be greater weight attached by government to protecting wildlife sites, eco-systems and other environmental resources.[4] Sustainable development is defined as the balancing of urban development with the conservation of environmental resources – land, air, water, forests, energy, etc.

The definition of the meaning of 'sustainable' by the UK Government in response to its international agreement is rather timid. More radical definitions are being promulgated by environmental campaigners. Typical is that by Brenda and Robert Vale who define a sustainable society as being

> one which can maintain its existence in the long term without threatening by its actions the existence of other forms of life. Sustainability implies that there should be no irreversible pollution, no reliance on finite resources, and a stable population.[5]

Such a definition is difficult to meet in the timescale of decisions normally taken by governments. As a vision of environmental harmony the Vale's definition is commendable but as a realistic target for European societies in the 1990s it contains too much utopianism. In Britain's case, in particular, an abundant supply of oil and gas from the North Sea (currently providing 75 per cent of the nation's energy needs) undermines attempts at limiting reliance upon fossil-fuel resources. What is emerging in the UK is a patchy policy framework, moving towards sustainable principles in some fields (especially on pollution control) but continuing to pursue non-sustainable policies in others. There are signs of a conflict in government between those ministries (such as the DOE) which favour resource conservation and those elsewhere (such as the DTI) which think technological innovation rather than self-sacrifice will play a larger part in advancing towards 'sustainability'.

The UK Strategy contains a thinly argued analysis of principles, a summary of the implications of sustainability on economic growth, and a number of general policies within ten key areas of the national economy. Three are of particular interest to developers and construction professionals – the sections on 'Development and construction', on 'Waste', and on 'Transport'.

Implications for the construction industry

Under 'Development and construction' there are five summary points on sustainable development which seek to accommodate an anticipated 14 per cent increase in the number of households over the next 20 years in a fashion which balances growth with environmental constraints.[6]

The strategy seeks to:

- promote attractive and convenient urban areas, in which people will want to live and work;
- encourage new development in locations that are likely to minimize energy consumption;
- encourage the regeneration of urban land and buildings, and the restoration to use for development or open space of derelict and contaminated land;
- integrate the development which is necessary to sustain the rural economy with the protection of the countryside for its landscape, wildlife, agricultural, forestry, recreational and natural resource value;

---

[2]*Sustainable Development: The UK Strategy (Summary Report)* January 1994, Cm2426, p 7.
[3]*Ibid.*, p 8.
[4]*Ibid.*

[5]Brenda and Robert Vale, Building the sustainable environment, Andrew Blower (ed.) *Planning for a Sustainable Environment* Town and Country Planning Associates, 1993, p 93.
[6]*Sustainable Development* p 15.

Figure 28.1
Making better use of existing buildings by imaginative adaptation conserves the resources of towns and helps promote sustainable development. (Hugh Martin and Partners©.)

- promote an understanding of sustainable development among all those who have an interest in the development process.

Many of the principles embodied in these five points favour the use of professional design skills, rather than procurement by other means such as Design and Build.

The creation of 'attractive and convenient urban areas' presupposes an element of design skill where the tastes and needs of people at home and at work are considered. Architects and other design professionals pride themselves on meeting consumer expectations in a fashion which creates beauty, amenity and commodity. Attractive places to live and work are robust in the long term, thereby

Figure 28.2
Sustainable development implies a new approach not just to buildings but the spaces between them. (Brian Edwards©.)

allowing the buildings to be adapted over time to suit the varying needs of different generations. A town like Bath is as popular today as it was 200 years ago, and having paid the initial investment in environmental costs, it can be periodically upgraded at relatively low resource cost by successive users. By way of comparison the peripheral estate of Easterhouse on the eastern edge of Glasgow built between 1955-65 to house 60 000 people is currently occupied by only 12 000 people. The poor quality of the built environment, the lack of diversity of house types, and the shortage of social and leisure facilities has led to the rejection of the estate by the people it was designed to house. Thus an unattractive and inconvenient urban area has led to great waste in the use of land, energy and building resources.

The encouragement of new development to locations that minimize energy consumption favours places well connected to the present infrastructure of public transport. Existing cities are generally well served by rail and bus services and it is to here that one can expect to see development directed rather than to green field sites.

Changes in UK planning guidelines in 1994 (particularly PPGs 12 and 13) and EU policy expressed in the Green Paper on the Urban Environment and Directive 92/43 herald further changes to legislation to bring this about. The Planning Policy Guidance Note 12 (PPG12) on 'Development Plans and Regional Planning Guidance' advocates putting 'sustainable development at the heart of strategic planning in the UK' and offers guidance on how to bring this about. The lack of a consensus or reliable methodology has hitherto discouraged town and country planners from playing their part in establishing sustainable patterns of development. PPG12 encourages the concept that environmental capacity should determine the level of development. As 25 per cent of global warming gas production is the result of transportation, this element of the strategy for sustainable development will presumably see a shift from car to rail use by encouragement being given to locating new development where it can readily be served by public transport. A likely consequence of this policy is to speed the regeneration of land in the inner cities and to intensify development around suburban rail stations.

Related to this point is the strategy to encourage the regeneration of urban land and buildings either for development through restoration or as open space. Existing buildings represent a resource in labour, energy and materials. It makes sense to recycle buildings, converting and adapting them to new uses, rather than demolishing them. The fine grain of design skill possessed by many architects, engineers and surveyors is well suited to the adaptation of buildings. Volume builders and contractors are less well suited to dealing with the complexities of existing structures. If this element of the strategy favours the employment of architectural skills, the concentration upon 'derelict and contaminated land' will have the further effect of creating a market for professional expertise. As Chapter 24 argues, the preference given to the redevelopment of contaminated land is generating a demand for specialist advisers able to offer a service which embraces pollution control, engineering and landscape design.

Construction is a major user of energy resources, and the structures and buildings created support economic development and contribute towards the quality of life. As the life of buildings is about fifty years decisions made today have an impact upon the environment well into the next century when energy, land and raw materials may be restricted. It is in the interests of clients and design professionals to prolong the productive lifespan of buildings by ensuring they are flexible in use, attractive to those who live and work in them, and minimize energy consumption and hence CO_2 emissions. The latter point is particularly significant since global warming will increase the demand for summer-time cooling which has energy implications especially in the commercial sector.

The strategy dealing with 'Waste' impacts upon building construction less directly. The need to minimize waste in the construction process, the use of sustainable resources for the production of building materials, the recycling of materials, all reduce the need for landfill and for the extraction and production of raw materials.[7] The relationship between production and waste is a close one in the building industry: decisions made by designers and contractors can greatly influence the amount and type of waste generated. The aim should be to minimize the amount of waste produced and to make the best use of the waste generated. Waste in the form of packaging of building products, of loss due to poor management or workmanship, of the lack of appreciation by contractors, specifiers and designers of the environmental costs of waste, all conspire to construction being a highly wasteful activity. Effective waste management normally contains a hierarchy of decisions from a reduction in the need for materials and packaging, to a policy of reuse of waste, to recovery (including recycling of products such as bricks, doors, etc. and energy recovery from the latent fossil-fuel element) and finally disposal by incineration or landfill. Not many architects ask themselves what the waste implications are of the products they intend to employ, and too few suppliers and manufacturers of building components provide information which allows the specifier to choose a low waste option. When the EC eco-labelling scheme (Regulation 880/92/EEC and Directive 94/2/EEC) is extended to building products, the task of implementing the UK strategy on sustainable development will be a great deal easier.

Buildings and transport are together responsible for 75 per cent of UK energy use (about 72 per cent of Europe's as a whole) and three-quarters of the CO_2 emissions. Hence development and where it is located has a significant impact upon the production of global warming gases. Traffic has grown rapidly over the last forty years with a trebling of car usage and freight movements by road. The environmental costs in terms of carbon dioxide production, pollution (growing concern over the health of urban people exposed to permanent low levels of air contamination), congestion, noise and disturbance to communities along busy roads has resulted in European and UK governments beginning to take steps to curb car and lorry use, and to redirect investment towards public transport. Rail and water-borne transport are emerging as the most favourable options when transport costs reflect both the needs of the economy and the environment.

The main goal for sustainable development in the transport sector is the need to 'meet the economic and social needs for access to facilities with less need for travel and in ways which do not place unacceptable burdens on the environment'.[8] The Government plans to influence the rate of traffic growth by restricting investment in motorway plans, balance individual choice in transport with environmental objectives, make transport policy decisions equitable across modes, and encourage the use of less polluting vehicles. It is also seeking to influence land-use policies through the review of Structure Plans to enable

---

[7] *Ibid.*, p 16.

[8] *Ibid.*

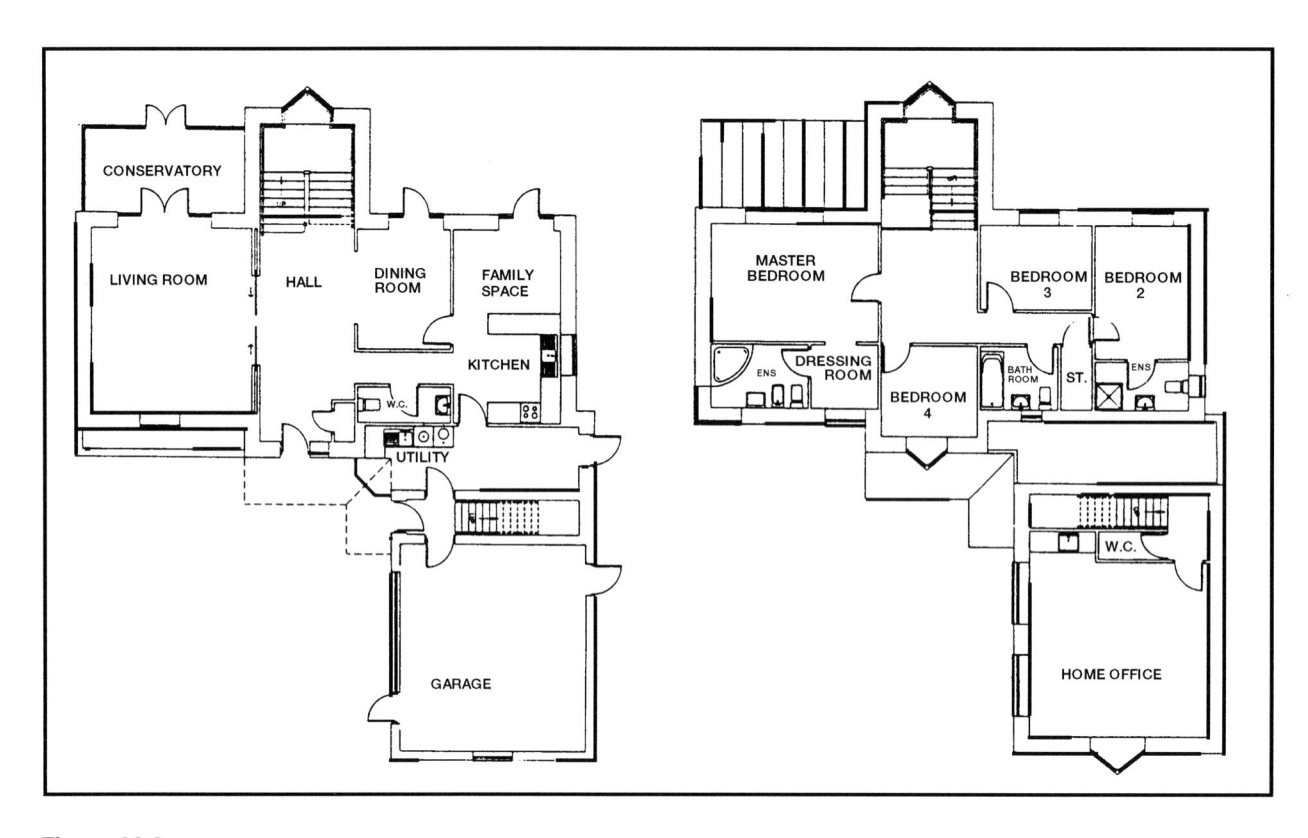

Figure 28.3
House designed for working from home at Futureworld, Milton Keynes. Note the self-contained office over the garage. (CNT©.)

people and business to take advantage of locations well served by public transport, and to encourage the use of less polluting means of transport such as cycling. Increased urban density and the close integration of different land uses favours journeys by bus, tram, cycle and on foot. The UK strategy for 'sustainable development' marks a significant shift in transport policy which has been dominated by the road sector for the past generation. Questions of urban density raise the spectre of more liveable cities where the close grain of streets and buildings not only reduce transport energy costs, but also lead to safer places for the pedestrian and an enhanced quality of design. As we saw with the policies for development, the whole thrust of sustainability favours the sophisticated and integrating skills of the design professional, rather than the simplistic methods of building procurement provided under Design and Build which is better suited to green field sites.

Under the dual influences of the urban and environment policies of the EU and the UK's moves towards a strategy for sustainable development, the construction industry faces a significant shift in direction over the next generation. The twenty year view of the UK strategy will embrace a large proportion of the working life of those currently employed in the construction industry. The White Paper of 1990 *This Common Inheritance* marked the first tentative steps towards a strategy for the environment which Agenda 21 of the Rio Summit and the UK Strategy for Sustainable Development build upon. Though few would deny the weaknesses of the UK Strategy, particularly the inadequate definition of sustainability and the lack of integration between the policies for the ten key sectors, most commentators welcomed the attempt in 1994 to achieve a more sustainable pattern of development for the next century.

Guidelines for sustainability and land-use planning in the UK

In 1993 the DOE published the guide *Environmental Appraisal of Development Plans* which introduced elements of a green agenda into the UK planning system. Whilst the guide predated by a few months the *UK Strategy on Sustainable Development* report, it adopted similar principles. Where the guide differs from the Strategy report is in its greater focus upon land-use matters. The guide is not a statutory document but an advisory report aimed at giving planning authorities a green framework for assessing planning applications and, perhaps more importantly, providing a methodology for the production of green development plans.

The guide advises local and regional planning authorities how to include environmental appraisal at each stage of development plan making and for each type of development plan – structure, unitary, district, minerals or waste.[9] It can, therefore, be seen as parallel advice to the UK Strategy report, with the same general aims now tailored to the specific function of town planning. The main interest lies in making legitimate green questions in a planning system which hitherto had not been encouraged to take much interest in energy. The guide lists green questions which may be asked at the planning application stage, and prescribes sets of environmental priorities which planning authorities should themselves address in their development plans.

The three sets of environmental priorities are:

- *Global sustainability*: questions of climate change, the effect of energy use and carbon dioxide (CO_2) production, encouragement of energy-efficient transport and buildings, the exploitation of renewable energy, the maintenance and creation of biodiversity, the use of woodland to take up CO_2.
- *Natural resource management*: air and water quality, the creation of healthy urban and rural environments, the wise husbanding of land and its minerals.
- *Local environmental quality*: 'liveability' of the urban environment, access to open space, conservation and enhancement of towns and the landscape, cultural heritage, building quality.

These broad environmental targets, each supported by the completion of a resource and database, provide the basis for assessing the value of environmental qualities. Such value, when set alongside social and economic targets, provide the framework of balance for inclusion in development plans. The guide offers several concepts for qualitative environmental assessment, some overlapping elements of the UK Strategy report. Four evaluative concepts are proffered:

- *Environmental stock*, where things which have environmental value are listed and monitored.
- *Critical environmental capital*, where elements whose loss or damage would be serious are measured.
- *Environmental capacities*, where the ability of a particular resource to perform its natural function is closely reviewed.
- *Precautionary principle*, where environmental damage may occur but knowledge is incomplete, decisions should err on the side of caution.

The guide marks a significant step towards placing sustainability at the centre of the UK planning system. It does not require all planning authorities to put environmental priorities at the top of their deliberations but the guide provides a methodology for those which wish to do so. If the guide avoids suggesting how economic development and environmental protection are to be reconciled in a competitive world, it does provide the basis for equating environmental costs and benefits in a systematic way.

Implementing sustainable development: the role of Planning Policy Guidance Note 12

Soon after the UK Government published the Summary Report on Sustainable Development (in January 1994), a number of guidance documents were released to help translate national policy into local action. One such was Planning Policy Guidance Note 12 (PPG12) on 'Development Plans and Regional Planning Guidance'. It seeks to provide advice to planning authorities on how specifically to balance environmental concerns with development pressures. On the question of conservation issues PPG12 proposes that local authorities should[10]

- maintain a regularly updated environmental resource database;
- determine a site's environmental capacity beyond which further development could not be sustained;
- use the planning process to maintain richness and diversity in the landscape by, for instance, overcoming degradation by habitat creation;
- maintain cultural diversity through the preservation of historic buildings, historic areas, diversity of land uses, street patterns, traditional settlement forms, etc., and by avoiding cumulative peripheral growth;
- maintain a clear zone between town and country through effective green-belt policies, so reducing travel distances and creating wildlife corridors and green wedges;
- establish effective monitoring of progress towards sustainability.

A parallel document 'Landscape Assessment Guidance' sets out how to measure the quality and capacity of the countryside.

---

[9] *The Architects' Journal* 26 January 1994, p 33.

[10] Jeremy Dodd, Call for sustainability, *The Architects' Journal* 12 January 1994, p 23.

Taken together PPG12, and related documents provide a framework for balancing development with the conservation of natural and man-made resources. Though limited in scope and tentative in its adoption of parameters for sustainable development, the guidance note is an important beginning. Its chief value is to signal a change of direction – a shift from development dominated policies of the post-war period to a new concern for balancing growth with the capacity of the environment to support it in the long term. The guidance note also signals a line of demarcation between local planning authorities and pollution control bodies with regard to contaminated land. The effect is to discourage planning authorities from duplicating the functions of other pollution agencies, but to encourage consultation between planning and pollution control authorities at the planning consent stage. Risk assessment with regard to releases into the atmosphere and the danger posed by contaminated sites are matters where planning authorities are required to heed advice from pollution control bodies, rather than develop their own independent expertise.

29

Case studies of sustainable urban development

Some UK planning authorities are beginning to put sustainability at the heart of their land-use policies. In Europe developments such as Ecolonia in Holland have already tested, albeit on a small scale, the necessary integration of land-use, transport, design and landscape design necessary for sustainable development. The following six case studies explore at different scales and with various types and methods of development how such matters can be absorbed within the normal responsibilities of national, regional and local governments, and tested by enlightened developers.

The Hertfordshire Structure Plan: a case study of applying sustainable principles

The review of Hertfordshire's Structure Plan published in May 1994 devises a strategy for sustainable development which extends beyond the normal fifteen-year timescale for such plans to a more ambitious long-term view shaping action to 2050. The plan defines sustainability roughly in line with the UK Strategy and then links environmental issues with social and economic objectives using the DOE's *Environmental Appraisal of Development Plans, 1993* as a guide. This interconnection of interests in a town planning context allows the revised Structure Plan to develop policies for land use which seek to 'reduce overall demand for resources' and help 'maintain biological diversity'.[1] Central to the plan are policies for growth in retail, office and residential demands upon land which attempt to reduce car use by a mixture of encouraging development of relatively dense mixed uses and directing new development towards under-used or contaminated land in existing urban areas.

The Hertfordshire example highlights the way sustainable principles impact upon council activity across a broad front. The future planning of towns which are the foci for energy use, environmental destruction and resource consumption is of prime concern for those seeking to build a strategy for sustainable development into public policy documents such as county structure plans. The Hertfordshire example looks at how policies for urban, rather than rural, areas can be made more environmentally sensitive. The plan asserts that towns must be viewed as systems, not separate activities, and systems which can by their interaction be made more sustainable. Within the structure plan for Hertfordshire each township in the region will (if the plan is adopted by the Secretary of State for the Environment) be required to audit its operational as well as physical characteristics to ensure that sustainability is achieved in relation to 'resource and energy use and movement'.[2] The methodology for such an audit is not well established and local communities have yet to display a willingness to forego the benefits of the private car. However, the revised structure plan begins to pave the way for sustainable development which is integrative across a broad front and looks at both the energy and land needs over an extended time period. By involving community groups in the consultation on the plan other concerns have emerged, such as poor air quality and health, which impact upon transport policies. Though flawed, the Hertfordshire example points to the benefit of seeing towns as energy and resource systems, even if there is a need to develop a firmer methodology for testing and applying sustainable principles at the local level.

Towards sustainable development: the Leicester initiative

Being closer to the people than central government, local authorities are well placed to explore community initiatives

---

[1] Anthony Fyson, To the heart of a sustainable future, *Planning Week* 19 May 1994, p 16.

[2] *Ibid.*

Case studies of sustainable urban development

a

b

c

Figure 29.1
Energy demonstration houses at Milton Keynes. (Milton Keynes Development Corporation©.)

in the field of sustainable development. An example is the city of Leicester in central England which in 1990 was designated Britain's first Environment City by the Royal Society for Nature Conservation, Civic Trust and UIC 2000. Using a grant of 1.2 million ecus (about £1 million) from the European Community, the Leicester Environment City Project is endeavouring to develop a model of sustainability in the urban environment. The plan is necessarily long term with targets of environmental and resource management extending over a thirty year time period.

The project has defined sustainable development as 'integrating urban development with resource management'.[3] Using the Environment City concept local leaders with businesses and voluntary groups are seeking to formulate a co-ordinated model for energy, transport, waste and pollution, food and agriculture, economy and work, built environment, natural environment and social environment.[4] The programme is unique in the UK in that it attempts to synthesize different and often divergent strands of development around these eight broad themes. The working groups tackling each theme are composed of public, private and voluntary sector representatives who have the task of auditing the environment in their fields and developing a long-term policy framework for the town. The subject groups are co-ordinated by a national steering group (chaired by the Royal Society for Nature Conservation) which seeks to integrate the eight themes (energy, transport, etc.) into a model of sustainable development for Leicester. The advantage of chairing the

---

[3]Leicester City Environment, promotionary broadsheet (no date).
[4]*Ibid.*

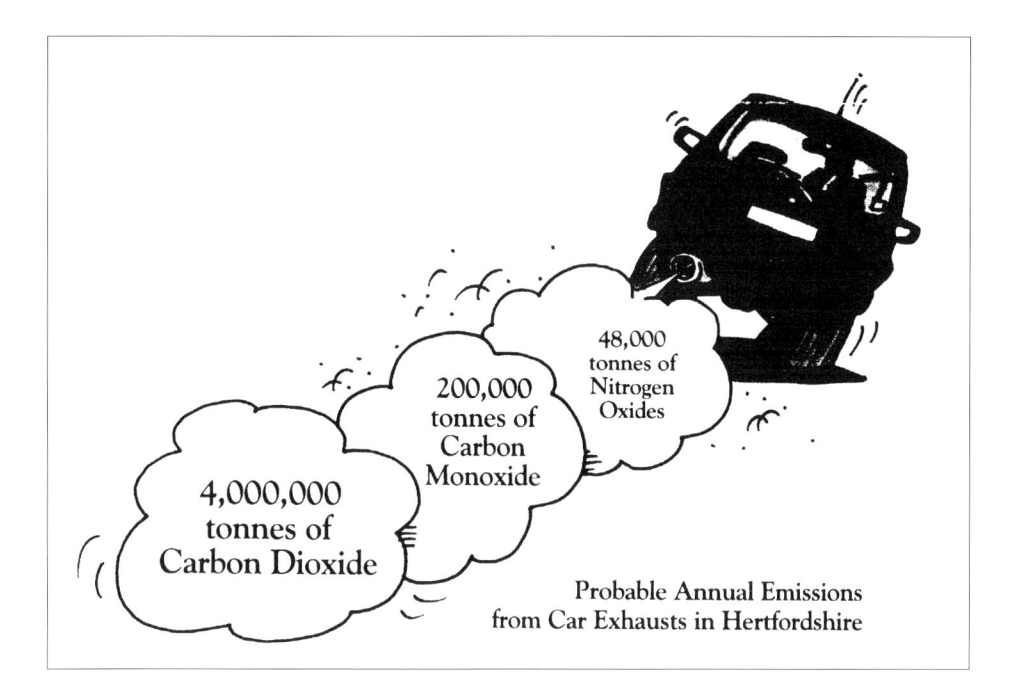

Figure 29.2
Extract from Hertfordshire County Council's Structure Plan brochure. The message is clear in terms of the changed attitude required of sustainable development. (Hertfordshire County Council©.)

national group by a body separate from the city council is that it can better keep abreast of international environment initiatives similar in nature, and can act independently when hard policy decisions have to be made.

The Leicester Environment City Project has the long-term goal of reaching a sustainable pattern of development over a thirty year period (known as Agenda 2020) and the adoption of more immediate initiatives to raise public awareness of green issues in the short term. These consist of such things as traffic calming, greening business premises, the development of combined heat and power schemes, the construction of an Eco House providing a working demonstration project, the establishment in the city of cycle routes, local nature reserves, recycling schemes, the planting of a city forest, and the adoption by the City Council of an environmental audit scheme for its own services. In addition, the town is hosting energy and ecology workshops targeted particularly at local business leaders. The project also funds green events in schools and runs environmental competitions for local residents. These and other initiatives aim to fulfil Leicester City Council's commitment to reducing CO_2 emissions by 50 per cent of 1990 levels by the year 2025.

Under the EC funding rules, Leicester is intended to be the first of a network of British cities established as models of environmental excellence. The task for the steering group is to raise awareness of green issues and to strive for 'practical solutions to the challenge of urban sustainability.'[5] Although the main thrust of the Leicester

[5]*Ibid.*

Figure 29.3
Eco-house, Leicester. (Leicester City Council©.)

Environment City Project is concerned with formulating a working model of sustainable development for medium-sized cities in Europe, the scheme also provides an advisory service through an independent charitable trust on energy management, setting up recycling schemes and environment business partnerships. To date (1994) a matrix for decision makers has been developed which allows policy on matters such as transportation to be tested against its environmental efficacy.

The main lessons to date of the Leicester Environment City Project concern the importance of public, private and

Case studies of sustainable urban development

voluntary partnerships in securing environmental improvement and awareness. Moves towards the green city involve decisions by individuals as well as councils, and local businesses (for example Leicester City Football Club) and the churches. The synthesis of interests embraced within a broadly conceived plan of action bodes well for the city. Whether the generous funding from the EC leads in the end to tangible lessons and pointers towards sustainable development applicable elsewhere remains to be seen. Irrespective of the ambitious thirty-year vision which the project seeks, the short-term action already evident in the town has begun to improve its image and environmental performance. Other local authorities such as Kirklees Council in West Yorkshire are undertaking less ambitious steps towards greater environmental awareness. The annual Kirklees Green Festival focused upon Huddersfield seeks to raise public awareness of environmentally friendly transport, cycling, walking, green products and services, and the role of the local authority in raising questions of a more sustainable lifestyle. These projects, though modest when set against the scale of environmental damage inflicted on a daily basis, are precursors of things to come.

Sustainable development via an Environmental Charter: Central Regional Council, Scotland

The adoption in 1992 by the Central Regional Council in Scotland of an 'Environmental Charter' represents a different manifestation of the move towards sustainable development. It is less land-use focused than the example of Hertfordshire and less concerned with balancing development and conservation than Leicester. The main value of the Central Regional Council's initiative is the inclusion of environmental policies into the wide raft of responsibilities it fulfils as a large local authority, from education to strategic planning, transportation to water quality and pollution control. Unlike in England and Wales, the regional councils in Scotland are bigger and more powerful bodies than the traditional pattern of county councils. This breadth of statutory duty has become the platform for integrated environmental planning and management.

The Council is aware that in the provision of services, in the buying of products, and in its relationship with others (EC, UK Government, district councils, voluntary groups, etc.) it can set an example of environmental resource planning. The Charter embraces eight fields, each significant in themselves but each integrated through a new committee structure of the Council, and a five yearly Action Plan. By adopting the guidelines in *Environmental Practice in Local Government* published in 1990[6] the Council has put the issue of environmental management above all other priorities.

The main objectives of the Central Regional Council's Environmental Charter are:[7]

- to promote 'sustainable development';
- to promote the conservation and sustainable use of natural resources;
- to preserve and improve the environment, both natural and man-made;
- to increase the public's awareness of environmental issues;
- to ensure that decision making at all levels respects the environment.

The Action Programme reviewed annually has become the means of assessing how successfully the Council is meeting its environmental objectives. Some policy areas such as the introduction of recycling measures can be achieved fairly readily, others such as introducing energy conservation into the planning process take longer, not least because of the lack of guidance from central government on the relationship between town planning and energy planning.

The eight topic areas which are the focus for Council action are each monitored and have a special budget to speed through changes. Each also looks to external funds for help and involves professional bodies, trade unions and voluntary groups where appropriate. The topic areas are 'Acting Locally, Energy Conservation, Transport, Built and Natural Environment, Economic Development, Education, Pollution and Recycling, and Communication'. The list highlights the broad impact a seat of regional government can have in introducing elements of a strategy for sustainable development, even if it cannot influence or implement all of them. Under 'Acting Locally' the Council has put in place an environmental management system for its estate of 800 buildings and extensive land holdings. With 41 000 children at school in its buildings, the measures taken and evidence of environmental commitment can help sway the values of the next generation. In terms of Council buildings, CFCs and tropical hardwoods are banned, the emphasis is upon using recycled materials, and only biodegradable cleaning materials are purchased. The Council has also established an Energy Management Unit to advise on energy measures to adopt with regard to its own estate (£6.0 million is spent per year by the Council on the purchase of energy), and provide a service to developers. Some measures already taken, such as the replacement of street lights by more energy-efficient lamps have

---

[6]*Environmental Practice in Local Government* Association of County Councils, District Councils and Metropolitan Authorities, 1990.
[7]Central Regional Council *Environmental Charter* 1992, Stirling, Scotland, p 6.

been commended by the Audit Commission. Unlike many other local administrations, the Council has encouraged the use of bicycles to work, and their use in local work journeys.

The 100 or so measures per year taken by the Council under the Action Plan display a genuine commitment to the environment. From environmental teaching in primary schools to the creation of urban forests in the Falkirk and Bowness areas, the strength of the approach by Central Regional Council is its integrative nature. Rather than establish a Council Department of the Environment, the decision was made to put environmental measures into the programmes and policies of every department. Whether the broad front of environmental and ecological concern is sufficiently targeted to tackle the major problems of global warming and ozone depletion remains to be seen. Like many bodies Central Regional Council has taken the view of the *Caring for the Earth*[8] report that local rather than global action is needed to solve wider environmental problems.

The various measures adopted under the Action Plan provide a sound basis for undertaking 'environmental audits'. As the EC moves towards requiring local, regional and national governments to undertake environmental audits as a condition of grants under initiatives such as the Urban Programme, the framework of the Environmental Charter adopted by the Council permits an evaluation of social and economic benefit against environmental cost.

Lessons from Denmark

With its scarce supplies of fossil-fuel energy and a reluctance to take the nuclear option, Denmark has pioneered a variety of green initiatives. In the ten years between 1975 and 1985 the energy consumption nationwide for heating buildings was reduced by 30 per cent.[9] This has been achieved by the following measures.

Subsidized energy conservation measures

Government grants of about DKK 3bn a year tied to advice from specially trained energy consultants (educated at the expense of the state) who deliberately targeted existing buildings, resulted in large energy savings. The state grants were matched by some DKK 10bn attracted from the private sector. Together it is estimated that financial savings of some DKK 2000 per year per Danish citizen were made. The total invested in conservation measures to houses, shops, industrial and commercial properties was recovered in the decade.

---

[8]*Caring for the Earth* IUCN/UNEP/WWF, October 1991.
[9]*Denmark uses Energy better* Danish Building Agency, 1986.

Energy conservation in public buildings

Government agencies and regional and local authorities were required by a law of 1981 to upgrade insulation levels and improve energy-conscious design. Government buildings were seen as potential demonstration projects.

Higher energy standards in new buildings

The Danish Building Regulations effectively doubled the insulation standards of new buildings in an amendment of 1977. At the same time technical standards for heating plant were revised to improve efficiency. The tightening of insulation standards was matched by relaxations in the space, building heights and room relationship rules for small houses. This flexibility with parallel improvement in conservation levels led to a wave of new 'green' housing development, much of it for young people.

Operation and maintenance

New standards for heating installations with improved maintenance schemes resulted in a 27 per cent improvement in energy use. By targeting heating plant efficiencies, expanding district heating schemes, and switching from oil- to gas-fired systems major savings in energy costs were achieved. The increased use of computerized control of technical installations was helped by government training schemes.

Energy-conscious habits of consumption

Education programmes sought to make consumers more conscious of the benefits of conserving energy and reducing the production of greenhouse gases. Massive, sustained information campaigns linked energy measures to wider problems of environmental decay and climate change. Education through television advertising and energy teaching in schools and universities, ensured that the population was conscious of a wider energy responsibility even in a period of falling fuel prices.

These measures not only help Denmark with its balance of payments deficit, but have created a body of energy expertise and 'green' product development which the country can now export. Danish kit houses built to higher insulation standards than elsewhere are now regularly exported to 'green' consumers in Canada and USA. Danish engineers are also helping with the development of Combined Heat and Power schemes in Germany and Holland, and the building of 'waste' power stations in England (see Chapter 12). The industrial advantages of the initiatives listed above which led, amongst other projects, to the construction of the influential 'Sol and Vind' housing commune in Beder, near Arhus in the 1980s, mean that Denmark is well placed to take advantage of opportunities outside its boundaries.

Case studies of sustainable urban development

Ecolonia: An energy and environment demonstration village in Holland

In 1989 the Dutch government published the National Environmental Policy Plan (NMP), the first by an EC Member State. Inspired by the Brundtland Commission (1988) with its warnings of growing environmental problems, the Policy Plan targeted the construction industry in particular. Conscious that buildings and urban development were the main source of environmental pollution and wasteful energy use, it was here that the Dutch government decided to focus its attention. Under the National Environmental Policy Plan the Dutch building industry was charged with achieving the following by the year 2000:[10]

- examine the environmental consequences of construction methods and products;
- reduce the use of finite natural resources with particular regard to tropical forest products;
- double the level of recycling of building and demolition waste;
- substitute materials whose extraction, use and waste has serious environmental consequences;
- save 25 per cent in energy consumption in heating buildings;
- reduce risk values in internal environmental quality.

The demonstration project, known as Ecolonia, grew out of the NMP though it had been mooted as an idea a few years earlier. The adoption of the NMP provided the impetus to build Ecolonia and the means to fund it. Through NOVEM, the Netherlands state agency for energy and the environment, Ecolonia sought to implement three broad policies in the village:

- energy conservation;
- life-cycle management;
- quality improvement in choice and durability.

These broad policies were translated into specific action areas by the development team of local officials, councillors and representatives of house builders. This secondary list included the avoidance of tropical hardwoods, radon penetration, limestone and sandstone use, and the encouragement of the use of crushed concrete waste. As for resources, the houses were to achieve an energy usage of no more than 200 MJ/m^3 through the use of insulation levels well above norms, a high degree of envelope airtightness, and solar water heaters. As for waste, this was to

---

[10]This list adapted for brevity from that in *Ecolonia* a report by the Netherlands Agency for Energy and Environment, 1992, p 3.

Figure 29.4
Ecolonia in Holland is the closest Europe has come to building a demonstration village based upon a combination of ecological and social principles. Working with house builders, each employing a different architect, a range of approaches to the design of low-energy houses have been constructed. (Novem©.)

be separated into three categories at each household and waste water was to be recycled.

Ecolonia is a small, simple village of 100 dwellings embraced within a larger development of 300 houses and a business park master-planned by the Belgian architect Lucien Kroll. In symbolic fashion the village is grouped around a central park with irregular lake which acts as an ecological resource and a practical benefit since rainwater and cleaned waste water is discharged here rather than into local streams. Since it is a closed system, diversity will grow more quickly, and the fluctuating water level will directly reflect the patterns in nature. The park and lake provide the ordering system for a canal and fingers of tree planting which intersect the village.

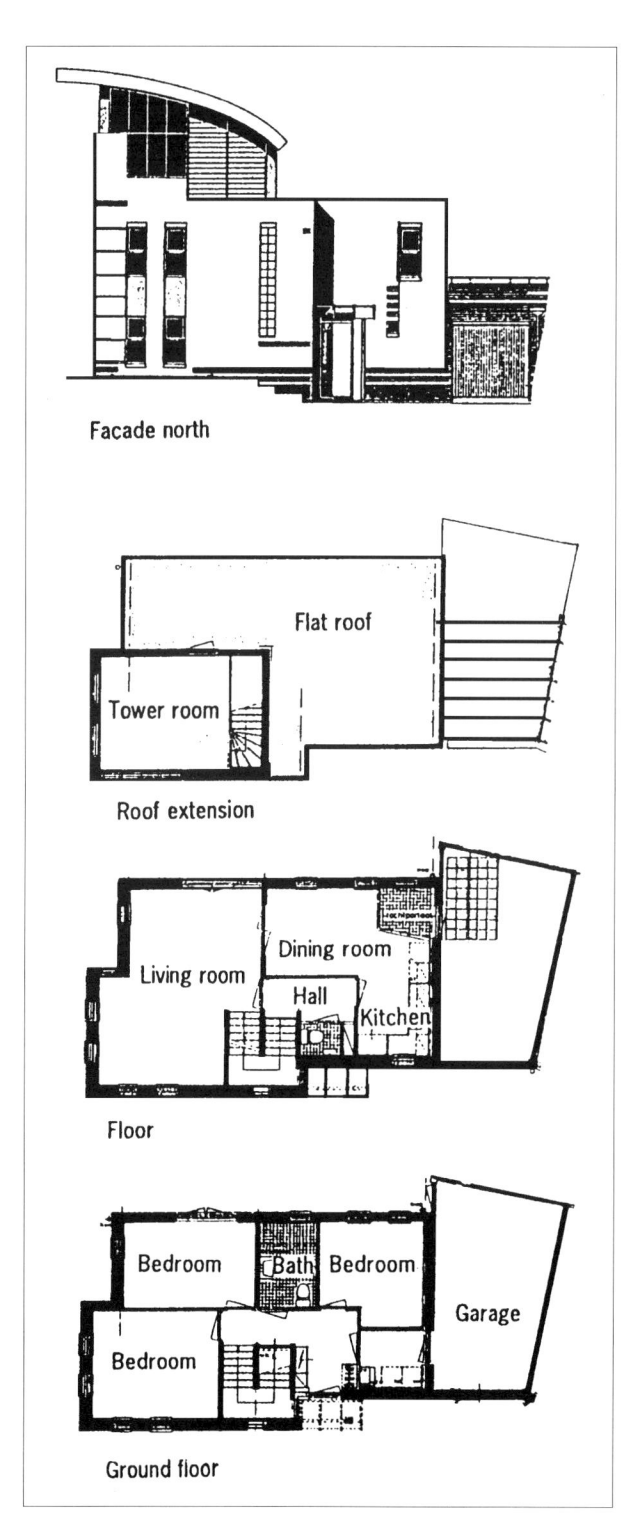

Case studies of sustainable urban development

Figure 29.5
Design for a house at Ecolonia based upon the use of natural materials and a tower to aid natural ventilation. (Novem©.)

Ecolonia is geared to the pedestrian who moves by walking, cycling or taking the train (a new station has been provided as part of the village development). Roads are not defined but left to meander as access courts to the different housing clusters. Exterior lighting is geared not for car users but pedestrians. The effect of these measures is to discourage car use (cars contribute about 20 per cent towards CO_2 production) and where they are used to slow them down.

The village is split into parcels of development of 10 to 18 houses or apartment units. Each is designed by a different architect, employing a different housing developer, and adopting different energy strategies. Hence, a variety of solutions to energy and environmental management are being subject to practical experiment. The village is in effect a test-bed for ideas with design, construction and market appeal being monitored under an EC Thermie Project. Since a number of different, and to UK eyes somewhat outlandish, solutions are being tried at Ecolonia, the village has the air of a demonstration project rather than a village. This is evident in the general design of buildings, the relationship between houses and the common spaces (such as the courtyards), and in the construction of the buildings themselves.

Kroll's masterplan with its emphasis upon picturesque informality and synthesis of buildings and nature provides a robust framework for the energy experiments. The different designs, once evaluated by experts from Dutch universities and research centres, are not only built but systematically monitored against criteria such as energy consumption, durability, internal air quality and user satisfaction. One secondary benefit of the project has been to question aspects of Dutch building law, and to introduce regulatory reforms in support of the national energy plan (NMP). Many regulations as they existed in 1989 prevented the construction of buildings which contained desirable principles from an energy point of view.

Many architects suggested designs or constructional methods which failed to win the support of technical experts, or did not square with the aspirations of house builders. Risk assessment, an essential part of the evaluation of tendered designs, found unacceptable potential problems in many cases. Since Ecolonia was to test mass budget housing, architects have had to make practical and stylistic concessions. This has had the effect of watering down the visual radicalism of the village – energy consciousness is not a particularly striking element of the estate. However, Ecolonia does demonstrate that significant savings in energy use and environmental impact can be achieved by optimizing existing building materials and methods. By paying particular regard to orientation (south, east and west facing housing – not north), to differential window areas according to aspect, to increased levels of insulation and efficient boiler systems, Ecolonia has met the target in the NMP of a 25 per cent reduction in household energy use.

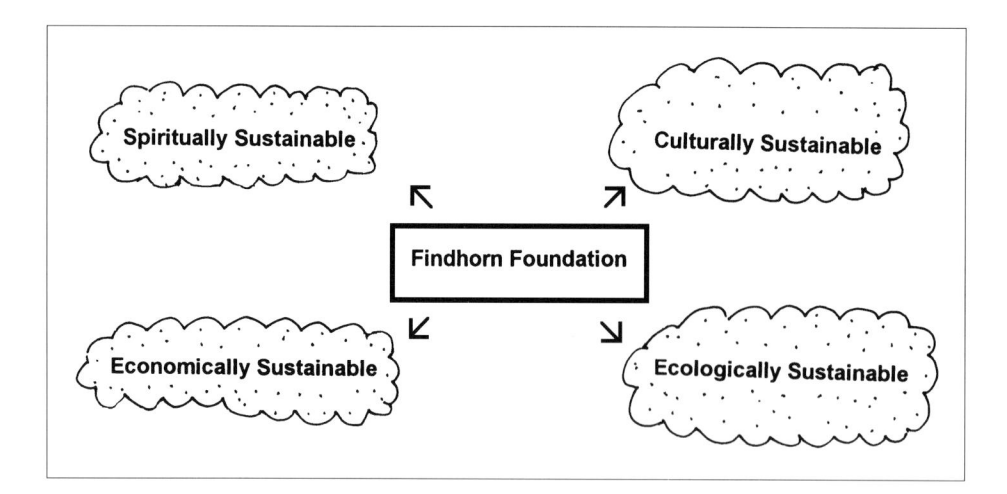

Case studies of sustainable urban development

Figure 29.6
Conceptual framework of sustainability at the village of Findhorn in Scotland.

On the negative side the monitoring of the village shows that:[11]

- compressed wood cellulose insulation carries risks with the entry of moisture (rotting may occur);
- heating and ventilation must be considered jointly if internal air quality is to be safeguarded. Sealed buildings and sophisticated heating systems must be coupled with proper use of ventilation by occupants;
- photovoltaic energy systems are too expensive and unreliable for use in housing;
- water saving is possible (by the reuse of 'grey' water) but compost toilets are insufficiently reliable in service.

Sustainable development, case study of Findhorn, Scotland

Findhorn is a small ecologically balanced community on the cold north-east coast of Scotland. Formerly a caravan site it has grown over the past decade into an important testbed for environmentally sensitive design. Findhorn consists of a community of 300 people living in a selection of self-built or architect designed, mainly detached houses. The houses in their different ways apply a range of ecologically based principles whether in the selection of building materials, the use of energy, or the application of new environmental technologies.

The village, set amongst sand-dunes and pine trees, has been developed by the Findhorn Foundation, a charitable trust whose purpose is to promote new spiritual and environmental awareness through education and demonstration projects. From relatively small beginnings in 1962 Findhorn has grown into one of the leading centres in the UK for a holistic approach to design predicated upon the German 'Baubiologie' principle, i.e. the integration of building and biology.

Healthy building, sustainable lifestyles, and self-sufficiency in food and resource production are the guiding aspirations behind Findhorn. The village has a distinct 'green' philosophy based upon the analogy that buildings are our 'third skin' which, like our skin ('first skin') and our clothes ('second skin') 'needs to function naturally and in harmony with our human organism'.[12] This analogy means that buildings need to breathe and function as a regulator, protector and insulator.

The main design principles embodied in 'Baubiologie' are:

- Houses located away from centres of industry and main traffic routes.
- Houses located in spaciously planned developments with 'green' areas.
- Use of non-toxic and untreated natural building materials.
- Use of wall, floor and ceiling materials that allow air diffusion.
- Use of building materials that are hygroscopic (can absorb and release water vapour) to help moderate indoor air humidity.
- Interior surface materials that allow air filtering and neutralization of air pollutants (i.e. materials capable of 'sorption').
- Balancing heat storage (thermal mass) and thermal insulation levels to provide a comfortable interior living temperature.

---

[11]*Ibid.* Adapted from conclusions in the *Ecolonia* report.

[12]John L Talbott *Simply Build Green* The Findhorn Foundation 1993, p 1–11.

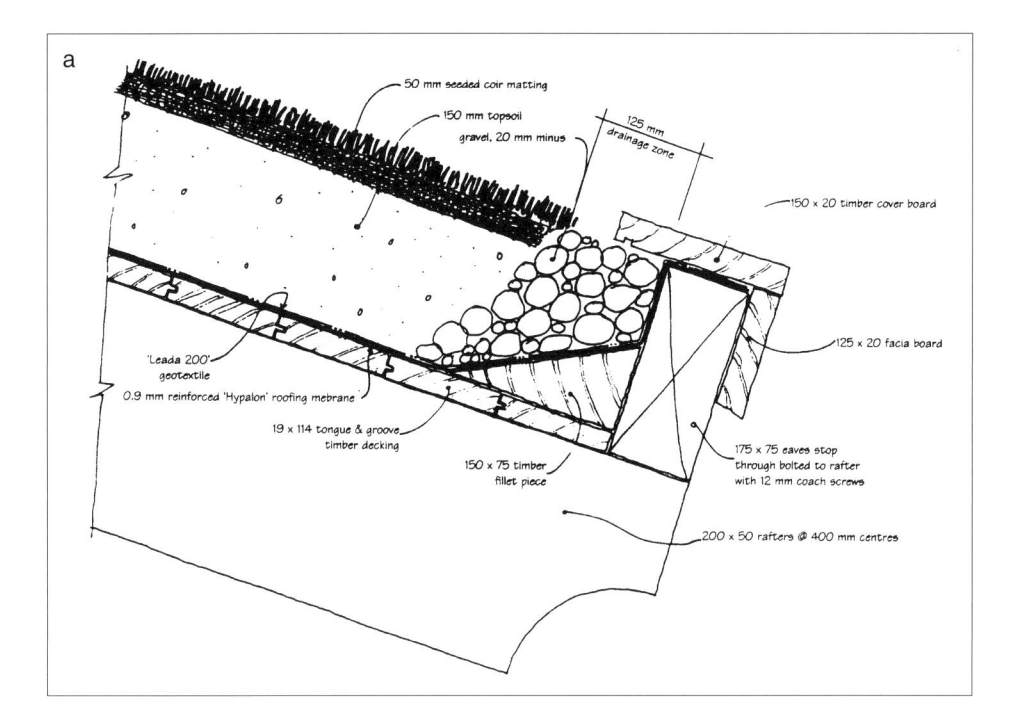

Figure 29.7
Construction details: roof (a) and wall (b) used at Findhorn. (Findhorn Foundation©.)

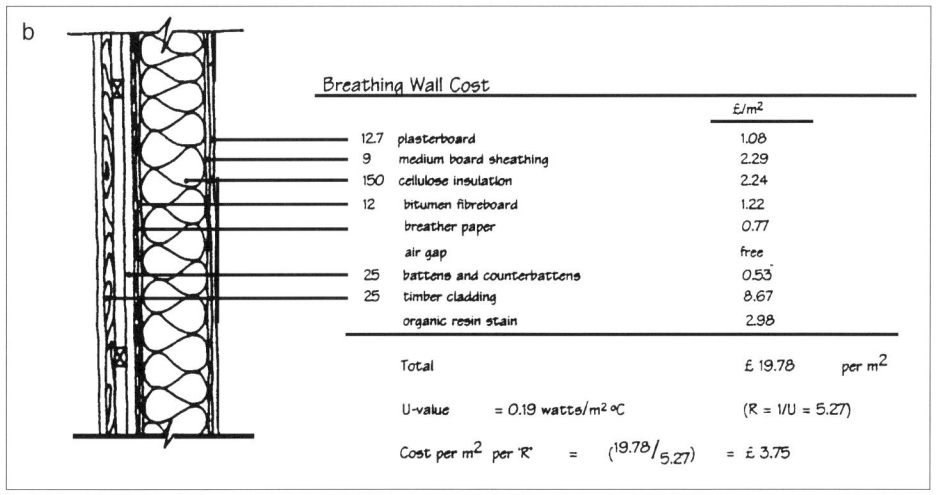

- The use of radiant heating and the use of solar energy wherever possible.
- Adequate protection from noise and infrasound vibration.
- Maximum use of natural daylighting and colours in the interior.
- Minimizing artificial electromagnetic fields while maintaining natural magnetic and electrical fields.
- Use of construction materials that do not contribute environmental degradation or pollution in any aspect of extraction, manufacture, installation and use, and do not exploit limited or endangered natural resources.

Not all of these principles are applied at Findhorn but the list represents design aspirations for those who wish to build in the village. As with all demonstration projects, a number of village houses are being monitored to assess their overall performance and to see how certain techniques (such as breathing walls) and constructional details (e.g. turf roofs) perform.

Findhorn presents two dilemmas. First, the use of mainly detached houses negates many of the benefits of shared wall and roof which are essential for effective energy conservation. Houses grouped into terraces or flats also create climate sheltering groupings. By constructing principally single family houses in their own gardens the model of Findhorn (like that of Energy World at Milton Keynes in 1986) is not readily transferable to the problems of the urban environment more generally. Second, by building near to the sea Findhorn begins with a severe climatic disadvantage. Though the community has planted many trees Findhorn is not where one would wish to start creating a model of sustainability in the first place.

Putting aside these reservations Findhorn has many lessons for other rural communities. To maintain the 'green' integrity of the village developers are required to appoint their own architect whose design is reviewed by Findhorn's in-house planning group. Once approved the plans are submitted to the local planning authority which, after initial reservations, is a whole-hearted supporter of the project.

Working to the guidelines of 'Baubiologie' Findhorn has now developed this checklist into the following principal features. Where the German inspiration was mainly concerned with the interaction between health and building, the new Findhorn principles are more broadly based. Energy and community well-being have emerged as equal concerns thereby moving the culture of Findhorn from a rural retreat for idealistic individuals to a self-sufficient village of people with shared purpose and wider social values.

Green aspects of design or construction used at Findhorn[13]

- Use of passive solar features where possible through orientation and window layout.
- Use of solar panels for domestic hot water heating.
- A district heating system using a gas condensing boiler for highest fuel efficiency.
- High levels of insulation (U-values of 0.2 W/m^2°C in roof, walls and floors).
- Use of low-energy light bulbs.
- Triple glazing (U=1.65 W/m^2°C).
- Use of cellulose insulation (made from recycled paper).
- Non-toxic organic paints and wood preservatives throughout.
- Composite boarding manufactured without the use of toxic glues or resins.
- Locally grown and harvested timber from managed forests.
- Local stone for skirting, patios and pathways.
- Roofing with natural clay tiles.
- Innovative 'breathing wall' construction with a controlled exchange of air and vapour.
- Suspended timber floors for better air circulation to avoid a build-up of radon gas.
- Isolated electrical circuits to reduce electromagnetic field stress.
- Water conservation (showers, low-flush toilets and self-closing taps).
- Collection and recycling of rainwater for garden use.
- Shared facilities (laundry, kitchens, lounges) avoiding unnecessary duplication.
- Simple timber frame construction and detailing suitable for self-build.

Demonstration projects tend to be expensive and those who build in the village accept higher construction costs than in conventional housing. The breathing wall, for example, costs 9 per cent more than the use of standard timber frame construction though the energy efficiency is doubled (0.19 W/m^2°C as against 0.38 W/m^2°C).[14] The payback period is about four years. Similarly, the roof costs 28 per cent more mainly because British suppliers were unable to produce tiles which were considered ecologically sound. For many materials and products used, the developers at Findhorn have had to use French, German and Scandinavian suppliers to obtain the guarantees on green efficacy required by the Foundation. The additional cost of going outside Britain for ecologically benign products has been partly offset by the use of self-build and other forms of voluntary labour. Construction at Findhorn is seen as a spiritual process as well as a means of training building workers in new green technologies.

---

[13]*Ibid.*, p 1–12.

[14]*Ibid.*, p 5–21.

Part 9
The Future of Design

30
New laws, new responsibilities

The complex detail of EC directives should not blind us to the general drift of policy emanating from Brussels. The various legislative measures add up to a potent raft of fresh environmental controls (Table 30.1). The combination of current directives and those mooted mean that Europe is moving towards a state where the impact of development upon the physical environment and the health of people will need to be predicted and made known publicly before buildings are constructed. This will throw architecture open to public scrutiny in a fashion quite unprecedented. The effects of development upon the environment, whether the latter is defined in cultural, aesthetic, social or resource terms, will need to be collected in new ways and made subject to fresh levels of debate. At their bottom line EC directives have the effect of adding to the democratic control over development. In countries like the UK such public consultation has a long tradition (though generally excluding questions of energy use and ecological impact), in other countries, for instance Italy and Spain, the directives bring a fresh current of public accountability.

If EC directives expose large-scale development to unprecedented levels of public accountability in terms of its environmental impact upon a specific site, other directives (such as the eco-labelling and eco-management schemes) seek to measure and make known the ecological

Figure 30.1
Green buildings make worthy landmarks. Here at the Atlantis Building in East London designed by Paul Hyett Architects, the energy and natural ventilation strategy leads to distinctive architecture. (Joss Reiver Barry©.)

New laws, new responsibilities

Table 30.1
Key EC treaties, regulations and directives and their effects on the construction industry and building design

Subject	Number	Effect

Construction products	89/106/EEC see also 93/5068/EEC	• standardizes performance criteria of building products
		• introduces six essential requirements including:
		  - safety in use
		  - environmental health
		  - energy conservation

CFCs	80/372/EEC Regulations 3332/88/EEC 594/91/EEC 3952/92/EEC	• banning of production of CFCs • phasing out HCFCs and halons
Air pollution	91/692/EEC 93/5059/EEC	• reduce permitted levels of discharge into atmosphere • encourage 'clean' burning
Environmental impact assessment	85/337/EEC	• requires assessment of impacts based upon formalized 'environmental statement' for major construction projects
Health and safety	76/579/EEC 79/343/EEC 79/640/EEC 83/477/EEC 86/188/EEC 87/217/EEC 91/382/EEC	• formalizes safety needs and responsibilities on construction sites • improves internal workplace environment • reduces adverse effects of office machines • sets limits to exposure to dangerous conditions
Recycling	75/442/EEC 91/156/EEC	• encouragement of recycling measures
Eco-labelling	94/2/EEC and Regulation EEC/880/92	• introduces a European scheme for eco-labelling • will, in time, provide information on embodied energy and environmental cost of materials
Eco-management	Regulation EEC/1836/93	• introduces a European scheme for the formulation of environmental management systems
Biodiversity	92/43/EEC	• strengthens protection given to natural habitats, flora and fauna • introduces new conservation categories

Sustainable development	Maastricht Treaty & Single European Act	• introduces 3 environment objectives:
		  - preserve, protect and improve environmental quality
		  - contribute towards protecting human health
		  - ensure a prudent and rational use of natural resources
		• introduces 3 environmental principles:
		  - prevention is better than cure
		  - environmental damage should be rectified at source
		  - the polluter should pay

Table 30.2 New and expanded environmental responsibilities for architects within the RIBA 'Plan of Work'

A. Inception	• Brief client on new environmental duties
	• Place 'environmental duty of care' within brief
	• Advise on environmental consequences of site choice
B. Feasibility	• Test the feasibility of environment-friendly design
	• Advise on appointment of 'green' consultants
	• Investigate environmental consequences/opportunities of site
C. Outline proposals	• Develop 'green' strategies in design
	• Obtain approval for unusual energy use or environmental aspects of design
D. Scheme design	• Finalize environmental parameters within design
	• Check the 'green' approach to design and construction against cost and legislative controls
E. Detail design	• Obtain final approvals for environmental design strategy
	• Check 'benignity' of materials to be specified
	• Undertake broad appraisal of 'life-cycle assessment' of components
F. Production information	• Ensure that design, details and specification are in line with current environmental duties and using up to date knowledge
G. Bills of quantities	• Check that bills of quantities allow contractors to realize their environmental duties in building
H. Tender action	• Obtain 'Environmental Policy Statement' from tenderers
	• Advise tenderers of environmental duties
J. Project planning	• Advise appointed contractor of environmental duties and standards
K. Operations on site	• Monitor site operations to ensure good environmental practice is followed
	• Undertake spot checks of environmental performance
L. Completion	• Ensure building is environmentally sound
	• Check environmental controls are working and understood
	• Compile Environmental Statement for building
M. Feedback	• Monitor environmental performance of building
	• Disseminate results of environmental initiatives in journals
	• Prepare a user manual for all subsequent owners/occupiers

effects of a multitude of small impacts upon the global environment. How much energy is embodied in a building material (in terms of the manufacturing processes which made it), what the effect of the use of certain timbers is upon the survival of rainforests or global biodiversity, what the impacts are of particular products and finishes upon the realization of 'sustainable development' are all questions now to be asked. The consequences are twofold: first, the public will be better able to veto poor environmental or energy practice using the new legislation to curb bad design. Second, architects, engineers and contractors will have new measures of environmental benignity to achieve, and new legal responsibilities to explain to their clients. If they fail to offer this advice or take appropriate action, professionals face a litigious future. The RIBA 'Plan of Work' provides a useful framework for measuring the scale of changes required (see Table 30.2). The table shows that environmental considerations need to be integrated from the briefing and establishment of design objectives stage to detailed design, site supervision and post-occupancy monitoring.

If the new controls seek to make us aware in a systematic fashion of the environmental and ecological effects of development, other EC measures are aimed not at achieving wider environmental well-being but the health of those who use buildings. Since Europeans spend 90 per cent of their time indoors, the effect of building materials, products and finishes upon human health is also emerging as a field of new legislative concern. Indoor air quality, the health of office workers using VDUs, and the environmental safety of factory workers, are increasingly attracting the attention of legislators in Brussels.

The deterioration of the urban environments of Europe, concerns over loss of global biodiversity, and the increasing prospect of global climate change are the external equivalent to parallel problems caused to those who inhabit buildings. There is a growing body of evidence which suggests that asthma and certain cancers are caused by poor interior environments. There are no easy solutions to complex problems and not always a consensus that buildings and the man-made environment are the sole or prime cause of many of today's problems. In a period of uncertainty it is, however, prudent to act within the 'precautionary principle'.

Materials and technologies which may pose a threat should not be specified: natural products are more benign in their effects than man-made; renewable energy should be exploited rather than that derived from fossil fuels or

New laws, new responsibilities

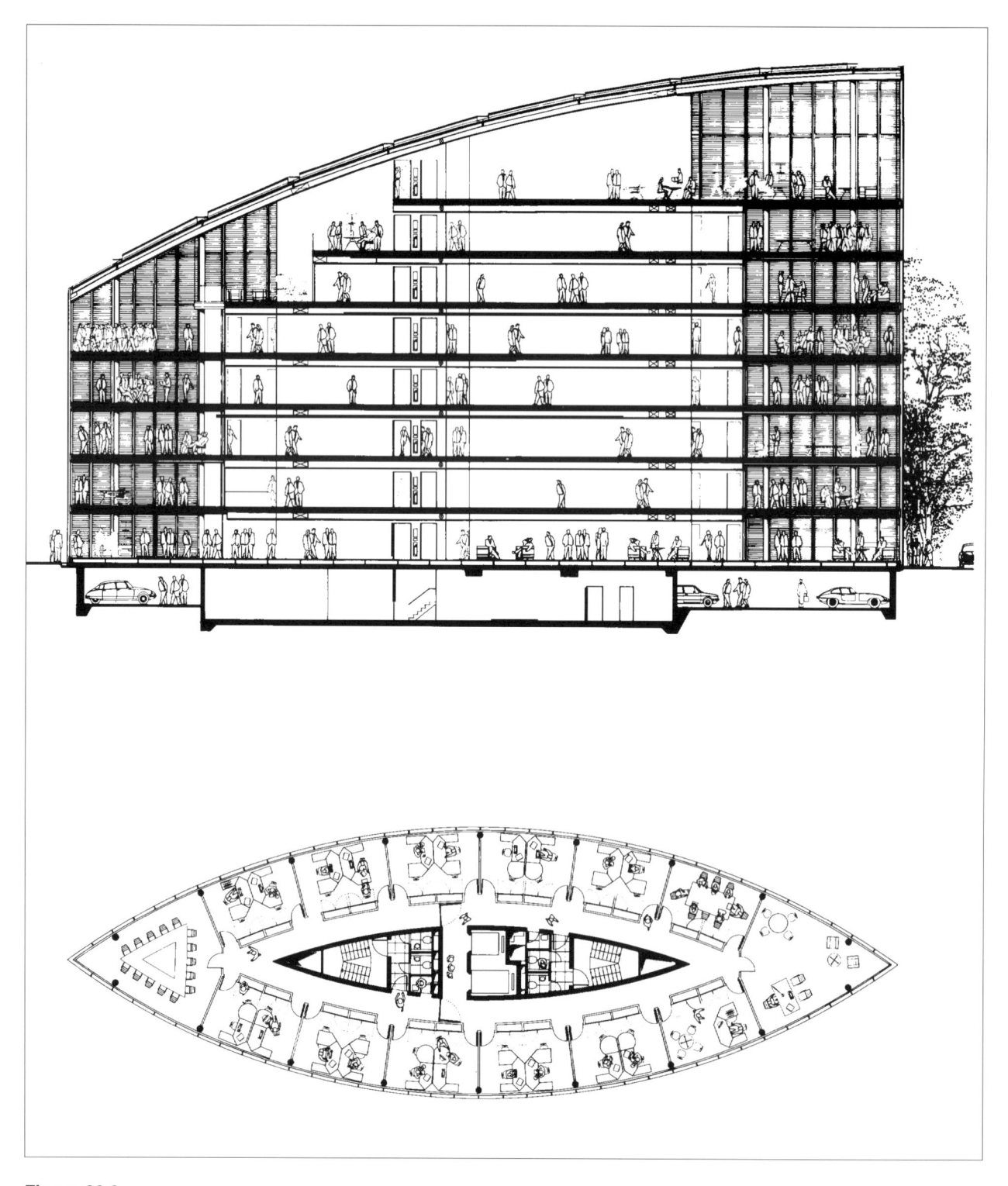

Figure 30.2
This naturally ventilated office utilizing roof mounted photovoltaic panels in Duisburg, Germany designed by Sir Norman Foster & Partners hints at the aesthetic opportunities of good environmental design. (Sir Norman Foster & Partners©.)

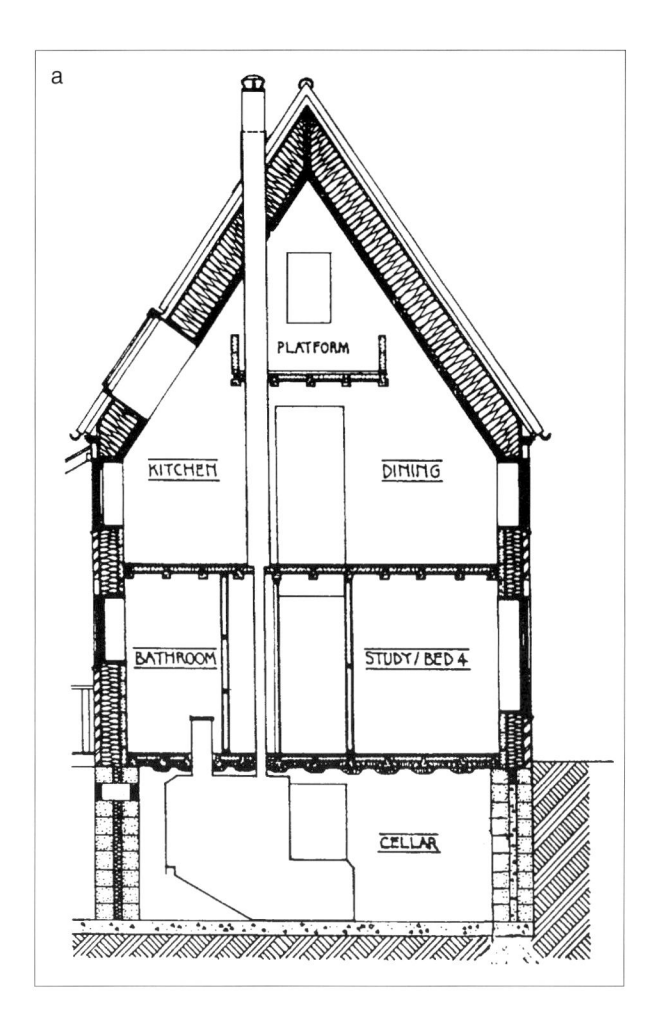

nuclear power. Ventilation and daylight by natural means should be the norm for most building types. Planting should be used to create shelter and improve internal and external air quality. Facilities should be provided at the urban and building level to encourage movement by bicycle and on foot. Patterns of development need to encourage rather than thwart the use of public modes of transport. Many more measures could be listed (and most can be found elsewhere in this book) which accumulatively and over time could greatly reduce the adverse effects of buildings upon the environment. Since architecture almost uniquely impacts upon the global system and local subsystems simultaneously, the designer needs to consider both the whole and the part, employing the best environmental knowledge and theory.

The EC measures and principles which currently control and shape development point towards a new age for European architecture. As substitute low-impact technologies are employed, a fresh aesthetic emerges. Construction and building services are becoming more user-friendly, organic materials are beginning to replace artificial or heavily engineered ones, natural means of lighting and ventilating buildings are replacing the sealed envelopes of earlier systems, and nature is informing designers and engineers in a fresh way. Buildings are using landscape as a climatic buffer, regional patterns of development are being rediscovered, and cities are being valued again as reservoirs of built resources to be recycled. New laws add fresh values which in turn produce a new architecture. In his Reith lectures of 1995 Richard Rogers predicted that the drive for sustainability will lead to a 'New Enlightenment' in architecture.

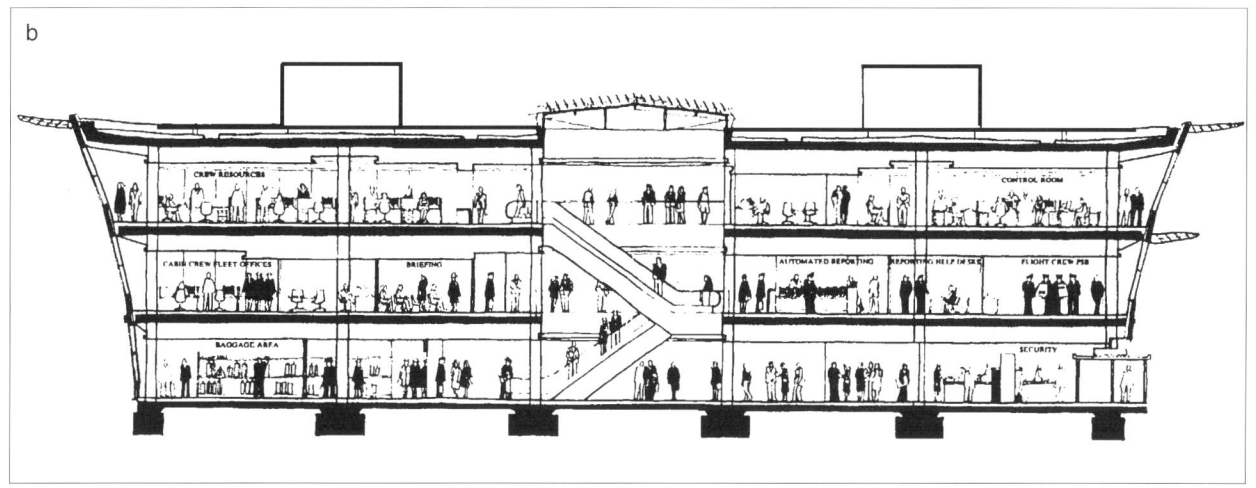

Figure 30.3
The section of buildings in particular will change as environmental considerations become paramount. These two common building types, a house (a) and an office (b), put green principles to the fore. (Robert and Brenda Vale© and Nicholas Grimshaw & Partners©.)

New laws, new responsibilities

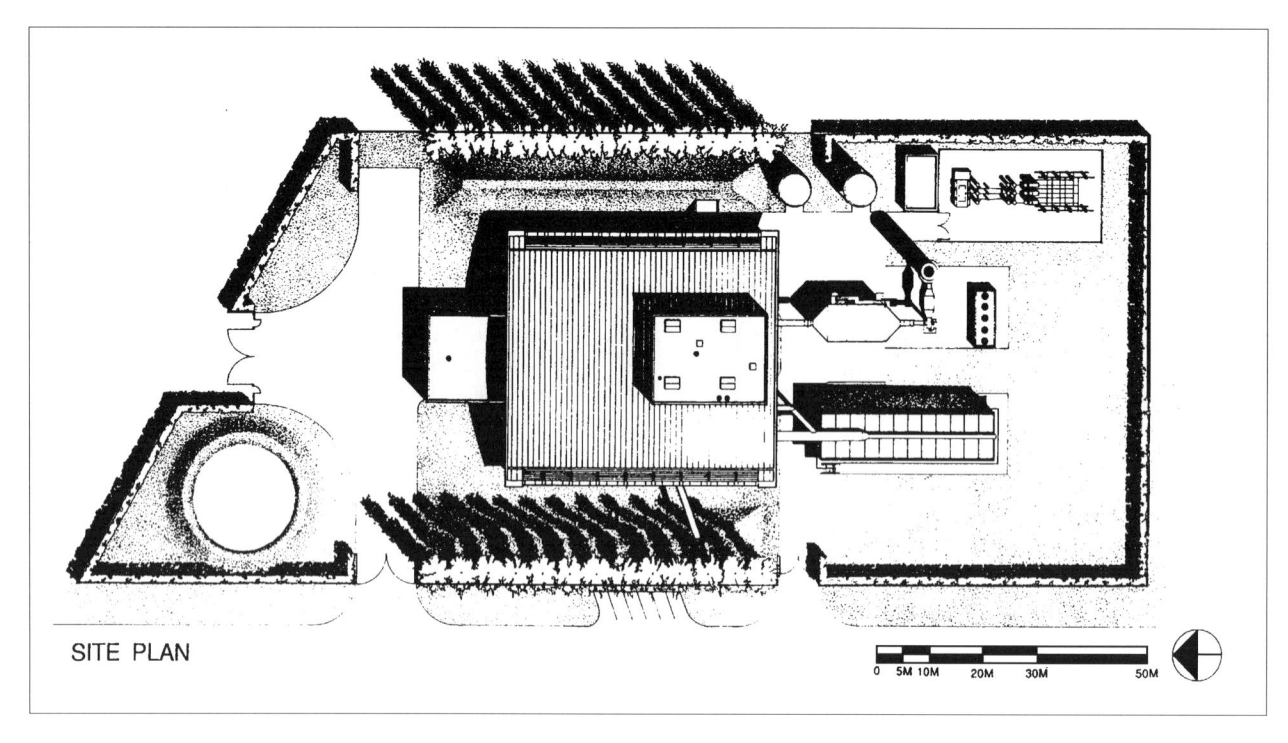

Figure 30.4
Eye Power Station, Suffolk by Lifschutz Davidson. Designs like this could become the model for small power plants integrated into urban areas. Notice how planting forms a perimeter for the development and effectively screens the larger buildings. (Lifschutz Davidson©.)

The 'green' age holds the prospect of a style of building as distinctive as the styles of earlier ages. As building technology changes and methods of construction alter, so there emerges a new aesthetic order. In Germany, Denmark and Holland evidence of the new approach to architecture is commonplace; in Britain green development is still relatively rare. As the UK becomes absorbed into the culture of Europe, and its legislative measures, such architecture will become the norm here too. At a cultural level green buildings hold the prospect of a new distinctive layer of development to stand alongside the buildings of earlier periods. The case studies seek to show that emergent environmental design principles will produce a visually rich and formally different architecture. Perspectives of beauty will increasingly reside in questions of ecological impact, not in the remoter reaches of fine art which has dogged much recent architecture.

The challenge for today's designers is to extend these beginnings into a coherent, intellectually refined architecture where the justification for the 'new style' is based entirely upon environmental factors. Such buildings will necessarily leave a small footprint upon the planet (no building is entirely ecologically benign), yet the impacts will be known in advance and the environmental costs will achieve the maximum social, economic and cultural benefits. In the next century buildings will be seen as a resource, not a commodity, and urban development as reaping the greatest advantages across a broad front for the minimum ecological and resource impact. Just as the 1970s heralded an age of 'long life, loose-fit, low energy buildings', the 1990s will extend these paradigms by the addition of 'minimum ecological impact'.

Although the detail of EC law affecting development inevitably changes, the principles endure. New statutes may change the focus of attention but the wide drift of policy remains much the same. The examples in this book and the analysis of EC regulation point to significant changes in the parameters of architecture. As fresh priorities emerge for design based upon minimum environmental damage, there grows a need to change practices, to alter philosophies, to explore new materials, to develop substitute technologies, and to modify how we teach architecture. Building design has not had to face such a ground swell of changes since the universal introduction of modernism between the wars. The new green age could be seen as the final refinement of modernist design thinking or the emergence of an architecture of the post-industrial age. Whichever position is adopted should not undermine

New laws, new responsibilities

Figure 30.5
Photovoltaic panels incorporated into the façades of buildings provide an effective way to reduce energy consumption. This demonstration project at the University of Northumbria at Newcastle was funded with an EC Thermie grant. (Ove Arup & Partners©.)

the importance of the changes brought about by the green tide of opinion embodied in various EC treaties, directives and regulations.

Since buildings are the source of about half of the production in Europe of greenhouse gases and ozone depleting chemicals, it is here that much new legislation is directed. Under the 'polluter pays' principle, clients and their designers have a responsibility to create development which is largely pollution free. The 'polluter pays' principle enables third parties to seek compensation from the original polluter, thereby exposing clients and their professional advisers to new levels of risk. It is vital that the client is made aware of the need to address environmental legal considerations by his architect, that designers use the best available knowledge and skills to reduce their liability for pollution and consequential clean-up costs. This is no easy task with current technology and a culture which measures cost rather than value. Buildings which cast a small footprint on the planet tend to be expensive initially – the energy cost savings may take a decade to be recovered. Yet if the control of pollution at source (another EC principle) is to be universally adopted, those who design, construct and procure buildings need to embrace new environmental technologies. Whilst the directives provide a fresh legal framework for design, ignoring them or their consequences at the client briefing stage may expose the construction professional to claims of negligence. As the eco-labelling and eco-management schemes take effect, designers will in the future be able to advise their clients of the environmental costs of different building materials. New laws will create new demands for knowledge which in turn will generate new skills and fresh opportunities.

New laws, new architecture

The raft of the issues raised by this book suggests a move from standardized building solutions to diversity based upon the specific dictates of environmental and ecological imperatives. Europe is increasingly concerned with

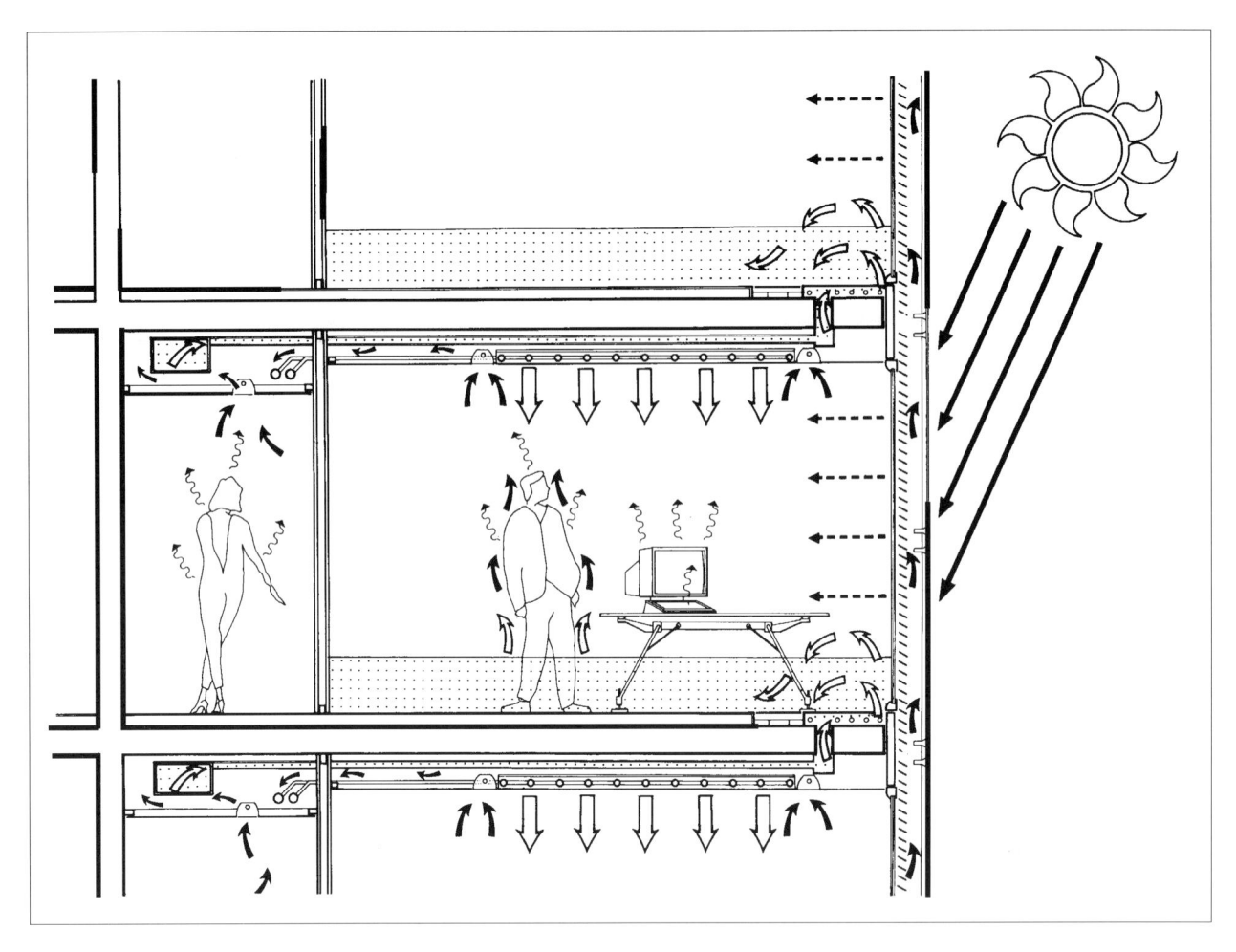

New laws, new responsibilities

Figure 30.6
Questions of energy use, amenity and health will drive the next generation of office buildings. (Sir Norman Foster & Partners©.)

questions of sustainable development, and personal and global health. The need to preserve fossil fuels for future generations, the protection of inherited environmental richness, whether natural or built, the drive for improved public health in the face of smothering pollution, are all legitimate concerns of government. New environmental laws from Brussels seek, as many UK ones do, the creation of ecologically safe and healthy buildings, and the wise use of diminishing resources. In this sense new laws will herald a new approach to architecture and building engineering.

The 1990s have seen a search for design solutions which exploit the specifics of place, resources and culture. The idea that standard precedents of plan or social organization can be imposed is dated. Today new concerns for sustainability, local tradition and diversity bred of environmental sensitivity are driving design into new forms and fresh fields. The imperative of maintaining ecological richness, and using the minimum of resources to achieve the maximum of diversity, smoothes the path into a humane, socially responsive and environmentally benign architecture. Development has changed its face over the decade: where buildings were once sealed to exclude climate, they now respond to climate, ruffling their feathers like a bird in response to changing temperature. Where they were once similar in form from one end of Europe to another, they now take on differences in response to climate, natural resources and regional cultures.

The fire of environmental revolution, fanned by the 160 signatories to the Rio Summit, is now sweeping through Western societies. Global climate change and ozone depletion are of such proportions that few governments can avoid their consequences. New laws and regulations are

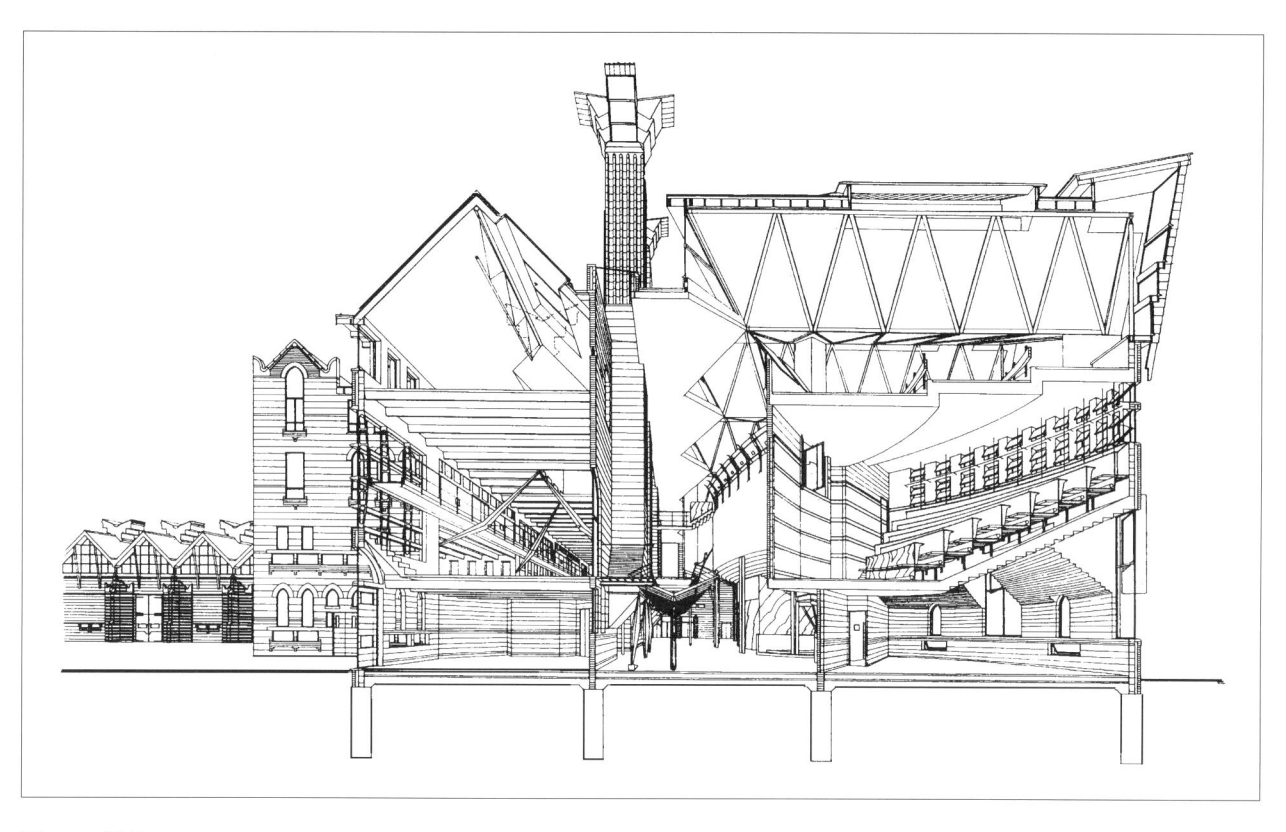

Figure 30.7
The section rather than the plans of buildings illustrate green thinking as here at the Queen's Building at De Montfort University. (Short Ford & Partners©.)

rapidly being enacted to encourage a more rational and harmonious pattern of development, and one which does not destabilize the world's climate. Several companies (such as Sainsbury and Salvesen Brick) and local authorities (such as Leicester City Council and Central Regional Council) have pointed the way with 'green' development strategies. Though flawed in concept or part, these beginnings are important precursors to the wider cultural changes needed. Elsewhere in Europe (such as Ecolonia in Holland) professionals have already charted a path which others can follow.

Developers and their architects have always broadly speaking served social needs. As these have changed new patterns of development and fresh professional skills emerge. The post-war reconstruction of European cities required a particular brand of entrepreneur and designer, the post-Rio Summit age will require another. As Ken Collins noted in the foreword, Europe has moved from protecting the environment to being conscious of the need to create environmental richness, reduce resource needs and repair environmental damage by the action of mankind. This involves forming environmental havens, recreating lost habitats, designing structures and places which reduce the demand for energy use, avoiding the use of climate damaging chemicals, and banning tropical hardwood products. European law has tended to be ahead of national laws, not just in Britain, but in most of Europe.

New laws have created the market for fresh design skills and substitute technologies. Professionals with new aptitudes and environmental sensibilities will find their services needed whilst those wedded to the old system of development and patronage will find themselves increasingly at the margin of popular and political ambition. This represents a challenge for education and for continuing professional development for those currently in practice. The scale of change needed, in how both new development is designed and existing buildings are adapted, is enormous. Since much environmental damage and wasteful consumption of energy and resources is the result of the existing development pattern and design of buildings, this is where effort needs to be directed. With rates of renewal of buildings in Europe currently at 2 per cent of the total stock per year, retrofit measures emerge as central to moves towards sustainable development. The

New laws, new responsibilities

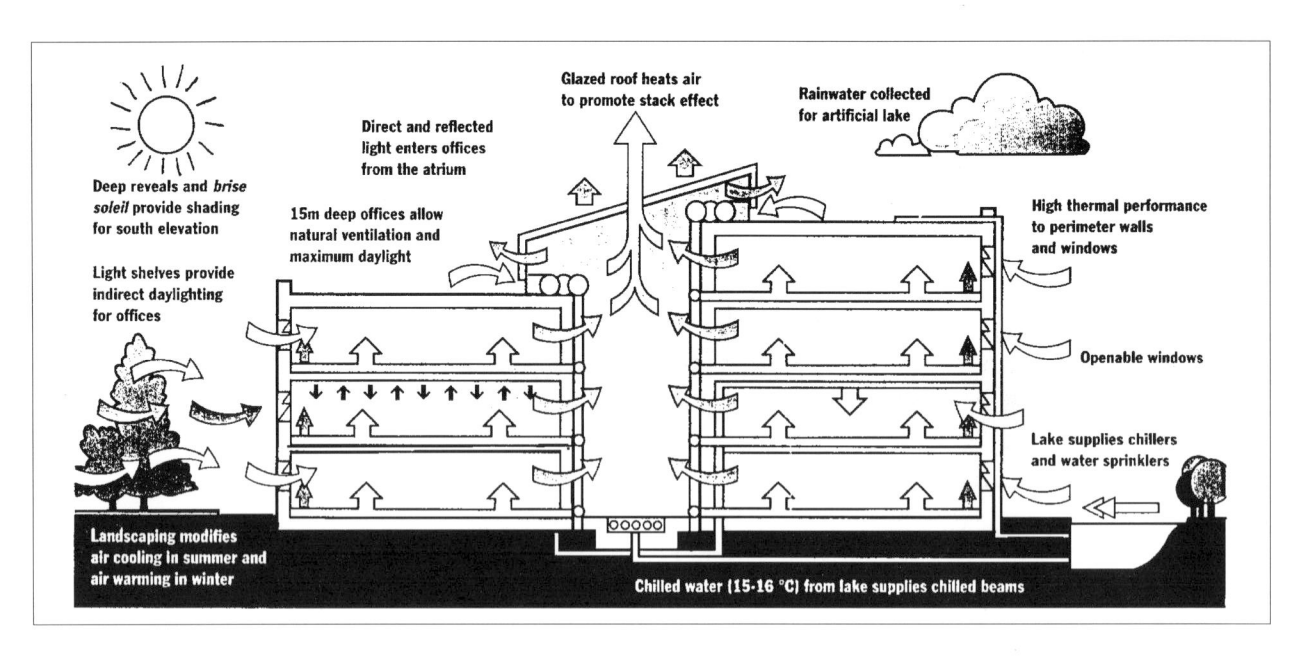

Figure 30.8
The shape of offices to come. Barclaycard headquarters by Fitzroy Robinson & Partners. (Matthew Bell©.)

Figure 30.9
Small, more community-based power stations, often burning biomass, will become commonplace in the future. (Lifschutz Davidson©.)

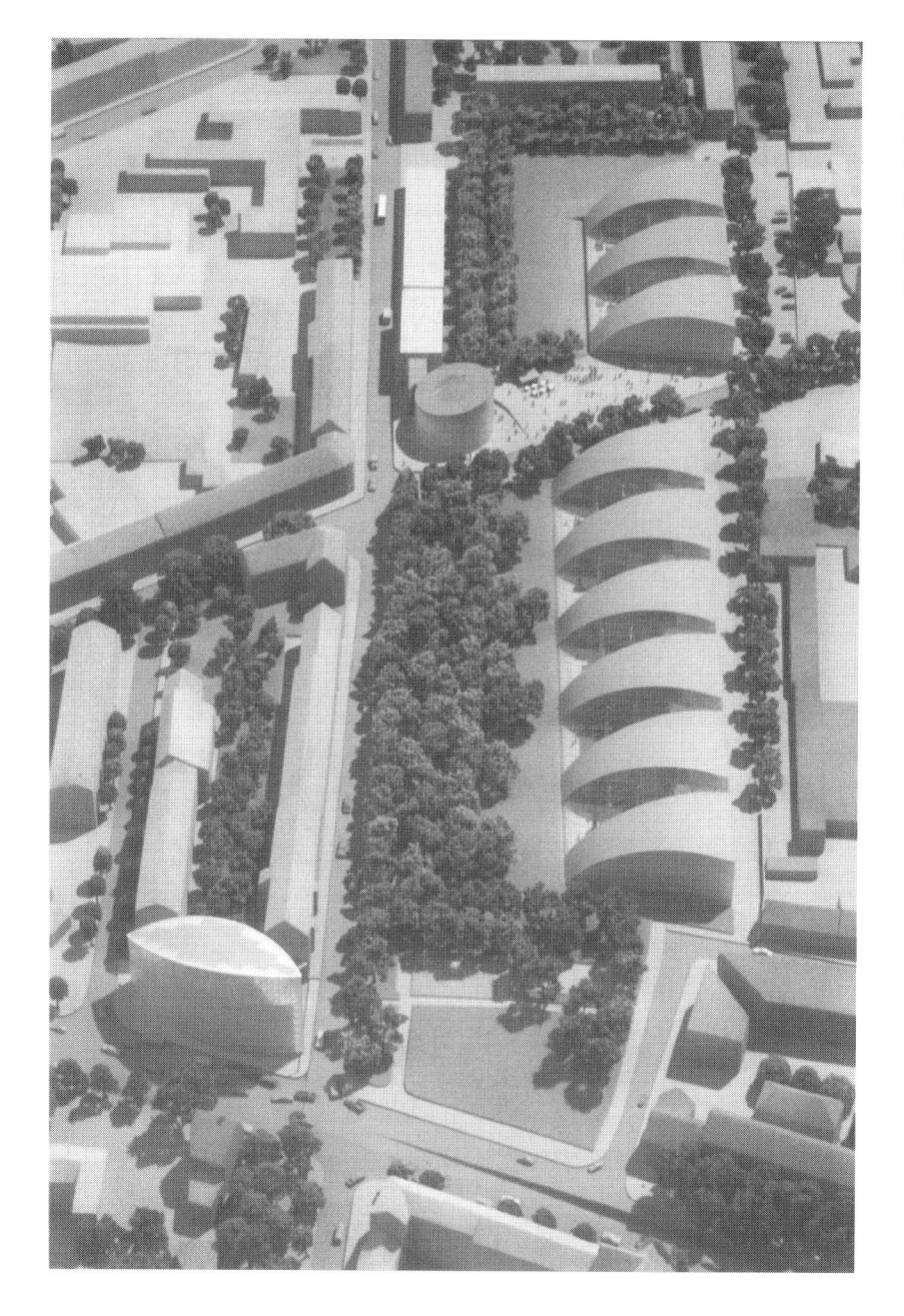

Figure 30.10
Expanding Environment Laws will inevitably generate a new age for architecture, but buildings of the future will require new skills and knowledge. Model of Technology Park, Duisburg, Germany, designed by Sir Norman Foster & Partners. (Sir Norman Foster & Partners©.)

problem is particularly significant with regard to existing office buildings (those built between 1960–90) where more heat is generated from lighting, equipment and solar gains than is lost through the building fabric. Air conditioning, the traditional solution, carries such environmental costs that fundamental redesign is required.

In Europe our cities are mainly already made, other parts of the world are less fortunate. The challenge for Britain and other Member States is to upgrade buildings and towns to fresh environmental standards, using new benign technologies. Since markets are open in Europe, unless UK professionals develop the skills and knowledge to undertake this work, it will fall to architects and engineers from Holland, Germany and Denmark who have already tackled these problems at home.

The EC Green Paper on the Urban Environment (1990) highlighted the importance of the traditional pattern of development in European cities to perceptions of European culture. The survival of the compact distinctiveness of countless cities and towns of Europe requires the same kind of attention which is currently directed to the Common Agricultural Policy (CAP). As EC law

New laws, new responsibilities

Figure 30.11
Sustainable development will focus attention upon cities and lead to a revival of urban housing types. (McGurn, Logan, Duncan and Opfer©.)

recognizes in its various clauses, the health and wealth of cities is dependent upon them moving in a more sustainable direction. Development needs to pay greater regard to questions of durability, energy use, pollution, public health, resource conservation, heritage and biodiversity. Sustainable development cannot be achieved quickly (if at all) but it is a goal towards which Europe aspires. Laws and regulations are an important means by which these changes can be brought about. Some companies such as ICI began to change environmental direction before forced to by law, others have had to adapt to the stricter timescales of regulatory change. Astute developers and designers are already building to much higher energy and health standards than laws require, believing that the moral argument will win favour with discerning clients and ultimately the public at large. In time the examples of 'green' building from Duisburg to Findhorn will not be rare exceptions to the pattern of European development but the norm.

The environmental revolution encapsulated in recent EC legislation will not go away. The near doubling of the human population of the world every forty years puts huge pressures on resources, both natural and built. A construction industry once dominated by questions of growth and land colonization now finds itself caught in new ideological currents. This book is written to help construction professionals to find their way through the details and principles of unfolding European laws on development and environmental protection. The case studies illustrate the new approach to building and show that a green architecture can be visually rich, technologically sound, socially responsive and ecologically benign. Sustainable development is the beginning of a process for which sustainable architecture is one of the ends.

Table 30.3
Comparison of energy use between air-conditioned office and natural ventilated office

Energy use	Typical air-conditioned office	Good practice open plan office with natural ventilation
Heating and hot water	222	95
Lighting	67	32
Fans and pumps	61	5
Refrigeration	33	0
Catering	7	4
Total	390	136

Source: Energy Consumption Guide 19, BRECSU
Note: The units are measured in kilowatt hours/m²

Glossary

Acid rain – Cloud and rain droplets containing a solution of sulphur oxides (SO_2 and SO_3) and nitrogen dioxide (NO_2).

Agenda 21 – A commitment entered into at the Rio (Earth) Summit (1992) to introduce specific policies to help stabilize world temperatures and move towards sustainable development.

Appropriate design – The use of the minimum energy input and the lowest level of technological sophistication to achieve effective, efficient and healthy conditions.

Artificial lighting – The use of non-natural means of providing internal or external illumination. Artificial lighting is usually dependent upon fossil-fuel use.

Biodiversity – The diversity of living things – eco-systems, species and genetic complexity.

Brown field sites – Land in urban areas which has already seen development and is lying vacant. In the UK about 40 per cent of urban land falls into this category.

Chlorofluorocarbons (CFCs) – These are man-made chemicals which cause the thinning of the ozone layer (about one half are used in building). CFCs are also a greenhouse gas.

Climate – The modified climate close to a building usually due to man's intervention.

Cross ventilation – The use of wind, temperature and pressure differences to ventilate a building naturally usually via windows or vents.

Daylight – Natural source of light which determines the internal 'Daylight Factor' (DF). This is dependent upon direct light, external reflected light, and internal reflected light. Daylight itself consists of sunlight, cloud diffused sunlight, and both reflected by the ground and adjoining surfaces.

Energy conservation – The conservation of energy by reducing the outward transmission of heat, by controlling ventilation, and by exploiting renewable sources of energy such as sunlight. Energy conservation is also a matter of balancing heating and lighting needs, and addressing energy use, energy controls and energy generation as related factors.

Environmental audit – A term used by companies to measure and understand the environmental implications of their operations, particularly with regard to pollution.

Environmental contamination – The damage to the environment and its eco-systems caused by contaminants of various kinds. Such damage can be either irreversible or reversible.

Environmental cost – A measure of the cost in resource or financial terms of environmental damage or degradation.

Environmental Impact Assessment (EA) – The assessment and evaluation of the impact of development upon a specific site or location. It usually consists of three analytical stages: impact identification, evaluation and comparison. Environmental Impact Assessment and Environmental Assessment are synonymous terms.

Environmental Impact Statement – A quantitative and qualitative statement of a broad range of impacts (from ecological to social), whether direct, indirect or cumulative. It is usually a publicly available document prepared by a developer.

Environmental review – The review of operations by a company to determine performance against selected environmental criteria. Usually an introduction to developing an environmental policy or action programme.

Environmental value – The value attached to an environmental resource in social, economic or cultural terms.

Environment-friendly – Materials and processes which seek to have the minimum impact upon the environment throughout their life-cycle (manufacture, use, disposal).

Evaporative cooling – Utilizing the cooling effect of the change in state of a liquid (usually water) to vapour. The evaporative cooling effect can be maximized by increasing the water/air contact area and speed of interface.

Glossary

Fossil fuels – Finite sources of carbon-based energy (mostly oil, gas and coal) which are burnt to produce heat and other sources of power.

Green field sites – Land in rural areas which is primarily in agricultural or forestry use.

Greenhouse effect (of a building) – The warming of a building due to the absorption, usually through glass, of shortwave solar energy which is stored as heat by elements of construction and prevented from being re-emitted as longwave radiation by the glass.

Greenhouse effect (of the planet) – The warming of the planet due to the increase in density of trace greenhouse gases in the atmosphere. They have the effect of increasing the absorption of sunlight by preventing the outward radiation of heat from the Earth.

Halons – These are CFCs used, for instance, in fire fighting equipment.

Hazardous waste – Particular types of waste which pose direct risks to personal or environmental health.

Interior amenity – A sense of amenity in the interior environment based upon spatial quality, extent of natural daylight and interior air quality.

Mixed-mode ventilation – Natural ventilation involving openable windows combined with mechanical air change usually with an emphasis upon local control of the environment.

Natural cooling – The use of ground cooling, night-time radiation heat loss, cross ventilation and evaporative cooling to naturally reduce internal temperatures.

Optimal daylight – The satisfactory provision of lighting based upon a combination of daylight and artificial light at the lowest level for effective work.

Ozone layer – A layer of protective gas some 10–40 km above the earth which absorbs ultraviolet radiation from the sun.

'Polluter pays' principle – The principle that the polluter is responsible for damage even to third parties and in perpetuity.

Pollution – The contamination of natural resources (water, air, land) or eco-systems by man-made actions and a human reaction to that physical effect.

'Pollution at source' principle – The principle that pollution should be dealt with at source, rather than through remedial action later.

Precautionary principle – Where doubts exist one should err on the side of caution rather than risk. This implies an anticipatory and preventative approach.

Recycled materials – Products which are manufactured from the resources previously existing in waste.

Recycling – The reuse of the resource potential locked within a waste product, including a redundant building.

Solar gain – The increase in temperature inside a building due to trapping and storing sunlight.

Solar radiation – The amount of sunlight on a building or site, usually dependent upon the position of adjoining buildings, planting or landform.

Solar shading – The protection of a building from sunlight radiation by external (and sometimes also internal) means of shading. Since the sun moves both seasonally and during the day, such shading is often adjustable.

Stack effect ventilation – The use of thermal currents driven primarily by utilizing passive solar gain to ventilate the interior of buildings.

Sustainable development – Development which meets present needs without compromising the ability of future generations to achieve their needs and aspirations (Brundtland Commission definition). Alternatively, Sustainable Development is based upon development which

(1) utilizes renewable resources at rates less than the natural rate at which they regenerate;
(2) optimizes the efficiency with which non-renewable resources are used.

Temperature gradient effect – The exploitation of different temperatures of air (and hence density and pressure) to create currents and hence ventilate a building, usually by natural means. See also 'stack-effect ventilation'.

Thermal comfort – A variable level of perceived comfort based upon a combination of metabolism, clothing, skin temperature, room temperature and relative humidity.

Urban microclimate – The local climate in a town, usually modified by the configuration of streets and buildings and the presence of planting.

Visual comfort – The perception of vision based upon relative brightness, clarity and even colour spread. Generally, glare free conditions and artificial lighting colours close to natural lighting are preferred.

Waste management – The management of waste to reduce the amount generated and to recycle the resources which exist within it.

Bibliography

Books

Baden-Powell, Francis, *Building Overseas* Butterworth Architecture, Oxford, 1993.

Beaumont, J. R. and Keys, P., *Future Cities: Spatial Analysis of Energy Issues* John Wiley & Sons, Chichester, 1982.

Burke, T. and Hill, J., *Ethics, Environment and the Company* The Institute of Business Ethics, London, 1990.

Commission of the European Communities, *Green Paper on the Urban Environment* COM(90) 218, Brussels, 1990.

Commission of the European Communities *Energy Conscious Design: A Primer for Architects* Batsford, London, 1992.

Curwell, S. R. and March, C. G., *Hazardous Building Materials: A guide to the selection of alternatives* E & F Spon, 1986.

Curwell, S. R., Fox, R. C. and March, C. G., *The Use of CFCs in Buildings* Friends of the Earth, London, 1988.

Curwell, S. R., March C. G. and Venables, *Buildings & Health: The Rosehaugh Guide to the Design, Construction, Use & Management of Buildings* RIBA Publications, London, 1990.

Davidson, J., *How Green is Your City* Bedford Square Press, London, 1988.

Dubin, F. S. and Long, C. G., *Energy Conservation Standards: for Building Design, Construction & Operation* McGraw-Hill, 1978.

Earnshaw, R. A. (ed.), *State of the Art in Stereo and Terrain Modelling* Conference Proceedings, British Computer Society, 1986.

Elkin, T., McLaren, D. and Hillman, M., *Reviving the City: towards sustainable urban development*, Friends of the Earth, London, 1991.

Energy in Architecture – European Passive Solar Handbook Batsford CEC.

Girardet, H., *The Gaia Atlas of Cities: New Directions for Sustainable Urban Living* Gaia Books Ltd, London, 1992.

Gordon, D., *Green Cities: Ecologically Sound Approaches to Urban Space* Black Rose Books, 1990.

Hay, A., and Wright, C., *Once is not Enough* Friends of the Earth, London, 1989.

Hill, J. *Towards Good Environmental Practice* Institute of Business Ethics, London, 1992.

Holdsworth, B. and Sealey, A., *Healthy Buildings: A Design Primer for a Living Environment* Longman, 1992.

Internation Energy Agency Task XI, *Passive and Hybrid Solar Commercial Buildings* Harwell Laboratory, Oxford, 1990.

JT Design and Build – Going Green, The Green Construction Handbook.

Knight's European Construction Documents Charles Knight Publishing, 1992.

Leinster, P. and Mitchel, E., *Health and Safety: A Review of Indoor Air Quality and its Impact on the Health and Well-being of Office Workers* Commission of European Communities, Luxembourg, 1992.

Lewis O. and Goulding J. (eds.), *European Directory of Energy Efficient Building 1993*, James & James, London, 1993.

Maver, T. W., 'Visual Modelling in Architectural Design' J. Lansdown (ed.), *Computer Graphics in Art Animation and Design* Springer-Verlag, 1989.

Owens, S. and Owens, P., *Environment, Resources and Conservation* Cambridge University Press, Cambridge, 1991.

Pearce, D., Markandya, A. and Barbier, E., *Blueprint for a Green Economy* Earthscan, London, 1989.

Sherlock, H., *Cities are Good for Us* Transport 2000, London, 1990.

Bibliography

Speaight, A. and Stone, G., *Architect's Legal Handbook: The Law for Architects* (Fifth Edition) Butterworth Architecture, Oxford, 1990.

Spencer Chapman, N. F. and Grandjean, C., *The Construction Industry and the European Community* BSP Professional Books, London, 1991.

This Common Inheritance CM1200 HMSO, London, 1990.

Vale, B. and Vale, R., *Green Architecture: Design for a Sustainable Future* Thames & Hudson, London, 1991.

Whyte, W. H., *City: Rediscovering the Centre* Doubleday, New York, 1988.

The World Commission on Environment and Development (The Brundtland Commission), *Our Common Future* Oxford University Press, Oxford, 1987.

Papers and Journals

Baker, N., *The Atrium Environment* The Martin Centre, University of Cambridge.

Baldwin, R., Leach, S. C., Doggart, J. and Attenborough, M., *An Environmental Assessment for new Office Design* BREEAM: Building Research Establishment, Watford UK, 1990.

BRE Digest 350 – Parts 1, 2 and 3.

BRE Report 129, Daylighting as a Passive Solar Energy Option.

Building and Buildings: the Construction Products Regulations, HMSO, 1991.

Building and Health: Indoor Climate and Effective Energy Use Stockholm: Swedish Council for Building Research, 1991.

Building Research Establishment (BRE) *Good Practice Guide Energy Efficiency in Advanced Factory Units*, Watford, 1992.

CEC Proceedings: Building 2000 Workshops, 1988.

CIBSE, 'Sick building syndrome: The CIBSE View' *CIBSE Journal*, Vol 11, No 6, June 1989, pp 31–3.

Energy 85, Energy Use in the Built Environment Stockholm: Swedish Council for Building Research, 1985.

Environment Business Forum Handbook CBI, London, 1994.

ETSU Report S 1160/4 – South Staffordshire Water Company.

Going Green (guide), Ove Arup & Partners, London, 1993.

Heating Cooling and Lighting – design methods for architects Norbert Lechner (Wiley Interscience).

IEA Task Group XI Passive & Hybrid Solar Commercial Buildings ETSU, Harwell Laboratories, Oxfordshire.

Indoor Air Quality Research WHO EURO Researches and Studies 103, Copenhagen, World Health Organization, 1986.

Mant, D. C. and Gray, J. A. M., *Building Regulations and Health* BRE Report, Building Research Establishment, 1986.

Maver, T. W. (ed.), 'Landscape and planning design' *Computer Aided Design* Vol 19, No 4.

Osborne J. (ed.) *The Construction Products Directive of the European Communities* Building Technical File, London, 1989.

Petric, J., 'Visual impact analysis transmission lines' *Power Technology International*, 1991.

Public Works Contract Regulations HMSO, 1991.

Public Works Supply Contract Regulations, HMSO, 1991.

RIAS Practice Information: March 1990: Section V: EK1: Roger Talbot, 'Buildings, energy and the greenhouse effect: the problem and the solution'.

RIAS Practice Information: Spring 1991: Section V: EK23: Roger Talbot, 'Environmental audits'.

Royal Institute of British Architects, *Environmental Policy Statement RIBA* London, 1990.

Russel, J. S., 'Indoor air quality: The Architect's Role' *Architectural Record*, November, 1990, pp 105–6.

The Environmental Charter for Local Government, Friends of the Earth, London, 1989.

UK Strategy for Sustainable Development: Consultation Paper Department of the Environment, London, July 1993.

Working in the City CEC Publication (available through University College Dublin – Architecture Department).

Index

Page references in **bold** are those of illustrations and tables.

ABACUS, 73
Abbey Hanson Rowe, **12**
Acid rain, **41**
Adhesives, 121
Agenda 21, 181
Aggregates, 121
Air-consuming, 39–40, 70, 121–2, 211
Air leakage, 70
Air pollution, 41–2
Air quality, 129
Aluminium, 72–3, 122
Architects' Directive, 26–8
Architects' Journal, The, 60
Arup, Facade Engineering Group, 83–4
Asbestos, 122
Asphalt, 122
Atlantis Building, London, 56, **201**
Avonmouth Sewage Works, 87, **87**

Barcelona, 3
Barclaycard Headquarters, **210**
Barn owls, 169, 171, 173
Bath, 38, 184
Bats, **171**, 172, 173
Baubiologie principles, 196–7
Belgian 'Greenbus', 45–6
Bio-climatic design, 64
Biodiversity, 168-73, 81
Bio-drier, 85
Biological walls and roofs, **172**, 175, **175**, **177**, 197
Biomass, 79, 82, 178
Birley Health Centre, Sheffield, 55
Blocks, 122
Boards, 122
BP Solar, 83
BRECSU, 53, 70
BREEAM, 37, 58, 63
Bricks, environmental impacts, **116**, 122
British Gas, 56–7, 58
British Gas energy demonstration offices, Leeds, 56–8, **57**

Broadacre City, 46
Brundtland Report, 182, 194
BSRIA, 70
Building Design Partnership, **6**, 28, 63
Building Research Establishment, 52, 54, 59, 155, 159
Built form, 64
Buro Happold, 153
Business in the Environment Report, 116

CAD in environmental assessment, 102–3, 104–10, **105**, **107**, **108**
Calatrava, Santiago, 28
Canary Wharf, London, 40
Capital, energy costs, 71–2
Carbon dioxide (CO_2), 32–8, 48, 174–5, 176
Carbon dioxide emissions, from central heating, **36**
Carbon tax, 37
Castle Henllys, Dyfed, 125
CDM regulations, **136**, 136–7
CE Mark, 24
Cement, 122
Ceramics, 122
Chlorofluorocarbons (CFCs), 32, **39**, 39–40, 115, 116, 141–2
Chronology of EC, **16**, **17**
Climate change, 33, 181
Climate related design, 61–3
Collins, Ken, 6, 181, 209
Colt International, 84
Comité Européan de Normalisation (CEN), 24–5
Combined Heat and Power (CHP), 41, 78, 79–81, **80**, **81**
Comfort, 61–2, 65–71
Constable Terrace, University of East Anglia, 52–3
Construction Products Directive, 21–5, **25**, 28, 133, 139
  environmental consequences, 23–4
  influence on design, 23
Contaminated land, 139–40, 154–60, **156**, 185
  methods of treatment, 156–7
Cultural heritage, 118–20
Cycling, provision, 122

217

Index

Davis Langdon & Everest, 54, 71
De Montfort University, School of Engineering, 59–60
Declaration on the Environment , 11
Denmark, 80, 90, 92, 93, 193–4
Directives , vii-viii, **13**, **14**, 16–18, 201–3, **202**, 206–7
Displayment ventilation, 70
Display screen, pollution from, 134
Dublin, Temple Bar , **xvi**
Duisburg, Germany, 84–5, **204**, **211**

Earth Summit , xiv-xv, 8, 181
East Anglia, University of, 52–3
EC environment policy, **xiv**, 138-9
EC institutions and powers, **18**
EC Joule Programme, 85, 152
EC Law , xii, 16–8
EC Thermie Programme, 58, 83, 85, 94
EC Treaties, **xv**
ECD Partnership, 54
Eco-House, Leicester, **191**
Eco-labelling, 111, 117, 142, **163**, 163–5, **165**, 167
Ecology, 168-173
Ecolonia, Holland, 194–6, **194**, **195**, 208
Eco-management, 111, 163
EDAS, University of Strathclyde, 73, 75
Edinburgh, 38, **51**
　Bonnington Bond, 77, **77**
　1 Castle Street, 75–6, **76**
　Victoria Quay, 73–5, **74**
Ellis-Miller, Jonathan, 54
Energy case studies, 73–7
Energy Conservation Index, 54
Energy conservation, institutional barriers, 52
Energy consumption, 4, **43**, 46–7
Energy, design approach, 61–3
Energy economy and heat retention, 21, 22
Energy Efficiency Office (UK), 35, 53
Energy Research Group, Dublin, 86
Energy targets, xiii, 35
Energy use, 31–8
Energy World, Milton Keynes, 53–4
Environment Agency, 155
Environment City, Leicester, 189–192
Environmental Agreements, xiii
Environmental Appraisal of Development Plans, 103, 186, 189
Environmental audits, 37, 111–7, **113**, **114**
Environmental Charter, 192
Environmental effects of manufacturing companies, **116**
Environmental health, 132–4
Environmental Impact Assessment, 90, 92–3, 94, **97**, **98**, 97–104
Environmental impacts (of building materials), 121–6
Environmental Improvement Plan, 116

Environmental Protection Act, 1990, 139–142, 155
Environmental responsibilities, xiv, 114, 201–12
Environmental Statement, 90, 93–4, 98, 99–102, 104
Equipment gains, 70
Essential Requirements (of CPD), 21–2
European Committee for Standardisation, 25
European Community, xiii, 16–8
European Environment Agency, vii
European Parliament, vii
EU Action Plan on renewable energy, 81, 93
EU energy strategy, 81
European Union, vii-viii, xiv, 16, 45
Eye Power Station, Suffolk, **82**, 151–2, **206**

Fixed shading, 66
Findhorn, Scotland, 196–8
Foggo, Peter, 56, 57
Fordham, Max & Partners, 59
Foster, Sir Norman & Partners, 28, 83, 84–5
Foster Wheeler Energy, 152
Fourth Framework Environment Programme, 118
Fifth Framework Environment Programme, 138, 139, 168
Future World, Milton Keynes, 54

Glare, 65
Glasgow, 3, 6, **33**, 184
Glasgow, Scottish Power Offices, **67**, **68**, **76**, **77**, 76–7
Glass, 72, 123
Glass, type of (for energy conservation), 67–8, 85–6
Global warming, 31–8, 42, 48, 185
　how it works, 32–3
　make up of, 000
　role of design, 36–7
'Going Green' report, 121
Green development strategy, 43–5
Green Paper on the Urban Environment, vii, 3–5, 44–5, 80, 104, 119, 184, 212
Green shading, 66
Greencode, 143, 144
Greenhouse gases, **32**, 32–3, **34**
Greenwich Enterprise Board, 59
Greenwich, low-energy business units, **58**
Grimshaw, Nicholas & Partners, 83

Halifax Building Society, **12**
Halons, 39, 40, 141–2
Health and safety, 135–7, **136**
Heat absorbing glass, 67–8
Hertfordshire Structure Plan, 189, **191**
Historic character, 4
Horizontal measures, vii
Hospitals, 52, 143–4

Index

Hydrochlorofluorocarbons HCFCs, 39–40, 142
Hydrogen power, 45–6
Hygiene, health and environment, 21, 22
Hyett, Peter, 56

IBM, 152–3
ICI, 39, 80, 113
Ionica Building, Cambridge, **50**, **64**
Industrial buildings, 51–2
Institute of Business Ethics (IBE), 111
Insulation materials, 72
Internal environment, 130-1
Internal finishes, 73

Kaiser Bautechnik, 85
Kroll, Lucien, 194, 195

Leeds, energy demonstration offices, 56–8, **57**, **69**
Legionnaire's Disease, 131
Lethaby, William, 38
Life-cycle analysis, 111, **112**
Lifschutz Davidson, 152
Lighting, 65
Linacre College, Oxford, 54–5
Liverpool, John Moores University, 114
Low emissivity glass, 68
Lutyens, Edwin, 169

Maastricht Treaty, xv, 8–10, 11–2, 15, 28, 78
Major John, 11
Materials, 63, 71–3
Mather Rick, 53
Mechanical resistance and stability, 21, 22
Milton Keynes, 49, **49**, 53–4, **186**, **190**
Mixed-mode ventilation, 69–70
Montreal Protocol, 39, 141
Moveable shading, 66
Murray O'Laorire, **xvi**

National Environment Policy Plan, 194
National forests initiative, 169
Natural environment, 4
Natural ventilation, 68–9
Nature Conservancy Council, 94
NHS Environment Forum, 143–4
Nitrogen oxide (NO$_2$), 39
Non-Fossil Fuel Obligation (NFFO), 83
Northumbria, University of, 83–4, **83**, **84**, **207**
NOVEM, 194–5
Nuisance, 142–3

Offices, energy use, 50–1
Ozone layer, 39–40, 141–2
Ovenden Moor, Yorkshire, **88**, 93–4
Owl box, **172**
Oxford, Linacre College, 54–5

Paints, 123–4
Pennyland, Milton Keynes, **49**, 53
Photovoltaic electricity generation, 83–5, **83**, **84**
Phillips Niall, 125
Piquér, Carlos Robles, 81
Planning Policy Guidance (PPG 12), 184, 185, 187–8
Planning Policy Guidance (PPG 13), 42, 184
Plastics, 124
Polluter pays, 11, 207
Pollution, 73, 129–131, 133–4, 140–1, 207
Precautionary principle, 11
Preservatives, 124
Prior, Edward, 38
Protection against noise, 27–8
Public procurement, 27–8

Radon, 124, 133–4
Rainforests, 55, 169, 171, 181
Rape methyl ester (RME), 79
Recycled buildings, 150–1
Recycling, 147–53
Reflective glass, 68
Regulations, 16
Renewable energy, 42, 78–87, 88–94
Revenue, energy costs, 71–2
Rio Conference (Earth Summit), 42, 208–9
RMJM Scotland, 73, 74
Rogers, Richard, 205
Royal Institute of British Architects (RIBA), 26, 27
RIBA Future World Competition, 54
RIBA Plan of Work, new environmental duties, 203, **203**
Royal Society for Nature Conservation, 190
Royd Moor, Yorkshire, 93

Safety:
  in buildings, 129–131
  in use, 21, 22
Sainsburys, 156, 158–60
Salvesen Brick, 116–7
Schools, energy use, 52
Scottish Office, Leith, **62**, 73–5, **74**
Sea level rises, 33, **35**
Settlement patterns, 46
Seville, Expo Pavilion, 83
Sewage sludge, power from, 87
Sheffield, 55–6

Index

Single European Act, xiv, 11, 26, 138
Site, energy design of, 63–4
Solar cooling, 85, **86**
　gain, 47–50, 53–4, 56–7, 62, 65, **66**
　protection, 66–7
Sources of information, 17–8
Space heating, 47
Stansted, CAD case study, **108**, 108–10
Steel, 72–3, 124
Stone, 124
Sustainable development, xv, 9, 11, 181–8, 201–12
　case studies of, 189–98
　definition of, 182
Sweden, 80

Task Force Report (on the environment), 5
Temperature rises (global), 33, **35**
Timber, 123
Torness power lines (CAD case study), **107**
Toyne Report, 52, 60
Treaty of Rome, 11, 138
Turf roofs, 126, **172**, **175**, **177**, **197**

Universities, energy use, 52

Urban density and gasoline consumption, **35**
　forestry, 176–8
　planning, 3–4

Vale, Robert and Brenda, 55–6, 182
Ventilation, 68
Vertical measures, vii
Voysey, CFA, 38

Waste management, **147**, 147–153, 185
Whicheloe Macfarlane, 87
Wind energy, 78–9
　power, **78**, **88**, 88–94
　turbines, 89, 91–4
Woodhouse Medical Centre, Sheffield, 55–6
Wood, David, 54
World population growth, 7
Wright, Frank Lloyd, 46

York, 38
Yorkshire Electricity, 93
Yorkshire Water, 93
Yorkshire Windpower, 93–4